# The MORAL of the STORY

# The MORAL of the STORY

## Timeless Tales to Cherish & Share

COMPILED AND EDITED BY

**Jerry Newcombe**

BROADMAN
&HOLMAN
PUBLISHERS

Nashville, Tennessee

© 1996 by Jerry Newcombe
All rights reserved

Published by Broadman & Holman Publishers, Nashville, Tennessee
Acquisitions & Development Editor: Janis Whipple
Published in association with the literary agency of
Alive Communications, Inc.,
1465 Kelly Johnson Blvd., Suite 320, Colorado Springs, CO 80920.
Page Design and Typography: TF Designs, Mt. Juliet, Tennessee
Printed in the United States of America

4261-99
0-8054-6199-X

Dewey Decimal Classification: 241
Subject Heading: CHRISTIAN ETHICS / MORAL EDUCATION
Library of Congress Card Catalog Number: 96-8383

Unless otherwise noted, Scripture quotations are from the Holy
Bible, New International Version, copyright © 1973, 1978, 1984 by
International Bible Society. Verses marked TLB are from The Living
Bible, copyright © Tyndale House Publishers, Wheaton, Ill., 1971,
used by permission.

**Library of Congress Cataloging-in-Publication Data**
Newcombe, Jerry.
    The moral of the story : timeless tales to cherish and share /
compiled and edited by Jerry Newcombe
        p.   cm.
    ISBN 0-8054-6199-X
    1. Christian fiction, American.  2. Didactic fiction, American.
I. Title.
    PS3564.E8756M67      1996
    813'.54—dc20

96-8383
CIP

96  97  98  99  00  5  4  3  2  1

This book is dedicated to my family,
Kirsti, Annie, and Eric,
who have shown unlimited patience
as I labored to put the book together.
In particular, my wife, Kirsti,
has helped me in innumerable ways,
including finding many stories
and even translating several of them
from Nordic languages.

# Contents

### PART II
# The Seven Deadly Sins

## PART III
# Faith, Hope, and Love

## PART IV

# Just for Fun

# FOREWORD

by D. James Kennedy, Ph.D.

W e live in an age where ungodly and perverted themes often fill the airwaves, the newspapers, the magazine racks, and the bookshelves. Furthermore, much of modern literature is pointless—reflecting either a nihilistic or an existentialist point of view. In contrast, what a refreshing thing it is to read positive, uplifting stories—many of which were written *before* the turn of the century. Western civilization is rich with such stories, many of them with overt and covert Christian themes. This is important because it matters which nature we feed, our new one or the old one. Let me explain.

When we are born again, we receive a new nature, a perfectly sinless nature that is not capable of sinning. However, the new nature then dwells within us, coexisting with the old nature, which can do nothing *but* sin. That sin may be of a repulsive nature or it may be a very "respectable" sin. It may be committed by a drunkard, a wino in an alley; it may be the sin of a president of a great corporation or the mayor of a city. But it is still sin. Both of these natures living within the Christian create a struggle, a warfare within. Paul said that he saw these two natures warring within himself. We have within us, as it were, a Dr. Jekyll and Mr. Hyde. So the question is, which nature is winning? To which nature do we yield? Above all, which nature are we *feeding?*

Dr. Bill Bright, founder of Campus Crusade for Christ and recent recipient of the Templeton Prize on Religion, used to tell a story that described the old and new natures as two dogs: a black dog and a white dog that were wont to fight viciously. He said, "Which dog will win is determined by which dog you feed. Feed the black dog and starve the white dog, and the black dog will win; feed the white dog and starve the black dog, and the white dog will win."

Which nature are *you* feeding? Unfortunately, in light of today's mostly immoral entertainment establishment, you are often feeding your old, sin-filled nature when you watch TV, or go to a movie, or read a novel or magazine, or listen to modern music. Not always, but often. There's a lot of trash out there, and even many professing Christians have succumbed to viewing, reading, and listening to it.

That's why I am delighted to recommend this new book by one of my staff members, Jerry Newcombe. His book, *The Moral of the Story,* is geared toward starving the old nature while feeding the new. Jerry, who has faithfully served my television outreach for more than a decade now, seems to have a knack for finding relevant—but often obscure—facts or stories for my television ministry. In this book, he's found both old classics and new tales that glorify Christ and build up His Church.

*The Moral of the Story* provides both *pleasurable* and *worthwhile* reading. Whether you're looking for a story to relax at bedtime or you're looking for a selection to read to your children or you're a teacher in search of tales for your students to read, you will find them in this timely book. I trust *The Moral of the Story* will become a time-less classic in its own right.

# INTRODUCTION

J esus went around telling stories, and He changed the world! Now, it wasn't only because He told stories that He accomplished so great a feat, but surely that was a major part of His ministry. A good story with a good moral can often teach more effectively than straightforward didactic teaching can.

The purpose of *The Moral of the Story* is to provide families and individuals hours of uplifting and interesting reading—material that makes a good point. Have you ever read something that perhaps held you along throughout its many pages, and then when it was over you stopped and thought, *What was that all about?* The point is that in our nihilistic age a lot of books and stories make no point, or if they do, they often make the wrong point. The stories in this book have been carefully chosen to make the right point.[1]

These stories deal with both sin and redemption, good and evil. The moral of each of these stories, however, has been chosen to conform to a biblical theme of one sort or another.

*The Moral of the Story* is so titled because each story selected has a moral to it, stated or implied; none of the stories are meaningless, reflecting the cynicism of our age. (Note that included in these selections are a few poems, songs, or speeches, which are not stories per se but are included because each tells a story in its own way.)

---

1.   In today's relativistic age, some would chafe at the idea that there is such a thing as right and wrong, but I'm starting from this premise: God has revealed Himself in the Scriptures, and He has told us what is right and what is wrong. As Abraham Lincoln once said, upon receiving a Bible as a gift: "In regard to this great book, I have but to say, it is the best gift God has given to men. All the good the Savior gave to the world was communicated through this book. But for it we could not know right from wrong." Abraham Lincoln, "Remarks upon the Holy Scriptures, in Receiving the Present of a Bible from a Negro Delegation," 7 September 1864, *Life and Works of Abraham Lincoln: Centenary Edition*, Volume 5, Marion Mills Miller, ed., (New York: The Current Literature Publishing Co., 1907), 209.

I hope you enjoy all of these selections. Skip around if you like. In this book, I am using as my major categories: the Imitation of Christ (including stories on Christ, His birth, and following Him), the Seven Deadly Sins (Pride, Greed, Envy, Anger, Lust, Gluttony, Sloth), Faith, Hope, and Love, and finally come stories that are "Just for Fun." While some people may feel that the seven deadly sins are too out-dated, I wouldn't agree. I daresay if you pick up *today's* newspaper you will find all sorts of news stories related to people committing some of the seven deadly sins. I think the ancients were on to something when they classified those seven sins as root causes of a host of many other evils, and I firmly believe we can learn from them in terms of what we should avoid.

Scattered throughout the book you will find many selections from the classics. A lot of the great writers of centuries past were deeply committed Christians with great spiritual insights. Thus, included here are selections by Augustine, Milton, Bunyan, Dostoyevsky, and others. I hope this provides for some at least a superficial introduction to some of the Christian classics. Of course, there are some Bible selections here too, especially in the section on the seven deadly sins. For example, in the realm of lust, one would be hard-pressed to find a better story than that of David and Bathsheba or of David's children, Amnon and Tamar! Other selections included here are from earlier in this century from great Christian writers like C. S. Lewis or G. K. Chesterton. Also in the mix are stories from contemporary writers. And finally there are even a couple of stories I commissioned specifically for *The Moral of the Story*.

Each story includes a short commentary at the beginning and even at the *end*. In my chosen field (I serve as a TV producer for Coral Ridge Ministries, D. James Kennedy's television outreach), there's an old rule of thumb in broadcasting: "Tell them what they're going to see. Let them see it. Then tell them what they just saw." At the risk of overstating the obvious, I've tried to do that here.

*The Moral of the Story* contains some long and meaty selections as well as some short and sweet ones. I have tried to design this to be both a family-friendly and a faith-friendly book. Its tales can be read aloud or read alone. Families, huddled around the fireplace, could enjoy stories from this book. Or individuals could curl up on the couch and enjoy reading a story or two at a time. I trust that Christian high schools or colleges could find *The Moral of the Story* useful. That includes home schoolers. I also hope that ministers and those involved in communicating the Christian message might find the book a helpful resource. Above all, *The Moral of the Story* has been compiled with the goal that you will find the stories both entertaining and edifying—entertaining enough so that you read them and edifying enough so that you receive some new insights into the things of God and a fresh picture of sins to avoid, so that your walk with Him will be strengthened!

Now, on to the stories. . . .

# PART I

## The Imitation of Christ

The following stories deal
with the Person of Jesus Christ,
what He has accomplished,
and the privilege and price of following Him.

# SECTION 1

# JESUS CHRIST: HIS BIRTH
# (CHRISTMAS-RELATED STORIES)

J esus Christ is "the Man who changed the world," to borrow a phrase from the eminent scholar and author Herbert J. Lockyer. No one has exerted a greater or more positive influence on life on this planet than Him. The initial stories in this book focus on Him—first, His birth; second, His life and ministry; and third, the imitation of Him.

Christmas time is the most wonderful time of the year. That's because the Savior's birth permeates many aspects of our culture. Even nonbelievers can often feel it.

Christmas is the time when charitable giving is the highest. It's the time when "love thy neighbor" is most often attempted.

It boggles the mind that God Almighty became one of us—and a baby at that! Furthermore, He came in such humble circumstances that no one in the world has to look up to Him, as they would someone born in a much higher class or caste. As to why He did this, C. S. Lewis once put it this way, "The Son of God became a man that men might become the sons of God."

Sometimes Christians complain about the materialism that often eclipses the meaning of Christmas. That's true. But it's also true that the gift-giving is an indirect reflection of these truths:

1. The first gift was the Son of God to us from God the Father.

2. The first material Christmas gifts given were from the wise men to the Christ Child.

And Christians have been giving gifts ever since. The important thing in our celebration is not to forget the origin of it all, which we too often do. The following stories reflect the significance and joy of the true meaning of Christmas.[1]

---

1. If you enjoy these stories, take a look at the *Christmas in My Heart* books by Dr. Joe Wheeler. This is a series of anthologies of beautiful, heart-warming Christmas stories.

*This selection is suitable for children.*
*The moral of the story is Christ has shared in our humanity and our suffering.*

# THE REVOLT IN HEAVEN

### from "Declare His Glory in a Suffering World"[2]
#### by Samuel Kamaleson

In the mid-1980s, there was a book by a rabbi that received national attention. The book was *Why Bad Things Happen to Good People* by Harold Kushner. The gist of his answer was that God is good but not really omnipotent. Therefore, He can't really prevent bad things from happening to good people, but He cares about them nonetheless. The Christian rebuttal is much more in line with the Hebrew Bible than the rabbi's answer: Man has fallen and is at enmity with God. There really are no good people, no, not one. We don't deserve good things from God, only His wrath. But because of His mercy, He forgives us through the death of His Son. Unfortunately, proclaiming this straightforward message, despite its truthfulness, does not put a book on the secular best-sellers lists.

The problem of evil causes many people to question whether there is a God or that He is good, if indeed He exists. But in Christ we know that God is and that He is indeed good.

The following story, a short excerpt from an excellent speech on missions, is told by a native of India, Samuel Kamaleson. The story is so hypothetical that it is impossible. For there could be no revolt among humans in heaven. Theologically, the story is based on an absurd premise. But, if you will, suspend that for a brief moment, and you will be rewarded by a story that gives a surprisingly simple and straightforward perspective on the problem of suffering in the world. Also note, this story was told in the 1970s when Bangladesh was among the poorest nations. Today, we might refer instead to a refugee camp in Somalia or Rwanda.

---

There was a revolt up in heaven. A small band of people got into a huddle and they said, "The one who is in charge here doesn't know

---

2. An excerpt from Samuel Kamaleson, "Declare His Glory in a Suffering World" found in David Howard, ed., *Declare His Glory among the Nations*, Urbana '76 transcripts (Downers Grove, Ill.: InterVarsity Press, 1977), 118–19.

what's happening down below. How can he ever properly govern it. We ought to go and talk to him." And they began to talk about things he did not know.

One said, "He doesn't know what poverty is."

Another said, "He doesn't know what it means to be in a refugee camp in Bangladesh."

Another said, "He doesn't know what injustice is."

And then a small man who had been silent until then suddenly jumped up. He was the kind of character who finds words inadequate to give vent to emotion. Every time he spoke his nostrils punctuated his emotions by dilating. He spoke emphatically, "Does God know about death? What does he know about the threat of non-existence?"

So they said, "We'll go and talk to him."

As they began to move, a little child came close to a very tall, beautiful woman, clad in a lovely sari. And she pulled at the end of the sari and when the woman bent down to listen, the child whispered, "I'm too small and too young to talk to God. But when you get there, would you ask him a question for me?"

And the beautiful woman said, "What do you want me to talk to God about?"

"Would you ask him if he knows anything about being illegitimate?"

The beautiful woman in the beautiful sari was considered a "fallen woman," so she bent down and picked up the little girl and said, "Honey, I'll carry you. You ask God."

So they went to the presence of God. And God said, "What is it that you want?"

And they said, "God, you don't know anything about what's going on on earth. You don't know what it means to suffer. You don't know what pain is."

And the little girl jumped up and said, "God, do you know what death is? Do you know what illegitimacy is?"

God said, "What do you think I ought to do?"

They said, "You should spend at least a week in Bangladesh."

And God had a friend on earth whose name was Isaiah. He called him and said, "Isaiah, proclaim it." And this is how Isaiah proclaimed it:

*For unto us a Child is born; unto us a Son is given; and the government shall be upon his shoulder. These will be his royal titles: "Wonderful," "Counselor," "The Mighty God," "The Everlasting Father," "The Prince of Peace"* (Isa. 9:6, TLB).

---

Jesus knows our every weakness and sorrow. He knows hunger firsthand, for He went without food for forty days. He knows homelessness firsthand, for the Son of man had no place to rest His head. He knows what it was like to be shunned by people, to be hated by His enemies, and even what it's like to be rejected by His friends. He even knows the anguish of death, for He, of course, underwent death for us. There's no one in the world who is undergoing some sorrow or rejection who cannot look to Christ for help, strength, and encouragement.

*This story is suitable for children.*
*The moral of the story is that God rewards those who humbly serve Him,*
*love Him, and give to Him, even out of their meager and humble means.*

## "WHY THE CHIMES RANG"

by Raymond Macdonald Alden

Dr. Raymond Macdonald Alden (1873–1924) was an English professor who earned his Master's degree at Harvard and his Ph.D. at Rollins College in Florida. He taught primarily at Stanford University and at the University of Illinois. He was the author of several books, including *The Rise of Formal Satire in England* and *The Art of Debate*. Perhaps he's best known, though, for the following story, "Why the Chimes Rang." This story, first published in 1909, is a Christmas tale, told in beautiful simplicity.

The story reminds me of the biblical point that God opposes the proud but He exalts the humble. This story is a perfect selection to read aloud for the whole family. I find it difficult to read with dry eyes!

———————

There was once, in a faraway country where few people ever traveled, a wonderful church. It stood on a high hill in the midst of a great city; and every Sunday, as well as on sacred days like Christmas, thousands of people climbed the hill to its great archways, looking like lines of ants all moving in the same direction.

When you came to the building itself, you found stone columns and dark passages, and a grand entrance leading to the main room of the church. This room was so long that one standing at the doorway could scarcely see to the other end, where the choir stood by the marble altar. In the farthest corner was the organ; and this organ was so loud, that sometimes when it played, the people for miles around would close their shutters and prepare for a great thunderstorm. Altogether, no such church as this was ever seen before, especially when it was lighted up for some festival, and crowded with people, young and old. But the strangest thing about the whole building was the wonderful chime of bells. At one corner of the church was a great gray tower, with ivy growing over it as far up as one could see. I say as far as one could see, because the tower was quite great enough to fit the great church, and it rose so far into the sky that it was only in very fair weather that anyone claimed to be able to see the top. Even then one could not be certain that it was in sight. Up, and up, and up climbed the stones and the ivy; and, as the men who built the church had been dead for hundreds of years, every one had forgotten how high the tower was supposed to be.

Now all the people knew that at the top of the tower was a chime of Christmas bells. They had hung there ever since the church had been built, and were the most beautiful bells in the world. Some thought it was because a great musician had cast them and arranged them in their place; others said it was because of the great height, which reared up where the air was clearest and purest: however that might be, no one who had ever heard the chimes denied that they were the sweetest in the world. Some described them as sounding like angels far up in the sky; others, as sounding like strange winds singing through the trees.

But the fact was that no one had heard them for years and years. There was an old man living not far from the church, who said that his mother had spoken of hearing them when she was a little girl, and he was the only one who was sure of as much as that. They were Christmas chimes, you see, and were not meant to be played by men or on common days. It was the custom on Christmas Eve for all the people to bring to the church their offerings to the Christ-child; and when the greatest and best offering was laid on the altar, there used to come sounding through the music of the choir the Christmas chimes far up in the tower. Some said that the wind rang them, and others that they were so high that the angels could set them swinging. But for many long years they had never been heard. It was said that people had been growing less careful of their gifts for the Christ-child, and that no offering was brought, great enough to deserve the music of the chimes.

Every Christmas Eve the rich people still crowded to the altar, each one trying to bring some better gift than any other; without giving anything that he wanted for himself, and the church was crowded with those who thought that perhaps the wonderful bells might be heard again. But although the service was splendid, and the offerings plenty, only the roar of the wind could be heard, far up in the stone tower.

Now, a number of miles from the city, in a little country village, where nothing could be seen of the great church but glimpses of the tower when the weather was fine, lived a boy named Pedro, and his little brother. They knew very little about the Christmas chimes, but they had heard of the service in the church on Christmas Eve, and had a secret plan, which they had often talked over when by themselves, to go to see the beautiful celebration.

"Nobody can guess, Little Brother," Pedro would say, "all the fine things there are to see and hear; and I have even heard it said that the Christ-child sometimes comes down to bless the service. What if we could see Him?"

The day before Christmas was bitterly cold, with a few lonely snowflakes flying in the air, and a hard white crust on the ground. Sure enough, Pedro and Little Brother were able to slip quietly away early in the afternoon; and although the walking was hard in the frosty air, before nightfall they had trudged so far, hand in hand, that they saw the lights of the big city just ahead of them. Indeed, they were about to enter one of the great gates in the wall that surrounded it, when they saw something dark on the snow near their path, and stepped aside to look at it.

It was a poor woman, who had fallen just outside the city, too sick and tired to get in where she might have found shelter. The soft snow made of a drift a sort of pillow for her, and she would soon be so sound asleep, in the wintry air, that no one could ever waken her again. All this Pedro saw in a moment, and he knelt down beside her and tried to rouse her, even tugging at her arm a little, as though he would have tried to carry her away. He turned her face toward him, so that he could rub some of the snow on it, and when he had looked at her silently a moment he stood up again, and said:

"It's no use, Little Brother. You will have to go on alone."

"Alone?" cried Little Brother. "And you not see the festival?"

"No," said Pedro, and he could not keep back a bit of a choking sound in his throat. "See this poor woman. Her face looks like the Madonna in the chapel window, and she will freeze to death if nobody cares for her. Every one has gone to the church now, but when you come back you can bring someone to help her. I will rub her to keep her from freezing, and perhaps get her to eat the bun that is left in my pocket."

"But I can not bear to leave you, and go on alone," said Little Brother.

"Both of us need not miss the service," said Pedro, "and it had better be I than you. You can easily find your way to the church; and you must see and hear everything twice, Little Brother—once for you and once for me. I am sure the Christ-child must know how I should love to come with you and worship Him; and oh! if you get a chance, Little Brother, to slip up to the altar without getting in any one's way, take this little silver piece of mine, and lay it down for my offering, when no one is looking. Do not forget where you have left me, and forgive me for not going with you."

In this way he hurried Little Brother off to the city, and winked hard to keep back the tears, as he heard the crunching footsteps sounding farther and farther away in the twilight. It was pretty hard to lose the music and splendor of the Christmas celebration that he had been planning for so long, and spend the time instead in that lonely place in the snow.

The great church was a wonderful place that night. Everyone said that it had never looked so bright and beautiful before. When the organ played and the thousands of people sang, the walls shook with the sound, and little Pedro, away outside the city wall, felt the earth tremble around him.

At the close of the service came the procession with the offerings to be laid on the altar. Rich men and great men marched proudly up to lay down their gifts to the Christ-child. Some brought wonderful jewels, some baskets of gold so heavy that they could scarcely carry them down the aisle. A great writer laid down a book that he had been making for years and years. And last of all walked the king of the country, hoping with all the rest to win for himself the chime of the Christmas bells. There went a great murmur through the church, as the people saw the king take from his head the royal crown, all set with precious stones, and lay it gleaming on the altar, as his offering to the holy Child. "Surely," everyone said, "we shall hear the bells now, for nothing like this has ever happened before."

But still only the cold old wind was heard in the tower, and the people shook their heads; and some of them said, as they had before, that they never really believed the story of the chimes, and doubted if they ever rang at all.

The process was over, and the choir began the closing hymn. Suddenly the organist stopped playing as though he had been shot, and everyone looked at the old minister, who was standing by the altar, holding up his hand for silence. Not a sound could be heard from anyone in the church, but as all the people strained their ears to listen, there came softly, but distinctly, swinging through the air, the sound of the chimes in the tower. So far away, and yet so clear the music seemed—so much sweeter were the notes than anything that had been heard before, rising and falling away up there in the sky, that the people in the church sat for a moment as still as though something held each of them by the shoulders. Then they all stood up together and stared straight at the altar, to see what great gift had awakened the long silent bells.

But all that the nearest of them saw was the childish figure of Little Brother, who had crept softly down the aisle when no one was looking, and had laid Pedro's little piece of silver on the altar.

---

The Bible contains a repeated theme that God has chosen the poor things to humble the rich, the weak to shame the strong, the foolish things to confound the wise. Does all our pomp and ceremony—even when it's outwardly religious—impress the Lord? Not necessarily. For man looks at the outward appearance, but God looks at the heart. It's refreshing to be reminded of such truths from an English professor.

*This selection is suitable for children.*
*The moral of the story is that Jesus has changed the world for the better.*

# "IF HE HAD NOT COME"

by Nan F. Weeks

One of the best-loved movies of all time is *It's a Wonderful Life* (1946) directed by Frank Capra. In this movie, starring Jimmy Stewart and Donna Reed, the main character gets to see what life would be like had he never been born. In 1938, eight years *before* that movie came out, the following Christmas story was written by Nan F. Weeks, dealing with what if Jesus had not come.

The editor is very familiar with that theme. I cowrote a book with D. James Kennedy, Ph.D. on that very subject: *What If Jesus Had Never Been Born?* (Nashville, Tenn.: Thomas Nelson, Publishers, 1994). A nonfiction work, it documents the positive aspects the life of Christ has had on our society and continues to have. For example, we show that if Jesus had never been born, there would be no salvation, no Salvation Army, no Red Cross, no YMCA, probably no universities, no modern science, no capitalism, no widespread literacy, and so on.

Along the same lines, "If He Had Not Come" shows that Christ has had a positive impact on the world. Had He never come, things would be much worse.

---

It was Christmas Eve, and after Bobby had carefully hung his stocking by the fireplace, he went off to bed. Usually Bobby did not like to go to bed early, but tonight he was eager to get to sleep so as to be sure to wake up early to see his gifts.

For their daily Bible lesson that day Bobby and his father had read Jesus' own words to his friends found in John 15:22. Five words had stayed in Bobby's mind, and he kept saying them over and over again until he fell asleep. They were the words, "If I had not come."

It seemed as if he had not been asleep any time when a cross, harsh voice said: "Get up, get up, I tell you. It's time to get up."

Thinking about the skates he wanted and the flashlight and the motor and the books for which he'd been wishing, Bobby got up and hurried into his clothing and went downstairs. But all was still. No one was there to greet him; no stocking hung beside the fireplace; no wreaths were in the window, no splendid tree was there.

Hurrying to the door, Bobby looked down the street. The factory was open and he could hear the rumble of the machinery. He grabbed his cap and sweater and raced down the street to the factory door, and there stood a grim-looking foreman.

"What's the factory running for on Christmas?" asked Bobby.

"Christmas?" asked the man. "What do you mean? I never heard that word. This is one of our busy days, so you clear out of here."

Filled with wonder, Bobby hurried on down the street toward the stores, and to his amazement he found them all open. The grocer, the dry-goods man, the baker, each one was busy and cross, and each said in reply to his question, "Christmas? What's Christmas?"

When Bobby tried to explain, "It's Jesus' birthday," and that the first part of the word "Christmas" means "Jesus," he was gruffly ordered to move along as this was a very busy day.

Going round the corner, he thought: "I'll go to church, our own church, for there's to be a Christmas service there." All at once Bobby stopped short before a big vacant field, and he mumbled to himself: "I guess I'm lost. I was certain our church was here. I know it was." Then he noticed a signboard in the center of the big vacant lot, and on going nearer to it he read the words, "If I Had Not Come."

Suddenly the meaning of it all dawned on the puzzled boy, and he said, "Oh, I know, 'If I Had Not Come'—that's why there's no Christmas day nor any church."

He was wandering along in a gloomy way, when he thought of the box of toys and games his class had sent to the Orphans' Home, and he said, half aloud, "I guess I'll go up to the Home and see the children get their presents." But when Bobby reached the place, instead of seeing the name of the Home over the gateway, he read these same five words, "If I Had Not Come," and beyond the archway there was no fine building.

Seeing an old man, feeble and ill, by the roadside, Bobby said: "I guess you're sick, mister. I'll run to the hospital and tell them to send an ambulance for you." But when he reached the grounds no splendid building was to be seen, nothing but signs and posters bearing the words, "If I Had Not Come."

As Bobby hurried back to the corner where the Rescue Mission had been he said, "I'm sure they'll take the poor old man in there, anyway." But men with angry faces were gambling and swearing and over the door Bobby saw, instead of the name of the mission, the same words, "If I Had Not Come."

Thinking still about the poor old man, Bobby hurried home to ask his father and mother to help him. On his way across the living-room he waited to look up in a Bible these words, "If I Had Not Come." Turning past the pages of the Old Testament, he found that there was no new part. After Malachi all the pages were blank, and as he held them up to the light on each he could see a faint outline of the words, "If I Had Not Come."

With a sigh Bobby said, "Oh, what a terrible world this is—no Christmas, no churches, no homes for little orphan children, no hospitals, no rescue missions, no almshouses, nothing but jails and gambling-houses and police patrols and sickness and wrong and—"

Just then there came the sound of bells. The chimes were playing. Bobby listened, and sure enough it was his favorite hymn "Joy to the world, the Lord is come," and then he heard his mother's cheery voice saying, "Merry Christmas, Bobby!"

With a joyous bound Bobby was out of bed, and kneeling down, he said, "O Lord Jesus, I thank You that You did come, and I'll show You how thankful I am by always trying to be the kind of boy You want me to be."

------

If you have had the privilege of traveling to different countries, as I have, you can see quite clearly the difference Christianity can make in the foundations of a culture. For example, look at the lack of religious freedom that exists in many of the countries where other religions are in charge. I recently met a man from Nepal who faces six years in prison if he sets foot again in that Hindu country. His crime? He faces three years for becoming a Christian (converting to any religion but the state religion), and an additional three years for having been baptized. Unfortunately, there is often a lack of freedom in many Islamic countries as well. But in those countries where Christianity, evangelicalism in particular, has held sway, we tend to find the greatest religious, economic, and political freedom. If He had not come, nor would these things have come. Above all, there would be no salvation for the soul!

*This selection is suitable for children.*
*The moral of the story is that there was no room in the inn for Christ*
*when He came; however, when recognized for who He is, wise men still*
*seek and receive Him.*

# "THE INNKEEPER OF BETHLEHEM"

from *The Glorious Galilean*[3]
by J. W. G. Ward

It's incredible that when the Son of God was born on earth, there was no room for Him at the inn. He could have been born in an ivory palace. He could have come as the rightful King. Instead, He was born in humble estate.

His accommodation at the time of His birth was a smelly stable, and He was laid in a manger. Most people don't even know what that is; they think of it as some sort of special crib for Jesus. But a manger was a feeding trough for animals! When our daughter was a baby, we stayed one time in a room where there was no crib for her, but there was a dressing cabinet drawer that we put her in. It became her makeshift crib. And so it was for Jesus. The manger in that stable became His makeshift crib.

Most of the people at the time of Jesus' arrival on earth had no idea who He was and how important He was. But when they understood, as the innkeeper of Bethlehem does in this fictional story, then they paid Him the homage due.

J. W. G. Ward wrote a wonderful book in 1936, entitled *The Glorious Galilean,* which contains about ten stories of people with whom Christ came in contact. I have used a few of them in this book. The first is "The Innkeeper of Bethlehem."

─────────────

We had concluded our business with Shammuz, the wealthy trader of Jerusalem. And we were seated in his luxurious home.

"Did you, by any chance, know the Galilean whose fame was so great in these parts?" we asked.

Shammuz looked up in surprise. That one from afar should inquire of the Preacher seemed unusual.

Shammuz rose from the divan and crossed to the casement, overlooking the market place. Then he said: "Yonder sits one who can tell

─────────────

3. Minor portions of this text have been edited without the use of ellipses.

of the strange happenings, should he be so disposed. At times, he talks freely. Then again, when the mood so moves him, he will say nothing. On the contrary, he drives away those who seek to question him, and with scorn and burning reproaches bids them leave him in peace. A curious fellow indeed."

We looked in the direction indicated. Within the shadow of a tattered awning sat an aged man. His face was tanned and wrinkled. He was listening to the bartering going on between a seller of rugs and a would-be purchaser, and his gnarled fingers were stroking the flowing white beard which fell upon his breast.

"Who is he?" we asked. "Does he always spend his days listening to the talk of the traders?"

"Why, all men know Jeshua," came the reply. "He was the innkeeper of Bethlehem for many a year. Now he lives with his daughter in Jerusalem. Yet he loves to be where the merchants gather that he may hear their talk. Besides, some of them have lodged at his inn. Go speak with him, my friend, if you would hear his tale. At least, your ears will be tickled by his wit—should he see fit to talk to what he knows."

"We thank you, O Shammuz. We will do so."

Taking our leave of the merchant, we walked across the marketplace, and saluted the venerable old man.

"Greeting, O Jeshua of Bethlehem! Nay, do not rise. It is we who come to sit at your feet. Last night, we slept at a hostelry once famed for its host. Like lingering fragrance such as spices yield the memory of your care of passing travelers abides. We have sought you out to tell you so."

Jeshua grunted. Then raising his hand deprecatingly he replied, "You have well spoken. Manon, my father, built that inn, and I took up his task, and for fifty years I served, as did he, the needs of men. If only my son—"

"You have a son, then?" we inquired.

"Yea, but one little worthy of the name—no longer a youth, and yet always a youth in mind. Would he tarry where I labored? Would he be at men's beck and call? Nay; he would rather join those idle fellows who tend the sheep. 'O father Jeshua,' he would say as I reproached him, 'let those who like it have the prison walls of an inn to enclose them. I want to range the vales of Judea, where the winds blow and the stars peer forth by night.' And to think that my inn should pass to strangers!"

Garrulous with age, Jeshua rambled on. We, however, saw our chance.

"Full many a man of note has been sheltered in that abode of yours. Embassies from afar; mayhap King Herod himself has honored your house with his presence? Is that so?"

Jeshua, not ill-pleased at the remark, replied, "Nay; now your tongue runs wildly. Herod slept not beneath my roof. And yet a king, as some have said, was once born there."

Concealing the thrill of interest we felt, we asked, "Born beneath your roof? What king would seek Bethlehem as his birthplace! Would he not be encompassed with royal purple and marble courts?"

"You are altogether foolish," retorted Jeshua, bridling up. "What man can seek any place wherein to be born? If you will listen, verily, I can tell you that which, strange though it may sound, is nonetheless true. I, Jeshua, alone can tell you of him that was born in yonder inn at Bethlehem."

Having successfully lured the old man on, we settled down to hear his story.

"It is even as you said," went on the innkeeper. "This king was not born under my roof. Yet he was, as one might say. It was in the khan where the cattle rest. Nay; look not so unbelieving. It is even so. And I shall yet tell you that at which you may truly wonder.

"Some forty years ago—it must be so, though it seems to be but yesterday—Caesar Augustus, whom God requite for his deeds!—demanded a census of our nation. And for this purpose, every man had to return to the city of his fathers. From north to south, from east to west, many journeyed. Glad were the hearts of those of us whose livelihood was to afford shelter to the traveler.

"Now, in the city of Bethlehem stands the inn where I carried on the work of my father. And right merry was my heart at the sight of wayfarers from afar who sought food and rest. Most of them were of godly stock. They knew the means whereby the rough places of life are made easy, and their purses were well filled. So also was my house! Truly, not since the days of David were our streets so crowded.

"It was long past evening, when there came a knock at my door. Have you ever thought how a man reveals himself by his manner of knocking? Of course not! Well, there is the fierce hammering of him who travels in the king's name; none may brook his anger should he be kept unduly without. There is the firm, confident hand of the merchant who can pay for what he requires, and requires what he pays for. Then there is also the timid tapping of him who has but slender means, and is anxious that he should be accepted with good grace.

"That night, came the sound of one who was in need, yet who was afraid that his coming might be untimely, as indeed it was. Have I not already told you? The hour was late, and the inn full. No messenger of the emperor, nor merchant's hand knocked thus. I mused, as I turned to the door. It was like the sound of a suppliant. Yea; and by the light of the lamp as I stood at the portal I saw that I was right. It was a man from the north country. His garb showed that. Moreover, I knew by his speech that he was from Galilee even before he told me his name. He came, said he—for the bidding of the Roman none dare disobey—to be enrolled in the city of his fathers. But the way had been sore and long, and his wife was faint. Thus they had journeyed slowly, for they had been hindered by the throngs. Men's desire to reach the gates before nightfall, as you can understand, was hot within them. And this was the stranger's request. Could he find shelter for his wife and for himself?

"That sounded fair to my ears, for—it was my pride as it is now my shame—I loved to bargain where I could. There might, I reasoned, be two whom I could well turn out were I to be recompensed aright. So, naming the sum which would warrant me finding room for them, I waited. But it was in vain! This man, Joseph, shook his head. He was poor—a carpenter, forsooth! Then as he turned away, something struck his dull mind. He came back, and whispered in mine ear. Well did I know his guile. To take in the woman would mean that he would later demand a place so that he might shield her from harm. But I would have none of them. He had said that he himself would be well content with a bed of straw in the stable. Why, then, let him and his wife take it. Was not the place large enough for them both? And besides, they were only peasant-folk."

"You sent the woman there in her plight?" we queried.

"Yea; but misjudge me not. Wait, and you shall hear all. How did I know that this man spoke truly? Besides, the hour was late. I was weary, and I had to be astir betimes. You have forgotten what duties lay upon me. Again, that night, a few hours later, my door resounded with the beating of hands. I listened, resolved at first to let them knock. Then thinking of their anger should the guests be disturbed, I went forth from my bed. This time it was Eleazar, my son. With him were certain other shepherds. But before I could demand what senseless folly had brought him to my door, he cried, 'Jeshua, my father, where is he—the king?' I thrust him aside, and sought to close the door. Doubtless, the lad was hot with some folly. 'King?' I said angrily. 'Would you were as concerned for your kin. Begone! get back to those silly sheep; they are fit company for such as you.' Yet the lad was not to be silenced. He told of a sight on which none may look and still live. May Jehovah forgive me, but such was my thought! It was a vision of angels which they had seen on the hillside. The darkness of that Syrian night had been swallowed by light celestial. Clear as the voice of a herald, said they, one had proclaimed, 'I bring you good tidings of great joy. . . . For unto you is born this day in the city of David a Saviour, which is Christ the Lord.' Then followed a great burst of angelic music. And the burden of their song was, 'Glory to God in the highest, and on earth peace, good will toward men.'

"Well I knew that the lad had been witless, irresponsible, and vain. He had proved that in refusing to follow his father's trade. But now I deemed him mad. Yet when I bade him to go and dream again, he demanded of his fellows if he did not speak the sober truth. I was bitter of tongue, and I answered, 'You did well in coming to your father for news of the city. Little happens that I do not learn. Yet no king, least of all the Christ, has been born here in Bethlehem.'

"They seemed convinced at length. Then, by some strange chance, there came back to me the whispered words of that traveler to whom I had given shelter in the khan.[4] Could it be that Eleazar spoke of them? But how could that be? What king was ever born in such a place? However, to satisfy myself, yea, also to quiet my own soul, I led the way to the stable, and bade them follow. A dim light was burning therein. As we peered inside, lo! there was the young mother. A babe lay upon her breast, and Joseph stood looking with fixed gaze upon them both. I turned to speak to my son, but he had fallen upon his knees. The others stood by in rapt wonderment. The very dogs which had followed them from the fields seemed to sense that which clamored for answer within my brain. Then beckoning to the others, we returned to the house. It was no place for us. What we

---

4. A place to sleep.

had looked upon, yea, and that which also I had heard from their lips, left me amazed. To Sarah, my wife, I gave the news of the child's birth, though there was no need to impart to her the tidings which our son had brought. It was a time for deeds, not words. Then, leaving the men to go back to their flocks, I sought my rest.

"Sleep was impossible! The words of that careless lad rang in my ears: 'A Saviour, which is Christ the Lord.'—Could it be that the shepherds were mistaken? They could not all have dreamed the same thing! Yet, perchance, Eleazar had been filling their minds with his weird fancies. He was ever one to let his thoughts run riot.

"But, as I was saying, I could not sleep. Then, for the third time that night, came the sound of eager hands on my door. Anger filled my heart! If Caesar's edict meant that one must obey man's summons night and day, life were too toilsome to endure. Let them knock, said I to myself. Again I thought of the wrath of the guests from whose eyelids sleep was driven, and so of necessity I went forth. Day had dawned as I flung open the door. And in the dim light, I beheld the strangest figures I have ever seen. Three men were there. Two bestrode their camels, while one stood imperiously before me. He demanded to know where the King of the Jews lay!

"I could not at first find words to answer him. My eyes were fixed upon these visitors from afar. All three were gorgeously clad as befitting those who would do homage to a king. I took it all in instantly— the jeweled turbans, the shimmering silk of their robes, the fine trappings of their beasts. What could one say?"

"What indeed?" we replied. "You told them that no King of the Jews was born in Bethlehem?"

"Nay; I thought it wise to leave them to answer their own questions. I asked them to follow me. But even as I walked to the stable, my mind was filled with misgiving. They might perhaps think I was playing a sorry jest upon them. What if they fell upon me in anger? But I resolved to show them the babe, and tell them that the child had been born that very night. Yet whether he were a king or not, none but the wise could say!

"My fears, however, were baseless! They dismounted without a word at the entrance to the khan. Then, as though they had forgotten my presence, they passed in. I caught Sarah's eye, and with unaccustomed obedience to my will she withdrew. Together we watched. The three went forward, doing obeisance to the child as unto the great Caesar himself. What they said we could not hear, but from their robes, each drew forth that which they unwrapped with great care. Again prostrating themselves before the babe and his mother, they laid their gifts before him. We saw what they were. There was an offering of gold, another of frankincense, and a third of myrrh. It flashed through my mind that these were gifts ill-fitting a child born of peasant parents. Since then, as I have pondered the matter, I have wondered if it were indeed a king—the King of the Jews—whom they thus had sought and found!"

"And what do you think now? Do you believe that they were divinely led? Was this the king of our race?"

"That too I have meditated upon through the passing years. Eleazar's story of the angelic vision I might have dismissed as a vain fancy were it not for these men. For, harken! I have told you no idle tale; and if mine be true, why not his? Besides—but I weary you? You must pursue your way?"

"Not until you have told us all. Speak on, Jeshua."

"Well, not many days after, came one who told of what Herod had done. These three men who had visited the inn that night had deemed that the palace of the king could alone shelter one born of the royal house. Following a wondrous star, they had first gone to the abode of Herod the Great. There they had asked for news of the babe born to sovereignty. The king was plainly disturbed. You can understand why?"

"Truly! Was not Herod's father an Edomite, for whose services Pompey had made him governor of Palestine? This office reverted to his son, Herod, who went to Rome, where, by a judicious use of bribes and flattery, he gained the title of the King of the Jews."

"That is right." Jeshua spoke bitterly, and then spat contemptuously on the ground. "A king by bribery must always fear a king by birth! Yea, Herod was afraid lest there might be indeed a king born of the true line. So he summoned the Elders. He was, as you may know, supposedly a convert to our faith. He therefore knew something of our Scriptures, and demanded where this Messianic Prince should be born when Jehovah fulfilled his promise to our nation. The answer was given. And the depth of his subtlety can be seen in what followed. He ordered those who had come to honor the divine king, to go to Bethlehem, to find the child, and then to return to the palace that he might also know where the babe was."

"And did they?"

"Have you never heard that the three were wise men? They found the child. But instead of going back to Herod, they took another course homeward. Although they had suspected the king's duplicity, they could not thwart his wicked purpose. He noted the time when the child was born. Then he issued his decree. All children under the age of two years were ruthlessly slaughtered. That was Herod's way. He slew his own sons because he feared them. Yea, it was rumored that Caesar once said, with biting humor, that he would rather be one of Herod's swine than his son!"

"Yea, so we have heard," we answered. "But what did the guests say next day? Did you tell them of these strange happenings? It seems hard to believe that none should have passed the night without offering to yield place to those pilgrims."

"That also will I speak of. You will laugh when you hear of their diverse moods. There was one, Cushi—if I recall his name aright. He was the spice merchant from Damascus, and one of right bitter speech. I remember that well. He protested with such violence that, if the walls had ears, as some say, they would have been deafened by his fury. 'Never did I spend so long and wearisome a night,' said he. 'Did I not covenant with you for a place to sleep? Then will I pay nothing, for lo! slumber has not visited my eyes. It is monstrous that an honest man should be thus mistreated.'

"And I replied, for my temper was hot, 'If you are an honest man, you will pay what you owe. I covenanted with you neither for sleep nor rest, but only for shelter.'"

The old man laughed silently at the recollection of his shrewdness.

"You see, I was careful to frame my words aright. But even as I was explaining the thrice-repeated blows upon my door, another spoke up. He was Beniah, also a merchant of the same city, and no friend of Cushi. He pretended to be likewise wroth, but I saw an eyelid droop while he unburdened himself.

"'Why did you not find lodgment for this poor mother and her babe?' he asked. 'That the house was full signifies nothing. There were some I know who might have found good fellowship and intelligence akin to their own with the asses and cattle.'

"'And, pray, what does that mean?' inquired Cushi. He was a man of dull wit, but much pride. But the question remained unanswered, for another who stood by, purse in hand to pay what was due, spoke to us all. He was one who had often stayed at my inn. His name was Shealtiel, a venerable man of good repute, and a deep student of our sacred writings.

"'Is it not written that out of Bethlehem should the Anointed come?' he inquired. 'What if this child born here last night were he? What did you say Jeshua, of the strange men who came, and of the costly gifts they offered to this babe?'

"I was about to repeat what I had already said when Cushi raised his hand for silence.

"'These are but old wives' tales. Is it not also written that he should be a Prince of David's house? Yet Jeshua has already avowed that they were but common people—and from Galilee. How do you answer that?'

"I was no longer able to stay. Taking the silver from Cushi's unwilling hands, I left them to their disputings, for I had much to do. Yea, moreover, I was also weary of their words. But let me tell the rest of my story, lest you also grow weary."

"That can never be," we replied. "But what of the child? What became of him? We would hear more."

"Truly, could I with certainty tell you more, I would myself be happier in my age. What I know is only hearsay. Since that night when I turned his parents from my door, peace has been a stranger to my heart. Would that I could undo what I did, or, do what I left undone! The child? Some have freely said that he escaped the sword only to find a cross. I cannot tell. It is that which troubles me. By night, they say, he was taken into the south lands, where he remained until Herod's wrath was extinguished by the waters of death. Then he went to the home of Joseph, in distant Galilee. Long years have passed since then, and I do not recall anything of his doings at that time, except that he was known as the carpenter's son. But one did come who declared himself the forerunner of the Christ. He was known to Eleazar, my son. The lad heard him speak of the Messiah, and he told this Baptist what he had seen in those early days—of the vision of angels, and of a child born in his father's stable. The preacher did not seem surprised. It was even as though he already knew the story.

"Then later, I have heard, that same child came forth from the silent years to speak of the kingdom of God. Verily, I intended to journey to his side and ask whether he were indeed the same. Yet there were many coming and going in those days. Trade with the south was increasing. Caravans were continually passing my way, and the inn required all my strength. Still, I heard many strange things of this Galilean. He was reputed to have power over the ills that torment us. He could give healing to the sick, sight to the blind, life to the dead. Nay, more, to the troubled soul he could afford peace. They even said that he was the Christ, that his kingdom was at hand, and yet— yet—I wonder how that could be when Jehovah let him die a felon's death?"

"What does Eleazar say?"

"Verily, now that is indeed beyond my power to explain. I am old. Fourscore years, even as has been written, are indeed labor and sorrow if one would unlearn old truths, and learn the new. But what my son believes I have heard from his own lips."

"Concerning this Jesus?"

"Ay, even so! Ten years have passed since he was condemned by our elders, and slain as a deceiver upon the cross. But his friends say that he still lives. Some saw him and talked with him after his death. And he was not as one from the place of shadows. He was rather as the Prince of life. Nor is that all! Many have followed the new way. My son is among them. He has told them of that night in which the babe lay in my stable, and they declare that this Jesus is the same. It is that which sorely troubles me. Can this be the Christ?"

The innkeeper turned his keen eyes upon us.

"Do you sincerely ask that?" we said. "Then if the story is ended, let us speak. We also have studied the Holy Writings of Israel. Like yourself we read there of one who was to come forth of the royal line. The time seemed full ripe for him. And the hour brought the man! But we have also read the records written by some who had been the Galilean's most intimate friends. They tell how his disciples were often perplexed about the conflict stirred by the teacher and his mighty works. Yet slowly, like the mists which enshroud Hermon, their doubts had faded as with the rising sun. They perceived not only what Jesus did, but also what he was!

"We resolved to search out for ourselves more perfectly the things we had read. Thus we went to Bethlehem. There we learned that you had been the keeper of that inn. And following the directions which one gave to us, at last we came to learn the truth from your own lips. We have succeeded beyond what we could have hoped. This story has answered questions which have long perplexed us. Now do we declare that that child born at your inn is indeed the Christ of God, the long-desired."

Jeshua looked us full in the eyes.

"You have been the messenger of God unto me. Now I understand! The song of the angels, the star, the slaying of the babes—and your testimony. Though once I denied him the shelter of my inn, now shall he have place in my heart! Yea, verily, for this is indeed the Christ, the Saviour of the world."

---

That fateful night that Joseph "timidly" knocked on his door, the innkeeper of Bethlehem acted in ignorance. How was he to know whom he was turning away from the inn? But today, in too many sectors of our society, there is still no room for Christ in the inn. Only these people should know better because now we know who Jesus is. It's incredible, as some point out, that after 2,000 years, there's *still* no room for Him in many of our homes, in the schools, in the public square, and even in some of our churches! At least the innkeeper (of this fictional account) finally found room after all for Christ.

*This story is suitable for children.*
*The moral of this Christmas story is that Christ is the real reason for the season, and those who receive His free gift of eternal life have received something very special, akin to receiving a million dollars, only far greater.*

# "MERRY TIFTON!"

## by D. James Kennedy

What if you weren't invited to your *own* birthday party? Well, that's sort of how it is often for Jesus Christ at Christmas time. Here's a story from D. James Kennedy about how people celebrate *Christ*mas but don't have a clue about *Christ*.

Dr. Kennedy is one of the great Christian leaders of our time. He serves as the pastor of Coral Ridge Presbyterian Church in Ft. Lauderdale. He is the founder and director of Evangelism Explosion. He's the featured speaker on "The Coral Ridge Hour" (television), "Truths that Transform" (radio), and "The Kennedy Commentary" (radio); his messages are broadcast throughout the nation and on many outlets in other parts of the world. Dr. Kennedy is also the chancellor of Knox Theological Seminary. He is the author of more than twenty books, including *Evangelism Explosion, Why I Believe,* and *What If Jesus Had Never Been Born?* (for which I served as coauthor).

This is a parable based on the old television program called *The Millionaire,* in which a very wealthy man would pick a person out of the blue—anybody—and give him a million dollars. The secretary of the rich man would bring a cashier's check in person. The program would then demonstrate how this new-found wealth would change the life of the recipients. In real life, how much more does receiving God's gift in Christ, the free gift of eternal life, change our lives for the better?

---

Long ago and far away, there lived a man named John Beresforth Tifton, a man whose teeming wealth stretched beyond the farthest dreams of avarice, a man in the strange habit of bestowing $1,000,000 to unsuspecting individuals of his inscrutable choice. Mr. Tifton would dispatch his secretary—Michael Anthony, replete with hat on head, umbrella under arm and briefcase in hand—to deliver not only this bountiful gift of money but legal papers showing that the selected individual had been formally adopted into Mr. Tifton's family and given his name.

You can imagine how radically the gift transformed the lives of its recipients. No matter what his previous financial circumstances, each individual became part of what amounted to a special millionaires' club. Receiving the name of Tifton elevated each one to a new level of prestige and respect he could never have won by himself.

First dozens, then hundreds, and finally thousands all over the world received the benefactions of John Beresforth Tifton. In his will, Tifton explicitly instructed his executors that from the incalculable holdings of his vast estate this practice was to continue down through the years. Thousands upon thousands had their lives transformed as they entered the rarefied atmosphere of the millionaire.

As centuries passed, the people who had received the gift decided it would be a very good idea if they could get together in groups around the world to specially celebrate the birth of their great benefactor. They did! Remember, the only people interested in celebrating Mr. Tifton's birthday were those who had received the gift. Nobody else would have any interest in it. How could they?

As the celebrations continued and grew, Mr. Tifton had hymns written and sung to his praise, pictures drawn of him and essays written about his character, especially his benevolence—all to honor the memory of a man who had changed untold lives.

Then an unusual thing happened here in America. A few people overheard that a party was in progress. After determining its location, they went there and slipped in unnoticed. They didn't grasp what was going on, but they did pick up the idea that somebody had given wonderful gifts to these people who in turn were celebrating that deed. The party crashers thought it was a neat idea; so they told their friends, who told their friends, who told their friends, and on and on and on. Soon non-Tiftons began to celebrate Tifton's birthday too! After all, it occurred in the middle of winter, a very drab time of year, and the celebrations brightened things up a bit.

Believe it or not, the idea spread. Before long, almost everyone was celebrating Tifton Day. It is even true that Tifton Day became a national holiday. As the years rolled on, it was celebrated every year by the masses.

The department stores and other entrepreneurs, with their keen perception, liked this new holiday and were quick to put it to use for their profit. First, they put forth their "Tifton Specials" and people bought their merchandise. Then came the Tifton card, and then even the Tifton tree, though strange to say, it did not even grow in the land of Mr. Tifton's birth.

Years later, on Tifton Eve, two gentlemen from Mr. Tifton's far-off land disembarked from a ship in New York harbor. They were genuine Tiftons, and as they walked down the gangplank, one said, "Would it not be wonderful if we could find one who had received the gift, with whom we could celebrate our benefactor's birthday tomorrow?"

The other replied, "Ah, yes! But in such a large land as this, it is highly unlikely that in so short a period of time we should be so fortunate."

In Mr. Tifton's home country, the celebrations of his birthday continued in their purity: only those who had received the gift entered into them. Thus, our friends were quite unprepared for what befell them.

As they walked down Fifth Avenue, they came upon a department store window which said, "Only one more day until Tifton." Their hearts leaped for joy; what good fortune they had met. Excitedly they read another sign near the first which said, "Tifton Specials, One-Half Off!"

"We are in luck! We have found a Tifton!" one shouted gleefully to the other. "This gentleman has used his million dollars well: he has bought a department store. How strange, though, that he calls himself 'Macy's.' Americans are an odd lot."

As the two started to go into the department store to meet the owner, they heard somebody cry out from across the street, "Merry Tifton!"

Startled to find a second Tifton so soon, they turned to pinpoint the man when someone from their own side of the street cried back, "Merry Tifton to you!"

Before they knew it, a whole chorus of voices was shouting "Merry Tifton and a Happy New Year!" The two gentlemen could hardly believe their ears. "Certainly," one said to the other, "Mr. Tifton has been very prodigal with his gifts in America, unlike anything we have ever seen in his own land." As the two gentlemen made inquiries to one person on the street, they were invited to a Tifton Eve celebration that night.

The celebration was in full swing at a large home when the two Tiftons arrived and was, in fact, a peculiarly American innovation: the

Tifton Eve cocktail party. Enthusiastic before entering, they grew uneasy as they surveyed the scene inside. They heard the tinkling of glasses, raucous laughter, and music blaring through loudspeakers. Wispy clouds of smoke wafted throughout the crowded rooms. Some people were staggering about, almost falling down, because they were drunk.

The two Tiftons stood bewildered. Mr. Tifton would never have approved of this kind of conduct; it certainly did not honor his memory. This prompted one to comment, "I say, dear brother, did you notice this afternoon that some of the people who proclaimed, 'Merry Tifton' were not dressed as elegantly as one would expect?"

"Why yes, I did. I just didn't want to say anything, but they did not look like millionaires to me."

After walking around briefly, each on his own, they reunited by the fireplace and compared notes.

"You know, dear brother," one said, "I cannot begin to understand these 'Tifton cards.' Most of them do not say anything about Mr. Tifton. Instead, they show a picture of a fat man in a green suit pulled about in a chariot drawn by reindeer. What in the world has he got to do with Tifton?"

"Yes, I spoke with some people about him," the other said. "The fat man is a character that has been invented. Uriah Surper, commonly known as St. U. Surper, is his name. It's all quite confusing. We need to investigate further."

They grabbed the attention of the man nearest them and asked, "Excuse us, please. Pray tell us, sir, when did you receive your $1,000,000 from Mr. Tifton?"

"How's that?"

"I said, when did you receive your million dollars from Mr. Tifton?"

"My $1,000,000? Mac, I had to borrow $300 to buy my Tifton presents this year. What are you talking about?"

Our friends looked at each other and said, "Could you please tell us, then, why are you celebrating Tifton?"

"Sure! By the way, Bootstraps is the name, Benny Bootstraps. You are strangers here, too, I see. Just came up from Atlanta for the holidays myself. Tifton Day, eh? Well, I'm no expert on the matter, but as I understand it, Mr. Tifton's life is written up in a big book. Most families have a copy of it in their homes but none of them read it much. I'd like to read it more than I'm able; just don't get much time for it.

"Anyway, this book tells about the life of Mr. Tifton. He was a very rich man. I think he was from the South somewhere, maybe Dallas. He made heaps of money and in this book he tells us how to do it. It's sort of a how-to-get-rich recipe. We are supposed to read it and apply those principles. Then, we will get rich, too."

Our friends looked at one another in utter amazement, for how this explanation of Tifton Day ever cropped up was beyond them.

They continued to inquire, finding yet another man to speak to. "Excuse us, sir, but could you tell us why you are celebrating Tifton?"

"Why am I celebrating Tifton? What's the matter with you? Everybody celebrates Tifton. I've celebrated Tifton all my life. I was brought up that way. My mother celebrated Tifton, and her mother celebrated Tifton. I remember when I was just a kid, I used to hang my Tifton stocking from the mantelpiece. Why do you question our custom? Don't you have Tifton where you come from? Ours is a tradition, an old tradition. That's what it is."

Their perplexity continued, but they collared one more fellow in hope of ascertaining what Tifton Day meant to these people. "This fellow is well dressed. Perhaps he can give a sensible explanation."

"Excuse me, Mr. Tifton, my friend and I are also Tiftons, and we would like to acquire a better understanding of your celebration over here. It seems so——."

"Tifton? My name isn't Tifton. It's Mick Mythology. What a coincidence that your names are Tifton. You must get kidded a lot this time of year."

"Yes, of course," they replied. "Well, er, why do you celebrate Tifton?"

"You really don't know?"

"No, we don't."

"There was this fellow named Tifton, who lived far away and long ago. Some people claim he actually lived, but the truth is that we really don't know that. In fact, with our scientific progress and sophisticated technology, we now know that he didn't live.

"Tifton had a habit of giving presents to people—ties, handkerchiefs, cologne, and the like. It's a fable, but it's a nice idea, so we picked up on it and started giving gifts ourselves. We've changed it around a little bit, but that is basically the idea."

"So you don't really think Tifton lived and gave important gifts to people?"

"No, but like I said, it's a nice idea."

"Yes. I can see from that purple tie with the orange stripes you are wearing," one of the Tiftons retorted, "that this is a very significant day in your life."

Thoroughly bewildered, the two gentlemen heard a knocking at the door. When no one answered, it opened, and through its way stepped in the perennial descendant of Michael Anthony, umbrella under one arm and briefcase in hand. The two friends from far away looked at each other with glad joy. At this party, someone was going to receive the gift. At least one person would come to know what Tifton Day was truly all about.

Mr. Anthony said, "Excuse me, please," but nobody paid him any mind; the music was so loud he could hardly be heard. Trying to talk over all the laughter and hubbub of the party, over all the tinkling of the glasses, he spoke again, "I beg your pardon, but I have here with me. . . ." His voice was drowned out. Yet he stepped up to the closest man, tapped him on the shoulder, and said, "Pardon me, sir, but I represent—."

The fellow interrupted, saying, "Hey, Mac, this is Tifton Eve. We don't do business on Tifton Eve. Come see me on Monday morning. Here, have a drink and celebrate. Merry Tifton to you!"

Without further ado, but dumbfounded by the disregard he received, Mr. Anthony turned and left as unnoticed as he entered. No one received the gift.

The Tifton celebration went on—undisturbed.

---

And so it goes every year with millions celebrating Christmas but knowing nothing of Christ, whose birth they supposedly celebrate. Someone once pointed out that people who wouldn't think of worshiping the adult Christ who died and rose again have little problem celebrating the birth of Jesus—since the baby makes no demands on them. The encouraging aspect of Christmas is that many *can* and *do* grasp its true meaning since it is often openly proclaimed, for example, in Christmas carols.

The apostle Paul said, "Thanks be unto God for His unspeakable gift" (2 Cor. 9:15, KJV), which is eternal life in Christ Jesus our Lord. The gift that Christians have received far outshines the gift Mr. Tifton had to bestow. If you haven't received that gift, I suggest you turn to the appendix.

# SECTION 2

# JESUS CHRIST: HIS LIFE AND MINISTRY

Question: What have you accomplished in the last three and a half years? Stop and think back. Where were you then? What were you doing? Now consider that in the same length of time Jesus Christ performed His public ministry and ultimately changed the world! (Hey, don't feel bad. I didn't accomplish that much either!) Seriously, think about what He accomplished in a mere span of forty-two months. Here you have a wandering rabbi, who goes around "doing good," two thousand years ago, and today He is the focal point of history. The date of this very year is in reference to His birth. Today, scores of millions of people make it their aim to serve Him first and foremost in their lives. Jesus Christ has changed the world!

If you want to know what the God of the universe is like, look at the face of Jesus. He is the visible representative of the invisible God. When God was on earth among us, He went about doing good.

One of my favorite quotes about Jesus says it all. This comes from Napoleon, who may have been converted in his last years (it certainly sounds like it from some of his later writings). He said this of Jesus: "I know men, and I tell you, Jesus is not a man. Superficial minds see a resemblance between Christ and the founders of empires and the gods of other religions. That resemblance does not exist. . . . There is between Christianity and whatever other religions the distance of infinity."[1]

The following stories focus on Jesus' life and ministry.

---

1. Quoted in *The Encyclopedia of Religious Quotations,* Frank S. Mead, ed. (Old Tappan, N.J.: Fleming H. Revell, 1965), 56.

*This selection is suitable for children.*
*The moral of the story is that God is the source of all life.*

# "THE CREATION"

### from *God's Trombones*
### by James Weldon Johnson

James Weldon Johnson (1871–1938) was a great American poet, who accomplished many diverse things. He was the first black to pass the Florida bar exam. He was the editor of *New York Age*. His poem, "Lift Every Voice and Sing" (1900), which was set to music by his brother, became the unofficial black anthem in the 1940s. He was also foreign consul to Venezuela and later Nicaragua. He served as a professor at Fisk University.

But Johnson is perhaps best known for some of his poetry, including his book of poetry, *God's Trombones* (1927). This book was called "dialect sermons in verse," and it became popularized in school recitations. Here is the first poem of that book, the classic poem, "The Creation," based loosely on Genesis 1 and 2.

The poem takes obvious poetic license with the subject matter and, from time to time, would appear to be in conflict with the overall teaching of the Bible. For example, it says that God made us because He was lonely. On the contrary, the Bible reveals God as self-sufficient, needing nothing, implying He is therefore not in need of human companionship either.[2] But the poem should be enjoyed as just that—a poem—and not as the straightforward teaching of doctrine. The moral of the story is that God is the source of all life on earth. I have placed it in the first part of the book because the Bible reveals Christ as the co-Creator: "Without him [Jesus] nothing was made that has been made" (John 1:3).

———————

And God stepped out on space,
And he looked around and said,

———————————————————

2. Theologian Dr. Walter Elwell, editor of the massive *Baker Encyclopedia of the Bible* writes, "God's *independence* or self-existence indicates that he is not dependent on anything outside himself. He is self-sufficient in his existence, in his decrees, and in all his works." Walter Elwell, gen. ed., *Baker Encyclopedia of the Bible*, vol. 1 (Grand Rapids, Mich.: Baker, 1988), 878. (Emphasis his.)

"I'm lonely—
I'll make me a world."

And far as the eye of God could see
Darkness covered everything,
Blacker than a hundred midnights
Down in a cypress swamp.

Then God smiled,
And the light broke,
And the darkness rolled up on one side,
And the light stood shining on the other,
And God said, "That's good!"

Then God reached out and took the light in His hands,
And God rolled the light around in His hands
Until He made the sun
And He set that sun a-blazing in the heavens.
And the light that was left from making the sun
God gathered up in a shining ball
And flung against the darkness,
Spangling the night with the moon and stars.
Then down between
The darkness and the light
He hurled the world;
And God said, "That's good!"

Then God himself stepped down—
And the sun was on His right hand,
And the moon was on His left;
The stars were clustered about His head,
And the earth was under His feet.
And God walked, and where He trod
His footsteps hollowed the valleys out
And bulged the mountains up.

Then He stopped and looked and saw
That the earth was hot and barren.
So God stepped over to the edge of the world

And He spat out the seven seas;
He batted His eyes, and the lightnings flashed;
He clapped His hands, and the thunders rolled;
And the waters above the earth came down,
The cooling waters came down.

Then the green grass sprouted
And the little red flowers blossomed,
The pine-tree pointed his finger to the sky,
And the oak spread out his arms;
The lakes cuddled down in the hollows of the ground,
And the rivers ran down to the sea;
And God smiled again,
And the rainbow appeared,
And curled itself around His shoulder.

Then God raised His arm and He waved His hand
Over the sea and over the land,
And He said, "Bring forth! Bring forth!"
And quicker than God could drop His hand,
Fishes and fowls
And beasts and birds
Swam the rivers and the seas,
Roamed the forests and the woods,
And split the air with their wings,
And God said, "That's good!"

Then God walked around,
And God looked around
On all that He had made.
He looked at His sun,
And He looked at His moon,
And He looked at His little stars;
He looked on His world
With all its living things,
And God said, "I'm lonely still."
Then God sat down
On the side of a hill where He could think;
By a deep, wide river He sat down;

With His head in His hands,
God thought and thought,
Till He thought, "I'll make me a man!"

Up from the bed of the river
God scooped the clay;
And by the bank of the river
He kneeled Him down;
And there the great God Almighty
Who lit the sun and fixed it in the sky,
Who flung the stars to the most far corner of the night,
Who rounded the earth in the middle of His hand—
This Great God,
Like a mammy bending over her baby,
Kneeled down in the dust
Toiling over a lump of clay
Till He shaped it in His own image;

Then into it He blew the breath of life,
And man became a living soul.
Amen. Amen.

---

It has been said, "We can't figure out where we're going if we don't know where we came from." This story, fanciful as it is in parts, spells out where we came from.

Jesus is the Author of life. He not only created life; He sustains it. Every beat of your heart is by His grace. The Scriptures say of Christ: "He is before all things, and in him all things hold together" (Col. 1:17, NIV).

*This selection is suitable for children.*
*The moral of the story is that Christ is the light of the world. He that*
*follows Him will never walk in darkness.*

## "THE MAN BORN BLIND"

### from *The Glorious Galilean*
### by J. W. G. Ward

"Before I was blind, but now I can see" is the sentiment that any true Christian can express. Becoming a Christian opened our eyes to what life is all about. Jesus took us from spiritual blindness to spiritual insight.

When He was on earth, Jesus did many miracles that represented who He was and what His mission was. He changed water into wine because He had come to give us joy and an abundant life. He fed thousands of people with merely a few loaves of bread because He was the bread of life. And He opened the eyes of the blind because He was the light of the world.

"The Man Born Blind" creatively tells what happened to the man born blind to whom Christ gave sight. This can be found in John 9. This is another story from J. W. G. Ward's *The Glorious Galilean*.

---

"Ask me not concerning Jesus, the Christ," he answered.

We looked at him with astonishment, for we had found him only after a long walk through the tortuous and narrow streets of Jerusalem. And it was the first time we had been rebuffed.

"Why not, pray? Are you not he who was born blind?" we persisted. "Did not Christ give you the priceless gift of sight?"

He regarded us with a whimsical smile, and at once we knew we had judged him hastily.

"Truly did he. That is why I said do not ask me about him. My reason? Because no tongue can utter, no words convey a thousandth part of the gratitude that swells within my bosom. And I would do myself a wrong were I to attempt that which is beyond the powers of man."

It was with some relief that we listened. And then we said, "Friend, you are right. Yet for the sake of those who love the Lord and would love him more, try even the impossible and tell us of your experience of his grace."

"Well, the world into which I came was enshrouded with gloom. Now that I can see I begin to realize what I had missed. No radiant east in saffron robes proclaimed the coming day. No golden splendor of the west glowed as the sun set. No diamond-mantled skies overspread my couch at night. The birds that chirp upon the boughs, yonder solemn hills clothed with majesty, the flower-decked valleys stretching there far beyond the walls—of these I had heard from my companions, but to me they were but empty words. And now—

"My parents were poor, and too long had I been a burden to them. So I had to take the only course then open to men like me: I sat to beg the charity of passersby. My days had been tedious but for a way I devised of snatching some little interest from the people who sometimes spoke to me. I learned to know the voice and what it revealed of the inner man. Ah! you never guessed that the soul is laid bare even by the tone? That is how I cheated the hours of their grievous weight. One day a group of strangers paused near where I sat. At once I placed them by their speech as from the north country. Beyond Samaria, it must be Galilee. And as I mused over this, I was greatly surprised, because they spoke of my affliction.

"'Master, who did sin, this man or his parents, that he was born blind?' Immediately I knew who they were. The word 'Master' would have told me that, even had I not located the place whence they came. For my friends and I had heard much of Jesus. We knew him to be a prophet, mighty in deed. Yea, some had further said that he could also remove human misery. But my mind hung upon their words. It was an old question—that problem of suffering. Many a time had I demanded of myself why Jehovah should permit some to be so blessed with riches and all the heart can wish, while others were denied even the ordinary faculties which men esteem so lightly until they have them not. But, although I had never found any satisfactory explanation, I had never heard anyone ascribe affliction or pain to the sin of a man before he was born. What folly the wise can utter! But I found myself waiting, listening intently for the Master's reply. And I declare that never had I heard a voice that moved my inmost soul as did his. Then he replied, 'Neither hath this man sinned, nor his parents, but that the works of God should be made manifest in him. I must work the works of him that sent me.'

"Suddenly, I sprang to my feet and flung myself prostrate before him. Imploring his mercy and help, I remember how I turned my sightless eyes upon him, stretching out my arms in entreaty. Would he be moved by the cry of a forlorn beggar? The favors of the great were freely bestowed only upon those who could make some adequate recompense. And I—naught could I offer by way of bribe, inducement, or reward. Thus it flashed across my darkened mind how vain and futile such a plea as mine.

"But even while I thus reasoned, I felt his hands pressing moist clay gently upon my eyelids. Then came the commanding word, 'Go wash in the pool of Siloam.' Without a word, unquestioning the sincerity of his implied promise, I began to thread my way through the streets. That was indeed a test both of patience and faith—patience, for you, to whom eyes are not as precious as the costliest gems that ever merchant found, cannot know how hard is the path of the sightless; and my faith also was tried, for, evil though I know now those thoughts to be, as I wandered on, doubts arose in my mind like the fever-laden vapors of the swamp. What could it mean? Was it only a pretense? Perhaps it was to rid himself of my importunity, and while I pursued some foolish quest, I was losing what little gain might otherwise be mine.

"Then my heart rose in revolt against such unworthy thoughts. Had I trained myself to read the soul in a man's voice in vain? I knew that Jesus would not, yea, could not, mock one in such a plight. And thus to Siloam's waters I came. As I stood by the edge and laved my eyes, lo! it was as though the curtains of night had been suddenly torn aside. There lay the pool like a silver mirror, the blue sky above my head, and people leisurely passing along the highway beyond. It was all so unbelievable, so wonderful! I now stumbled on my way to the synagogue. My brain was set on fire. Two things I must do. First I must render thanks to the Almighty Benefactor of the race for the mercy that was mine. Then I must search him to whom I owed so much. Even though none might tell me where he was, though I did not know his face, I had but to hear once more that soul-compelling voice to find my Master and Lord.

"Hard by the Temple, whom should I encounter but some of our neighbors. They recognized me. And one could not but be amused at their surprise. 'Is not this he that sat and begged?' asked one. 'This is he,' replied some. While others, unconvinced as they might well be, remarked, 'He is like him.' I decided it for them, however, by saying, 'I am he!' You ought to have seen the wonder with which they gazed upon me, as though doubting their very senses. They could not credit it, but verily I could scarcely do so myself. At once they assailed me with eager questions. 'How were thine eyes opened?' All I could tell them was the bare facts. 'A man that is called Jesus made clay, and anointed mine eyes, and said unto me, Go to the pool of Siloam, and wash' and I went and washed, and I received sight.' They evidently knew Jesus, certainly better than I, for they demanded excitedly, 'Where is he?' Probably it was the first time his miraculous power had come so closely to them. But I could not tell them where he was. I had never seen him.

"The matter, however, was not to end there. Whether it was to prove that the people's estimates of Jesus were correct and the rulers' wrong, I cannot say. Possibly they wanted to give proof of their faith to those who had maligned him. But they led me to the Pharisees in triumph. One thing had, I think, escaped them. It was the Sabbath day, and this work of healing had been performed thereon! The elders stared at me as my friends spoke, and then one of them inquired curtly how my sight had been given to me. I am sure they would have branded me as a cheat—one who had made pretense of being blind—had not these men spoken so vehemently. In very truth, I was beginning to feel wrathful at their unbelief, and so I answered, 'He put clay upon my eyes, and I washed and do see.'

"They were in a difficulty. They could not deny the testimony of those about me, nor could they doubt that my infirmity had been removed. Therefore, unable to dispute the fact, they sought to discredit Jesus and poison the minds of the people against him. 'This man is not of God,' they said, authoritatively, 'because he keepeth not the Sabbath day.' But, oddly enough, another of their number asked, 'How can a man that is a sinner do such miracles?' To cover their confusion, he who had spoken first demanded, 'What sayest thou of him, that he hath opened thine eyes?' And I replied, 'He is a prophet.'

"The news had spread quickly. My parents had come to the synagogue to worship as was their custom, and word had reached them. They came up at this moment, thrusting the neighbors aside to greet me. And at once the elders questioned them. 'Is this your son, who ye say was born blind? how then doth he now see?' My father spoke up. 'We know that this is our son, and that he was born blind. But by what means he now seeth, we know not; or who hath opened his eyes, we know not: he is of age; ask him: he shall speak for himself.' I understood why he evaded the responsibility of a direct answer. The elders had already threatened that if any man acknowledged Jesus as the Christ he should be expelled from the synagogue.

"They confronted me once more. 'Give God the praise,' they said, piously. 'We know that this man is a sinner.' But by this time I was thoroughly angry, for I had perceived their crafty purpose, and I did not care what might happen to me. 'Whether he be a sinner or no, I know not: one thing I know, that, whereas I was blind, now I see!' But they were still unwilling to admit defeat before the people, and they asked me again, 'What did he to thee? how opened he thine eyes?' And now, blazing with indignation at their unscrupulous ways, I cried, 'I have told you already, and ye did not hear: wherefore would ye hear it again? will ye also be his disciples?'

"Savagely they reviled me. 'Thou art his disciple; but we are Moses' disciples. We know that God spake unto Moses: as for this fellow, we know not from whence he is.' It was my turn to be bitter now, and I said, 'Why, herein is a marvelous thing, that ye know not from whence he is, and yet he hath opened mine eyes. Now we know that God heareth not sinners: but if any man be a worshiper of God, and doeth his will, him he heareth. Since the world began was it not heard that any man opened the eyes of one that was born blind. If this man were not of God he could do nothing.'

"It would have done your heart good to have noted their helplessness in view of the facts. 'Thou wast altogether born in sins,' they cried, 'and dost thou teach us?' And they hustled me down the steps to the crowded street. But what cared I? I was no longer a blind beggar, no longer a pitiful mendicant, but a man! I could see!

"Two things were clear in my mind. I must not involve my aged parents any further, for the Jews would avenge their discomfiture upon them. Moreover, I had still to find my Benefactor to express my gratitude to him. But he it was who found me. He had heard of the controversy, and that I had been cast out of the synagogue by the elders. He was all solicitude. He knew from personal experience what their enmity might mean, for I would be handicapped enough having to gain a new means of livelihood without having them set men's hands against me. Yet did I not construe his purpose when he asked, 'Dost thou believe on the Son of God?' All I could blurt out

was, 'Who is he, Lord, that I might believe on him?' I was sorely perplexed by the happenings of the day, and I could not think clearly.
That is why I said that. Then as though he had resolved to commit
some weighty secret to my keeping, he said, 'Thou has both seen
him, and it is he that talketh with thee.'

"What could I do? Like that moment when the darkness fled from
my eyes beside the pool, I saw at once what it all meant. Why should
the elders have vowed to punish any who affirmed this to be the
Christ if they were not half-convinced of it themselves? Why were
they so anxious to discredit his miraculous powers if that were not so?
And now, impelled by the truth I saw, I bowed before him saying,
'Lord, I believe!' He laid his hand in blessing on my head. Then he
said, 'For judgment I am come into this world, that they which see not
might see; and that they which see might be made blind.'

"Often have I turned those words over in my mind. What could
they mean? Was it that those who followed the light they had, and
used the part-knowledge vouchsafed to them, should have fuller truth
revealed; and that those who boasted they were enlightened, but did
not live up to what they enjoyed, should have the light withdrawn?
Yea, I am sure it were so. Use or lose is ever the law of life. And
because I had not become embittered by mine affliction, nor reviled
the Almighty for having dealt hardly with me, but awaited the out-
working of his will, because I had inwardly received what Jesus had
given to me, I passed from faith in him as a prophet to acknowledge
him the Prince of David's house and of Jehovah's promise. This is the
Christ of God.

"Now you understand why, at the outset, I bade you not ask me
concerning him. My love to Jesus is like unto the waters of the Jordan, fed by the melting snows of Hermon, swift, turbulent, yet revivi-
fying. And yet, though I put it so, the figure is but a poor one, I
cannot tell you what he has done for my soul. Only the divine Son of
God could have taken the darkness from my eyes; only he could
have satisfied the longings of my heart. And from that distant day to
this hour I have grown more fully thankful that to me was the promise of our ancient prophet Isaiah, fulfilled: 'The people that walked in
darkness have seen a great light. They that dwell in the land of the
shadow of death, upon them hath the light shined.' Yea, a living faith
in Christ is, as I have said, like our noble river. But a superficial
pretense of religion may best be likened to yonder Dead Sea. It

receives all to itself; it gives forth nothing. It takes the bounty of God; it turns naught to account. Therefore it is dead. For in that sea no fish cleave the waters. No luscious vegetation clothes its shores. No bird will even wing its way across its sullen expanse. Rightly it is called dead. But is not the hollow profession of religion also dead and profitless? Tell me, do I not speak true? And what, therefore, shall our own faith be likened to? But to be responsive to the touch of Christ, to obey his bidding, is, verily, to see indeed!"

---

If you know the Lord, then you can truly echo what this formerly blind man said, "All I know is that before I was blind, but now I see." And why is that? Because of the difference Christ has made. If you cannot truly say that for yourself and your own life, I'd like you to turn to the appendix of this book and read it right now. It could make all the difference in the world for your eternal state.

*This selection is suitable for children.*
*The moral of the story is Jesus was a wonderful Savior, who underwent terrible agony for our sakes.*

# THE STARTLING PAINTING [3]

### from *The Idiot*
### by Fyodor Dostoyevsky

One of the greatest writers of all time was the nineteenth-century Russian novelist, Fyodor Dostoyevsky (1821–81). He was also a Christian and it shows in his writings.

Dostoyevsky's work reflects his remarkable sensitivity. Having been sentenced to death for revolutionary activities, he received a reprieve at just the last minute and was then sent to Siberia. Many of the characters of his novel suffer much personal torment. Thus, many of his great works are psychological dramas.

When he was a prisoner, he came across a New Testament, which he read over and over. It had a profound impact on him. So, often in his novels, we see many people who despair of joy and purpose in this life, while we also see a solid Christian character, who shines like a light in the book. This is seen in his great works, including his masterpiece, *Brothers Karamazov*, a portion of which we will feature later in this book.

This short excerpt is from one of his lesser-known works, *The Idiot,* which was written in 1869. The description of the painting is a beautiful word picture of what our Savior accomplished for us through His own agony in our stead.

---

The picture represented Christ who has only just been taken from the cross. I believe artists usually paint Christ, both on the cross and after He has been taken from the cross, still with extraordinary beauty of face. They strive to preserve that beauty even in His most terrible agonies. In Rogozhin's picture there's no trace of beauty. It is in every detail the corpse of a man who has endured infinite agony before the crucifixion; who has been wounded, tortured, beaten by the guards and the people when He carried the cross on His back and fell beneath its weight, and after that has undergone the agony of crucifixion, lasting for six hours at least (according to my reckoning). It's true it's the face

---

3. Excerpted from *The Idiot,* part 3, chapter 6.

of a man only just taken from the cross—that is to say, still bearing traces of warmth and life. Nothing is rigid in it yet, so that there's still a look of suffering in the face of the dead man, as though he were still feeling it (that has been very well caught by the artist). Yet the face has not been spared in the least. It is simply nature, and the corpse of a man, whoever he might be, must really look like that after such suffering. I know that the Christian Church laid it down, even in the early ages, that Christ's suffering was not symbolical but actual, and that His body was therefore fully and completely subject to the laws of nature on the cross. In the picture the face is fearfully crushed by blows, swollen, covered with fearful, swollen and blood-stained bruises, the eyes are open and squinting: the great wide-open whites of the eyes glitter with a sort of deathly, glassy light. But, strange to say, as one looks at this corpse of a tortured man, a peculiar and curious question arises; if just such a corpse (and it must have been just like that) was seen by all His disciples, by those who were to become His chief apostles, by the women that followed Him and stood by the cross, by all who believed in Him and worshiped Him, how could they believe that that martyr would rise again? The question instinctively arises: if death is so awful and the laws of nature so mighty, how can they be overcome? How can they be overcome when even He did not conquer them,[4] He who vanquished nature in His lifetime, who exclaimed, "Maiden, arise!" and the maiden arose—"Lazarus, come forth!" and the dead man came forth? Looking at such a picture, one conceives of nature in the shape of an immense, merciless, dumb beast, or more correctly, much more correctly, speaking, though it sounds strange, in the form of a huge machine of the most modern construction which, dull and insensible, has aimlessly clutched, crushed and swallowed up a great priceless Being, a Being worth all nature and its laws, worth the whole earth, which was created perhaps solely for the sake of the advent of that Being.

---

Speaking of beautiful and moving pictures of Christ's sufferings, there's a classic tale of a wealthy man in Europe in the seventeenth century. Count Zinzendorf had much of what this world

---

4. They were disappointed that He couldn't prevent His death since He could obviously conquer death in the case of Lazarus or others. Meanwhile, the Gospels point out that the disciples really weren't expecting Him to rise from the dead. Only after they saw Him risen did they believe (and even then, some doubted, Matt. 28:17).

has to offer—money, position, success. But one day he saw a painting of Christ with attention paid to His sufferings. A caption at the base of the picture read: "This I did for thee. What hast thou done for Me?" Zinzendorf was so touched by this painting that he dedicated the rest of his life to the spread of the gospel. He founded the Moravian Church, which was extremely missions-minded. He underwrote significant missionary activities, and he himself served as a missionary to Indians in North America—and all from the inspiration of a painting!

*This selection is suitable for children.*
*The moral of the story is that Christ died and rose again for the salvation*
*of us sinners.*

## "ALIVE"

### from *No Wonder They Call Him the Savior*[5]
by Max Lucado

There are stories in this book that come straight from the pages of Scripture. But because of my assumption that the vast majority of the readers of this book are already somewhat familiar with the Bible, I have generally tried to limit the number of stories directly from the Bible. (But when it comes to the subject of envy, how can one ignore the story of Cain and Abel? When it comes to lust, how can you skip David and Bathsheba?)

Now when it comes to the life of Christ, virtually every incident is well-known. Therefore, I have tried to find stories that somehow approach the subject afresh. I have tried to find examples where these stories are retold with such creative flair that we discover anew just how magnificent Jesus Christ really is.

Now how do you tell afresh the crucifixion and resurrection of our Lord? His is the most famous death of anyone's in the world. The symbol of that death is seen all over the world—even in fashion jewelry! So my goal was to find a creative retelling of the most important event in the history of the world, Jesus' death and rising again.

Max Lucado, one of our most creative and popular contemporary Christian writers has, in my opinion, filled the need. He wrote of the cross and empty tomb by using a continuous flow of one-word sentences. This is "story in staccato," if you will. I hope it will jar your thinking about what Jesus Christ accomplished by His death and resurrection.

---

Road. Dark. Stars. Shadows. Four. Sandals. Robes. Quiet. Suspense. Grove. Trees. Alone. Questions. Anguish. "Father!" Sweat. God. Man. God-Man. Prostrate. Blood. "NO!" "Yes." Angels. Comfort.

5. Max Lucado, *No Wonder They Call Him the Savior* (Portland, Oreg.: Questar Publishers, 1986), 113–15.

Footsteps. Torches. Voices. Romans. Surprise. Swords. Kiss. Confusion. Betrayal. Fearful. Run! Bound. Wrists. Marching.

Courtyard. Priests. Lamps. Sanhedrin. Caiphas. Sneer. Silk. Arrogance. Beard. Plotting. Barefoot. Rope. Calm. Shove. Kick. Annas. Indignant. Messiah? Trial. Nazarene. Confident. Question. Answer. Punch!

Peter. "Me?" Rooster. Thrice. Guilt.

Proceedings. Court. Rejection. Prosecute. Weary. Pale. Witnesses. Liars. Inconsistent. Silence. Stares. "Blasphemer!" Anger. Waiting. Bruised. Dirty. Fatigued. Guards. Spit. Blindfold. Mocking. Blows. Fire. Twilight.

Sunrise. Golden. Jerusalem. Temple. Passover. Lambs. Lamb. Worshipers. Priests. Messiah. Hearing. Fraud. Prisoner. Waiting. Standing. Shifting. Strategy. "Pilate!" Trap. Murmurs. Exit.

Stirring. Parade. Crowd. Swell. Romans. Pilate. Toga. Annoyed. Nervous. Officers. Tunics. Spears. Silence. "Charge?" "Blasphemy." Indifference. Ignore. (Wife. Dream.) Worry. Interview. Lips. Pain. Determined. "King?" "Heaven." "Truth?" Sarcasm. (Fear.) "Innocent!" Roar. Voices. "Galilean!" "Galilee?" "Herod!"

9:00 A.M. Marchers. Palace. Herod. Fox. Schemer. Paunchy. Crown. Cape. Scepter. Hall. Elegance. Silence. Manipulate. Useless. Vexed. Revile. Taunt. "King?" Robe. Theatrical. Cynical. Hateful. "Pilate!"

Marching. Uproar. Prisoner. Hushed. Pilate. "Innocent!" Bedlam. "Barabbas!" Riot. Despair. Christ. Bare. Rings. Wall. Back. Whip. Slash. Scourge. Tear. Bone. Moan. Flesh. Rhythm. Silence. Whip! Silence. Whip! Silence. Whip! Thorns. Stinging. Blind. Laughter. Jeering. Scepter. Slap. Governor. Distraught. (Almost.) Eyes. Jesus. Decision. Power. Freedom? Threats. Looks. Yelling. Weak. Basin. Water. Swayed. Compromise. Blood. Guilt.

Soldiers. Thieves. Crosspiece. Shoulder. Heavy. Beam. Heavy. Sun. Stagger. Incline. Houses. Shops. Faces. Mourners. Murmurs. Pilgrims. Women. Tumble. Cobblestone. Exhaustion. Gasping. Simon. Pathetic. Golgotha.

Skull. Calvary. Crosses. Execution. Death. Noon. Tears. Observers. Wails. Wine. Nude. Bruised. Swollen. Crossbeam. Sign. Ground. Nails. Pound. Pound. Pound. Pierced. Contorted. Thirst. Terrible. Grace. Writhing. Raised. Mounted. Hung. Suspended. Spasms. Heaving. Sarcasm. Sponge. Tears. Taunts. Forgiveness. Dice. Gambling. Darkness.

Absurdity.

Death. Life.
Pain. Peace.
Condemn. Promise.
Nowhere. Somewhere.
Him. Us.
"Father!" Robbers. Paradise. Wailing. Weeping. Stunned. "Mother."
Compassion. Darkness. "My God!" Afraid. Scapegoat. Wilderness. Vinegar. "Father." Silence. Sigh. Death. Relief.

Earthquake. Cemetery. Tombs. Bodies. Mystery. Curtain. Spear.
Blood. Water. Spices. Linen. Tomb. Fear. Waiting. Despair. Stone.
Mary. Running. Maybe? Peter. John. Belief. Enlightenment. Truth.
Mankind. Alive. Alive. Alive!

---

Amen. Amen. Amen.

*This selection is suitable for children.*
*The moral of the story is that Jesus the Savior will not fail us, even when everybody else does. Though the world, the flesh, and the devil try to tear us down, only He can save us.*

# THE STORY OF THE FAITHFUL FRIEND AND ITS EXEGESIS IN A MEDIEVAL SERMON

(summary of *Everyman,* one of the best-known morality plays of the Middle Ages)
Adapted in Modern English[6]

During the late Middle Ages, morality plays were performed in parts of Europe. The morality plays, judged by many today as weak plays with wooden characters, often had characters who were named the part so you wouldn't lose the meaning. Some sixty of these plays have survived to this day. *Everyman* is one of the survivors. What we have here is a summary of the play, not an excerpt of the play itself. This summary, as paraphrased here, is the essence of the story of *Everyman.*

---

I find a tale that there was sometime a man that had four friends. And in three of them especially he laid great affection in, but in the fourth he had but little affection in. So it befell on a time that he had trespassed against the king of the land, and so had violated the law to the point that he was to be executed. And when he was arrested and should be brought to judgment, he pleaded with them that took him that he might speak with his friends before he died. They granted his request.

He came to his first friend, that he trusted most in, and asked him for his help, if he would assist him as he appealed to the king for mercy. But the first friend answered him this way: "The king's felon I will not help, for thou art worthy to die; but I will do this for thee: I will buy thee a cloth to bury thee in." He had no other answer.

He went away sorrowfully and came to his second friend, beseeching him of his help against the king, that he would grant him his life. And his second friend answered him and said that the king's felon

---

6. This story summarizes the plot of *Everyman.* It is here adapted in a slightly modernized form from a sermon, probably of the late fourteenth century, in W. O. Ross, ed., *Middle English Sermons* (London EETS O.S. 209, 1940), 86–88. First published in G. A. Lester, ed., *Three Late Medieval Morality Plays: Mankind, Everyman, Mundus et Infans* (London: A & C Black, 1981, 1990), 104–105. I have updated several of the antiquated words.

should have no other favour of him but that he would himself lead the king's traitor unto death! But the felon slipped away, and he went unto his third friend.

When he found the third friend, he asked if he would be willing to go with him to help him plead for mercy before the king. The third friend answered him and said that he would not help him; but rather, since he was the king's traitor, he would help to hang him!

Then he went to seek the help of his fourth friend, the one he trusted the least, and he asked him that he would go with him and plead for him to the king that he would forgive him his trespass. And then the fourth answered him and said: "Inasmuch as thou request this of me, though thou have but little deserved it, yet I will go with thee to the king and pray the king to forgive thee thy trespass; and rather than thou should be dead, I will die for thee myself."

Here's the explanation of this parable. Now the first friend that mankind seeks help from the most is the world. But what does the world give to mankind after his death? In this life, the world may grant to many men riches and pomp. But what friendship does the world show to a man at the end of his life? Nought else but an old sheet of the earth to wrap him in! This is a worthless friendship.

The second friend that mankind has in this world is his father and his mother, his brothers and sisters, his wife and his children. But what friendship do these show unto him? They weep and cry and wail his death, and bring him to his grave, and there they leave him; and after a while they have forgotten him. . . .

The third friend that comes to mankind is the devil, to whom many men are inclined these days to obey his bidding, whatever that he bid them do. For many a person is more obedient to the devil than he is to his pastor, his wife, or her husband. And as soon as such a man is dead, the thief [the devil] is ready to bring the soul into pain.

Then since these three friends fail in the time of need, we then come to the fourth friend, that is Christ, whose friendship and whose love we may not be without, for his friendship delivers us from the bitter pains of hell, and restores us to everlasting life.

---

While others may fail us, Jesus never will. He is a friend that "sticketh closer than a brother."

# SECTION 3

# IMITATING CHRIST

We live in an age where there is a dearth of real heroes. When asked who are their heroes, young people today list all sorts of rock stars and movie stars, whose names rotate from time to time. However, many of these people would be found wanting when evaluated by the "content of their character," to borrow a phrase from Dr. Martin Luther King.

There's no question that we face a character crisis in this country. Many of our national leaders, in all sorts of fields—not just politics, but business, academia, and even religion—have been proven to have feet of clay.

But there is One we can emulate, who is the ultimate hero, and that is Jesus Christ. He has the most perfect character of anyone the world over. In His own day, Jesus asked His critics—not His friends, His critics—"Which of you can convict me of sin?" But they responded in silence.

Even skeptics and nonbelievers have commented on Christ's flawless character. For example, W. E. Lecky of Dublin, a skeptic and historian said, "Christ has exerted so deep an influence that it may be truly said that the simple record of three short years of active life has done more to regenerate and soften mankind than all of the disquisitions of philosophers, and all the exhortations of moralists."[1] Lord Byron, the poet, put it this way: "If ever man was God, or God man, Jesus Christ was both."[2] And the great French infidel, Ernest Renan,

---

1. William Lecky, *History of European Morals from Augustus to Charlemagne,* as quoted in Josh McDowell, *Evidence that Demands a Verdict: Historical Evidences for the Christian Faith,* revised edition (San Bernardino, Calif.: Here's Life Publishers, 1972, 1979), 132–33.

2. As quoted in Frank S. Mead, *The Encyclopedia of Religious Quotations* (Old Tappan, N.J.: Fleming H. Revell Company, 1965), 51.

said, "Whatever may be the surprises of the future, Jesus will never be surpassed."[3]

From time to time, we read in the papers an inconceivable story: a very wealthy man or woman who "has it all" kills him or herself. *How could they do that?* we wonder. They were set for life. But in reality their lives were empty, for they were not fulfilling the purpose for which they were created.

God created us for fellowship with Him. And when we follow Him, come what may, including persecution, we are fulfilling the very purpose for which we were placed on earth: to glorify God and enjoy Him forever, as the Westminster shorter catechism puts it.

The following stories are all related to the joys and sacrifices of living a life in imitation of Christ. The moral of the stories that follow is that while there is a cost to following Christ, there is great joy as well.

---

3.   Quoted in McDowell, *Evidence that Demands a Verdict*, 129.

*This selection is NOT suitable for children (or is suitable with great caution). The moral of the story is that following Christ can be risky business, as all the apostles learned first hand.*

# THE DEATHS OF THE APOSTLES

from *Foxe's Book of Martyrs*
by John Foxe

One of the most depressing—and, at the same time, uplifting—books ever penned is *Foxe's Book of Martyrs*, written by John Foxe in the sixteenth century in England. Foxe (1516–87) was a Protestant historian, who chronicled the history of the Church, with particular attention to those who died for their faith, from the beginning up until 1563 when he published his book.

The portion of *Foxe's Book of Martyrs* that we excerpt here deals with the fate of the twelve apostles (minus Judas). Their testimony was sealed with their own blood. What happened to these men who were among the first to put their faith in Jesus? All but one underwent a martyr's death. John, who escaped such a fate, was exiled on the lonely and hot and humid island of Patmos. But they all kept with their commitment to the very end. None of them fell away.

Foxe's telling of this story is based on traditional accounts. It may not be possible for modern historians to completely authenticate all the details here, but the important point is that these early Christians gladly followed Jesus Christ, even when it cost them their very lives.

Interestingly, while martyrdom seems to have occurred only long ago and far away, in reality, this century has seen the greatest number of Christian martyrs who were specifically murdered for their faith. Dr. David Barrett, one of the greatest church statisticians alive today says that more Christians were killed for their faith in the last nine decades than in all previous centuries combined![4] This is in large part because of the fact that there are so many people alive now and also the fact that the Communists killed so many Christians. For example, the total number of Christians killed in the early Church by Rome over the span of three centuries was approximately two million persons. In contrast,

---

4. David B. Barrett and Todd M. Johnson, *Our Globe and How to Reach It: Seeing the World Evangelized by AD 2000 and Beyond* (Birmingham: New Hope, 1990), 18.

Stalin alone was responsible for killing between fifteen million and twenty million Christians simply because they were Christians. During the Great Proletarian Cultural Revolution in China, Mao's forces killed every known Christian they could lay their hands on. Barrett called this "history's most systematic attempt ever, by a single nation, to eradicate and destroy Christianity."[5] This attempt failed completely; the Church in China has now begun to grow significantly and rapidly. Many reports estimate that there are some eighty million Christians in China! (For further reading on this subject, see D. James Kennedy with Jerry Newcombe, *The Gates of Hell Shall Not Prevail*, chapter 11.)

One last introductory comment: The worldwide persecution and martyrdom of Christians is beginning to heat up in our day. Christians are being savagely treated in some spots on the globe, in particular some of the Islamic countries and the remaining Communist countries. The worst persecution is taking place in Sudan; there have even been reports of some Christian leaders being crucified on trees in that Muslim country. Despite a virtual media black out on all this, tens of thousands of Christians are martyred worldwide each year for the crime of either being a Christian or of spreading the gospel. For more information on this, contact International Christian Concern,[6] an agency which tracks the plight of the suffering Church worldwide. Interestingly, one of the most ardent voices on this issue is a Jew, Michael Horowitz. He has done an outstanding job to help awaken the Christian community to the plight of the persecuted Church.

Please note that the original text (dated 1563) of *Foxe's Book of Martyrs* is obviously in old English. Therefore, we have taken the liberty to "translate" much of it (not including those whom he quotes) into more modern language, while still attempting to be faithful to the text.

---

After the martyrdom of Stephen, the next to suffer such a fate was James the holy apostle of Christ, who was the brother of John. "When this James," said Clement, "was brought to the tribunal seat, he that brought him and was the cause of his trouble, seeing him to be condemned and that he should suffer death, was in such sort moved

---

5.  David B. Barrett, *Cosmos, Chaos, and Gospel: A Chronology of World Evangelization from Creation to New Creation* (Birmingham, Ala.: New Hope, 1987), 60.

6.  To reach the International Christian Concern (located in Silver Spring, Md.) to learn about the worldwide persecution of Christians, call 800-ICC-5441.

therewith in heart and conscience that as he went to the execution he confessed himself also, of his own accord, to be a Christian. And so were they led forth together, where in the way he desired of James to forgive him what he had done. After that James had a little paused with himself upon the matter, turning to him he saith 'Peace be to thee, brother;' and kissed him. And both were beheaded together, A.D. 36."[7]

Thomas preached to the Parthians,[8] Medes[9] and Persians,[10] also to the Carmanians,[11] Hyrcanians,[12] Bactrians[13] and Magians.[14] He was martyred in Calamina, a city of India, being slain with a dart. Simon— brother to Jude, and to James the younger, who were all the sons of Mary Cleophas and of Alpheus—served as Bishop of Jerusalem after James. He was crucified in a city of Egypt in the time of Trajan the emperor. Simon the apostle, formerly called Simon the Zealot, preached in Mauritania, and in the country of Africa, and in Britain: he was likewise crucified.

Mark, the evangelist and first Bishop of Alexandria, preached the Gospel in Egypt, and there he was drawn with ropes into the fire and was burned and afterwards buried in a place called "Bucolus." This happened during the reign of Trajan the emperor. Bartholomew is said also to have preached to the Indians [as did Thomas] and to have translated the Gospel of St. Matthew into their tongue. At last in Albinopolis, a city of greater Armenia, after various persecutions, he was beaten down with staffs, then crucified; and after that, they stripped off his skin and beheaded him.

Jerome wrote this about Andrew the apostle and brother of Peter: "Andrew did preach, in the year fourscore[15] of our Lord Jesus Christ, to the Scythians and Sogdians,[16] to the Sacae, and in a city which is

---

7. Thus, the very man who turned James in to be executed was so moved with remorse that he too became a Christian and was also executed with James, after the two reconciled.

8. Parthia was an ancient country in West Asia, in what is now part of Iran.

9. Media was an ancient country in Southwest Asia in the northwest part of modern Iran.

10. Persia changed its name to Iran in this century.

11. Carmania (also spelled as Carmana or Kerman) was an ancient country in what is now part of Iran.

12. Hyrcania was an ancient province of Persia (modern day Iran).

13. Bactria was an ancient country of southwest Asia, close to the Hindu Kush Mountains. Thomas was working his way eastward into India.

14. The Magians were a sect of philosophers in Persia.

15. A.D. 80.

16. Sogdiana was a province of the Persian empire.

called Sebastopolis, where the Ethiopians do now inhabit. He was buried in Patrae, a city of Achaia,[17] being crucified by Aegeas, the governor of the Edessenes." Both Bernard and St. Cyprian mention the confession and martyrdom of this blessed apostle. Partly from these two and partly from other credible sources, we are able to reconstruct what happened: When Andrew, through his diligent preaching, had brought many to faith in Christ, Aegeas the governor, came to Patrae so that he might compel as many as possible who believed Christ to be God to instead worship the old idols. By consent of the whole senate, the governor wanted to prevent the spread of this new faith so that the people might continue making sacrifices to the idols, giving divine honors to them. Andrew, thinking it good to resist the wicked counsel and the doings of Aegeas at the very outset, went to him, saying something to this effect: "it behooved him who was judge of men, first to know his Judge which dwelleth in heaven, and then to worship Him being known; and so, in worshiping the true God, to revoke his mind from false gods and blind idols."[18] This is the gist of what Andrew said to the proconsul.[19]

But Aegeas, greatly agitated by this, demanded to know if he was the same Andrew that "overthrew the temple of the gods," and persuaded men to join that superstitious sect [the Christians] which the Romans had recently commanded to be abolished and rejected. Andrew replied that the Roman princes did not understand the truth—that the Son of God, coming from heaven into the world for man's sake, taught and declared how those idols, whom they so honored as gods, were not only not *gods,* but were actually very cruel *devils.* They were enemies of mankind, teaching the people nothing else but that which offends God. Being so offended, He turns away and does not answer such prayers. And so, by the wicked service of the devil, men fall headlong into all kinds of wickedness. After they die, nothing remains of them but their evil deeds.

But the proconsul charged and commanded Andrew not to teach and preach such things any more; or, if he did, he should be fastened to the cross with all speed.

---

17. Achaia is a region in southern Greece.

18. In other words, You who are a judge of men would do well to first come to know the Judge (of all the earth) who dwells in heaven. Then worship Him who is the only true God and stop worshiping false gods and idols which can't see.

19. A proconsul was the governor or military commander of a Roman province.

Andrew, not wavering one bit, replied that he would not have preached the honor and glory of the cross, if he had feared death by the cross. When he said this, the sentence of condemnation was pronounced; that Andrew, teaching and promoting a new sect, and taking away the religion of their gods, ought to be crucified. On his way to his execution, seeing the cross being prepared for him, he changed "neither countenance nor color," nor did his blood shrink, nor did he fail in his speech. He didn't faint, nor was he upset. His understanding did not fail him, as happens to some who face torture and death. But out of the abundance of his heart, he spoke, and love broke forth as he said: "O cross, most welcome and long looked for! With a willing mind, joyfully and desirously, I come to thee, being the scholar of Him which did hang on thee: because I have always been thy lover, and have coveted to embrace thee."

Matthew, otherwise named Levi, who had first been a tax collector and then later an apostle, wrote his Gospel to the Jews in the Hebrew tongue. After he had converted Aethiopia[20] to the faith and all Egypt, Hircanus, their king, sent somebody to run him through with a spear.

Philip, the holy apostle, after he labored a lot among the barbarous nations in preaching the word of salvation to them, was also killed. In Hierapolis, a city of Phrygia,[21] he was crucified and stoned to death; and he was buried. (His daughters were with him.)

James, the brother of the Lord, governed the Church with the apostles. From the time of our Lord, he was well-respected and thought to be a just and perfect man. He drank no wine nor any strong drink. He ate no meat and no razor touched his head. Only he could enter into the holy place, for he was not clothed with wool, but with linen only; and he used to enter into the temple alone, and there, falling upon his knees, asked remission for the people. He prayed so much that his knees lost the sense of feeling; they became hardened like the knees of a camel. Because of his excellent and just life, he was called "the Just," and "the safeguard of the people."

When many of the Jewish leaders came to believe in Christ, there was a tumult among the Jews. The Scribes and Pharisees said that this was now becoming dangerous—that the people should not look at this Jesus as the Christ.[22] So they all went to James and said: "We

---

20. Presumably Ethiopia.
21. Phrygia was an ancient country in west central Asia Minor, in what is now Turkey.
22. Christ is a Greek word meaning "Messiah." (The English word is "Anointed One.")

beseech thee restrain the people, for they believe in Jesus, as though he were Christ; we pray thee persuade all them which come unto the feast of the passover to think rightly of Jesus; for we all give heed to thee, and all the people do testify of thee that thou art just, and that thou dost not accept the person of any man.[23] Therefore persuade the people that they be not deceived about Jesus, for all the people and we ourselves are ready to obey thee. Therefore stand upon the pinnacle of the temple, that thou mayest be seen above, and that thy words may be heard of all the people; for all the tribes with many Gentiles are come together for the passover."

And so these Scribes and Pharisees had James get way up on the top (on the battlements[24]) of the temple, and they cried to him, and said, "Thou just man, whom we all ought to obey, this people is going astray after Jesus which is crucified."

And he answered with a loud voice, "Why do you ask me of Jesus the Son of Man? He sitteth on the right hand of the Most High, and shall come in the clouds of heaven."

Many were thus persuaded (that Jesus was the Christ) and they glorified God because of James' witness. And they proclaimed, "Hosannah to the Son of David."

Then the Scribes and the Pharisees said among themselves, "We have done evil, that we have caused such a testimony of Jesus; let us go up, and throw him down, that others, being moved with fear, may deny that faith." And they cried out, saying, "Oh, oh, this just man also is seduced." Therefore they went up and threw this just man down. Yet he was not killed by the fall, but, turning, fell upon his knees, saying, "O Lord God, Father, I beseech thee to forgive them, for they know not what they do." And they said among themselves, "Let us stone the just man, James," which they then began to do, even though a priest said, "Leave off, what do ye? The just man prayeth for you." One of those present, a fuller,[25] took an instrument used to beat cloth, and smashed the just man on his head; and so he finished his testimony. And they buried him in the same place. He was a true witness for Christ to the Jews and the Gentiles.

---

23. In other words, you show no favoritism.

24. The battlements were structures on the sides of buildings, which had openings at the top, providing spaces for people to look down below (similar to what are found at the top of castle walls).

25. A fuller was one who "fulls" cloth—"to scour, cleanse, and thicken cloth in a mill."

Now let us comprehend the persecutions raised by the Romans against the Christians in the primitive age of the Church, during the space of three hundred years. It's amazing to see and read about the incredible number of innocent Christians who were tormented and slain. Their punishments may have varied, but the steadfastness they all showed was consistent. The power of the Lord was seen in them, even in their deaths. Jerome wrote: "There is no day in the whole year unto which the number of five thousand martyrs cannot be ascribed, except only the first day of January."[26]

The first of these ten persecutions was stirred up by Nero in about A.D. 64. The emperor exhibited a fierce and tyrannical rage against the Christians. How much? According to the Church historian Eusebius: "insomuch that a man might then see cities full of men's bodies, the old there lying together with the young, and the dead bodies of women cast out naked, without all reverence of that sex, in the open streets." Many Christians in those days, who, seeing the filthy abominations and intolerable cruelty of Nero, thought that he was the Antichrist.

In this persecution, among many other saints, the blessed apostle Peter was condemned to death. He was crucified, as some write, in Rome. (However, others are not quite sure about that.) Hegesippus says that Nero sought Peter to put him to death. When the people learned of this, they begged Peter to flee the city. They were so insistent that he was finally persuaded. He started to leave, but coming to the gate, he had a vision of Jesus coming to meet him. He worshiped Him and said, "Lord, whither dost Thou go?" To which the Lord answered, "I am come again to be crucified." By this, Peter understood that he [Peter] was supposed to suffer, so he returned back into the city. Jerome said that he was crucified upside down on his own insistence because he was not worthy to be crucified in the same form and manner as the Lord was.

Paul, the apostle, who before was called Saul, after his great travail and unspeakable labors in promoting the Gospel of Christ, suffered also in this first persecution under Nero. Abdias, declares that for his execution Nero sent two of his trusted military men, Ferega and Parthemius, to bring him word of his death. When they heard Paul

---

26. In other words: Virtually every day of the year but January 1 was an anniversary of some 5,000 Christians killed (during the first three centuries of Christianity). (Note: that conforms with the number of approximately 2 million Christians killed in that time frame.)

instructing the people, they desired him to pray for them, that they might believe. He told them that shortly after they should believe and be baptized at his sepulchre. After he said this, the soldiers came and led him out of the city to the place of execution, where he, after his prayers made, gave his neck to the sword. . . .[27]

The tyrants and instruments of Satan weren't satisfied with death only, to rob the life from the body. Whatever cruelness man could think up, they devised for the torturing and killing of Christians. These included: "stripes and scourgings, drawings, tearings, stonings, plates of iron laid unto them burning hot, deep dungeons, racks, strangling in prisons, the teeth of wild beasts, gridirons, gibbets[28] and gallows, tossing upon the horns of bulls." Moreover, after they were thus killed, their bodies were laid in heaps, and dogs were placed to guard the corpses, so that no one could remove them to bury them, neither would any request to obtain them be granted.

And yet, in spite of all these continual persecutions and horrible punishments, the Church increased daily—deeply rooted in the doctrine of the apostles and of apostolical men—and was watered abundantly with the blood of saints.

---

What an incredible and moving account of the courage of the early Christians! Sometimes, it's hard to relate to that intense persecution and commitment on the part of the believers. Unfortunately, the modern Church is plagued with a problem of "Easy Believism." We seem to be able to get people to make a "commitment to Christ," but it too often ends up to be a shallow one. Obviously, that was not a problem with the apostles, except, of course, Judas.

It was amazing, and disturbing, to look up all the obscure names of old countries mentioned in this account. Amazing because of the spread of the gospel to so many lands. Disturbing because Islam in the seventh century and beyond snuffed out the light of the gospel in some of those lands, most notably Persia.

Another point about this story is that, when understood in its historical context, it provides compelling evidence that Christ rose from the dead. After His death, the disciples were devastated and depressed. They had put "all their eggs in one basket" and

---

27. Unfortunately, Foxe says no more about Ferega and Abdias.

28. A kind of gallows where the deceased would be hanged in chains and there remain for a time, as a warning.

now the basket had fallen over and every egg shattered. But then Jesus returned from the dead, triumphant over the grave, and these men were overjoyed.

They were so confident that He had risen from the dead because they had seen Him themselves. And they boldly proclaimed His resurrection, even though they were told repeatedly to shut up. They continued to proclaim Him risen until all but one were martyred for their faith.

Keep in mind, the apostles weren't wild-eyed dreamers, poets, and mystics. These were fishermen and one was a tax collector— men of the earth. Most of them were rough and tumble men, not easily swayed by superstitions. Because Jesus rose from the dead, and because He appeared to them, they could not keep silent about Him, even though they had to pay with their lives. Thus, this portion of *Foxe's Book of Martyrs* reminds us that Christianity rests on a firm and unshakable foundation.

*This selection is suitable for children.*
*The moral of the story is that one person can have a powerful impact.*

# "IN THE ARENA"

### from *Loving God* [29]
### by Chuck Colson

There was a time when human beings were being killed for sport. In the gladiatorial contests of ancient Rome, slaves would fight until death. When Constantine professed to become a Christian, in the early part of the fourth century, he decreed that these games should cease. For a while that was so. But slowly they crept back into popularity, until one day in the next century when a humble monk, Telemachus, stumbled across one of these cruel contests in the arena. This story retells the remarkable events of that fateful day.

One of our time's greatest Christian communicators is Chuck Colson, formerly of the Nixon White House, who spent some time in prison for Watergate-related crimes. But he was changed through a personal encounter with Jesus Christ. He describes this transformation well in his classic book *Born Again*. Today Colson heads Prison Fellowship (which he founded), an effective ministry to inmates, and he has written many excellent inspirational books. Colson tells the true story of Telemachus in the gladiatorial arena in this excerpt from *Loving God*.

---

In the fourth century there lived an Asiatic monk who had spent most of his life in a remote community of prayer, raising vegetables for the cloister kitchen. When he was not tending his garden spot, he was fulfilling his vocation of study and prayer.

Then one day this monk named Telemachus felt that the Lord wanted him to go to Rome, the capital of the world—the busiest, wealthiest, biggest city in the world. Telemachus had no idea why he should go there, and he was terrified at the thought. But as he prayed, God's directive became clear.

How bewildered the little monk must have been as he set out on the long journey, on foot, over dusty roads westward, everything he

---

29. Chuck Colson, *Loving God* (Grand Rapids: Zondervan, 1983), 241–43.

owned on his back. Why was he going? He didn't know. What would he find there? He had no idea. But obediently, he went.

Telemachus arrived in Rome during the holiday festival. You may know that the Roman rulers kept the ghettos quiet in those days by providing free bread and special entertainment called circuses. At the time Telemachus arrived the city was also bustling with excitement over the recent Roman victory over the Goths. In the midst of this jubilant commotion, the monk looked for clues as to why God had brought him there, for he had no other guidance, not even a superior in a religious order to contact.

Perhaps, he thought, it is not sheer coincidence that I have arrived at this festival time. Perhaps God has some special role for me to play.

So Telemachus let the crowds guide him, and the stream of humanity soon led him into the Coliseum where the gladiator contests were to be staged. He could hear the cries of the animals in their cages beneath the floor of the great arena and the clamor of the contestants preparing to do battle.

The gladiators marched into the arena, saluted the emperor, and shouted, "We who are about to die salute thee." Telemachus shuddered. He had never heard of gladiator games before but had a premonition of awful violence.

The crowd had come to cheer men who, for no reason other than amusement, would murder each other. Human lives were offered for entertainment. As the monk realized what was going to happen, he realized he could not sit still and watch such savagery. Neither could he leave and forget. He jumped to the top of the perimeter wall and cried, "In the name of Christ, forbear!"[30]

The fighting began, of course. No one paid the slightest heed to the puny voice. So Telemachus pattered down the stone steps and leapt onto the sandy floor of the arena. He made a comic figure—a scrawny man in a monk's habit dashing back and forth between muscular, armed athletes. One gladiator sent him sprawling with a blow from his shield, directing him back to his seat. It was a rough gesture, though almost a kind one. The crowd roared.

But Telemachus refused to stop. He rushed into the way of those trying to fight, shouting again, "In the name of Christ, forbear!" The

---

30. In other words, stop this thing.

crowd began to laugh and cheer him on, perhaps thinking him part of the entertainment.

Then his movement blocked the vision of one of the contestants; the gladiator saw a blow coming just in time. Furious now, the crowd began to cry for the interloper's blood.

"Run him through," they screamed.

The gladiator he had blocked raised his sword and with a flash of steel struck Telemachus, slashing down across his chest and into his stomach. The little monk gasped once more, "In the name of Christ, forbear."

Then a strange thing occurred. As the two gladiators and the crowd focused on the still form on the suddenly crimson sand, the arena grew deathly quiet. In the silence, someone in the top tier got up and walked out. Another followed. All over the arena, spectators began to leave, until the huge stadium was emptied.

There were other forces at work, of course, but that innocent figure lying in the pool of blood crystallized the opposition, and that was the last gladiatorial contest in the Roman Coliseum. Never again did men kill each other for the crowds' entertainment in the Roman arena.

---

When the Emperor learned what happened that day, he ordered the complete cessation of the gladiatorial contests. Because of Telemachus, these savage games were finally stopped once and for all.

This story is a powerful example of the fact that one man or woman *can* make a big difference for good! Telemachus had no idea why he felt led to meander into that coliseum that day. And how could he have possibly known as he lay dying the impact he would have ultimately (until he entered into glory)? Telemachus is an example of bravery and self-sacrificing for the cause of Christ.

*This selection is suitable for children.*
*The moral of the story is that imitating Christ may cost us personally, but in the end, it is well worth it.*

## "THE MINISTRY OF EDWARD SPENCER"
by Jerry Newcombe

This tale is of an unsung and unknown hero who gave himself sacrificially, at the hour of need, on the eve of the Civil War.

I know this story because it took place in my home town, Winnetka, Illinois, a suburb on the north shore of Chicago. Yet your average Winnetkan doesn't know of Edward Spencer's ministry. I learned about it through a book I bought when I joined the Winnetka Historical Society's. At the time, I was in the seventh grade and was by far the society's youngest member. (When I would go to their teas, I was usually among octogenarians!) So great was my love for history that I went on to earn my B.A. in history from Tulane University.

My source for this story is Lora Townsend Dickinson's *The Story of Winnetka*, though Spencer is not its chief character.[31] In my version, however, without altering any of the known historical facts, Spencer is the focus. He imitated Jesus Christ, and his personal sacrifice saved many lives.

---

Those who don't know Jesus Christ as their Savior and Lord are spiritually drowning. It is the work of Christians to rescue the drowning with the life-changing gospel of Christ, which alone brings salvation. In the 1850s a young seminarian was preparing to rescue those who were spiritually perishing. Yet the day came when he was called upon to do this literally. This bittersweet story describes what was his only known ministry. His name was Edward Spencer.

Spencer was a student at Garrett Biblical Institute in Evanston, Illinois (forerunner to Garrett Theological Seminary, which is associated with Northwestern University). In the early morning hours of September 8, 1860, he was called to nearby Winnetka to save the surviving passengers of the sinking *Lady Elgin*.

---

31. The information for this story comes from Lora Townsend Dickinson, *The Story of Winnetka* (Winnetka, Ill.: Winnetka Historical Society, 1956), 62–66 and 200–201.

The *Lady Elgin* was a fancy paddle wheel boat en route back to Milwaukee, after having spent a day in Chicago. The boat was luxuriously furnished although, as it turns out, it had too few life boats. The day before, September 7, the *Lady Elgin* had been chartered by a group of about 400 Milwaukee residents, who went to Chicago to hear Democratic Senator Stephen Douglas rail against his political opponent, Abraham Lincoln. When the political rally ended at 11:30 that night, the passengers reboarded the *Lady Elgin* to travel back to Milwaukee.

The word *travel* comes from the word *travail*, for in ancient times travel was fraught with peril. And that night, the return voyage of the *Lady Elgin* would also prove to be perilous indeed.

Captain Wilson, according to some reports, questioned the wisdom of traveling back at that time, as a storm was brewing on Lake Michigan. (Having spent much time at Lake Michigan, I can testify that storms often rise in an instant, seemingly out of nowhere!) But the passengers, anxious to be home, persuaded the captain to return that night. The storm grew worse as the boat paddled on.

At about 2:30 the next morning, some of the passengers of the *Lady Elgin* slept, while others sang and danced the hours away; but about then a ship in the dark came dangerously close. It was the *Augusta*, a lumber ship sailing from Milwaukee to Chicago. Captain Wilson used a megaphone, barking orders at the crew of the *Augusta* to try and avert a collision. But it was too late! The front of the lumber ship cut a big gash in the side of the paddle boat, and then, for reasons that are not clear to historians, the *Augusta* sailed on to its destination, and left the *Lady Elgin* to its miserable plight. The disaster came some three miles off the shore of Winnetka. All known survivors came ashore on her beaches.

Many drowned right after the crash itself. The captain encouraged the rest to yank off doors, table tops, and whatever pieces of loose wood they could find to try and float to shore. As is the custom, Captain Wilson went down with the ship.

In Winnetka, word of the disaster spread quickly. There were less than 100 residents of the small, sleepy village at the time. People came out to try and help the survivors washing ashore. The local Catholic church was in the midst of mass, and the priest canceled the service to encourage everyone to go help the drowning.

Word reached south into Evanston, to the Garrett Bible Institute. Edward Spencer and his brother William quickly traveled the five miles or so to help. They fastened ropes around each other and dove into the icy waters to rescue whomever they could find.

Edward Spencer proved himself the strongest and bravest of the rescuers. He was a good swimmer, and for six long hours he went out again and again, always returning with someone new. Once he even brought back a husband and wife at the same time.

Many were saved from drowning that night though many more of the *Lady Elgin* passengers perished in Lake Michigan. In the months that followed, 269 bodies washed up on the beaches up and down the western shore of the lake, from Wisconsin through Illinois to Indiana.

On the morning of the disaster, Edward Spencer did all he could; God used the brave young man to save the lives of seventeen people, and his ministry kept them from the grave. On the plaque dedicated to him, which hangs today at the entrance to Patten Gymnasium of Northwestern University,[32] is this inscription: "In the delirium of exhaustion which followed [his daring rescue], his oft-repeated question was: 'Did I do my best?'"

After the rescue effort Edward Spencer himself did not fare so well. His health broke because of those six hours in the freezing waters of Lake Michigan. He never even graduated from Garrett and lived as an invalid for the next sixty-three years. It is said that not one of the seventeen people he saved thanked or corresponded with him, beyond whatever may have been said at the time of the rescue.

Edward Spencer never made it to the pulpit. But he answered the call at the hour of need and held back nothing. He gave everything he had, sacrificing his own life for the sake of the strangers he found in the freezing waters. Edward Spencer rose to the occasion, to imitate the Savior who gave up His life that we might live. His name should be well known in the history books because he provides a powerful example of heroism and bravery.

Nearly 140 years later, who knows how many are the progeny of the seventeen people he saved that day? There may be many; there may be few. But this we do know: every one of them owes his or her life to the ministry of Edward Spencer. Yes, he did do his best!

---

32. I trust the plaque still remains. My source here is a 1956 book.

This side of paradise, some may wonder if it was worth it. It may seem to some that Edward Spencer was a fool. If this life is all there was, indeed he would be. But this life is not all there is! Imagine instead his joyful homecoming. Picture the day Jesus Christ took him into His arms and said, "Well done, thou good and faithful servant!" Imagine his meeting in heaven with at least some of the people he saved years before. Our actions are judged by their eternal consequences, not just their temporal ones. Jesus, who gave His life, has inspired many to lay down their lives for their friends or even for strangers, as was true of Edward Spencer.

*This selection is suitable for children.*
*The moral of the story is that faith in Christ gives joy.*


# "FATHER ZOSSIMA'S BROTHER"

from *The Brothers Karamazov*[33]
by Fyodor Dostoyevsky

As stated before, the greatest works of Fyodor Dostoyevsky are psychological dramas. His masterpiece is *Brothers Karamazov.*

This volume is about a family, where each brother is different in his worldview and outlook. For example, there is Ivan, the humanistic unbeliever, and, at the other extreme, there is Alexey, the dedicated Christian. Alexey is portrayed in a much more attractive way than the nonbelievers in the book, reflecting Dostoyevsky's faith in Christ.

The following tale deals with a lesser character in the book, Father Zossima. He is a sincere monk who is dying at this point. As he reflects over his life, he tells the story of his older brother and how he came to faith despite a skeptical start.

---

Beloved fathers and teachers, I was born in a distant province in the north, in the town of V. My father was a gentleman by birth, but of no great consequence or position. He died when I was only two years old, and I don't remember him at all. He left my mother a small house built of wood, and a fortune, not large, but sufficient to keep her and her children in comfort. There were two of us, my elder brother Markel and I. He was eight years older than I was, of hasty irritable temperament, but kind-hearted and never ironical.[34] He was remarkably silent, especially at home with me, his mother, and the servants. He did well at school, but did not get on with his schoolfellows, though he never quarreled, at least so my mother has told me. Six months before his death, when he was seventeen, he made friends with a political exile who had been banished from Moscow to our town for freethinking, and led a solitary existence there. He was a

---

33. Fyodor Dostoyevsky, *The Brothers Karamazov,* trans. by Constance Garnett. Book 6, chapter 2, section A.

34. Another translation puts it this way: "He never teased me." Andrew H. MacAndrew, trans., *The Brothers Karamazov* (N. Y.: Bantam, 1970, 1981), 345.

good scholar who had gained distinction in philosophy in the university. Something made him take a fancy to Markel, and he used to ask him to see him. The young man would spend whole evenings with him during that winter, till the exile was summoned to Petersburg to take up his post again at his own request, as he had powerful friends.

It was the beginning of Lent, and Markel would not fast, he was rude and laughed at it. "That's all silly twaddle and there is no God," he said, horrifying my mother, the servants and me too. For though I was only nine, I too was aghast at hearing such words. We had four servants, all serfs. I remember my mother selling one of the four, the cook Afimya, who was lame and elderly, for sixty paper roubles, and hiring a free servant to take her place.

In the sixth week in Lent, my brother, who was never strong and had a tendency to consumption, was taken ill. He was tall but thin and delicate-looking, and of very pleasing countenance. I suppose he caught cold; anyway the doctor, who came, soon whispered to my mother that it was galloping consumption,[35] that he would not live through the spring. My mother began weeping, and, careful not to alarm my brother, she entreated him to go to church, to confess and take the sacrament, as he was still able to move about. This made him angry, and he said something profane about the church. He grew thoughtful, however; he guessed at once that he was seriously ill, and that that was why his mother was begging him to confess and take the sacrament. He had been aware, indeed, for a long time past, that he was far from well, and had a year before coolly observed at dinner to our mother and me, "My life won't be long among you, I may not live another year," which seemed now like a prophecy.

Three days passed and Holy Week had come. And on Tuesday morning my brother began going to church. "I am doing this simply for your sake, mother, to please and comfort you," he said. My mother wept with joy and grief, "his end must be near," she thought, "if there's such a change in him." But he was not able to go to church long, he took to his bed, so he had to confess and take the sacrament at home.

It was a late Easter, and the days were bright, fine, and full of fragrance. I remember he used to cough all night and sleep badly, but in the morning he dressed and tried to sit up in an arm-chair. That's how

---

35. Tuberculosis.

I remember him sitting, sweet and gentle, smiling, his face bright and joyous, in spite of his illness. A marvelous change passed over him, his spirit seemed transformed. The old nurse would come in and say, "Let me light the lamp before the holy image, my dear." And once he would not have allowed it and would have blown it out.

"Light it, light it, dear, I was a wretch to have prevented you doing it. You are praying when you light the lamp, and I am praying when I rejoice seeing you. So we are praying to the same God."

Those words seemed strange to us, and mother would go to her room and weep, but when she went into him she wiped her eyes and looked cheerful. "Mother, don't weep, darling," he would say, "I've long to live yet, long to rejoice with you, and life is glad and joyful."

"Ah, dear boy, how can you talk of joy when you lie feverish at night, coughing as though you would tear yourself to pieces."

"Don't cry mother," he would answer, "life is paradise, and we are all in paradise, but we won't see it; if we would, we should have heaven on earth the next day."

Everyone wondered at his words, he spoke so strangely and positively; we were all touched and wept. Friends came to see us. "Dear ones," he would say to them, "what have I done that you should love me so, how can you love anyone like me, and how was it I did not know, I did not appreciate it before?"

When the servants came in to him he would say continually, "Dear, kind people, why are you doing so much for me, do I deserve to be waited on? If it were God's will for me to live, I would wait on you, for all men should wait on one another."

Mother shook her head as she listened. "My darling, it's your illness that makes you talk like that."

"Mother, darling," he would say, "there must be servants and masters, but if so I will be the servant of my servants, the same as they are to me. And another thing, mother, every one of us has sinned against all men, and I more than any."

Mother positively smiled at that, smiled through her tears. "Why, how could you have sinned against all men, more than all? Robbers and murderers have done that, but what sin have you committed yet, that you hold yourself more guilty than all?"

"Mother, little heart of mine," he said (he had begun using such strange caressing words at that time): "little heart of mine, my joy, believe me, everyone is really responsible to all men for all men and for everything. I don't know how to explain it to you, but I feel it so, painfully even. And how is it we went on then living, getting angry and not knowing?"

So he would get up every day, more and more sweet and joyous and full of love. When the doctor, an old German called Eisenschmidt, came: "Well, doctor, have I another day in this world?" he would ask, joking.

"You'll live many days yet," the doctor would answer, "and months and years too."

"Months and years!" he would exclaim. "Why reckon the days? One day is enough for a man to know all happiness. My dear ones, why do we quarrel, try to outshine each other and keep grudges against each other? Let's go straight into the garden, walk and play there, love, appreciate, and kiss each other, and glorify life."

"Your son cannot last long," the doctor told my mother, as she accompanied him to the door. "The disease is affecting his brain."

The windows of his room looked out into the garden, and our garden was a shady one, with old trees in it which were coming into bud. The first birds of spring were flitting in the branches, chirruping and singing at the windows. And looking at them and admiring them, he began suddenly begging their forgiveness too, "Birds of heaven, happy birds, forgive me, for I have sinned against you too." None of us could understand that at the time, but he shed tears of joy. "Yes," he said, "there was such a glory of God all about me; birds, trees, meadows, sky, only I lived in shame and dishonoured it all and did not notice the beauty and glory."

"You take too many sins on yourself," mother used to say, weeping.

"Mother, darling, it's for joy, not for grief I am crying. Though I can't explain it to you, I like to humble myself before them, for I don't know how to love them enough. If I have sinned against every one, yet all forgive me, too, and that's heaven. Am I not in heaven now?" And there was a great deal more I don't remember. I remember I went once into his room when there was no one else there. It was a bright evening, the sun was setting, and the whole room was lighted up. He beckoned me, and I went up to him. He put his hands on my shoulders and looked into my face tenderly, lovingly; he said nothing for a minute, only looked at me like that.

"Well," he said, "run and play now, enjoy life for me too."

I went out then and ran to play. And many times in my life after-wards I remembered even with tears how he told me to enjoy life for him too. There were many other marvelous and beautiful sayings of his, though we did not understand them at the time. He died the third week after Easter. He was fully conscious though he could not talk; up to his last hour he did not change. He looked happy, his eyes beamed and sought us, he smiled at us, beckoned us. There was a great deal of talk even in the town about his death. I was impressed by all this at the time, but not too much so, though I cried a great deal at his funeral. I was young then, a child, but a lasting impression, a hidden feeling of it all, remained in my heart, ready to rise up and respond when the time came. So indeed it happened.

---

This story teaches us that Christ can transform the human heart and convert a miserable person into a happy person. Inter-estingly, psychological surveys show a correlation between reli-gious commitment and contentment with life. One article's title sums it up well: "Keep the faith and be happier."[36] Another point to this story is that life is short and we should enjoy each day the Lord gives us to the fullest. Furthermore, the story shows that faith in Christ prepares one well for dying.

---

36. *Washington Times,* April 15, 1988.

*This selection is suitable for children.*
*The moral of the story is that obedience to Christ will manifest itself in love toward others.*

# IN HIS STEPS[37]

### by Charles M. Sheldon

In the 1890s, Charles Sheldon, a minister of a Congregational Church in Topeka, Kansas, wrote a novel, *In His Steps*, based on the verse in 1 Peter 2:21, wherein the apostle states that we should follow in the Lord's steps. His purpose for writing this was to awaken a smug and cold-hearted churchgoing population.

The selection from *In His Steps* is a compilation of portions of the first two chapters. It sets the premise for the rest of the book. But this selection makes a nice story in and of itself. Something unusual happens at the First Church in the Midwestern town of Raymond. The incident jolts many of the members into a more serious commitment to the Lord. Their commitment in turn has a revolutionary impact on them, the church, and the town. In this portion of the story we see the catalyst for change and the commitment these church members make.

This 1896 novel was an immediate sensation. Translated into most of the major languages in the world, *In His Steps* has become one of the best-selling novels of all time. The year 1996 marked the one hundredth anniversary of this classic book.

---

It was Friday morning and the Rev. Henry Maxwell was trying to finish his Sunday morning sermon. He had been interrupted several times and was growing nervous as the morning wore away, and the sermon grew very slowly toward a satisfactory finish.

"Mary," he called to his wife, as he went upstairs after the last interruption, "if any one comes after this, I wish you would say I am very busy and cannot come down unless it is something very important."

"Yes, Henry. But I am going over to visit the kindergarten and you will have the house all to yourself."

The minister went up into his study and shut the door. In a few minutes, he heard his wife go out, and then everything was quiet. He

---

37. This selection contains portions of chapters 1 and 2 of *In His Steps* and has been edited without the use of ellipses.

settled himself at his desk with a sigh of relief and began to write. His text was from 1 Peter ii. 21: "For hereunto were ye called; because Christ also suffered for you, leaving you an example that ye should follow his steps."

He put down "Three Steps. What are they?" and was about to enumerate them in logical order when the bell rang sharply.

Henry Maxwell sat at his desk and frowned a little. He made no movement to answer the bell. Very soon it rang again; then he rose and walked over to one of his windows which commanded the view of the front door. A man was standing on the steps. He was a young man, very shabbily dressed.

"Looks like a tramp," said the minister. "I suppose I'll have to go down and—"

He did not finish his sentence but went downstairs and opened the front door. There was a moment's pause as the two men stood facing each other, then the shabby-looking young man said:

"I'm out of a job, sir, and thought maybe you might put me in the way of getting something."

"I don't know of anything. Jobs are scarce—" replied the minister, beginning to shut the door slowly.

"I didn't know but you might perhaps be able to give me a line to the city railway or the superintendent of the shops or something," continued the young man, shifting his faded hat from one hand to the other nervously.

"It would be of no use. You will have to excuse me. I am very busy this morning. I hope you will find something. Sorry I can't give you something to do here. But I keep only a horse and a cow and do the work myself."

The Rev. Henry Maxwell closed the door and heard the man walk down the steps. As he went up into his study he saw from his hall window that the man was going slowly down the street, still holding his hat between his hands. There was something in the figure so dejected, homeless and forsaken that the minister hesitated a moment as he stood looking at it. Then he turned to his desk and with a sigh began the writing where he had left off. He had no more interruptions, and when his wife came in two hours later the sermon was finished, the loose leaves gathered up and neatly tied together, and laid on his Bible all ready for the Sunday morning service.

"A queer thing happened at the kindergarten this morning, Henry," said his wife while they were eating dinner. "You know I went over with Mrs. Brown to visit the school, and just after the games, while the children were at the tables, the door opened and a young man came in holding a dirty hat in both hands. He sat down near the door and never said a word; only looked at the children. He was evidently a tramp, and Miss Wren and her assistant Miss Kyle were a little frightened at first, but he sat there very quietly and after a few minutes he went out."

"Perhaps he was tired and wanted to rest somewhere. The same man called here, I think. Did you say he looked like a tramp?"

"Yes, very dusty, shabby and generally tramp-like. Not more than thirty or thirty-three years old, I should say."

"The same man," said the Rev. Henry Maxwell thoughtfully.

"Did you finish you sermon, Henry?" his wife asked after a pause.

"Yes, all done. It has been a very busy week with me. The two sermons have cost me a good deal of labor."

"They will be appreciated by a large audience, Sunday, I hope," replied his wife smiling. "What are you going to preach about in the morning?"

"Following Christ. I take up the Atonement under the head of sacrifice and example, and then show the steps needed to follow His sacrifice and example."

"I am sure it is a good sermon. I hope it won't rain Sunday. We have had so many stormy Sundays lately."

"Yes, the audiences have been quite small for some time. People will not come out to church in a storm." The Rev. Henry Maxwell sighed as he said it. He was thinking of the careful, laborious effort he had made in preparing sermons for large audiences that failed to appear.

But Sunday morning dawned on the town of Raymond one of the perfect days that sometimes come after long periods of wind and mud and rain. The air was clear and bracing, the sky was free from all threatening signs, and every one in Mr. Maxwell's parish prepared to go to church. When the service opened at eleven o'clock the large building was filled with an audience of the best-dressed, most comfortable-looking people of Raymond.

The First Church of Raymond believed in having the best music that money could buy, and its quartet choir this morning was a source of great pleasure to the congregation. The anthem was inspiring. All the music was in keeping with the subject of the sermon. And the anthem was an elaborate adaptation to the most modern music of the hymn,

> "Jesus, I my cross have taken,
> All to leave and follow Thee."

The church was the first in the city. It had the best choir. It had a membership composed of the leading people, representatives of the wealth, society and intelligence of Raymond.

The sermon was interesting. It was full of striking sentences. They would have commanded attention printed. Spoken with the passion of a dramatic utterance that had the good taste never to offend with a suspicion of ranting or declamation, they were very effective. If the Rev. Henry Maxwell that morning felt satisfied with the conditions of his pastorate, the First Church also had a similar feeling as it congratulated itself on the presence in the pulpit of this scholarly, refined, somewhat striking face and figure, preaching with such animation and freedom from all vulgar, noisy or disagreeable mannerism.

Suddenly into the midst of this perfect accord and concord between preacher and audience, there came a very remarkable interruption. It would be difficult to indicate the extent of the shock which this interruption measured. It was so unexpected, so entirely contrary to any thought of any person present that it offered no room for argument, or for the time being, of resistance.

The sermon had come to a close. Mr. Maxwell had just turned the half of the big Bible over upon his manuscript and was about to sit down as the quartet prepared to arise and sing the closing selection,

> "All for Jesus, all for Jesus,
> All my being's ransomed powers,"

when the entire congregation was startled by the sound of a man's voice. It came from the rear of the church, from one of the seats under the gallery. The next moment the figure of a man came out of the shadow there and walked down the middle aisle. Before the startled congregation fairly realized what was going on the man had reached the open space in front of the pulpit and had turned about facing the people. "I've been wondering since I came in here"—they were the words he used under the gallery, and he repeated them—"if it would be just the thing to say a word at the close of the service. I'm not drunk and I'm not crazy, and I am perfectly harmless, but if I die, as there is every likelihood I shall in a few days, I want the satisfaction of thinking that I said my say in a place like this, and before this sort of crowd."

Mr. Maxwell had not taken his seat, and he now remained standing, leaning on his pulpit, looking down at the stranger. It was the man who had come to his house the Friday before, the same dusty, worn, shabby-looking young man. He held his faded hat in his two hands. It seemed to be a favorite gesture. He had not been shaved and his hair was rough and tangled. It is doubtful if any one like this had ever confronted the First Church within the sanctuary. It was tolerably familiar with this sort of humanity out on the street, around the railroad shops, wandering up and down the avenue, but it had never dreamed of such an incident as this so near.

There was nothing offensive in the man's manner or tone. He was not excited and he spoke in a low but distinct voice. Mr. Maxwell was conscious, even as he stood there smitten into dumb astonishment at the event, that somehow the man's actions reminded him of a person he had once seen walking and talking in his sleep.

No one in the house made any motion to stop the stranger or in any way interrupt him. Perhaps the first shock of his sudden appearance deepened into a genuine perplexity concerning what was best to do. However that may be, he went on as if he had no thought of interruption and no thought of the unusual element which he had introduced into the decorum of the First Church service. And all the while he was speaking, the minister leaned over the pulpit, his face growing more white and sad every moment. But he made no movement to stop him, and the people sat smitten into breathless silence. One other face, that of Rachel Winslow from the choir, stared white and intent down at the shabby figure with the faded hat. Her face was striking at any time. Under the pressure of the present unheard-of incident it was as personally distinct as if it had been framed in fire.

"I'm not an ordinary tramp, though I don't know of any teaching of Jesus that makes one kind of a tramp less worth saving than another. Do you?" He put the question as naturally as if the whole congregation had been a small Bible class. He paused just a moment and coughed painfully. Then he went on.

"I lost my job ten months ago. I am a printer by trade. The new linotype machines are beautiful specimens of invention, but I know six men who have killed themselves inside of the year just on account of those machines. Of course I don't blame the newspapers for getting the machines. Meanwhile, what can a man do? I know I never learned but the one trade, and that's all I can do. I've tramped all over the country trying to find something. There are a good many others like me. I'm not complaining, am I? Just stating facts. But I was wondering as I sat there under the gallery, if what you call following Jesus is the same thing as what He taught. What did He mean when He said: 'Follow me!' The minister said," here the man turned about and looked up at the pulpit, "that it is necessary for the disciple of Jesus to follow His steps, and he said the steps are 'obedience, faith, love and imitation.' But I did not hear him tell you just what he meant that to mean, especially the last step. What do you Christians mean by following the steps of Jesus?

"I've tramped through this city for three days trying to find a job; and in all that time I've not had a word of sympathy or comfort except from your minister here, who said he was sorry for me and hoped I would find a job somewhere. I suppose it is because you get so imposed on by the professional tramp that you have lost your interest in any other sort. I'm not blaming anybody, am I? Just stating facts. Of course, I understand you can't all go out of your way to hunt up jobs for other people like me. I'm not asking you to; but what I feel puzzled about is, what is meant by following Jesus. What do you mean when you sing 'I'll go with Him, with Him, all the way?' Do you mean that you are suffering and denying yourselves and trying to save lost, suffering humanity just as I understand Jesus did? What do you mean by it? I see the ragged edge of things a good deal. I understand there are more than five hundred men in this city in my case. Most of them have families. My wife died four months ago. I'm glad she is out of trouble. My little girl is staying with a printer's family until I find a job. Somehow I get puzzled when I see so many Christians living in luxury and singing 'Jesus, I my cross have taken, all to leave and follow Thee,' and remember how my wife died in a tenement in New York City, gasping for air and asking God to take the little girl too. Of course I don't expect you people can prevent everyone from dying of starvation, lack of proper nourishment and tenement air, but what does following Jesus mean? I understand that Christian people own a good many of the tenements. A member of a church was the owner of the one where my wife died, and I have wondered if following Jesus all the way was true in his case. I heard some people singing at a church prayer meeting the other night,

'All for Jesus, all for Jesus,
All my being's ransomed powers,
All my thoughts, and all my doings,
All my days, and all my hours,'

and I kept wondering as I sat on the steps outside just what they meant by it. It seems to me there's an awful lot of trouble in the world that somehow wouldn't exist if all the people who sing such songs went and lived them out. I suppose I don't understand. But what would Jesus do? Is that what you mean by following His steps? It seems to me sometimes as if the people in the big churches had good clothes and nice houses to live in and money to spend for luxuries, and could go away on summer vacations and all that, while the people outside the churches, thousands of them, I mean, die in tenements, and walk the streets for jobs, and never have a piano or a picture in the house, and grow up in misery and drunkenness and sin."

The man suddenly gave a queer lurch over in the direction of the communion table and laid one grimy hand on it. His hat fell upon the carpet at his feet. A stir went through the congregation. Dr. West half rose from his pew, but as yet the silence was unbroken by any voice or movement worth mentioning in the audience. The man passed his other hand across his eyes, and then, without any warning, fell heavily forward on his face, full length up the aisle. Henry Maxwell spoke:

"We will consider the service closed."

He was down the pulpit stairs and kneeling by the prostrate form before any one else. The audience instantly rose and the aisles were crowded. Dr. West pronounced the man alive. He had fainted away. "Some heart trouble," the doctor also muttered as he helped carry him out into the pastor's study.[38]

---

38. At this juncture comes the break between chapters 1 and 2.

Henry Maxwell and a group of his church members remained some time in the study. The man lay on the couch there and breathed heavily. When the question of what to do with him came up, the minister insisted on taking the man to his own house; he lived nearby and had an extra room. Rachel Winslow said:

"Mother has no company at present. I am sure we would be glad to give him a place with us."

She looked strongly agitated. No one noticed it particularly. They were all excited over the strange event, the strangest that First Church people could remember. But the minister insisted on taking charge of the man, and when a carriage came, the unconscious but living form was carried to his house; and with the entrance of that humanity into the minister's spare room a new chapter in Henry Maxwell's life began, and yet no one, himself least of all, dreamed of the remarkable change it was destined to make in all his after definition of the Christian discipleship.

The event created a great sensation in the First Church parish. People talked of nothing else for a week. It was the general impression that the man had wandered into the church in a condition of mental disturbance caused by his troubles, and that all the time he was talking he was in a strange delirium of fever and really ignorant of his surroundings. That was the most charitable construction to put upon his action. It was the general agreement also that there was a singular absence of anything bitter or complaining in what the man had said. He had, throughout, spoke in a mild, apologetic tone, almost as if he were one of the congregation seeking for light on a very difficult subject.

The third day after his removal to the minister's house there was a marked change in his condition. The doctor spoke of it but offered no hope. Saturday morning he still lingered, although he had rapidly failed as the week drew near its close. Sunday morning, just before the clock struck one, he rallied and asked if his child had come. The minister had sent for her at once as soon as he had been able to secure her address from some letters found in the man's pocket. He had been conscious and able to talk coherently only a few moments since his attack.

"The child is coming. She will be here," Mr. Maxwell said as he sat there, his face showing marks of the strain of the week's vigil; for he had insisted on sitting up nearly every night.

"I shall never see her in this world," the man whispered. Then he uttered with great difficulty the words, "You have been good to me. Somehow I feel as if it was what Jesus would do."

After a few minutes he turned his head slightly and before Mr. Maxwell could realize the fact, the doctor said quietly, "He is gone."

The Sunday morning that dawned on the city of Raymond was exactly like the Sunday of a week before. Mr. Maxwell entered his pulpit to face one of the largest congregations that had ever crowded the First Church. He was haggard and looked as if he had just risen from a long illness. His wife was at home with the little girl who had come on the morning train an hour after her father had died. He lay in that spare room, his troubles over, and the minister could see the face as he opened the Bible and arranged his different notices on the side of the desk as he had been in the habit of doing for ten years.

The service that morning contained a new element. No one could remember when Henry Maxwell had preached in the morning without notes. As a matter of fact he had done so occasionally when he first entered the ministry, but for a long time he had carefully written every word of his morning sermon, and nearly always his evening discourses as well. It cannot be said that his sermon this morning was striking or impressive. He talked with considerable hesitation. It was evident that some great idea struggled in his thought for utterance, but it was not expressed in the theme he had chosen for his preaching. It was near the close of his sermon that he began to gather a certain strength that had been painfully lacking at the beginning.

He closed the Bible and, stepping out at the side of the desk, faced his people and began to talk to them about the remarkable scene of the week before.

"Our brother," somehow the words sounded a little strange coming from his lips, "passed away this morning. I have not yet had time to learn all his history. He had one sister living in Chicago. I have written her and have not yet received an answer. His little girl is with us and will remain for the time."

He paused and looked over the house. He thought he had never seen so many earnest faces during his entire pastorate. He was not able yet to tell his people his experiences, the crisis through which he was even now moving. But something of his feeling passed from him to them, and it did not seem to him that he was acting under a careless impulse at all to go on and break to them this morning something of the message he bore in his heart.

So he went on:

"The appearance and words of this stranger in the church last Sunday made a very powerful impression on me. I am not able to conceal from you or myself the fact that what he said, followed as it has been by his death in my house, has compelled me to ask as I never asked before 'What does following Jesus mean?' I am not in a position yet to utter any condemnation of this people or, to a certain extent, of myself, either in our Christ-like relations to this man or the numbers that he represents in the world. But all that does not prevent me from feeling that much that the man said was so vitally true that we must face it in an attempt to answer it or else stand condemned as Christian disciples. A good deal that was said here last Sunday was in the nature of a challenge to Christianity as it is seen and felt in our churches. I have felt this with increasing emphasis every day since.

"And I do not know that any time is more appropriate than the present for me to propose a plan or a purpose, which had been forming in my mind as a satisfactory reply to much that was said here last Sunday."

Again Henry Maxwell paused and looked into the faces of his people. There were some strong, earnest men and women in the First Church.

He could see Edward Norman, editor of the Raymond Daily News. He had been a member of the First Church for ten years. No man was more honored in the community. There was Alexander Powers, superintendent of the great railroad shops in Raymond, a typical railroad man, one who had been born into the business. There sat Donald Marsh, president of Lincoln College, situated in the suburbs of Raymond. There was Milton Wright, one of the great merchants of Raymond, having in his employ at least one hundred men in various shops. There was Dr. West, who although still comparatively young was quoted as an authority in special surgical cases. There was young Jasper Chase, the author, who had written one successful book and was said to be at work on a new novel. There was Miss Virginia Page, the heiress, who through the recent death of her father had inherited a million at least, and was gifted with unusual attractions of person and intellect. And not least of all, the great soprano Rachel Winslow, from her seat in the choir, glowed with her peculiar beauty of light this morning because she was so intensely interested in the whole scene.

There was some reason, perhaps in view of such material in the First Church, for Henry Maxwell's feeling of satisfaction whenever he considered his parish as he had the previous Sunday. There was an unusually large number of strong, individual characters who claimed membership there. But as he noted their faces this morning he was simply wondering how many of them would respond to the strange proposition he was about to make.

"What I am going to propose now is something which ought not to appear unusual or at all impossible of execution. Yet I am aware that it will be so regarded by a large number, perhaps, of the members of this church. But in order that we may have a thorough understanding of what we are considering, I will put my proposition very plainly, perhaps bluntly. I want volunteers from the First Church who will pledge themselves, earnestly and honestly for an entire year, not to do anything without first asking the question, 'What would Jesus do?' And after asking the question, each one will follow Jesus as exactly as he knows how, no matter what the result may be. I will of course include myself in this company of volunteers, and shall take for granted that my church here will not be surprised at my future conduct, as based upon this standard of action, and will not oppose whatever is done if they think Christ would do it. Have I made my meaning clear? At the close of the service I want all those members who are willing to join such a company to remain and we will talk over the details of the plan. Our motto will be, 'What would Jesus do?' Our aim will be to act just as He would if He was in our places, regardless of immediate results. In other words, we propose to follow Jesus' steps as closely and as literally as we believe He taught His disciples to do. And those who volunteer to do this will pledge themselves for an entire year, beginning with today, so to act."

Henry Maxwell paused again and looked out over his people. It is not easy to describe the sensation that such a simple proposition apparently made. Men glanced at one another in astonishment. It was not like Henry Maxwell to define Christian discipleship in this way. There was evident confusion of thought over his proposition. It was understood well enough, but there was, apparently, a great difference of opinion as to the application of Jesus' teaching and example.

He calmly closed the service with a brief prayer. The organist began his postlude immediately after the benediction and the people began to go out. There was a great deal of conversation. Animated groups stood all over the church discussing the minister's proposition. It was evidently provoking great discussion. After several minutes he asked all who expected to remain to pass into the lecture room which joined the large room on the side. He was himself detained at the front of the church talking with several persons there, and when he finally turned around, the church was empty. He walked over to the lecture-room entrance and went in. He was almost startled to see the people who were there. He had not made up his mind about any of his members, but he had hardly expected that so many were ready to enter into such a literal testing of their Christian discipleship as now awaited him. There were perhaps fifty present, among them Rachel Winslow and Virginia Pate, Mr. Norman, President Marsh, Alexander Powers the railroad superintendent, Milton Wright, Dr. West and Jasper Chase.

He closed the door of the lecture-room and went and stood before the little group. His face was pale and his lips trembled with genuine emotion. It was to him a genuine crisis in his own life and that of his parish.

It seemed to him that the most fitting word to be spoken first was that of prayer. He asked them all to pray with him. And almost with the first syllable he uttered there was a distinct presence of the Spirit felt by them all. As the prayer went on, the presence grew in power. They all felt it. The room was filled with it as plainly as if it had been visible. When the prayer closed there was a silence that lasted several moments. All the heads were bowed. Henry Maxwell's face was wet with tears.

"We all understand," said he, speaking very quietly, "what we have undertaken to do. We pledge ourselves to do everything in our daily lives after asking the question, 'What would Jesus do?' regardless of what may be the result to us. Some time I shall be able to tell you what a marvelous change has come over my life within a week's time. I cannot now. But the experience I have been through since last Sunday has left me so dissatisfied with my previous definition of Christian discipleship that I have been compelled to take this action. I did not dare begin it alone. I know that I am being led by the hand of divine love in all this. The same divine impulse must have led you also.

"Do we understand fully what we have undertaken?"

"I want to ask a question," said Rachel Winslow. Every one turned towards her. Her face glowed with a beauty that no physical loveliness could ever create.

"I am a little in doubt as to the source of our knowledge concerning what Jesus would do. Who is to decide for me just what He would do in my case? It is a different age. There are many perplexing questions in our civilization that are not mentioned in the teachings of Jesus. How am I going to tell what He would do?"

"There is no way that I know of," replied the pastor, "except as we study Jesus through the medium of the Holy Spirit. We shall all have to decide what Jesus would do after going to that source of knowledge."

"What if others say of us, when we do certain things, that Jesus would not do so?" asked the superintendent of railroads.

"We cannot prevent that. But we must be absolutely honest with ourselves. The standard of Christian action cannot vary in most of our acts."

"And yet what one church member thinks Jesus would do, another refuses to accept as His probable course of action. What is to render our conduct uniformly Christ-like? Will it be possible to reach the same conclusions always in all cases?" asked President Marsh.

Mr. Maxwell was silent some time. Then he answered, "No; I don't know that we can expect that. But when it comes to a genuine, honest enlightened following of Jesus' steps, I cannot believe there will be any confusion whether in our own minds or in the judgment of others. We must be free from fanaticism on one hand and too much caution on the other. If Jesus' example is the example for the world to follow, it certainly must be feasible to follow it. But we need to remember this great fact. After we have asked the Spirit to tell us what Jesus would do and have received an answer to it, we are to act regardless of the results to ourselves. Is that understood?"

All the faces in the room were raised towards the minister in solemn assent. There was no misunderstanding that proposition. Henry Maxwell's face quivered again as he noted the president of the Endeavor Society with several members seated back of the older men and women.

They remained a little longer talking over the details and asking questions, and agreed to report to one another every week at a regular meeting the result of their experiences in following Jesus this way. Henry Maxwell prayed again. And again as before the Spirit made Himself manifest. Every head remained bowed a long time. They went away finally in silence. The pastor shook hands with them all as they went out. Then he went into his own study room and kneeled. He remained there alone nearly half an hour. When he went home he went into the room where the dead body lay. As he looked at the face he cried in his heart again for strength and wisdom. But not even yet did he realize that a movement had begun which would lead to the most remarkable series of events that the city of Raymond had ever known.

---

This story reminds me of a godly man I've heard about who used to live in Birmingham, Alabama, who had the nickname "religion in shoes"—because he "went about doing good." Clearly, we have a challenge before us to replace the smug, complacent type of religion that marks so many of our lives with a vibrant life of love—love to God first and to our fellow man second. The year-long challenge here—to face every decision by first asking the question "What would Jesus do?"—is a tall order, but is well worth it for those willing to take up the adventure!

PART II

The following stories are related to the
Seven Deadly Sins—as warnings to that against
which we should guard our hearts.

# INTRODUCTION

For centuries, Christians have been concerned about what are known as the "seven deadly sins." They are not only sins that are committed, but they are attitudes of the heart.

The seven deadly sins are:

- Pride

- Greed (or Avarice)

- Envy

- Anger (or Wrath)

- Lust

- Gluttony

- Sloth

The earliest record to which I can trace these back to is from the sixth century. Both St. John Cassian and St. Gregory the Great are believed to be the first ones to use these seven categories.[1] It's not that these sins are necessarily worse than other sins. You'll notice that murder is not even on the list! Yet the point is that these sins *engender* other sins. They are root causes that lead to murder, that lead to war and adultery and stealing and all manner of evils.

I believe we can gain spiritual insight in terms of what sins we are to avoid by looking at stories related to these sins. So I have searched far and wide to find stories that address these root evils in the human heart. I believe these stories, like the parables of Christ (a few of which are contained in this next section), can teach us how we should then live.

---

1. *Catechism of the Catholic Church* (Libreria Editrice Vaticana: Pauline, 1994), 457.

# SECTION 1

# PRIDE

Some modern people actually have trouble looking at pride as a sin. That's partly because they think of pride as dignity or self-respect, which are worthy goals. But pride, which is defined by Webster's as "an overly high opinion of oneself: conceit," is the first of the seven deadly sins.

The Christian view of pride contrasts sharply with the world's view. The Christian view is that we are *creatures*, made in the image of God—therefore, we are naturally endowed by the Creator with dignity. However, our attitude should not be haughty, but rather grateful. When I feel "proud" of something, I try to instead think (and say) I am "thankful" for it. After all, as Paul asks, "What do you have that you did not receive?" (1 Cor. 4:7). Everything we have, including life itself, is a gift from God. Every beat of our hearts is by the grace of Jesus Christ. Therefore, who are we to puff ourselves up and swell with pride?

C. S. Lewis had some enlightening things to say about the subject: "The essential vice, the utmost evil, is Pride. Unchastity, anger, greed, drunkenness, and all that, are mere fleabites in comparison: it was through Pride that the devil became the devil. . . . It is Pride which has been the chief cause of misery in every nation and every family since the world began. Other vices may sometimes bring people together: you may find good fellowship and jokes and friendliness among drunken people or unchaste people. But Pride always means enmity—it *is* enmity. And not only enmity between man and man, but enmity to God."[2]

Pride, arrogance, and haughtiness blind our vision so that we don't see as we ought. Pride leads to a fall. "Pride goes before destruction, a haughty spirit before a fall" (Prov. 16:18). There-

---

2. C. S. Lewis, *Mere Christianity* (New York: Macmillan, 1960), 109, 110–11.

fore, we must "not think more highly of ourselves than we ought" (Rom. 12:3). First Peter summarizes how we should then live: "'God opposes the proud but gives grace to the humble.' Humble yourselves, therefore, under God's mighty hand, that he may lift you up in due time" (1 Pet. 5:5–6 NIV).

*This selection is suitable for children.*
*The moral of the story is that the Word of God is the key to overcoming*
*the temptation to sin.*

# THE TEMPTATION OF CHRIST

### from the Gospel According to Luke (NIV)

As stated above, much of this book deals with what the medieval Church called the "seven deadly sins." To understand this section of the book, we need to see exactly how Christ overcame sin.

At the outset of His ministry, Jesus fasted for forty days in a row (there's an antidote to gluttony!). He prayed. And He was tempted—not that He brought this last item upon Himself, but He was acted upon. And He passed the test. He's the only human being who has passed that test and who ever will. For there is none righteous, no not one (Rom. 3:10). Since we are to imitate Christ, to walk in His steps, as Peter commands us to, then how are we to deal with temptation? He shows us how in this passage. He uses the Word of God to overcome the evil one.

At the root of these temptations was pride. *"If* you are the Son of God" implies that if Jesus did not do this, then He wasn't the Son of God. The devil was appealing to pride in all three of these temptations, especially the second one.

This passage is from Luke 4:1–13.

---

Jesus, full of the Holy Spirit, returned from the Jordan and was led by the Spirit in the desert, where for forty days he was tempted by the devil. He ate nothing during those days, and at the end of them he was hungry.

The devil said to him, "If you are the Son of God, tell this stone to become bread."

Jesus answered, "It is written: 'Man does not live on bread alone.'"

The devil led him up to a high place and showed him in an instant all the kingdoms of the world. And he said to him, "I will give you all their authority and splendor, for it has been given to me, and I can give it to anyone I want to. So if you worship me, it will all be yours."

Jesus answered, "It is written: 'Worship the Lord your God and serve him only.'"

The devil led him to Jerusalem and had him stand on the highest point of the temple. "If you are the Son of God," he said, "throw yourself down from here. For it is written:

"'He will command his angels concerning you
to guard you carefully;
they will lift you up in their hands,
so that you will not strike your foot against a stone.'"

Jesus answered, "It says: 'Do not put the Lord your God to the test.'"

When the devil had finished all this tempting, he left him until an opportune time.

---

In this scenario, it's obvious Christ didn't have a concordance or some other Bible reference book at His fingertips. Instead, it appears He had available to Him that which He had memorized. Clearly, He had put to memory numerous passages and knew how to apply them right then and there. Here is our model. Memorize Scripture verses related to the sins you struggle with. Then recite those verses at the moment of temptation. I remember John MacArthur once talking about this and remarking: "I can't sin without first thinking about a hundred Bible verses!"

One other point about this story: it's very enlightening to see that the devil quotes Scripture. He did at the time of Christ, and he has through the ages. That's why it's so important to know the overall message of the Bible and the overall context of Scriptures so we're not easily fooled by those who wrench passages out of place to serve their own agenda. The proliferation of numerous cults in our day is another evidence of the truth that the devil can quote the Bible!

*This selection is suitable for children.*
*The moral of the story is God opposes the proud but will exalt those who
humble themselves.*

# THE PARABLE OF THE PHARISEE
# AND THE PUBLICAN

### from the Gospel According to Luke (NIV)

The parables that Christ told go straight to the heart of the matter. This parable demolishes self-righteousness and shows that it wins no favor with God. Instead, those who humble themselves and recognize their sinfulness before Him are recognized by Him.

Here is a story He told to an audience that included a lot of self-righteous hearers who thought they were on their way to heaven because they performed various works of the law (and a lot of man-made rules as well, some of which effectively nullified God's actual law). The story has two characters: one is a Pharisee (a Jewish leader of the time, who meticulously kept the letter of the law but not necessarily the spirit of it); the other is a tax collector, who, by virtue of his profession at that time, was likely a cheat and a fraud—someone who was getting rich at the expense of his neighbor (that's why tax collectors were so hated). Jesus commends him for his humility and true remorse over his sin, something I fear we have lost in many portions of the Church today.

This passage is from Luke 18:9–14.

———

To some who were confident of their own righteousness and looked down on everybody else, Jesus told this parable: "Two men went up to the temple to pray, one a Pharisee and the other a tax collector. The Pharisee stood up and prayed about himself: 'God, I thank you that I am not like other men—robbers, evildoers, adulterers—or even like this tax collector. I fast twice a week and give a tenth of all I get.'

"But the tax collector stood at a distance. He would not even look up to heaven, but beat his breast and said, 'God, have mercy on me, a sinner.'

"I tell you that this man, rather than the other, went home justified before God. For everyone who exalts himself will be humbled, and he who humbles himself will be exalted."

---

Isn't it amazing how we often read that story and then think, *Dear God, I thank You that I'm not like that self-righteous, hypocritical Pharisee!*

The Publican feels so genuinely sorry for his sins and admits to God the truth of how unworthy he is. Jesus commends him for this. While this may not be popular theology in today's self-esteem milieu, it's true nonetheless. To some degree, we're all as sinful as that Publican . . . only some of us don't know it.

*This selection is recommended for children, but the language is difficult.*
*The moral of the story is to not judge by mere outward appearances.*

# THE CASKET SCENES FROM *THE MERCHANT OF VENICE* [3]

### by William Shakespeare

It must be deep in the race to make judgments based on superficial criteria. Jesus said not to judge by "mere appearances" (John 7:24). We've all heard the cliche "Don't judge a book by its cover." I remember reading about a man behind the booth at a convention who essentially shooed away a casually dressed woman based on her appearance alone. It turned out she represented a huge client that could have given them a great potential for profit, but her casual dress and demeanor didn't give that away. Subsequently, he lost out big time. We can miss a lot by superficial judgments.

The moral of this story is not to judge on outward appearances alone. For "all that glitters is not gold." People often judge poorly because their pride blinds them.

In Shakespeare's classic play *The Merchant of Venice*, there is a beautiful woman, Portia, who is being highly sought after, like a prize, by noble suitors. Her father devises a way to test the hearts of these potential husbands for his daughter. He uses three caskets—one gold, one silver, and one lead—for his exam and places her portrait in one of them. The suitor that picks the correct casket wins her hand. The gold one bears this inscription: "Who chooseth me shall gain what many men desire." The silver one carries this promise: "Who chooseth me shall get as much as he deserves." The lead casket warns: "Who chooseth me must give and hazard all he hath."

Portia herself does not know the solution to the riddle. Attempting to win her hand are the Prince of Morocco, the Prince of Aragon, and Bassanio (the hero). There are three scenes where each of these men has a turn at opening one of the caskets.

In act 2, scene 7, the Prince of Morocco goes first. He reasons that Portia is worthy to be represented only by gold, so he

---

3.  Summarized here by the editor. The occasional quotes are excerpts from act 2, scenes 7 and 9, and act 3, scene 2.

chooses that casket. When he opens it, he finds a symbol of
death and a scroll. He reads it aloud:

> All that glitters is not gold—
> Often have you heard that told;
> Many a man his life hath sold
> But my outside to behold;
> Gilded tombs do worms infold:
> Have you been as wise as bold,
> Young in limbs, in judgment old,
> Your answer had not been inscrolled.
> Fare you well, your suit is cold.

The Prince of Morocco leaves, bitterly disappointed.

In act 2, scene 9, the Prince of Arragon gets his turn to try and
solve the riddle. As he contemplates his options, he's intrigued by
the promise on the silver casket: "Who chooseth me shall get as
much as he deserves." He essentially reasons that he deserves
her. So he chooses this casket. Arragon is disappointed when he
opens it up. He remarks:

What's here? The portrait of a blinking idiot, . . .
How much unlike art thou to Portia!
How much unlike my hopes and my deservings!
"Who chooseth me shall have as much as he deserves."
Did I deserve no more than a fool's head?
Is that my prize? Are my deserts[4] no better?

Apparently not. He too exits in shame and disappointment.

Later, in act 3, scene 2, Bassanio, the one Portia was hoping all
along to be her suitor, tries his hand at the puzzle. As he reviews
the caskets, he perceptively observes, "The world is still deceived
with ornament." Bassanio continues:

Therefore, thou gaudy gold,
Hard food for Midas, I will none of thee;
Nor none of thee, thou pale and common drudge[5]
'Tween man and man:[6] but thou, thou meagre lead,

---

4. That which is deserved.
5. The silver casket. See the next note.
6. In those days, silver was used as common currency "between man and man."

Which rather threaten'st than dost promise aught,
Thy plainness moves me more than eloquence,
And here choose I. Joy be the consequence!. . .
[Opening the leaden casket] What find I here?
Fair Portia's counterfeit![7]. . .
Here's the scroll,
The continent[8] and summary of my fortune.

> You that choose not by the view[9]
> Chance as fair and choose as true.
> Since this fortune falls to you,
> Be content and seek no new.
> If you be well pleased with this
> And hold your fortune for your bliss,[10]
> Turn you where your lady is
> And claim her with *a loving kiss.*

·"All that glitters is not gold" is a great reminder for our glitzy age with its "Who's Hot" and "Who's Not" type of lists. Pride blinds our correct vision so we make judgments by superficial and inaccurate criteria, often with disastrous consequences.

---

7. Portrait.
8. The contents.
9. In other words, you that choose not by mere outward appearance.
10. In other words, if you view your luck [in attaining Portia's hand] as the height of your happiness . . . .

*This selection is generally NOT recommended for children as the language is too difficult.*

*The moral of the story is that because of his pride, the devil forfeited his place in Paradise and successfully convinced man to fall as well, although man can find forgiveness.*

## PARADISE LOST[11]

by John Milton

Of man's first disobedience, and the fruit
Of that forbidden tree, whose mortal taste
Brought death into the world, and all our woe,
With loss of Eden, till one greater Man
Restore us, and regain the blissful seat.

So states John Milton in the opening of his classic poem, *Paradise Lost*. This poem is, as one scholar put it, is "the greatest epic in the English language."[12] Yet it's one of those classics of literature that everybody seems to be vaguely familiar with, but few in our time seem to have actually read. But it is worth the reading! The Old English language is difficult, and throughout the work are numerous cultural allusions, many of which are obscure to the average reader. It's not an easy book to read, but it rewards the reader. One can gain a greater understanding of the big picture of the story of man by absorbing its message.

The Puritan writer John Milton (1608–74) lived in the tumultuous seventeenth century, which was rocked by political and religious conflicts. Although he eventually became completely blind and had to dictate his writings, Milton had much greater insight into spiritual matters than do most people who can see very well. *Paradise Lost* is one of the greatest Christian compositions of all time.

*Paradise Lost* is a lengthy poem broken into several different "books" (sections). It's the story of the fall of Satan and his demonic host, the fall of man, and God's plan to redeem man through His Son. In book 1, the story opens with the devil and

---

11. Summarized here by the editor. Included are excerpts from book 1, book 2, and book 3 of *Paradise Lost*.

12. Kerry M. Wood, Helen McDonnell, John Pfordresher, Mary Alice Fite, and Paul Lankford, *Classics in World Literature* (Glenview, Ill.: Scott, Forseman, and Company, 1989), 500.

his minions (one-third of all the former angels, now having become demons)—smarting and sore, having just lost the battle in heaven to try and unseat the Almighty. They now are experiencing the horrors of hell for the very first time, but still Satan is unrepentant. Although he's in pain, he says:

"All is not lost; the unconquerable will,
And study of revenge, immortal hate,
And courage never to submit or yield:
And what is else not to be overcome?
That glory never shall his wrath or might
Extort from me. To bow and sue for grace
With suppliant knee.

. . . . . . . . . . . . .

"Is this the region, this the soil, the clime[13],"
Said then the lost Archangel, "this the seat
That we must change for heaven, this mournful gloom
For that celestial light? Be it so, since he
Who now is sovran[14] can dispose and bid
What shall be right: fardest[15] from him is best,
Whom reason hath equaled, force hath made supreme
Above his equals. Farewell, happy fields,
Where joy for ever dwells! Hail, horrors, hail,
Infernal world, and thou, profoundest hell,
Receive thy new possessor: one who brings
A mind not to be changed by place or time.
The mind is its own place, and in itself
Can make a heaven of hell, a hell of heaven.
What matter where, if I be still the same,

. . . . . . . . . . . . .

Here we may reign secure, and in my choice
To reign is worth ambition, though in hell:
Better to reign in hell than serve in heaven."

In book 2, after being a little more adjusted to their new terrible dwelling place, Satan and some of the leading demons—

---

13. Region of the earth.
14. Sovereign.
15. Farthest.

including Moloch, Belial, Beelzebub, and Mammon—discuss plans of revenge on heaven. While Moloch suggests "open war" on heaven, Belial points out that the "towers of heaven" are "impregnable." The demonic leaders discuss this back and forth. Finally, Beelzebub points out a more practical way they could get their revenge on heaven. There's a new creature in the works (man). What if Satan and Company could somehow tamper with man in order that they might get their revenge on the Creator? Beelzebub says:

"What if we find
Some easier enterprise? There is a place
(If ancient and prophetic fame in heaven
Err not), another world, the happy seat
Of some new race called man, about this time
To be created like to us, though less
In power and excellence, but favored more
Of him who rules above; so was his will

. . . . . . . . . . . . . . .

Thither let us bend all our thoughts, to learn
What creatures there inhabit, of what mold
Or substance, how endued, and what their power,
And where their weakness, how attempted best,
By force or subtlety. Though heaven be shut,
And heaven's high Arbitrator sit secure
In his own strength, this place may lie exposed,
The utmost border of his kingdom, left
To their defense who hold it; here perhaps
Some advantageous act may be achieved
By sudden onset, either with hell fire
To waste his whole creation, or possess
All as our own, and drive as we were driven,
The puny habitants; or if not drive,
Seduce them to our party, that their God
May prove their foe, and with repenting hand
Abolish his own works. This would surpass
Common revenge, and interrupt his joy

In our confusion, and our joy upraise
In his disturbance; when his darling sons,

Hurled headlong to partake with us, shall curse
Their frail original, and faded bliss,
Faded so soon. Advise if this be worth
Attempting, or to sit in darkness here
Hatching vain empires." Thus Beelzebub
Pleaded his devilish counsel, first devised
By Satan, and in part proposed; for whence,
But from the author of all ill, could spring
So deep a malice, to confound the race
Of mankind in one root, and earth with hell
To mingle and involve, done all to spite
The great Creator?[16] But their spite still serves
His glory to augment.[17]

After articulating Satan's idea of corrupting man in order to procure the demons' revenge against God, Beelzebub states that it's critical they send just the right one to pull off this scheme: "On whom we send, the weight of all our last hope relies." There is silence at first after his proposal. No one seconds or opposes the plan. They "all sat mute," pondering the perilous plan. Finally, Satan himself breaks the silence:

"I should ill become this throne, O Peers,
And this imperial soveranty,[18] adorned
With splendor, armed with power, if aught[19] proposed
And judged of public moment, in the shape
Of difficulty or danger could deter
Me from attempting."[20]

Satan thus goes off to earth to seek to somehow wreak havoc with God's new creation, man. In the introduction to book 3, Milton writes, "God, sitting on his throne, sees Satan flying towards this world, then newly created; shows him to the Son, who sat at his right hand; foretells the success of Satan in perverting mankind; clears his own justice and wisdom from all imputation, having cre-

---

16. In other words, who else but Satan himself could come up with such a diabolical plan?
17. In other words, God in His sovereignty glorifies Himself even through their diabolical plan.
18. Sovereignty.
19. Any part; the smallest detail.
20. In other words, Satan is saying, "I don't deserve this throne if I don't at least try this plan."

ated man free and able enough to have withstood his tempter; yet declares his purpose of grace towards him, in regard he fell not of his own malice, as did Satan, but by him seduced." Here is an excerpt of what God the Father says to God the Son in that scene:

"Only begotten Son, seest thou what rage
Transports our Adversary? Whom no bounds
Prescribed, no bars of hell, nor all the chains
Heaped on him there, nor yet the main abyss
Wide interrupt can hold; so bent he seems
On desperate revenge, that shall redound[21]
Upon his own rebellious head. And now
Through all restraint broke loose he wings his way
Not far off heaven, in the precincts of light,
Directly towards the new-created world,
And man there placed, with purpose to assay[22]
If him by force he can destroy, or worse,
By some false guile pervert; and shall pervert;
For man will hearken to his glozing[23] lies,
And easily transgress the sole command,
Sole pledge of his obedience; so will fall
He and his faithless progeny. Whose fault?
Whose but his own? Ingrate, he had of me
All he could have; I made him just and right,
Sufficient to have stood, though free to fall.
Such I created all the ethereal Powers
And Spirits, both them who stood and them who failed;
Freely they stood who stood, and fell who fell.
Not free, what proof could they have given sincere
Of true allegiance, constant faith or love,
Where only what they needs must do, appeared,
Not what they would? What praise could they receive?

.    .    .    .    .    .    .    .    .    .    .    .

I formed them free, and free they must remain,
Till they enthrall themselves: I else must change
Their nature, and revoke the high decree

---

21. Be sent back.
22. To attempt.
23. Flattering.

Unchangeable, eternal, which ordained
Their freedom; they themselves ordained their fall.
The first sort by their own suggestion fell,
Self-tempted, self-depraved; man falls deceived
By the other first; man therefore shall find grace,
The other none. In mercy and justice both,
Through heaven and earth, so shall my glory excel.
But mercy first and last shall brightest shine."

And the rest is history. Satan deceived Adam and Eve, who sinned of their own free will, and the world was plunged into woe. But God didn't destroy the world—"abolish His own work"—as Beelzebub assumed He would. Instead, He came up with a brilliant plan, whereby the Son of God would redeem a portion of humankind. Just a few lines later from where I stopped, when this divine plan was hatched, it says this of Jesus:

Beyond compare the Son of God was seen
Most glorious; in him all his Father shone
Substantially expressed, and in his face
Divine compassion visibly appeared,
Love without end, and without measure grace.

This story puts the history of the universe into perspective. You can't really understand what the world is all about unless you understand the fall and redemption of man, which is inseparably linked to the fall of Satan and his demons.

C. S. Lewis wrote an interesting novel, *The Great Divorce,* that relates to one of the themes of *Paradise Lost.* In *The Great Divorce,* there are many characters who have the opportunity to go to heaven, but actually prefer to choose hell, rather than submit to God. This reminds me of Satan's classic line above: "[It's] better to reign in hell than serve in heaven." Wow. There's the deadly sin of pride in a nutshell!

*This selection is suitable for children.*
*The moral of the story is not to be proud, in the sense of being haughty.*

## BEN FRANKLIN ON PRIDE
from *Poor Richard's Almanack*[24]

Ben Franklin contributed a lot to everyday American life. He invented all sorts of devices to improve the quality of our lives. He also contributed greatly to the cause of American freedom. As one of the Pennsylvania delegates to the Second Continental Congress, he signed the Declaration of Independence, which was virtually the same as signing his death warrant if the British caught him. As he said at the time with characteristic wit, "We shall all hang together or most assuredly we shall all hang separately."

Ben Franklin was not an orthodox Christian. As a young man, he was turned off by the numerous religious debates over theological points.[25] Paraphrasing him, he thought that many a theological discussion could be abridged to this: "It is so." "It is not." "It is too." "No, it's not."

Nor was Franklin an atheist either. He clearly recommended the Bible and labeled it as one of the greatest purchases one could make. And he remonstrated with Thomas Paine for writing his anti-Christian book, *Age of Reason.* Furthermore, during the Constitutional Convention, when the delegates got bogged down and couldn't agree on specifics, Franklin rose and gave an important speech, suggesting that the new nation look to God for help and to pray about this matter. It is reported that his suggestion helped break the impasse.

The Philadelphia printer had a great wit about him, and he collected his many pithy statements under the pseudonym of Poor Richard. *Poor Richard's Almanack*, first published in 1732, is a delightful collection of his witty aphorisms. Many of the statements reflect biblical truth as well. Some of them don't. He's the

24. Ben Franklin, *Poor Richard's Almanack, BEING the choicest Morsels of* Wisdom, *written during the Years of the Almanack's Publication, By that well-known* Savant, *Dr. Benjamin Franklin of Philadelphia.* (Mt. Vernon, N.Y.: Peter Pauper Press, undated), 12, 17, 32, 38, 41, 47, 55, 56, 66, 68, 71, 74.

25. John Eidsmoe deals thoroughly with Ben Franklin and his religion in his wonderful book, *Christianity and the Constitution: The Faith of Our Founding Fathers* (Grand Rapids: Baker Book House, 1987), chapter 12.

one who coined the phrase, with its unbiblical message, "God helps those who help themselves."

However, we can glean from him much wisdom on many sins that plague us. As I went through *Poor Richard's Almanack*, I was fascinated to see how much there was on each category of the seven deadly sins (except envy). So for six of the seven, I have collected the pithy commentary of Ben Franklin on that particular subject. The first one included here is pride. These are the thoughts of one of our founding fathers on the subject of sinful pride.

---

- The Devil wipes his Breech with poor Folks' Pride.

- As Pride increases, Fortune declines.

- Pride dines upon Vanity, sups on Contempt.

- Great Merit is coy, as well as great Pride.

- People who are wrapped in themselves make small packages.

- The first degree of folly, is to conceit one's self wise; the second to profess it; the third to despise counsel.

- Despair ruins some, presumption many.

- Presumption first blinds a man, then sets him a running.

- He that falls in love with himself, will have no rivals.

- Fond pride of dress is sure an empty purse.

- The proud hate pride—in others.

- Pride gets into the coach, and shame mounts behind.

- Vain-glory flowereth, but beareth no fruit.

- Pride breakfasted with plenty, dined with poverty, supped with infamy.

- To be proud of knowledge, is to be blind with light.

- He that would rise in court, must begin by creeping.

We'll hear more from Franklin next when we deal with the sin of greed. Franklin's derision of pride is also seen in the epitaph he prepared for himself (but which was never used):

The body of

B. Franklin, printer

(Like the cover of an old book,

Its contents torn out

And stripped of its lettering and gilding),

Lies here, food for worms.

But the work shall not be lost;

For it will (as he believed) appear once more

In a new and more elegant edition,

Revised and corrected

*By the Author.*[26]

This is a clever way of showing how pride is leveled by death. Note that the only real basis on which anyone can truthfully say something along these lines is if they have put their trust in Jesus Christ alone for salvation.

---

26. Franklin's epitaph, quoted in Eidsmoe, *Christianity and the Constitution,* 212.

*This selection is suitable for children.*

*The moral of the story is that we need to humble ourselves before Almighty God, that because of pride some of our calamities, personal and corporate, have come upon us.*

# PROCLAMATION OF A NATIONAL FAST DAY[27]

### March 30, 1863
### by Abraham Lincoln

Abraham Lincoln had great insights on pride. They come out in his humble, simple, yet profound, speeches. He rose from an unassuming and poor background to the highest office in the land, but he never seemed to forget from whence he came. Lincoln never became a haughty man.

In March of 1863 the nation was engaged in the greatest crisis we've ever faced, the Civil War. During that month, President Lincoln called for a day of humiliation, fasting, and prayer to occur the next month. (He also called for one near the outset of the war, August 12, 1861.)

This was at a time when the South had won more victories over the North. His request for fasting and prayer came at a time when the outcome of the war was very much uncertain. Gettysburg had not yet been fought.

Lincoln's proclamation makes the point that nations, as well as individuals, can grow haughty and forget God and assume that all they've accomplished has been their own doing. But we must never forget that it is God who gives us the opportunity to succeed in the first place.

---

It is the duty of nations as well as of men to own their dependence upon the overruling power of God; to confess their sins and transgressions in humble sorrow, yet with assured hope that genuine repentance will lead to mercy and pardon; and to recognize the sublime truth, announced in the Holy Scriptures and proven by all history, that those nations only are blessed whose God is the Lord. . . .

We know that by his divine law nations, like individuals, are subjected to punishments and chastisements in this world; may we not

---

27. Marion Mills Miller, ed., *Life and Works of Abraham Lincoln*, vol. 6 (New York: The Current Literature Publishing Co., 1907, 156–57.

justly fear that the awful calamity of civil war which now desolates the land may be but a punishment inflicted upon us for our presumptuous sins, to the needful end of our national reformation as a whole people? We have been the recipients of the choicest bounties of Heaven. We have been preserved, these many years, in peace and prosperity. We have grown in numbers, wealth, and power as no other nation has ever grown; but we have forgotten God. We have forgotten the gracious hand which preserved us in peace, and multiplied and enriched and strengthened us; and we have vainly imagined, in the deceitfulness of our hearts, that all these blessings were produced by some superior wisdom and virtue of our own. Intoxicated with unbroken success, we have become too self-sufficient to feel the necessity of redeeming and preserving grace, too proud to pray to the God that made us:

It behooves us, then, to humble ourselves before the offended Power, to confess our national sins, and to pray for clemency and forgiveness:

Now, therefore, in compliance with the request, and fully concurring in the views, of the Senate, I do by this my proclamation designate and set apart Thursday, the 30th day of April, 1863, as a day of national humiliation, fasting, and prayer. And I do hereby request all the people to abstain on that day from their ordinary secular pursuits, and to unite at their several places of public worship and their respective homes in keeping the day holy to the Lord, and devoted to the humble discharge of the religious duties proper to that solemn occasion.

---

What happened after this national day of prayer? The next month, Stonewall Jackson[28] was killed. Three months later came the turning point of the war, Gettysburg, which might have been a Confederate victory had Jackson lived.

---

28. I know I may sound like I'm speaking out of both sides of my mouth on this point . . . but I admire Stonewall Jackson as a hero. He was a great Christian whose motivation for fighting for the Confederacy lay solely in his defense of Virginia and what he perceived as states' rights. He did a great deal for African Americans before the war—for example, at a time when most of them could not read or write, he taught literacy to some, using the Bible as his text. During the war, he sent some of his tithes to his former students for their well-being at a time when they would have no means of income. The Civil War was not the simple cut-and-dry conflict over slavery some modern revisionists make it out to be, although that was certainly the catalyst issue. As to his death coming the month after the national day of fasting and prayer, it was just as well for the preservation of the Union, for Jackson was extremely effective on the battlefield.

This 1863 proclamation is one of the finest descriptions of pride and haughtiness I think I've ever read! Lincoln gets right to the root of pride: We have forgotten God. Paraphrasing him, in vain have we imagined that we alone have produced all these choice blessings in this country. Drunk with success after success, we have become too proud to pray.

This applies to America today as well. We have forgotten God. America has been so blessed by Him for so long, but we have turned our backs on the source of that blessing. No wonder we are now plagued with so many problems. The need is great for Christians to rediscover fasting and humiliation. Many leaders today think America's only real hope lies in revival. This kind of humiliation and prayer and fasting is a key antidote to pride.

*This selection is suitable for children.*
*The moral of the story is that each culture and country may have some-*
*thing to contribute.*

# OUR SOLID AMERICAN CITIZEN
### by Ralph Linton[29]

The world today is like a global village, and while there are many serious and deep differences between different cultures, countries, and religions, there are some things we can learn from each other. There are customs from other cultures that we can easily assimilate into our own, and as you'll see, we already have.

The following isn't so much a story as a brief description of how we have already assimilated many of our daily traditions and everyday items from other countries and cultures. The moral of the story is to challenge our pride that manifests itself in the form of a snug, cultural imperialism.

---

Our solid American citizen awakens in a bed built on a pattern which originated in the Near East but which was modified in Northern Europe before it was transmitted to America. He throws back covers made from cotton, domesticated in India, or linen, domesticated in the Near East, or silk, the use of which was discovered in China. All of these materials have been spun and woven by processes invented in the Near East. He slips into his moccasins, invented by the Indians of the Eastern woodlands, and goes to the bathroom, whose fixtures are a mixture of European and American inventions, both of recent date. He takes off his pajamas, a garment invented by ancient Gauls. He then shaves, a masochistic rite which seems to have been derived from either Sumer or Ancient Egypt.

Returning to the bedroom, he removes his clothes from a chair of southern European type and proceeds to dress. He puts on garments whose form originally derived from the skin clothing of the nomads of the Asiatic steppes, puts on shoes made from skins tanned in a process invented in Ancient Egypt and cut to a pattern derived from the classical civilizations of the Mediterranean, and ties around his neck a strip of bright-colored cloth which is a vestigial survival of the

---

29. Ralph Linton, *The Study of Man* (N. Y.: Appleton-Century-Crofts, 1936), 326–27.

shoulder shawls worn by the seventeenth century Croatians. Before going out for breakfast, he glances through the window, made of glass invented in Egypt, and if it is raining, puts on overshoes made of rubber, discovered by the Central American Indians, and takes an umbrella, invented in Southeastern Asia. Upon his head he puts a hat made of felt, a material invented in the Asiatic steppes.

---

Customs can differ and be neither good nor bad, but while cultural differences may be relative, that doesn't mean that *morality* is relative. Cannibalism and human sacrifice, for instance, are evil. They are practices that have ceased for the most part because of the spread of Christianity into the world. Nor is theology relative. Jesus Christ is set apart from any idol that is worshiped as a god. He alone is King of kings and Lord of lords.

*This selection is suitable for children and is geared toward them.
The moral of the story is to not think more highly of yourself than you
ought. You will be happier if you think of others' welfare instead of just
your own.*

## "THE TEAPOT"

by Hans Christian Andersen
translated by Kirsti Saebo Newcombe

Did you know that Hans Christian Andersen was Christian? I
don't mean only his middle name; I mean his worldview, his
writings, his demeanor. This has been a delightful discovery that
my wife brought to my attention. She's from Kristiansand, Norway, close to Denmark, Andersen's homeland. She has a multi-
volume set of all of his fairy tales. She pointed out to me how so
many of them have a Christian worldview and some of them
even directly talk about God or the Bible. This story is the first of
two fairy tales by Hans Christian Andersen reproduced in this
book.

This fairy tale underscores how wrong it is for one to think too
highly of himself. Here are the recollections of a teapot that
snootily looks down on the other members of the tea set since
their role is not as important as hers. Fortunately for the teapot,
by the end of the tale she learns her lesson. Unfortunately for us,
many teapots around us haven't seemed to learn their lessons
about the vanity of pride. I think Andersen wrote this story about
a teapot because we can all see how silly it is for a teapot to be
proud and arrogant. When we think we have plenty of reasons to
puff ourselves up and believe ourselves quite marvelous, we
often become as silly as the teapot in this fairy tale.

---

Once upon a time, there was a proud teapot, proud of her fine
porcelain, proud of her long spout, proud of her wide handle. She
had something in the front and something in the back, and that's all
she talked about. But she did not talk about her lid—there was a
crack and a chip in it. It was a shortcoming, that lid was, and one
does not talk about one's shortcomings. Others do that—quite willingly. The cups and the cream jug and the sugar bowl, the whole tea
set, remembered the shortcomings of the lid (and talked about it)

much better than the good handle and the excellent spout. The teapot knew that.

"I know them," she said to herself. "I also know my faults. I acknowledge them, which proves that I am humble and good-mannered. We all have our faults, but then, we have our strong points too. The cups, they all have a handle each, and the sugar bowls have a lid. I have both, plus something in the front—a spout, something they will never get. This makes me the queen of the tea table. The sugar bowl and the cream jug, they are servants of good taste at the table. But I, I am the one who gives, the one who is in charge, the one who spreads blessing to alleviate the thirst of mankind. In me are the Chinese leaves and the tasteless water transformed."

All these things said the teapot when she was young and arrogant. She stood on the most elegant tables and was lifted by the finest hands. But one day, the finest hand was clumsy, and the teapot fell. Her spout broke, her handle cracked. The lid's not even worth mentioning; we have said enough about that already. The teapot lay fainted on the floor and all the scalding hot water poured out. It was a hard blow, but the hardest was that they all laughed at the teapot—when they should have been laughing at the clumsy hand.

"I'll never live this down," said the teapot. "I was called a cripple and the very next day, I was given away to a beggar woman who begs for scraps at the door. Now I sank down into the deepest poverty, and I didn't know which way to turn. But everything turned out for the better. One can be one thing and then become something quite different.

"Dirt was laid in me, but it wasn't a funeral because they planted a flower bulb in that dirt. Who put it there and who gave it away, that I don't know. But I have it. It was a compensation for the Chinese leaves and the hot water. A compensation for the broken spout and handle. The bulb lay in the soil. It laid in me and became my heart. I had never had a heart before. There was life in me now and power. The pulse was beating the power of life, from which sprang forth a green shoot. From all the life and thoughts and feelings sprang forth a beautiful flower. I saw it. I was carrying it. I forgot myself for the glory of the flower.

"It is blessed to forget oneself for others! The flower didn't thank me. It didn't think about me. It was praised and adored. I was so happy and I'm sure the flower was too.

"One day, I heard them say that the flower deserved a better pot. They cracked me across the middle, and that hurt really bad. But the flower received a better pot, and I was thrown out into the yard. Here I lay, a broken piece here, an old chip there. But I have my memories, and I can never lose them."

---

When we focus on ourselves, our lives get out of whack. We get consumed with self-love. When we focus on others, our lives are in the proper perspective. I love the acrostic that teaches this so well: J.O.Y. (put *J*esus first, *O*thers second, *Y*ourself last).

*This selection is suitable for children.*
*The moral of the story is: Don't let success make you think too highly of yourself.*

# "THE GOOD THINGS OF LIFE"

### from *Through Many Windows*[30]

### by Arthur Gordon

In this particular story, the main character has allowed his success—ironically his success as a minister—to crowd out his relationship with the Lord. He has allowed his great achievements to blind him as to his ultimate mission. In this story, he returns to his simple ministry and realizes that he has forgotten his first love. It is a simple Christmas service that he himself is about to officiate that brings him to his senses. (I think a lot of people tend to return to the Lord at Christmas time.)

Arthur Gordon is a freelance writer who's published articles in *The Saturday Evening Post, Reader's Digest,* and *Redbook,* among others. He has served as editorial director for *Guideposts.* He's the author of *A Touch of Wonder* and a book of his own short stories, entitled *Through Many Windows.* There are three stories from this last book that I use in this present volume. "The Good Things of Life" is the first one.

---

Near the crest of the hill he felt the rear wheels of the car spin for half a second, and he felt a flash of the unreasonable irritability that had been plaguing him lately. He said, a bit grimly, "Good thing it didn't snow more than an inch or two. We'd be in trouble if it had."

His wife was driving. She often did, so that he could make notes for a sermon or catch up on his endless correspondence by dictating into the tape recorder he had built into the car. Now she looked out at the woods and fields gleaming in the morning sunlight. "It's pretty, though. And Christmasy. We haven't had a white Christmas like this in years."

He gave her an amused and affectionate glance. "You always see the best side of things, don't you, my love?"

---

30. Arthur Gordon, *Through Many Windows* (Grand Rapids: Revell, 1983), 58–63.

"Well, after hearing you urge umpteen congregations to do precisely that . . ."

Arnold Barclay smiled, and some of the lines of tension and fatigue went out of his face. "Remember the bargain we made twenty years ago? I'd do the preaching and you'd do the practicing."

Her mouth curved faintly. "I remember."

They came to a crossroads, and he found that after all these years he still remembered the sign: LITTLEFIELD, 1 MILE. He said, "How's the time?"

She glanced at the diamond watch on her wrist: his present to her this year. "A little after ten."

He leaned forward and switched on the radio. In a moment his own voice, strong and resonant, filled the car, preaching a Christmas sermon prepared and recorded weeks before. He listened to a sentence or two, then smiled sheepishly and turned it off. "Just wanted to hear how I sounded."

"You sound fine," Mary Barclay said. "You always do."

They passed a farmhouse, the new snow sparkling like diamonds on the roof, the Christmas wreath gay against the front door. "Who lived there?" he asked. "Peterson, wasn't it? No, Johannsen."

"That's right," his wife said. "Eric Johannsen. Remember the night he made you hold the lantern while the calf was born?"

"Do I ever!" He rubbed his forehead wearily. "About this new television proposition, Mary. What do you think? It would be an extra load, I know. But I'd be reaching an enormous audience. The biggest—"

She put her hand on his arm. "Darling, it's Christmas Day. Can't we talk about it later?"

"Why, sure," he said, but something in him was offended all the same. The television proposal was important. Why, in fifteen minutes he would reach ten times as many people as Saint Paul had reached in a lifetime! He said, "How many people did the Littlefield church hold, Mary? About a hundred, wasn't it?"

"Ninety-six," his wife said. "To be exact."

"Ninety-six!" He gave a rueful laugh. "Quite a change of pace."

It was that, all right. It was years since he had preached in anything but metropolitan churches. The Littlefield parish had been the beginning. Now, on Christmas morning, he was going back. Back for an hour or two, to stand in the little pulpit where he had preached his first hesitant, fumbling sermon twenty years ago.

He let his head fall back against the seat and closed his eyes. The decision to go back had not been his, really; it had been Mary's. She handled all his appointments, screening the innumerable invitations to preach or speak. A month ago she had come to him. There was a request, she said, for him to go back to Littlefield and preach a sermon on Christmas morning.

"Littlefield?" he had said, incredulous. "What about that Washington invitation?" He had been asked to preach to a congregation that would, he knew, include senators and cabinet members.

"We haven't answered it yet," she said. "We could drive to Littlefield on Christmas morning, if we got up early enough . . ."

He had stared at her. "You mean, you think we *ought* to go back there?"

She had looked back at him calmly. "That's up to you, Arnold." But he knew what she wanted him to say.

Making such a decision wasn't so hard at the moment, he thought wearily. Not resenting afterward—that was the difficult part. Maybe it wouldn't be so bad. The church would be horribly overcrowded, the congregation would be mostly farmers, but . . .

The car stopped; he opened his eyes.

They were at the church, all right. There it sat by the side of the road, just as it always had—if anything, it looked smaller than he had remembered it. Around it the fields stretched away, white and unbroken, to the neighboring farmhouses. But there were no cars, there was no crowd, there was no sign of anyone. The church was shuttered and silent.

He looked at Mary, bewildered. She did not seem surprised. She pushed open the car door. "Let's go inside, shall we? I still have a key."

The church was cold. Standing in the icy gloom, he could see his breath steam in the gray light. He said, and his voice sounded strange, "Where is everybody? You said there was a request . . ."

"There was a request," Mary said. "From me." She moved forward slowly until she was standing by the pulpit. "Arnold," she said, "the finest sermon I ever heard you preach was right here in this church. It was your first Christmas sermon; we hadn't been married long. You didn't know our first baby was on the way—but I did. Maybe that's why I remember so well what you said.

"You said that God had tried every way possible to get through to people. He tried prophets and miracles and revelations—and nothing worked. So then He said, 'I'll send them something they can't fail to understand. I'll send them the simplest and yet the most wonderful thing in all My creation. I'll send them a Baby . . .' Do you remember that?"

He nodded wordlessly.

"Well," she said, "I heard that they had no minister here now, so I knew they wouldn't be having a service this morning. And I thought . . . well, I thought it might be good for . . . for both of us if you could preach that sermon again. Right here, where your ministry began. I just thought . . ."

Her voice trailed off, but he knew what she meant. He knew what she was trying to tell him, although she was too loyal and too kind to say it in words. That he had gotten away from the sources of his strength. That as success had come to him, as his reputation had grown larger, some things in him had grown smaller. The selflessness. The humility. The most important things of all.

He stood there, silent, seeing himself with a terrifying clarity: the pride, the ambition, the hunger for larger and larger audiences. Not for the glory of God. For the glory of Arnold Barclay.

He clenched his fists, feeling panic grip him, a sense of terror and guilt unlike anything he had ever known. Then faintly, underneath the panic, something else stirred. He glanced around the little church. She was right, Mary was right, and perhaps it wasn't too late. Perhaps here, now, he could rededicate himself . . .

Abruptly he stripped off his overcoat, tossed it across the back of a pew. He reached out and took both of Mary's hands. He heard himself laugh, an eager, boyish laugh. "We'll do it! We'll do it just the way we used to! You open the shutters; that was your job, remember? I'll start the furnace. We'll have a Christmas service just for the two of us. I'll preach that sermon, all for you!"

She turned quickly to the nearest window, raised it, began fumbling with the catch that held the shutters. He opened the door that led to the cellar steps. Down in the frigid basement he found the furnace squatting, as black and malevolent as ever. He flung open the iron door. No fire was laid, but along the wall wood was stacked, and kindling, and newspapers.

He began to crumple papers and thrust them into the furnace, heedless of the soot that blackened his fingers. Overhead he heard the sound that made him pause. Mary was trying the wheezy old melodeon. "Ring the bell, too," he shouted up the stairs. "We might as well do the job right!"

He heard her laugh. A moment later, high in the belfry, the bell began to ring. Its tone was as clear and resonant as ever, and the sound brought back a flood of memories: the baptisms, the burials, the Sunday dinners at the old farmhouses, the honesty and brusqueness and simple goodness of the people.

He stood there, listening, until the bell was silent. Then he struck a match and held it to the newspapers. Smoke curled reluctantly. He reached up, adjusted the old damper, tried again. This time a tongue of flame flickered. For perhaps five minutes he watched it, hovering over it, blowing on it. When he was sure that it was kindled, he went back up the cellar steps.

The church was a blaze of sunlight. Where the window glass was clear, millions of dust motes whirled and danced; where there were panes of stained glass, the rays fell on the old floor in pools of ruby and topaz and amethyst. Mary was standing at the church door. "Arnold," she said, "come here."

He went and stood beside her. After the darkness of the cellar, the sun on the snow was so bright that he couldn't see anything.

"Look," she said in a whisper. "They're coming."

Cupping his hands round his eyes, he stared out across the glistening whiteness, and he saw that she was right. They were coming. Across the fields. Down the roads. Some on foot. Some in cars. They were coming, he knew, not to hear him, not to hear any preacher, however great. They were coming because it was Christmas Day, and this was their church and its bell was calling them. They were coming because they wanted someone to give them the ancient message, to tell them the good news.

He stood there with his arm round his wife's shoulders and the soot black on his face and the overflowing happiness in his heart. "Merry Christmas," he said. "Merry Christmas. And thank you. Thank you, darling."

When Christ addressed the Ephesian church in Revelation 2, He told them they were *doing* all the right things . . . but apparently with a poor motivation. For they were no longer in love with Jesus. It is refreshing to see the main character in this story humble himself and return to his first love.

A subtheme of this story deals with the beautiful, but often abandoned, country churches. New life needs to be breathed into the work of God, even in those places where there once may have been a vibrant church. We're all in need of renewal.

# SECTION 2

# GREED

Money is an idol to millions today, and it has been throughout the ages. The Bible doesn't condemn money per se, as some think it does, but it does speak ill of the *love* of money, which is the root of all kinds of evil (1 Tim. 6:10). Solomon the wise, one of the wealthiest men who ever lived, once said, "Whoever loves money never has money enough" (Eccl. 5:10). Amen.

Greed is a serious spiritual problem. But we are blind to it in America. "Greed has poisoned men's souls," said Charlie Chaplin on the eve of World War II.[1] That's well put. Greed is sometimes even viewed as a good thing by some quarters of our society. But the problem with the rat race, it has been said, is that even if you win, you're still a rat!

Many of the seven deadly sins involve the perversion of an otherwise healthy appetite. We are sexual beings because God made us that way; but lust goes beyond what He intended. We eat because He created us that way; but gluttony goes way beyond His intentions. Greed is also a perversion of the normal, positive God-given desire to earn a decent living.

The classic tale of Midas shows how the love of wealth can lead to ruin. Midas, you will recall, loved gold a great deal. One day his wish was granted to him that everything he touched would turn to gold. But this proved disastrous—he couldn't even eat! It even turned fatal for his daughter, whom he touched without thinking.

---

1. Charlie Chaplin, *The Great Dictator*, a 1940 film.

Another classic tale of greed is the one where the dog has a bone and sees his reflection in a pool of water. Thinking it another dog—with another bone—he drops his to grab the extra bone and loses the only one he had!

In the Bible, there's the story of Achan, who greedily horded a wedge of gold and some other items after the battle of Jericho in direct disobedience to God's command. His greedy act caused the Lord to withhold His supernatural blessing from Israel in battle. Thus, Achan's "sin in the camp" brought destruction on others, as well as himself and his family (Josh. 7).

Everyday in America, there are people who rob others for their own selfishness, to satisfy their greed. Theft has gotten way out of hand. Bill Bennett writes: "Ninety-nine percent of Americans will be victims of theft at least once in their lives. Eighty-seven percent will have property stolen three or more times." Wow, that's reassuring! *Ninety-nine percent!* The most amazing thing about that statistic is that we continue to take it.

The man with few possessions can also be greedy. He can be possessed with envy of others' goods. The dictionary defines *greed* as "an overwhelming desire to acquire or have, as wealth or power, in excess of what one requires or deserves." There's no condition put on greed that makes it a wealthy man's sin.

The following stories deal with greed. They underscore our need for less covetousness and more contentment.

*This selection is suitable for children.*
*The moral of the story is that envy leads to destruction.*

# NABOTH'S VINEYARD

### from the Book of 1 Kings (NIV)

Greed can lead to the murder of innocent people. This story from the Bible illustrates that.

One of the most wicked people in all of literature was Queen Jezebel in the Old Testament. She was the devil's servant, responsible for murdering God's servants and supplanting them with idol-worshiping priests. The worship of the true God was greatly arrested during her time because of her efforts. The true prophets of God were forced into hiding because of her, lest they be slain.

When her husband, Ahab, set his heart on aquiring the land of a certain man, Naboth, he expressed an interest to receive it. But he was refused. So Jezebel connived to get it for him illegitimately. Ahab's covetousness of Naboth's land was the driving force for this crime, which included murder.

This passage is found in 1 Kings 21:1–29.

---

Some time later there was an incident involving a vineyard belonging to Naboth the Jezreelite. The vineyard was in Jezreel, close to the palace of Ahab king of Samaria. Ahab said to Naboth, "Let me have your vineyard to use for a vegetable garden, since it is close to my palace. In exchange I will give you a better vineyard or, if you prefer, I will pay you whatever it is worth."

But Naboth replied, "The LORD forbid that I should give you the inheritance of my fathers."

So Ahab went home, sullen and angry because Naboth the Jezreelite had said, "I will not give you the inheritance of my fathers." He lay on his bed sulking and refused to eat.

His wife Jezebel came in and asked him, "Why are you so sullen? Why won't you eat?"

He answered her, "Because I said to Naboth the Jezreelite, 'Sell me your vineyard; or if you prefer, I will give you another vineyard in its place.' But he said, 'I will not give you my vineyard.'"

Jezebel his wife said, "Is this how you act as king over Israel? Get up and eat! Cheer up. I'll get you the vineyard of Naboth the Jezreelite."

So she wrote letters in Ahab's name, placed his seal on them, and sent them to the elders and nobles who lived in Naboth's city with him. In those letters she wrote: "Proclaim a day of fasting and seat Naboth in a prominent place among the people. But seat two scoundrels opposite him and have them testify that he has cursed both God and the king. Then take him out and stone him to death."

So the elders and nobles who lived in Naboth's city did as Jezebel directed in the letters she had written to them. They proclaimed a fast and seated Naboth in a prominent place among the people. Then two scoundrels came and sat opposite him and brought charges against Naboth before the people, saying, "Naboth has cursed both God and the king." So they took him outside the city and stoned him to death. Then they sent word to Jezebel: "Naboth has been stoned and is dead."

As soon as Jezebel heard that Naboth had been stoned to death, she said to Ahab, "Get up and take possession of the vineyard of Naboth the Jezreelite that he refused to sell you. He is no longer alive, but dead." When Ahab heard that Naboth was dead, he got up and went down to take possession of Naboth's vineyard.

Then the word of the LORD came to Elijah the Tishbite: "Go down to meet Ahab king of Israel, who rules in Samaria. He is now in Naboth's vineyard, where he has gone to take possession of it. Say to him, 'This is what the LORD says: Have you not murdered a man and seized his property?' Then say to him, 'This is what the LORD says: In the place where dogs licked up Naboth's blood, dogs will lick up your blood—yes, yours'!"

Ahab said to Elijah, "So you have found me, my enemy!"

"I have found you," he answered, "because you have sold yourself to do evil in the eyes of the LORD. 'I am going to bring disaster on you. I will consume your descendants and cut off from Ahab every last male in Israel—slave or free. I will make your house like that of Jeroboam son of Nebat and that of Baasha son of Ahijah, because you have provoked me to anger and have caused Israel to sin.'

"And also concerning Jezebel the LORD says: 'Dogs will devour Jezebel by the wall of Jezreel.'

"Dogs will eat those belonging to Ahab who die in the city, and the birds of the air will feed on those who die in the country."

(There was never a man like Ahab, who sold himself to do evil in the eyes of the LORD, urged on by Jezebel his wife. He behaved in the vilest manner by going after idols, like the Amorites the Lord drove out before Israel.)

When Ahab heard these words, he tore his clothes, put on sackcloth and fasted. He lay in sackcloth and went around meekly.

Then the word of the LORD came to Elijah the Tishbite: "Have you noticed how Ahab has humbled himself before me? Because he has humbled himself, I will not bring this disaster in his day, but I will bring it on his house in the days of his son."

---

If you ever find yourself admiring the possessions of others, be careful never to let a true and decent appreciation of what they have turn into a horrid greed and envy. It starts in the heart and, if unchecked, ends up in all manner of evil deeds. I would bet that if you browsed today's paper, you might well see many news items about crimes committed because of greed.

*This story is suitable for children.*
*The moral of the story is twofold: (1) faith sometimes goes beyond com-*
*mon sense, and (2) greed leads to destruction.*

# THE HEALING OF NAAMAN THE LEPER
# AND THE GREED OF GEHAZI[2]

retold by Jesse Hurlbut

This story has two parts. The second part deals with greed; the
first with faith. I include the story here primarily because of its
second half.

Faith sometimes requires our going beyond our natural understanding. What comes first? Understanding or faith? The answer is
faith. Faith comes first, then understanding. Not that it's an unreasonable faith. The Christian faith is based on the sure foundation
that Christ rose from the dead in human history on a particular
Sunday in the first century (most likely in April, A.D. 30). So Christianity does not demand a "blind faith." But we walk by faith, not
by sight.

In this story, we read about Naaman, a Gentile who was open
to the possibility that the Jewish God was *the* God, the God of
the universe. Naaman suffered from the horrible disease of leprosy, which in those days was enough to cause one to be ostra-
cized from the camp (at least among the Hebrews). He was
desperate enough to try something radical to rid himself of the
disease. Interestingly, his pride almost prevented him from
engaging in the advice that Elisha, God's prophet, gave him. But
his humble servant suggested he try it anyway.

The second part of the story is that we should avoid being
greedy—a lesson our culture seems to have forgotten. What happens to Gehazi, Elisha's servant, in this story is one of the all-time
great warnings against avarice.

This story is based on 2 Kings 5:1–27.

---

At one time, while Elisha was living in Israel, the general of the Syrian army was named Naaman. He was a great man in his rank and
power and a brave man in battle, for he had won victories for Syria.

---

2. This story by Jesse Hurlbut was originally entitled "How a Little Girl Helped to Cure a
Leper."

But one sad, terrible trouble came to Naaman. He was a leper. A leper was one with a disease called leprosy, which is still found in those lands. The leper's skin turns a deathly white and is covered with scales. One by one his fingers and toes, his hands, his feet, his arms and limbs decay, until at last the man dies, and for the disease there is no cure. Yet, strange to say, through it all, the leper feels no pain. Often he will not for a long time believe that he has leprosy.

There was in Naaman's house at Damascus, in Syria, a little girl who waited on Naaman's wife. She was a slave girl stolen from her mother's home in Israel and carried away as a captive to Syria. Even when there was no open war between Syria and Israel, parties of men were going out on both sides and destroying villages on the border, robbing the people and carrying them away to be killed or sold as slaves. But this little girl, even though she had suffered wrong, had a kind heart, full of sorrow for her master Naaman; and one day she said to her mistress:

"I wish that my lord Naaman might meet the prophet who lives in Samaria; for he could cure his leprosy."

Someone told Naaman what the little girl had said, and Naaman spoke of it to the king of Syria. Now the king of Syria loved Naaman greatly; and when he went to worship in the temple of his god, out of all his nobles he chose Naaman as the one upon whose arm he leaned. He greatly desired to have Naaman's leprosy cured; and he said, "I will send a letter to the king of Israel and I will ask him to let his prophet cure you."

So Naaman, with a great train of followers, rode in his chariot from Damascus to Samaria, about a hundred miles. He took with him as a present a large sum in gold and silver and many beautiful robes and garments. He came to the king of Israel and gave him the letter from the king of Syria. And this was written in the letter:

"With this letter I have sent to you Naaman, my servant; and I wish you to cure him of his leprosy."

The king of Syria supposed that as this prophet who could cure leprosy was in Samaria, he was under the orders of the king of Israel and must do whatever the king told him to do; and as he did not know the prophet, but knew the king, he wrote to him. But the king was greatly alarmed when he read the letter.

"Am I God," he said, "to kill men and to make men live! Why should the king of Syria send to me to cure a man of his leprosy? Do you not see that he is trying to find an excuse for making war, in asking me to do what no man can do?"

And the king of Israel tore his garments, as men did when they were in deep trouble. Elisha the prophet heard of the letter and of the king's alarm, and he sent a message to the king.

"Why are you so frightened? Let this man come to me, and he shall know that there is a prophet of the Lord in Israel."

So Naaman came with his chariots, his horses, and his followers and stood before the door of Elisha's house. Elisha did not come out to meet him but sent his servant out to him, saying:

"Go and wash in the river Jordan seven times, and your flesh and your skin shall become pure, and you shall be free from the leprosy."

But Naaman was very angry because Elisha had not treated with more respect so great a man as he was. He forgot, or he did not know, that by the laws of Israel no man might touch or even come near a leper; and he said:

"Why, I supposed that of course he would come out to meet me and would wave his hand over the leper spot and would call on the name of the Lord his God, and in that manner would cure my leprosy! Are not Abana and Pharpar, the two rivers of Damascus, better than all the waters in Israel? May I not wash in them and be clean?"

And Naaman turned and went away in a rage of anger. But his servants were wiser than he. They came to him, and one of them said:

"My father, if the prophet had told you to do some great thing, would you not have done it? Then why not do it, when he says, 'Wash and be clean?'"

After a little Naaman's anger cooled, and he rode down the mountains to the river Jordan. He washed in its water seven times, as the prophet had bidden him. And the scales of leprosy left his skin, and his flesh became like the flesh of a little child, pure and clean. Then Naaman, a leper no more, came back to Elisha's house with all his company, and he said, "Now I know that there is no God in all the earth, except in Israel. Let me make you a present in return for what you have done for me."

But the true prophets of God never gave their message or did their works for pay; and Elisha said to Naaman:

"As surely as the Lord lives, before whom I stand, I will receive nothing."

And Naaman urged him to take the present, but he refused. Then Naaman asked a favor that he might be allowed to take away from the land of Israel as much soil as could be carried on two mules, with which to build an altar; for he thought that an altar to the God of Israel could be made only of earth from the land of Israel; and he said:

"From this time I will offer no burnt offering or sacrifice to any other god except the God of Israel. When I go with my master, the king of Syria, to worship in the temple of Rimmon his god, and my master leans on my arm, and I bow down to Rimmon with him, then may the Lord forgive me for this, which will look as if I were worshiping another god."

And Elisha said to him, "Go in peace."

Then Naaman went on his way back to his own land. But Gehazi, the servant of Elisha, said to himself:

"My master has let this Syrian go without taking anything from him; but I will run after him and ask him for a present."

So Gehazi ran after Naaman, and Naaman saw him following and stopped his chariot and stepped down to meet him. And Gehazi said to him:

"My master has sent me to you to say that just now two young men of the sons of the prophets have come to his house; will you give them a talent of silver and two suits of clothing?"

And Naaman said, "Let me give you two talents of silver."

So he put two talents of silver in two bags, a talent in each bag, and gave them to Gehazi, and with them two suits of fine clothing; and he sent them back by two of his servants. But before they came to Elisha's house, Gehazi took the gifts and hid them. Then Gehazi went into the house and stood before Elisha. And Elisha said to him, "Gehazi, where have you been?"

And Gehazi answered, "I have not been at any place."

And Elisha said to him:

"Did not my heart go with you, and did I not see you when the man stepped down from his chariot to meet you? Is this a time to receive gifts of money and garments, or gifts of vineyards and olive yards and of sheep and oxen? Because you have done this wickedness, the leprosy of Naaman shall come upon you and shall cling to you and to your children after you forever!"

And Gehazi walked out from Elisha's presence, a leper, with his skin as white as snow.

---

Paul once said these things that occurred in the Old Testament, as severe as they may seem, happened to them so that people throughout the ages could avoid these sins (1 Cor. 10:11). God is not pleased with greed. What happened to Gehazi is an eternal reminder of that fact.

*This selection is suitable for children.*
*The moral of the story is to be generous to God, even if you don't have much money.*

# THE WIDOW'S MITE

### from the Gospel According to Luke (NIV)

We've been examining different stories related to greed. Here's one reflecting the opposite. This is a short story from the gospels showing a woman who was anything but greedy.

This story comes from Luke 21:1–4.

---

As he looked up, Jesus saw the rich putting their gifts into the temple treasury. He also saw a poor widow put in two very small copper coins. "I tell you the truth," he said, "this poor widow has put in more than all the others. All these people gave their gifts out of their wealth; but she out of her poverty put in all she had to live on."

---

Did you know that the Church is run by the widow's mite? In other words, precisely because of the generosity of people like this in the passage, the Church is able to do all its various works. Studies show that the more money people make, they often give less in proportion. Those who earn $50,000 or more tend to give less to the Church than those who make $10,000 or less! Wow. That's a sobering thought, since so many in our society seem to strive for more and more wealth. Many Americans have made an idol of wealth. They worship money. Even many professing Christians seem to serve mammon over serving Christ! But Jesus said no man can serve both God and wealth. He said: "No one can serve two masters. Either he will hate the one and love the other, or he will be devoted to the one and despise the other. You cannot serve both God and Money" (Matt. 6:24, NIV).

Amazingly, the more we accumulate, the tougher it is to be like this lady and to give generously. But as Christians we must view ourselves merely as stewards, not eternal owners, of our things. We must own things, but never let them own us.

*This selection is suitable for children.*
*The moral of the story is don't try to be greedy with God.*

# ANANIAS AND SAPPHIRA

### from the Book of Acts (NIV)

Abe Lincoln once said, "You can fool all the people some of the time and some of the people all of the time, but you can't fool all of the people all of the time."[3] And to that, I would add: "You can't fool God any of the time!" This next selection is a true story about two greedy people who tried to fool Him and, of course, could not.

This story comes from the book of Acts in the New Testament, specifically Acts 4:32–5:11. This was at a time when the Church was beginning to mushroom, and there was no place for those whose greed led them to lies and destruction.

---

All the believers were one in heart and mind. No one claimed that any of his possessions was his own, but they shared everything they had. With great power the apostles continued to testify to the resurrection of the Lord Jesus, and much grace was upon them all. There were no needy persons among them. For from time to time those who owned lands or houses sold them, brought the money from the sales and put it at the apostles' feet, and it was distributed to anyone as he had need.

Joseph, a Levite from Cyprus, whom the apostles called Barnabas (which means Son of Encouragement), sold a field he owned and brought the money and put it at the apostles' feet.

Now a man named Ananias, together with his wife Sapphira, also sold a piece of property. With his wife's full knowledge he kept back part of the money for himself, but brought the rest and put it at the apostle's feet.

Then Peter said, "Ananias, how is it that Satan has so filled your heart that you have lied to the Holy Spirit and have kept for yourself some of the money you received for the land? Didn't it belong to you

---

3. Abraham Lincoln, in a speech at Clinton, Illinois, 8 September 1858, as quoted in Gorton Carruth and Eugene Ehrlich, eds., *The Harper Book of American Quotations* (New York: Harper & Row, 1988), 351.

before it was sold? And after it was sold, wasn't the money at your disposal? What made you think of doing such a thing? You have not lied to men but to God."

When Ananias heard this, he fell down and died. And great fear seized all who heard what had happened. Then the young men came forward, wrapped up his body, and carried him out and buried him.

About three hours later his wife came in, not knowing what had happened. Peter asked her, "Tell me, is this the price you and Ananias got for the land?"

"Yes," she said, "that is the price."

Peter said to her, "How could you agree to test the Spirit of the Lord? Look! The feet of the men who buried your husband are at the door, and they will carry you out also."

At that moment she fell down at his feet and died. Then the young men came in and, finding her dead, carried her out and buried her beside her husband. Great fear seized the whole church and all who heard about these events.

---

When you read this story, you may wonder: *Why was God so harsh with these people? Didn't the punishment go beyond the crime?* But in reality, this was at the beginning of Christian history. And the Lord was purifying His Church. At the beginning of the Church, there was no place at all for gross immorality, for gross sins. Therefore, in this early stage, God severely judged a couple that sinned within the Church.

One other observation. All these people were engaged here in a *voluntary* giving project. (This wasn't communism, and it was to the *Church* that this money was given.) They could have given less if they had wanted to. Their sin was that they lied about it, apparently to give the impression to everybody how much money they gave to the Church—a sin motivated by greed (to hold back more) and pride (to make it seem like they were more generous).

*This selection is suitable for children.*
*The moral of the story is that people sometimes sin for no real reason but to engage in the evil act itself.*

# "THE STOLEN FRUIT"

### from *The Confessions of St. Augustine*[4]

One aspect of greed-motivated theft that's strange is that the greedy sometimes have no real need for the items they covet and steal. Here is a brief description from St. Augustine, commenting on his youth, wherein he violated God's commandment not to steal. His greed wasn't motivated by need, but rather the sheer desire to engage in what he knew was wrong.

St. Augustine (354–430) is said to have been one of the greatest thinkers in the history of the world. One of the great doctors of the Church, Augustine commands respect from both Catholic and Protestant alike. As Presbyterian theologian B. B. Warfield once said, "Every tendency of thought in the church was eager to claim for itself the support of his name."[5]

Augustine wrote two very important and influential books, *The Confessions of St. Augustine*, written as a prayer (a portion of which we present here), and *The City of God*, which is said to have laid "the foundations of a rational philosophy of history."[6]

Surely, Lord, your law punishes theft, as does that law written on the hearts of men, which not even iniquity itself blots out; what thief puts up with another thief with a calm mind? Not even a rich thief will pardon one who steals from him because of want. But I was willed to commit theft, and I did so, not because I was driven to it by any need, unless it were by poverty of justice, and dislike of it, and by a glut of evildoing. For I stole a thing of which I had plenty of my own and of much better quality. Nor did I wish to enjoy that thing which I desired to gain by theft, but rather to enjoy the actual theft and the sin of theft.

4. Trans. by John K. Ryan (Garden City, N.Y.: Doubleday, 1960), 69–70, 73.
5. B. B. Warfield, *Calvin and Augustine* (Philadelphia: The Presbyterian and Reformed Publishing Co., 1956), 309.
6. Ibid., 307.

In a garden nearby to our vineyard there was a pear tree, loaded with fruit that was desirable neither in appearance nor in taste. Late one night—to which hour, according to our pestilential[7] custom, we had kept up our street games——a group of very bad youngsters set out to shake down and rob this tree. We took great loads of fruit from it, not for our own eating, but rather to throw it to the pigs; even if we did eat a little of it, we did this to do what pleased us for the reason that it was forbidden.

Behold my heart, O Lord, behold my heart upon which you had mercy in the depths of the pit. Behold, now let my heart tell you what it looked for there, that I should be evil without purpose and that there should be no cause for my evil but evil itself. Foul was the evil, and I loved it. I loved to go down to death. I loved my fault itself. Base in soul was I, and destruction, and I sought nothing from the shameful deed but shame itself!

O rottenness! O monstrous life and deepest death! Could a thing give pleasure which could not be done lawfully, and which was done for no other reason but because it was unlawful?

---

Have you ever seen one of those signs by the highway that says "No hunting allowed" but is riddled with bullet holes? There's something about human nature—our sinful nature—that often relishes sin for sin's sake. In a later selection in this book, we'll continue with St. Augustine and find out how he became a Christian.

---

7. Morally noxious.

*This story is suitable for children.*
*The moral of the story is that the love of money is the root of all kinds of evil.*

# "THE PARDONER'S TALE" [8]

### from *The Canterbury Tales*
### by Geoffrey Chaucer

Greed can lead to all kinds of evil actions. People will take the life of another human being for money. It happens so often we get numb to it. But think of how evil that is! For example, a youngster fatally shooting another youngster for a $100-pair of basketball shoes. But there's nothing new about greed, as there is nothing new with all these sins, the categorization of which goes back to the early Medieval period. Here is a summary of a clever story from the Middle Ages, showing how greed can lead to death.

Geoffrey Chaucer (1340?–1400) wrote *The Canterbury Tales,* one of the earliest classics of the English language. It is a collection of tales (about a hundred or so) that a group of pilgrims told each other as they made their pilgrimage to the tomb of St. Thomas à Becket in Canterbury. Chaucer makes it clear that this group of pilgrims included the devout and sincere, along with rogues. Ironically, this tale was told by one of the rogues! He told it for an evil purpose (to extract money from the other pilgrims). Nonetheless, the story stands on its own and makes a powerful plea to avoid the deadly sin of greed.

---

In a tavern in Flanders drank three rowdy, young men of low character. They spent their days and nights carousing, imbibing, gambling, dancing, and gorging themselves. One morning, they heard the church bells ring out, signifying yet another funeral in the region. I say "yet another funeral" for there were so many in those days. One of the three inquired of the tavern worker to find out who it was that died:

---

8. Summarized here by the editor. The occasional quotes from the original are from the translation into modern English by Nevill Coghill (Middlesex, England: Penguin Books, 1951, 1970).

One of them called the little tavern-knave
And said, "Go and find out at once—look spry!—
Whose corpse is in that coffin passing by;
And see you get the name correctly too."
"Sir," said the boy, "no need, I promise you;
Two hours before you came here I was told.
He was a friend of yours in days of old,
And suddenly, last night, the man was slain,
Upon his bench, face up, dead drunk again.
There came a privy thief, they call him Death,
Who kills us all round here, and in a breath
He speared him through the heart, he never stirred.
And then Death went his way without a word.
He's killed a thousand in the present plague."

That was it! The three "rioters" flew into a drunken rage. They had had enough! Death had gone too far this time. He had been ravishing the region for too long. So the three rash young men arose, with swords in hand, to go and find Death that they might slay this wicked monster that was bringing so much unhappiness to the region. They swore, "If we can only catch him, Death is dead!"

The men stormed out of the tavern and came across an old man by the roadside. Disrespectfully, they demanded of him where they might find Death. They even threatened to kill *him* if he didn't answer them. One of them barked, "Say where he is or you shall pay for it!"

[The old man spoke:]
"Well, sirs," he said, "if it be your design
To find out Death, turn up this crooked way
Towards that grove, I left him there to-day
Under a tree, and there you'll find him waiting."

At once the carousers set out to find the particular tree the man described to them. When they came to it, they were surprised to find eight bushels of newly-minted gold coins! There was enough there to keep them going in their wicked lifestyle seemingly forever!

As they examined their discovery, they forgot all about their quest to find and slay Death. Now they were trying to figure out how to lug their treasure home. They thought it wise not to carry these baskets in broad daylight, for fear that they would be accused by the townspeople of having stolen it. They thought, "People would call us robbers." Thus, "our own property will make us hang," an obvious indication of their poor reputations among their neighbors.

So they decided to wait until dark to bring the bullion to their homes. But they were getting hungry, so they drew lots to see which of the three would go into town to fetch food and wine for all three. The youngest was chosen and he set off.

While he was beyond hearing range, the two decided that each of them would be the wealthier if they didn't have to split the gold three ways, but only two ways. So they plotted that when the young man returned, one would grab him from behind and the other would stab him.

Meanwhile, the young man also entertained greedy notions. He thought that if he could rid the two of them, he would keep the gold for himself. So he went to the office of a chemist and purchased a poison. Then he bought wine and food for all three, but he carefully put the poison into two of the flasks of drink.

When he arrived back, they pounced upon him as planned and killed him. They then sat down to enjoy the food he had brought. But they died when they drank the poisoned wine he had brought them.

Thus, the old man had been proven right. Death indeed *was* under that tree!

---

What a classic and timeless tale illustrating the biblical point that the love of money is the root of all kinds of evil.

*This selection is suitable for children.*
*The moral of the story is that greed is a vice to avoid.*

# BEN FRANKLIN ON GREED

### from *Poor Richard's Almanack*[9]

Ben Franklin was always striving to be a man of self-control. He kept checklists on his progress. He wanted to track how well he was doing in cultivating certain virtues and curbing certain vices.

We learn here what he had to say on the sin of greed, avarice, and covetousness. Also here are comments about money in general. Again having money is not to be equated with greed. But the love of money is. Over all, Franklin is cleverly calling for contentment, for saving, for living within your means, for not always craving more and more wealth.

---

- Avarice and happiness never saw each other; how then should they become acquainted?

- If you'd be wealthy, think of saving, more than of getting: The Indies have not made Spain rich, because her Outgoes equal her Incomes.

- Who is rich? He that rejoices in his Portion.

- Content makes poor men rich; Discontent makes rich Men poor.

- He who multiplies Riches multiplies Cares.

- Poverty wants some things, luxury many things, avarice all things.

- Light purse, heavy heart.

- The discontented man, finds no easy chair.

- He does not possess wealth, it possesses him.

---

9. Franklin, *Poor Richard's Almanack*, 9, 11, 12, 23, 30, 31, 33, 41, 43, 44, 46, 49, 52, 57, 59, 63, 66, 67, 68, 70.

- The thrifty maxim of the wary Dutch, is to save all the money they can touch.

- If man could have half his wishes, he would double his troubles.

- If you know how to spend less than you get, you have the philosopher's stone.

- Wish a miser long life, and you wish him no good.

- Sell not virture to purchase wealth, nor liberty to purchase power.

- Many a man would have been worse, if his estate had been better.

- He that pursues two hares at once, does not catch one and lets the other go.

- When will the miser's chest be full enough?
  When will he cease his bags to cram and stuff?
  All day he labours and all night contrives,
  Providing as if he'd an hundred lives,
  While endless care cuts short the common plan.

- Tell a miser he's rich, and a woman she's old, you'll get no money of one, nor kindness of the other.

- If your riches are yours, why don't you take them with you to the other world?

- What is more valuable than gold? Diamonds. Than diamonds? Virtue.

- Ambition often spends foolishly what avarice had wickedly collected.

- Content[ment] is the philosopher's stone, that turns all it touches into gold.

- He that's content hath enough. He that complains hath too much.

- Spare and have is better than spend and crave.

- Wealth and contentment are not always bedfellows.

- The generous mind least regards money and yet most feels the want of it.

---

Jesus once told us to "beware of covetousness" (Luke 12:15 KJV). Greed can be a form of idolatry (Col. 3:5). Paul even said that greed, left unchecked, can keep one from the kingdom of heaven! (1 Cor. 6:10). So greed is not only a vice to avoid—but a deadly sin from which to repent.

# SECTION 3

# ENVY

Envy is like a poisonous plant growing up in the human heart. The seed is sown when we realize that someone has something we don't have, or that they can do something we can't do, or that they can do something better than we can. Envy is the feeling we get when someone else has a position we think we should have. It's important that we recognize the seed of envy so we can pluck it out as soon as we feel ourselves envying someone else.

Envy is a condition of the human heart. It is defined as "resentful desire for another's possessions or advantages." Left unchecked, it can result in sins like lying and slander, stealing and murder. It is not restricted to any age or time or place. At different times in our lives, I daresay we've all felt envy creep up on us.

Envy can be compared to a sickness. In one language, it's called "the black sickness." In English, it's often associated with the color green—she was "green with jealousy."

A great deal of political conflicts boil down to envy. The whole communist movement has been nothing but a bloodbath for the sake of redistributing the wealth from one set of tyrants (in the case of the czar in Russia) to another set of tyrants (Lenin, Stalin, Mao, and company). Envy of power and property was the prime motivator. Even in America we find a similar feeling of envy of the wealthy, regardless of who's worked for what. There's even a term that particularly applies to shameless politicians who appeal to the down-and-outers' sense of envy—"class envy."

One classic story of envy—that, thankfully, has a happy ending—is that of Joseph and his brothers in the Book of Genesis. You will recall that they were jealous of him because of his father's affection for him. Of course, Jacob was wrong to show favoritism toward his son, when he had so many other sons. But Joseph's brothers were wrong to be jealous of him. They envied him so much, they took the first opportunity to do away with him when he was out in the fields. They threw him down a well and left him to die. Then when they saw a caravan, which happened to be on its way to Egypt, they decided to cash in on him and make a little profit. They sold him as a slave into Egypt.

But in the providence of God, Joseph eventually became the vice-regent of the whole land! He became the number two man in all of Egypt. And seven years before a time of famine that he had been warned about in advance by God, he wisely recommended that Egypt save grain during the fat years to cover the lean years, which is what the Egyptians did. Thus, Egypt was spared during the famine while many other lands were hurting.

Joseph's brothers eventually came to Egypt to seek grain and were reunited with their brother, who forgave them, in a touching scene wherein he declares: "You meant it for evil. But God meant it for good." This whole story, which comprises several chapters of the Bible (Genesis 37–45), is quite beautiful, despite its ugly beginning, which was fueled by envy.

The following stories, most of which do not end so pleasantly, show the destructive nature of envy. We must guard our hearts from it so that evil plant will not take root!

*This selection is suitable for children.*
*The moral of the story is that envy was the root cause of the first murder*
*on earth!*

# CAIN AND ABEL
### from the Book of Genesis (NIV)

The deadly sin of envy was the root cause of the first murder on earth. Just one chapter after man fell into sin, in Genesis 3, we come to the account of Cain and Abel. Already, morality was beginning to plunge. In fact, consider this: the first man born to a woman became a murderer! And envy was the motive.

In the passage it's clear that Cain had an out. He could have made his sacrifices in a way that pleased God, but he was so moved by jealousy against his brother that he killed him. The irony is that the thing he was envious of in the first place was God's approval. Abel received it; Cain didn't. Now, by committing murder, he was sure not to receive it!

This passage is found in Genesis 4:2b–16.

---

Now Abel kept flocks, and Cain worked the soil. In the course of time Cain brought some of the fruits of the soil as an offering to the LORD. But Abel brought fat portions from some of the firstborn of his flock. The LORD looked with favor on Abel and his offering, but on Cain and his offering he did not look with favor. So Cain was very angry, and his face was downcast.

Then the LORD said to Cain, "Why are you angry? Why is your face downcast? If you do what is right, will you not be accepted? But if you do not do what is right, sin is crouching at your door; it desires to have you, but you must master it."

Now Cain said to his brother Abel, "Let's go out to the field." And while they were in the field, Cain attacked his brother Abel and killed him.

Then the LORD said to Cain, "Where is your brother Abel?"

"I don't know," he replied. "Am I my brother's keeper?"

The LORD said, "What have you done? Listen! Your brother's blood cries out to me from the ground. Now you are under a curse and driven from the ground, which opened its mouth to receive your brother's blood from your hand. When you work the ground, it will no longer yield its crops for you. You will be a restless wanderer on the earth."

Cain said to the LORD, "My punishment is more than I can bear. Today you are driving me from the land, and I will be hidden from your presence; I will be a restless wanderer on the earth, and whoever finds me will kill me."

But the LORD said to him, "Not so; if anyone kills Cain, he will suffer vengeance seven times over." Then the LORD put a mark on Cain so that no one who found him would kill him. So Cain went out from the LORD'S presence and lived in the land of Nod, east of Eden.

---

John Steinbeck's classic novel, *East of Eden*, also deals with two brothers. It, too, is a story of envy and jealousy, where one brother is responsible for his brother's death (but indirectly, not directly). "East of Eden" is a good description of life after the fall.

*This selection is suitable for children.*
*The moral of the story is that envy, which is often fueled by pride, leads*
*to destruction.*

# SAUL AND DAVID[1]

retold by Jesse Hurlbut

King Saul had a lot going for him. He was handsome. He was tall. He was even humble—in the early days. He was flattered and thankful to be Israel's first king. But he grew arrogant over time. And he did not obey the Lord fully. So God started stripping away some of his power. Saul fought back in fear. Motivated by envy and fueled by pride, Saul couldn't stand to see David alive, knowing he was more popular than Saul and—probably—knowing that one day he might replace him. Saul was driven, as many are, by his envy to engage in rash and criminal acts.

The historical context of this story reveals that Saul is the king, but Samuel, the chief prophet at the time (and the one who had anointed Saul as king), has already secretly anointed David to be king. He was acting on God's instructions in this. This story begins soon after David's victory over Goliath.

This story is based on events in 1 Samuel 17:55–20:42.

————————

After David had slain the giant, he was brought before King Saul, still holding the giant's head. Saul did not remember in this bold fighting man the boy who a few years before had played [the harp] in his presence. He took him into his house and made him an officer among his soldiers. David was as wise and as brave in the army as he had been when facing the giant, and very soon he was in command of a thousand men. All the men loved him, both in Saul's court and in his camp, for David had the spirit that drew all hearts toward him.

When David was returning from his battle with the Philistines, the women of Israel came to meet him out of the cities, with instruments of music, singing and dancing, and they sang:

————————

1. This story by Jesse Hurlbut was originally entitled "The Little Boy Looking for the Arrows."

> "Saul has slain his thousands,
> And David his ten thousands."

This made Saul very angry, for he was jealous and suspicious in his spirit. He thought constantly of Samuel's words, that God would take the kingdom from him and would give it to one who was more worthy of it. He began to think that perhaps this young man, who had come in a single day to greatness before the people, might try to make himself king.

His former feeling of unhappiness again came over Saul. He raved in his house, talking as a man talks who is crazed. By this time they all knew that David was a musician, and they called him again to play on his harp and to sing before the troubled king. But now, in his madness, Saul would not listen to David's voice. Twice he threw his spear at him; but each time David leaped aside and the spear went into the wall of the house.

Saul was afraid of David, for he saw that the Lord was with David, as the Lord was no longer with himself. He would have killed David, but they did not dare kill him, because everybody loved David. Saul said to himself, "Though I cannot kill him myself, I will have him killed by the Philistines."

And he sent David out on dangerous errands of war; but David came home in safety, all the greater and the more beloved after each victory. Saul said, "I will give you my daughter Merab for your wife if you will fight the Philistines for me."

David fought the Philistines; but when he came home from the war, he found that Merab, who had been promised to him, had been given as wife to another man. Saul had another daughter, named Michal. She loved David and showed her love for him. Then Saul sent word to David, saying, "You shall have Michal, my daughter, for your wife when you have killed a hundred Philistines."

Then David went out and fought the Philistines, and killed two hundred of them; and they brought the word to Saul. Then Saul gave him his daughter Michal as his wife; but he was all the more afraid of David as he saw him growing in power and drawing nearer to the throne of the kingdom.

But if Saul hated David, Saul's son, Jonathan, loved David with all his heart. . . . Jonathan saw David's courage and nobility of soul, and loved him with all his heart. He took off his own royal robe and his sword and his bow and gave them all to David. It grieved Jonathan greatly that his father, Saul, was so jealous of David. He spoke to his father, and said: "Let not the king do harm to David; for David has been thankful to the king, and he has done great things for the kingdom. He took his life in his hand and killed the Philistine, and thus won a great victory for the Lord and for the people. Why should you seek to kill an innocent man?"

For the time Saul listened to Jonathan and said, "As the Lord lives, David shall not be put to death."

And again David sat at the king's table, among the princes; and when Saul was troubled again, David played on his harp and sang before him. But once more Saul's jealous anger arose and he threw his spear at David. David was watchful and quick. He leaped aside and, as before, the spear fastened into the wall.

Saul sent men to David's house to seize him; but Michal, Saul's daughter, who was David's wife, let David down out of the window, so that he escaped. She placed an image on David's bed and covered it with the bedclothes. When the men came, she said, "David is ill in the bed and cannot go."

They brought the word to Saul, and he said, "Bring him to me in the bed, just as he is."

When the image was found in David's bed, David was in a safe place, far away. David went to Samuel at Ramah, and stayed with him among the men who were prophets worshiping God and singing and speaking God's word. Saul heard that David was there and sent men to take him. But when these men came and saw Samuel and the prophets praising God and praying, the same spirit came on them and they began to praise and to pray. Saul sent other men, but these also, when they came among the prophets, felt the same power and joined in the worship.

Finally, Saul said, "If no other man will bring David to me, I will go myself and take him."

And Saul went to Ramah; but when he came near to the company of the worshipers, praising God and praying and preaching, the same spirit came on Saul. He, too, began to join in the songs and the prayers, and stayed there all that day and that night, worshiping God very earnestly. When the next day he went again to his home in Gibeah, his feeling was changed for the time and he was again friendly to David.

But David knew that Saul was at heart his bitter enemy and would kill him if he could as soon as his madness came upon him. He met Jonathan out in the field away from Saul's home. Jonathan said to David:

"Stay away from the king's table for a few days, and I will find out how he feels toward you and will tell you. Perhaps even now my father may become your friend. But if he is to be your enemy, I know that the Lord is with you and that Saul will not succeed against you. Promise me that as long as you live you will be kind to me, and not only to me while I live, but to my children after me."

Jonathan believed, as many others believed, that David would yet become the king of Israel, and he was willing to give up to David his right to be king, such was his great love for him. That day a promise was made between Jonathan and David that they and their children, and those who should come after them, should be friends forever.

Jonathan said to David, "I will find how my father feels toward you and will bring you word. After three days I will be here with my bow and arrows, and I will send a little boy out near your place of hiding, and I will shoot three arrows. If I say to the boy, 'Run, find the arrows, they are on this side of you,' then you can come safely for the king will not harm you. But if I call out to the boy, 'The arrows are away beyond you,' that will mean that there is danger, and you must hide from the king."

So David stayed away from Saul's table for two days. At first Saul said nothing of his absence, but at last he said:

"Why has not the son of Jesse come to meals yesterday and today?"

And Jonathan said, "David asked leave of me to go to his home at Bethlehem and visit his oldest brother."

Then Saul was very angry. He cried out, "You are a disobedient son! Why have you chosen this enemy of mine as your best friend? Do you know that as long as he is alive, you can never be king? Send after him and let him be brought to me, for he shall surely die!"

Saul was so fierce in his anger that he threw his spear at his own son Jonathan. Jonathan rose up from the table, so angry at his father and so anxious for his friend David that he could eat nothing. The next day, at the hour agreed upon, Jonathan went out into the field with a little boy. He said to the boy, "Run out yonder and be ready to find the arrows that I shoot."

And as the boy was running, Jonathan shot arrows beyond him, and he called out, "The arrows are away beyond you; run quickly and find them."

The boy ran and found the arrows and brought them to Jonathan. He gave the bow and arrows to the boy, saying to him, "Take them back to the city. I will stay here a while."

And as soon as the boy was out of sight, David came from his hiding place and ran to Jonathan. They fell into each other's arms and kissed each other again and again, and wept together. For David knew now that he must no longer hope to be safe in Saul's hands. He must leave home and wife and friends and his father's house, and hide wherever he could from the hate of King Saul.

Jonathan said to him, "Go in peace; for we have sworn together saying, 'The Lord shall be between you and me, and between your children and my children forever.'"

Then Jonathan went again to his father's palace, and David went out to find a hiding place.

---

How ugly is raw envy! How unhappy as well.

For those who don't know the rest of the story, both Saul and Jonathan met an untimely death on the battlefield against the Philistines. By that time, Saul had strayed far from God, and yet he still wanted to hear from God (about going into battle). But there was silence from heaven. Why should God answer him who was rejecting His laws and killing His servants? Saul, driven by desperation, even sought a medium to contact Samuel, though he was dead, so he could communicate with him. Whether it was Samuel or a demon impersonating him, the apparition condemned Saul and predicted his death and defeat in battle the next day, which is precisely what happened.

*This selection is suitable for children.*
*The moral of the story is that envy robs one of joy and can lead one down a destructive path.*

# "LITTLE SNOWDROP"

### A classic fairytale, retold by Dinah Craik

This classic tale of envy is better known as "Snow White and the Seven Dwarfs." I'm not sure when the name change was made, but I would assume that occurred when Walt Disney made the fairytale into the movie. This version is retold by Dinah Craik (1826–87). (Note that one sentence has been edited out of original to make this story acceptable for children.)

In this story, the Queen has just about everything a woman could possibly want—a loving husband, beauty, charms, power, and wealth. But she's not content with all these things unless she happens to rank number one in beauty. By striving for that alone and by being envious of anyone (in this case, it's Little Snowdrop) who supersedes her in this category, she loses all contentment and happiness. Instead, consumed by envy, she cannot rest until she has rid the land of someone more beautiful than she. Think of all the misery and unhappiness people bring upon themselves when they envy others!

In the 1962 book *Seven Deadly Sins*—edited by Ian Fleming (yes, the same one who created James Bond, who was guilty of lust and other deadly sins)[2]—Angus Wilson writes:

> All the seven deadly sins are self-destroying, morbid appetites, but in their early stages at least lust and gluttony, avarice and sloth know some gratification, while anger and pride have power, even though that power eventually destroys itself. Envy is impotent, numbed with fear, yet never ceasing in its appetite; and it knows no gratification save endless self-torment. It has the ugliness of a trapped rat that has gnawed its own foot in its effort to escape.

That certainly applies to the wicked queen in this story!

---

2.  Angus Wilson, "Envy," *The Seven Deadly Sins,* Ian Fleming, ed. (New York: William Morrow and Company, 1962), 11.

Once upon a time, in the middle of winter, when the flakes of snow fell like feathers from the sky, a queen sat at a window set in an ebony frame, and sewed. While she was sewing and watching the snow fall, she pricked her finger with her needle, and three drops of blood dropped on the snow. And because the crimson looked so beautiful on the white snow, she thought, "Oh that I had a child as white as snow, as red as blood, and as black as the wood of this ebony frame!"

Soon afterwards she had a little daughter, who was as white as snow, as red as blood, and had hair as black as ebony. And when the child was born, the queen died.

After a year had gone by, the king took another wife. She was a handsome lady, but proud and haughty, and could not endure that any one should surpass her in beauty. She had a wonderful mirror, and whenever she walked up to it, and looked at herself in it, she said:

"Little glass upon the wall,
Who is fairest among us all?"

The mirror replied:

"Lady queen, so grand and tall,
Thou art the fairest of them all."

And she was satisfied, for she knew the mirror always told the truth. But Snowdrop grew ever taller and fairer, and at seven years old was beautiful as the day, and more beautiful than the queen herself. So once, when the queen asked of her mirror:

"Little glass upon the wall,
Who is fairest among us all?"

It answered:

"Lady queen, you are grand and tall,
But Snowdrop is fairest of you all."

Then the queen was startled, and turned yellow and green with envy. From that hour she so hated Snowdrop, that she burned with secret wrath whenever she saw the maiden. Pride and envy grew apace like weeds in her heart, till she had no rest day or night. So she called a huntsman and said, "Take the child out in the forest, for I will endure her no longer in my sight. Kill her, and bring me her lungs and liver as tokens that you have done it."

The huntsman obeyed, and led the child away; but when he had drawn his hunting-knife, and was about to pierce Snowdrop's innocent heart, she began to weep, and said, "Ah! Dear huntsman, spare my life, and I will run deep into the wild forest, and never more come home."

The huntsman took pity on her, because she looked so lovely, and said, "Run away then, poor child!" —"The wild beasts will soon make an end of thee," he thought; but it seemed as if a stone had been rolled from his heart, because he had avoided taking her life; and as a little bear came by just then, he killed it, took out its liver and lungs, and carried them as tokens to the queen. [And the queen was momentarily fooled.] The poor child was now all alone in the great forest, and she felt frightened as she looked at all the leafy trees, and knew not what to do. So she began to run, and ran over the sharp stones, and through the thorns; and the wild beasts passed close to her, but did her no harm. She ran as long as her feet could carry her, and when evening closed in, she saw a little house, and went into it to rest herself. Everything in the house was very small, but I cannot tell you how pretty and clean it was.

There stood a little table, covered with a white table-cloth, on which were seven little plates (each little plate with its own little spoon)—also seven little knives and forks, and seven little cups. Round the walls stood seven little beds close together, with sheets as white as snow. Snowdrop, being so hungry and thirsty, ate a little of the vegetables and bread on each plate, and drank a drop of wine from every cup, for she did not like to empty one entirely.

Then, being very tired, she laid herself down in one of the beds, but could not make herself comfortable, for one was too long, and another too short. The seventh, luckily, was just right; so there she stayed, said her prayers, and fell asleep.

When it was grown quite dark, home came the masters of the house, seven dwarfs, who delved and mined for iron among the mountains. They lighted their seven candles, and as soon as there was a light in the kitchen, they saw that some one had been there, for it was not quite so orderly as they had left it.

The first said, "Who has been sitting on my stool?"
The second, "Who has eaten off my plate?"
The third, "Who has taken part of my loaf?"
The fourth, "Who has touched my vegetables?"
The fifth, "Who has used my fork?"
The sixth, "Who has cut with my knife?"
The seventh, "Who has drunk out of my little cup?"

Then the first dwarf looked about, and saw that there was a slight hollow in his bed, so he asked, "Who has been lying in my little bed?"

The others came running, and each called out, "Some one has also been lying in my bed."

But the seventh, when he looked in his bed, saw Snowdrop there, fast asleep. He called the others, who flocked round with cries of surprise, fetched their seven candles, and cast the light on Snowdrop.

"Oh, heaven!" they cried, "what a lovely child!" and were so pleased that they would not wake her, but let her sleep on in the little bed. The seventh dwarf slept with all his companions in turn, an hour with each, and so they spent the night. When it was morning, Snowdrop woke up, and was frightened when she saw the seven dwarfs. They were very friendly, however, and inquired her name.

"Snowdrop," answered she.

"How have you found your way to our house?" further asked the dwarfs.

So she told them how her stepmother had tried to kill her, how the huntsman had spared her life, and how she had run the whole day through, till at last she had found their little house.

Then the dwarfs said, "If thou wilt keep our house, cook, make the beds, wash, sew and knit, and make all neat and clean, thou canst stay with us, and shalt want for nothing."

"I will, right willingly," said Snowdrop. So she dwelt with them, and kept their house in order. Every morning they went out among the mountains, to seek iron and gold, and came home ready for supper in the evening.

The maiden being left alone all day long, the good dwarfs warned her, saying, "Beware of thy wicked stepmother, who will soon find out that thou art here; take care that thou lettest nobody in."

The queen, however, after having, as she thought, eaten Snow-drop's lungs and liver, had no doubt that she was again the first and fairest woman in the world; so she walked up to her mirror, and said:

"Little glass upon the wall,
Who is fairest among us all?"

The mirror replied:

"Lady queen, so grand and tall,
Here, you are fairest of them all;
But over the hills, with the seven dwarfs old,
Lives Snowdrop, fairer a hundredfold."

She trembled, knowing the mirror never told a falsehood; she felt sure that the huntsman had deceived her, and that Snowdrop was still alive. She pondered once more, late and early, early and late, how best to kill Snowdrop; for envy gave her no rest, day or night, while she herself was not the fairest lady in the land. When she had planned what to do, she painted her face, dressed herself like an old pedlar-woman, and altered her appearance so much, that no one could have known her. In this disguise she went over the seven hills, to where the seven dwarfs dwelt, knocked at the door, and cried, "Good wares, cheap! Very cheap!"

Snowdrop looked out of the window and cried, "Good-morning, good woman: what have you to sell?"

"Good wares, smart wares," answered the queen—"bodice laces of all colours"; and drew out one which was woven of coloured silk.

"I may surely let this honest dame in!" thought Snowdrop; so she unfastened the door, and bought for herself the pretty lace.

"Child," said the old woman, "what a figure thou art! Let me lace thee for once properly." Snowdrop feared no harm, so stepped in front of her, and allowed her bodice to be fastened up with the new lace.

But the old woman laced so quick and laced so tight, that Snow-drop's breath was stopped, and she fell down as if dead. "Now I am fairest at last," said the old woman to herself, and sped away.

The seven dwarfs came home soon after, at eventide, but how alarmed were they to find their poor Snowdrop lifeless on the ground! They lifted her up, and, seeing that she was laced too tightly, cut the lace of her bodice; she began to breathe faintly, and slowly returned to life. When the dwarfs heard what had happened, they said, "The old pedlar-woman was none other than the wicked queen. Be careful of thyself, and open the door to no one if we are not at home."

The cruel stepmother walked up to her mirror when she reached home, and said:

"Little glass upon the wall,
Who is fairest among us all?"

To which it answered, as usual:

"Lady queen, so grand and tall,
Here, you are fairest of them all;
But over the hills, with the seven dwarfs old,
Lives Snowdrop, fairer a hundredfold."

When she heard this, she was so alarmed that all the blood rushed to her heart, for she saw plainly that Snowdrop was still alive.

"This time," said she, "I will think of some means that shall destroy her utterly"; and with the help of witchcraft, in which she was skillful, she made a poisoned comb. Then she changed her dress and took the shape of another old woman.

Again she crossed the seven hills to the home of the seven dwarfs, knocked at the door, and cried, "Good wares, very cheap!"

Snowdrop looked out and said, "Go away—I dare let no one in."

"You may surely be allowed to look!" answered the old woman, and she drew out the poisoned comb and held it up. The girl was so pleased with it that she let herself be cajoled, and opened the door.

When the bargain was struck, the dame said, "Now let me dress your hair properly for once." Poor Snowdrop took no heed, and let the old woman begin; but the comb had scarcely touched her hair before the poison worked, and she fell down senseless.

"Paragon of beauty!" said the wicked woman, "all is over with thee now," and went away.

Luckily, it was near evening, and the seven dwarfs soon came home. When they found Snowdrop lifeless on the ground, they at once distrusted her stepmother. They searched, and found the poisoned comb; and as soon as they had drawn it out, Snowdrop came to herself, and told them what had happened. Again they warned her to be careful, and open the door to no one.

The queen placed herself before the mirror at home and said:
> "Little glass upon the wall,
> Who is fairest among us all?"

But it again answered:
> "Lady queen, so grand and tall.
> Here, you are fairest of them all;
> But over the hills, with the seven dwarfs old,
> Lives Snowdrop, fairer a thousandfold."

When she heard the mirror speak thus, she quivered with rage. "Snowdrop shall die," she cried, "if it costs my own life!"

Then she went to a secret and lonely chamber, where no one ever disturbed her, and compounded an apple of deadly poison. Ripe and rosy-cheeked, it was so beautiful to look upon, that all who saw it longed for it; but it brought death to any who should eat it. When the apple was ready, she painted her face, disguised herself as a peasant-woman, and journeyed over the seven hills to where the seven dwarfs dwelt. At the sound of the knock, Snowdrop put her head out of the window, and said, "I cannot open the door to anybody, for the seven dwarfs have forbidden me to do so."

"Very well," replied the peasant-woman; "I only want to be rid of my apples. Here, I will give you one of them!"

"No!" said Snowdrop, "I dare not take it."

"Art thou afraid of being poisoned?" asked the old woman. "Look here; I will cut the apple in two, and you shall eat the rosy side, and I the white."

Now the fruit was so cunningly made, that only the rosy side was poisoned. Snowdrop longed for the pretty apple; and when she saw the peasant-woman eating it, she could resist no longer, but stretched out her hand and took the poisoned half. She had scarcely tasted it, when she fell lifeless to the ground.

The queen, laughing loudly, watched her with a barbarous look, and cried, "O thou who art white as snow, red as blood, and black as ebony, the seven dwarfs cannot awaken thee this time!"

And when she asked the mirror at home:
> "Little glass upon the wall,
> Who is fairest among us all?"

The mirror at last replied:
    "Lady queen, so grand and tall,
    You are the fairest of them all."

So her envious heart had as much repose as an envious heart can ever know.

When the dwarfs came home in the evening, they found Snowdrop lying breathless and motionless on the ground. They lifted her up, searched whether she had anything poisonous about her, unlaced her, combed her hair, washed her with water and with wine; but all was useless, for they could not bring the darling back to life. They laid her on a bier, and all the seven placed themselves round it, and mourned for her three long days. Then they would have buried her, but that she still looked so fresh and life-like, and had such lovely rosy cheeks. "We cannot lower her into the dark earth," said they; and caused a transparent coffin of glass to be made, so that she could be seen on all sides, and laid her in it, writing her name outside in letters of gold, which told that she was the daughter of a king. Then they placed the coffin on the mountain above, and one of them always stayed by it, for even the wild animals came and mourned for Snowdrop: the birds likewise—first an owl, and then a raven, and afterwards a dove.

Long, long years did Snowdrop lie in her coffin unchanged, looking as though asleep, for she was still white as snow, red as blood, and her hair was black as ebony. At last the son of a king chanced to wander into the forest, and came to the dwarfs' house for a night's shelter. He saw the coffin on the mountain with the beautiful Snowdrop in it, and read what was written there in letters of gold. Then he said to the dwarfs, "Let me have the coffin! I will give you whatever you like to ask for it."

But the dwarfs answered, "We would not part with it for all the gold in the world."

He said again, "Yet give it me; for I cannot live without seeing Snowdrop, and though she is dead, I will prize and honour her as my beloved."

Then the good dwarfs took pity on him, and gave him the coffin. The prince had it borne away by his servants. They happened to stumble over a bush, and the shock forced the bit of poisoned apple which Snowdrop had tasted out of her throat. Immediately she opened her eyes, raised the coffin-lid, and sat up alive once more. "Oh, heaven!" cried she, "where am I?"

The prince answered joyfully, "Thou art with me," and told her what had happened, saying, "I love thee more dearly than anything else in the world. Come with me to my father's castle, and be my wife."

Snowdrop, well pleased, went with him, and they were married with much state and grandeur.

The wicked stepmother was invited to the feast. Richly dressed, she stood before the mirror, and asked of it:

"Little glass upon the wall,
Who is fairest among us all?"

The mirror answered:

"Lady queen, so grand and tall,
Here, you are fairest among them all;
But the young queen over the mountains old,
Is fairer than you a thousandfold."

The evil-hearted woman uttered a curse, and could scarcely endure her anguish. She first resolved not to attend the wedding, but curiosity would not allow her to rest. She determined to travel, and see who that young queen could be, who was the most beautiful in all the world. When she came, and found that it was Snowdrop alive again, she stood petrified with terror and despair. Then two iron shoes, heated burning hot, were drawn out of the fire with a pair of tongs, and laid before her feet. She was forced to put them on, and to go and dance at Snowdrop's wedding—dancing, dancing on these red-hot shoes.

---

Envy is cancer to the soul. It eats away at the insides of those who let it. Are you envious of others' success? It's natural to some degree. But these feelings must be checked. God has gifted different people with different talents and abilities. The key for us is to use ours for His glory and to rejoice with the success of others, not secretly to envy them.

Even in ministry, one can sometimes sense envy toward the success of others. But that's obviously a wrong attitude. When the apostle Paul was in prison, there were some misguided Christians who tried to provoke him to jealousy by preaching the gospel. Instead of the intended effect, he rejoiced that the gospel was being promoted, despite the motives of the messengers! (Phil. 1:15–18).

Sometimes an unhealthy overemphasis on competition can breed envy. Some pockets of our society seem to imply that if you're not *the* best, then you're nothing! I remember seeing a T-shirt with a message to the effect: "Show me the person who comes in second, and I'll show you the first loser." I disagree. I think a much more healthy and biblical attitude is summed up this way: Don't necessarily strive to be *the* best. But rather strive to be *your* best, using the unique combination of talents and gifts God has given you for His glory. Concentrate on that and envy will find no room in your heart.

*This selection is suitable for children, but it may be difficult for them. The moral of the story is that envy leads to destruction and can even lead to death.*

# IAGO'S INTENTIONS

*Othello* (Act 1, Scene 1)[3]

by William Shakespeare

One of the greatest tales of envy in all of literature is Shakespeare's *Othello*, written in 1604. Iago [Yah'-go] is the evil character, but he's a *fascinating* evil character at that. He is the slick-tongued assistant to Othello the Moor. He is his trusted advisor; Othello labels Iago a man "of honesty and trust." But Othello has put his trust in the wrong man!

In the very opening of the play, a portion of which we have here, Iago reveals his hatred of Othello to his friend Roderigo (a friend only inasmuch as Iago can manipulate him to his own ends). Iago is upset with Othello, his employer, because Othello has overlooked him for an important promotion. Iago had lobbied for the position of Othello's lieutenant; instead he was chosen only as his "ancient" or ensign (mere assistant). In this opening scene, Iago reveals the premise of the entire tragedy: because he has been so slighted, he is going to remain in Othello's service solely that he may enact revenge on him. This is one of the few scenes where the duplicitous Iago, a congenital liar, speaks the truth plainly. He declares, "I am not what I am" (I am not what I appear to be). Thus, the point of the entire play is brought to light here: *envy* drives Iago to seek revenge against Othello the Moor. Later in the play, Iago tells of feelings of envy against Cassio—the man who received the promotion Iago so coveted. Iago, the dishonest character, is naturally reproved by Cassio's honesty. As Iago puts it: "He hath a daily beauty in life that makes me ugly." Shakespeare had great insight into human depravity!

Iago's plan for revenge evolves to this: he will sow repeated seeds of doubt in the mind of Othello, the trusting husband, as to the faithfulness of his beautiful new bride, Desdemona, who

---

3. This is not the entire scene, but rather just a portion of the beginning, wherein the premise of the entire play is laid out. Nor is this a plot summary of the entire play, but rather a plot summary of highlights of the play, as it touches on *envy*.

has—in fact—been totally virtuous. He drops hints and suggestions that Desdemona has been committing adultery with Michael Cassio. Iago will not rest until he can, in his words, "put the Moor at least into a jealousy so strong that judgment cannot cure," which he succeeds at doing. By making misleading suggestions and by orchestrating circumstances, Iago manages to get Othello to work himself into a frenzy of rage and confusion of jealousy. At one point the Moor even collapses at Iago's feet, causing Iago to exclaim (to the audience, not Othello): "Work on, my medicine, work!"

Convinced the accusations are true, Othello, blind with jealousy (a variation of envy), strangles his lovely bride. His heart is pierced when he learns the truth. He wounds Iago (who is then led away to prison) and Othello kills himself.

Here are portions of act 1, scene 1 of *Othello,* wherein Iago reveals his evil intentions:

---

*Rod.* Thou told'st me thou didst hold him in thy hate.
*Iag.* Despise me if I do not. Three great ones of the city,
    In personal suit to make me his lieutenant,
    Off-capped to him;[4] and, by the faith of man,
    I know my price, I am worth no worse a place.
    But he, as loving his own pride and purposes,
    Evades them with a bombast circumstance,
    Horribly stuffed with epithets of war;[5]
    And, in conclusion,
    Nonsuits[6] my mediators; for, "Certes [certainly]," says he,
    "I have already chosen my officer."
    And what was he?
    Forsooth, a great arithmetician,
    One Michael Cassio, a Florentine,
    (A fellow almost damned in a fair wife),
    That never set a squandron in the field,[7]
    Nor the division of a battle knows
    More than a spinster; unless the bookish theoric,

---

4.  Iago is saying that he was recommended for the job of lieutenant by three great leaders in the city, who appealed to Othello with their hats in their hands ("off-capped to him").

5.  Othello, the veteran war hero, blows them off with lofty-sounding rhetoric about his war experiences.

6.  He does not grant the suit [the request].

7.  The man's never fought in a war! He's an "armchair warrior," at best.

Wherein the toged consuls can propose
As masterly as he.[8] Mere prattle, without practice,
Is all his soldiership. But he, sir, had th' election;[9]
And I (of whom his [Othello's] eyes had seen the proof
At Rhodes, at Cyprus, and on other grounds
(Christian and heathen) must be be-leed and calmed[10]
By debitor and creditor, this counter-caster [accountant].
He (in good time!)[11] must his lieutenant be,
And I (God bless the mark!) his Moorship's ancient [ensign].

*Rod.* By heaven, I rather would have been his hangman.

*Iag.* Why, there's no remedy; 'tis the curse of service.
Preferment goes by letter and affection,[12]
And not by old gradation [seniority], where each second
Stood heir to the first. Now, sir, be judge yourself,
Whether I in any just term am affined[13]
To love the Moor.

*Rod.* I would not follow him then.

*Iag.* O, sir, content you.
I follow him to serve my turn upon him.
We cannot all be master, nor all masters
Cannot be truly followed.[14]

---

Thus, the tragedy begins as Iago looks for the opportunities to "turn upon him." He soon finds them. If you haven't read the play, it's worth the time. It reflects Shakespeare's wisdom when it comes to human nature.

What a spiritual cancer is envy! It seeks to tear down rather than build up. What a cancer is the feeling of envy and pride when someone else gets promoted ahead of you. Sometimes that happens. Sometimes it happens unjustly. You feel that you're the more qualified for the job, but you get overlooked for whatever reason. To remonstrate appropriately and respectfully with that

---

8. The politicians in charge of the city ["the toged consuls"], who've not experienced the battlefield are as adept as Cassio, who's likewise inexperienced.

9. He was the one picked [not Iago].

10. "Stopped in my course."

11. An expression meaning (sarcastically): "Boy, that's just great!"

12. This decision was made by Cassio's letter [his standing/influence] and by Othello's personal taste.

13. Whether I am under any obligation.

14. Iago remains in his service for one object: to get his revenge.

decision is one thing. To secretly envy and plot out revenge, as Iago did, is quite another!

Chuck Swindoll once said, "Life is 10 percent circumstances and 90 percent how we react to those circumstances." A reaction of envy is a sinful response. Even if responding to an unjust decision, envy is an inappropriate response. And it can lead to devastating consequences, even if less severe than those in *Othello*.

*This selection is suitable for children.*
*The moral of the story is that envy can destroy relationships, even close ones.*

# "HEADMASTER BARD"

### from *En Glad Gutt*

by Bjornstjerne Bjornson, translated by Kirsti Saebo Newcombe

Envy between two brothers is as old as Cain and Abel. In this story it is a gold pocket watch that brings envy, strife, bitterness, pride, and hatred between Bard and Andrew. The story is taken from the novel: *En Glad Gutt* (A Happy Boy), chapter 3. It was published in 1860 and is by Bjornstjerne Bjornson (1832–1910), a Norwegian author, poet, and playwright.

The story takes place in a small farming community in the early 1800s. The names of the two main characters, Baard and Anders, have been anglicized to Bard and Andrew. (To make things simpler to follow, the unit of money has been changed to dollars.) It's a tragedy, even in fiction, to see envy destroy close relationships.

---

The headmaster's name was Bard, and he had a brother named Andrew. The two brothers were inseparable, they loved each other. They both enlisted in the army when the time came. They lived together in town; they served together in the war. They were both corporals, and served in the same unit. When they came home again, everybody thought they were such handsome young men.

Then their father died, and he had a sizable estate. It was hard to divide. They didn't want material things to come between them, so they decided to sell everything at auction. Then they could each buy what they really wanted and share the profit. And so they did. But the father had owned a great gold pocket watch; it was quite famous, and the only gold pocket watch people in these parts had ever seen. When the bidding started, several rich men wanted the watch; but when they saw that the brothers were bidding, they dropped out. Bard expected Andrew to let him have it, and Andrew was expecting the same of Bard. They bid once each, to test one another, looking at each other while bidding.

When the price reached twenty dollars, Bard thought that this wasn't nice of Andrew, and he continued bidding until the watch reached thirty dollars. He wondered if Andrew had forgotten how nice and kind he'd always been to his little brother. Andrew continued bidding too; and Bard thought that since he was the oldest, he should have the watch and he increased the price to forty. Andrew was thinking, if Bard could afford forty dollars, so could he. And if his brother didn't want him to have the watch, he would take it anyway, and he bid higher. Bard thought this was an outrage and a disgrace, and he bid again. It was now up to fifty dollars. There were a lot of people standing around, and Andrew didn't want Bard to get away with humiliating him in public like this, so he bid again. Bard laughed then and loudly proclaimed: "One hundred dollars and our brotherhood with it!" Bard turned on his heels and quickly left the house.

As he was saddling the horse he had just bought, a man came out to him and said, "The watch is yours, your brother gave up." As soon as Bard heard this, a shiver went through him as he thought of his brother, not the watch. The saddle was on, but his hand was frozen. He was uncertain whether he should ride off or not. Just then, a lot of people came out and Andrew was among them, and when he saw his brother over by the saddled horse, not knowing what Bard was just thinking, Andrew cried out, "Thanks a lot for the watch, Bard; you shall not see the day your brother follows in your footsteps again—neither the day I will darken your door!" Bard's face had gone white as he heard his brother. He then quickly swung himself onto the horse and rode off. The house where Bard and Andrew had lived with their father was never visited by either of them again.

A short while later Andrew got married and moved into a sharecropper's cottage. Bard was not invited to the wedding, neither was he at the church. The first year after Andrew was married his only cow was found dead by the northern wall of his cottage, where the cow had been grazing. Several other accidents were added to this one, but the worst was when his barn burned down in the middle of the winter with everything in it. Nobody knew how the fire got started. "This is done by someone who wants to harm me," said Andrew, and he wept all night long. Andrew became a very poor man, and he lost his will to work.

The night after the fire Bard showed up in Andrew's cottage. As soon as Bard stepped inside Andrew sprang to his feet and angrily asked, "What do *you* want?"

The two brothers stood there looking at each other and it took a while before Bard answered, "I want to help, Andrew. Things are not well with you."

"Things are as well as you wished me, Bard. You had better leave or I won't be able to control myself."

"You are mistaken, Andrew. I regret . . ."

"Go Bard, and God have mercy on both of us," said Andrew.

Bard backed up a couple of steps, and with a trembling voice he said, "If you want the watch, you can have it."

"Get out of here, Bard!" cried Andrew, and Bard left.

You shall now hear what led up to this day: As soon as Bard had heard that his brother Andrew was suffering, his heart softened toward his brother, but his pride held him back. He felt the need to go to church, and there he made resolutions to do good. But he couldn't carry through with them. Often he went towards his brother's house. But someone would come out of the door, or a stranger would be visiting, or Andrew would be chopping wood. Always. Always. Something would happen and he would lose his nerve and turn back.

One Sunday, in the middle of the winter, Bard was at church, and Andrew came too. Bard saw him; he was pale and thin. He had the same clothes as he had had when they were together—only now, the clothes were ragged and patched up. During the sermon, Bard looked up at the minister and thought him good and kind. Then he remembered his childhood and what a good and sweet brother Andrew had been. Bard took communion that day and gave God a solemn promise to reconcile himself with Andrew. As he took the wine, it flashed through his mind that the price might be high, but come what may, he would reconcile. Bard would have liked to go sit with his brother, but someone was sitting in the way; and Andrew didn't even look up. After the service there were too many people around Andrew. Bard didn't even know Andrew's wife, so he could not talk to her and reach Andrew in that way. So he thought it best to go home to Andrew in the evening and talk seriously with him. That night he went all the way to the cottage door and there he stopped and listened. The wife was talking. "He took communion today," she said. "He was thinking about you."

"No, he wasn't thinking about me," said Andrew. "I know him, he only thinks about himself."

For a long time, nothing was said. Bard was sweating where he stood, even though the night was cold. He could hear the wife working with a big pot over the fire. He also heard a baby cry from time to time; he also thought he heard Andrew rocking. Then the wife said these words, "I think both of you are thinking about each other, you just don't want to admit it."

"Let's talk about something else," said Andrew. A moment later he rose and went towards the door. Bard had to hide, so he hid in the woodshed. It was just where Andrew was heading, to fetch some logs. Bard was standing in the corner and could see him clearly. Andrew had taken off his ragged church clothes and was wearing his uniform—the one like Bard's, the one they had worn together in the war. They had sworn never to touch it again but to save it for their sons. Andrew's uniform was worn out. Andrew's once strong and well-formed body looked like a pile of rags. Bard could feel the pocket watch ticking in his pocket.

Instead of picking up the kindling wood and laying it on top of the logs, Andrew rested against a pile of wood. He looked out of the door, tilted his head back and looked at the clear, starry sky, and with a deep sigh, he said, "Well, well, well, Lord God, Lord God . . . ."

For the rest of his life, Bard could hear those words again and again. He wanted to make himself known, but just then Andrew cleared his throat, picked up the wood, and left. He walked so close to Bard that one of the branches hit him in the face; it stung.

Bard stood there for ten more minutes at the same spot, shivering in the cold winter night. He admitted that he was a coward, too scared to go in; therefore, he made another plan. Bard found a tinderbox and went to the barn. There he lit a little torch, so that he could find the hook his brother would use for his lantern when he came out to the barn in the morning. He found the hook and on it he hung the gold pocket watch. He extinguished his fire and closed up after himself. His heart was so light that he ran over the snow like a young boy.

The next day Bard got word that his brother's barn had burned down! Evidently, unnoticed by him, a spark must have fallen from his little torch while he hung up the watch. That day Bard just sat there as if he were sick. He took his hymnbook and sang hymn after hymn. The people who heard him wondered if something was really wrong with him. That night he went out, the moon was shining very bright on the snow, and he went to his brother's place. Bard dug through the burnt out ruins of the barn and found it—the watch—a little lump of melted down gold!

With the gold in his hand he approached his brother's house to explain what happened and ask for peace between them, and so he came face to face with his brother after all this time. We've already heard how that meeting went. Bard was heartbroken. He left his brother's house in a daze, knowing that Andrew believed he had burned down the barn on purpose.

A little girl had seen him digging in the burnt out ruins. Some boys, on their way to a dance, had seen him go over to his brother's house Sunday night, and the people living in the same house as him had told about his strange behavior the following Monday. Everybody knew that the two brothers were bitter enemies—so a police investigation was started and a hearing scheduled.

When Bard came to Andrew the next evening looking ill and pale, Andrew thought it must be out of repentance. He thought his brother must now be sorry for what he'd done. But for such a horrible deed against one's own brother there would be no forgiveness.

At the hearing Andrew heard how people had seen Bard going to his house the night of the fire. But nothing was proven. Nonetheless, Andrew believed *totally* that his brother was guilty. At the hearing Bard stood there in his good clothes, and Andrew in his worn-out ones.

Bard looked at his brother, and his eyes were begging so intensely that Andrew could feel it to the bottom of his soul. "He doesn't want me to say anything," thought Andrew, and when he was asked if he believed Bard had set the fire, Andrew answered loud and clear, "No!"

But Andrew started drinking heavily from that day on, and his life went downhill (even more) from there. Bard, even though he didn't drink, fared worse than his brother; he was hardly recognizable.

Late one night a poor woman came to see Bard in his small rented room. The woman asked him to come with her. He knew her—she was Andrew's wife. Bard understood immediately what kind of errand she was on. He became deadly pale and grabbed his coat and went with her, without saying a word. There was no path over the snow, but they followed the soft light from Andrew's window.

As Bard entered Andrew's house for the second time, a strange smell engulfed him and made him feel sick. They went inside. A child was sitting by the hearth eating coal. His face was black, but he laughed with white teeth; it was his brother's child. In a bed with all kinds of clothes piled on top, lay Andrew. He was emaciated, but his forehead was high and clear. Andrew was looking at Bard with hollow eyes. Bard trembled and sank down by the bedside and burst into tears. Andrew asked his wife to leave, but Bard gestured for her to stay.

Now, finally, the two brothers started talking. They told everything from the day they bid on the gold watch until this very moment. Bard ended by taking out the gold lump, which he always carried on him. It was evident that neither of them had one truly happy day all the years they were separated.

Andrew didn't say much, for he was quite weak, but Bard remained by the bedside as long as Andrew was sick.

"I'm totally well," said Andrew one morning, and continued, "Now, my brother, it's time for us to be together for the rest of our days and never part again, just as in the old days." But that very day Andrew died!

Bard took his wife and child home with him, and they were well taken care of. What the brothers had talked about that night by the deathbed leaked out the wall and spread all over the village. Bard became well-respected and honored. All greeted him kindly, as one who had carried much grief and sorrow and had now found happiness again. It was almost as if he had been gone for a long time and now returned.

Bard became strong in body and mind, and his heart became devoted to God—he was so grateful for having been forgiven. The old corporal wanted to do something important, so he set about and became a headmaster.

He engraved on the hearts and minds of the children one thing—love. He practiced it himself and instilled in them the knowledge that nothing is worth losing a loved one. The children loved him like a friend and a father rolled into one.

Today, more than 150 years later, we live in an even more materialistic society. The courts are clogged with all sorts of disputes over money, including inheritances. Families break up over fights over estates, as ugly as the breakup in this story.

Bjornson ends with this moral of the story in poetic form:

Do not step on your brother, you Christian soul,
Neither with shoes of iron or gold.
All who live are subject
To Love's recreative power,
When it is tried anew,
It blooms again as a flower.

# SECTION 4

# ANGER

With the deadly sin of gluttony, the question is what you eat. But with the deadly sin of anger, the question is what's eating you!

Anger is not only bad for the soul, it is bad for the body as well. In his book *Patience, My Foot!*, author Michael LeFan highlights some of the detrimental effects of uncontrolled anger:

> Medical experts say that anger causes physiological changes such as a red face, increased heart rate, raised blood pressure, surging stomach acid, even impotence, and a definite desire to punch out somebody's lights. They warn us that anger can be just plain unhealthy. It affects our performance and success in all areas of life. . . . Unfortunately, temper infuses a sense of power when we're feeling vulnerable. A blistering temper is exhilarating. It's an adrenaline high. However, temper addicts can end up with a hangover of headache, fatigue, nausea, and even black-outs. Guilt feelings also go along with temper outbursts.
>
> You can't enjoy productive, pleasant relationships if you vent your anger. It must be controlled, and that doesn't mean bottling it up—which can result in all sorts of unpleasantness. But the need to sometimes express anger doesn't give you license to scream, curse, and kick the dog any time you're annoyed.[1]

Well put. We'll be hearing more from Michael in this section on anger.

The strange thing about anger is that it is not always a sin. Anger is defined as "a feeling of great displeasure, hostility, indignation, or exasperation: wrath." Jesus got angry, but He never sinned. Paul said, "In your anger, do not sin"—implying there could be such a thing as anger without sin.

---

1. Michael LeFan, *Patience, My Foot!* (Joplin, Mo.: College Press, 1993), 64, 67.

Obviously, anger left *unchecked* is a sin. All sorts of evils are done in the world because people do not control their anger. Think of the numerous murders that occur regularly in the heat of anger.

Ben Franklin, with his characteristic wit, had this to say about anger:

- Take this remark from Richard, poor and lame,
  Whatever's begun in anger, ends in shame.

- Anger is never without a reason, but seldom with a good one.

And then there's my favorite:

- He that scatters thorns, let him not go barefoot.[2]

Ouch!

The following selections show what happens when anger gets out of hand. They underscore the need to keep this deadly sin at bay.

---

2. Franklin, *Poor Richard's Almanack*, 42, 47, 54.

*This selection is suitable for children.*
*The moral of the story is that you should forgive your brother since God has forgiven you. Anger can cause us to miss out on the grace of God.*

# THE PARABLE OF THE UNMERCIFUL SERVANT

### from the Gospel According to Matthew (NIV)

Jesus told stories that get right to the heart of the matter. For example, one day a lawyer, seemingly wanting to get around the biblical injunction of loving his neighbor, slyly ask the Lord, "And *who* is my neighbor?" Jesus' response was the classic parable of the good Samaritan. Our next selection, the parable of the unmerciful servant, is another such tale. It came in response to Peter's question as to the limits of our forgiveness.

Because the man in this story did not forgive his brother, but instead showed him anger, he missed out on the grace of God! He lost it all because he lost his temper.

This passage is found in Matthew 18:21–35.

Then Peter came to Jesus and asked, "Lord, how many times shall I forgive my brother when he sins against me? Up to seven times?"

Jesus answered, "I tell you, not seven times, but seventy-seven times.[3]

"Therefore, the kingdom of heaven is like a king who wanted to settle accounts with his servants. As he began the settlement, a man who owed him ten thousand talents[4] was brought to him. Since he was not able to pay, the master ordered that he and his wife and his children and all that he had be sold to repay the debt.

"The servant fell on his knees before him. 'Be patient with me,' he begged, 'and I will pay back everything.' The servant's master took pity on him, canceled the debt and let him go.

"But when that servant went out, he found one of his fellow servants who owed him a hundred denarii.[5] He grabbed him and began to choke him. 'Pay back what you owe me!' he demanded.

3. Or "seventy times seven."
4. About $10 million.
5. About $17.

"His fellow servant fell to his knees and begged him, 'Be patient with me, and I will pay you back.'

"But he refused. Instead, he went off and had the man thrown into prison until he could pay the debt. When the other servants saw what had happened, they were greatly distressed and went and told their master everything that had happened.

"Then the master called the servant in. 'You wicked servant,' he said, 'I canceled all that debt of yours because you begged me to. Shouldn't you have had mercy on your fellow servant just as I had on you?' In anger his master turned him over to the jailers to be tortured, until he should pay back all he owed.

"This is how my heavenly Father will treat each of you unless you forgive your brother from your heart."

Forgiveness starts in the heart and works its way into our words and actions. If you are truly a Christian, you *have* to forgive your brother. There's no other way around it. This is a command from the Lord Himself. We can become less angry when we realize how much we've been forgiven.

*This selection is suitable for children.*
*The moral of these stories is that anger is best to be avoided.*

# MICHAEL LEFAN ON ANGER

from *Patience, My Foot!* [6]
by Michael LeFan

If anybody should have the "right" to be angry, (not that anyone necessarily should), it would be Michael LeFan. LeFan is a
polio victim and has been since he was eight years old back in
the 1950s. He cannot walk. He cannot use his arms. He sleeps in
an iron lung. He can't even go to the bathroom without someone
else's help. And yet he is one of the most calm, relaxed, and
patient men I've ever met.

Some might think that Michael has every right to be angry.
Angry at his circumstances. Angry at life. Angry at God. But he
has chosen not to be. Michael is a dynamic Christian who loves
the Lord and loves life despite the difficulties.

I had the privilege of producing a feature on location in
Michael's home near Waco, Texas. This included interviewing
him and his parents for Coral Ridge Ministries television. He
accomplishes more with the physical limitations than do most
people without them!

Michael is the author of a book on patience, *Patience, My
Foot!*, wherein he has some interesting and humorous short anecdotes on anger. The following selection consists of some of these
anecdotes. It's nice to read something on the lighter side of what
can be a grim subject.

---

## The Church Directory

Our congregation decided once that we would produce our own
pictorial membership directory (big mistake). One of the men had a
fine new Polaroid camera, which he set up in one of the church
offices. The agreement was that he'd take your picture until he got a
photo which satisfied you—none of those driver's license mugshots,
thank you. All went reasonably well until this lady's turn came to be
in front of the camera.

---

6.   LeFan, *Patience, My Foot!*, 18–19, 46, 52, 64.

The first picture was too dark—even the photographer could see that. So they made a second picture. This time she felt her hair wasn't right. Okay, so they set up for a third one (after she'd made adjustments to her coiffure, of course). Well, this one had rather harsh, unflattering shadows on her face.

By the time they'd endured eight snaps of the shutter—thanks to exaggerated wrinkles, off-center poses, and other objections—nerves were fraying a bit. "I don't know why you can't get a good picture," protested the lady.

"Ma'am," snapped the photographer, "this camera can't take what's not there."

### The Cause of the Hatfield-McCoy Feud

Have you ever noticed that sometimes we get impatient, angry, and remain bitter with people and actually forget why we're so upset? Take the example of the notorious Hatfield-McCoy Feud.

It first hit newspaper front pages in the 1880s, when the Hatfield family feuded with the McCoy clan from across the border in Kentucky. Historians disagree on what started the feud—which captured the imagination of the nation during a ten-year course. Some cite Civil War tensions: McCoys sympathized with the Union, Hatfields with the Confederacy. Others say the feud began when the McCoys blamed the Hatfields for stealing hogs. As many as 100 men, women and children died from what probably began as anger between two anonymous individuals.

This tragedy had an agreeable ending. In May 1976, Jim McCoy and Willis Hatfield—the last two survivors of the original families—shook hands at a public ceremony dedicating a monument to six of the victims.

McCoy died Feb. 11, 1984, at age 99. He bore no grudges—and had his burial handled by the Hatfield Funeral Home in Toler, Kentucky.

### The Nasty Letter to His Father

Anger can cause us to do and say things we may deeply regret. George W. Martin tells the following true story:

I remember a fellow who once wrote a nasty letter to his father. Since we worked in the same office, I advised him not to send it because it was written in a fit of temper. But he sealed it and asked me to put it in the mail. Instead, I simply slipped it into my pocket and kept it until the next day. The following morning he arrived at the office looking very worried. "George," he said, "I wish I had never sent that note to my dad yesterday. It hurts me deeply, and I know it will break his heart when he reads it. I'd give fifty dollars to get it back!" Taking the envelope from my pocket, I handed it to him and told him what I had done. He was so overjoyed that he actually wanted to pay me the fifty dollars!

## An Overworked Imagination

Keith Hendricks (not his real name) has wrestled with a temper all his life. When his wife was late getting home from work recently, he sizzled with every tick of the clock. His imagination ran wild. He thought she was spending money. No, she was with a man. No, she was deliberately delaying in order to irritate him. Keith's anger worked his imagination overtime. In reality it was his wife who was working overtime. Her employer asked her to finish a report before a holiday vacation. She was only forty-five minutes later than usual, but Keith was so worked up that when his wife came in the door he yelled, cursed, slammed his fist through a wall, and broke his own hand in the process. That's the wages of impatience.

*This selection is NOT suitable for children.*
*The moral of the story is that sin can lead to a guilty conscience, which*
*can lead to confession.*

# "THE TELL-TALE HEART"

### by Edgar Allen Poe

The great American short-story writer Edgar Allen Poe (1809–49) was, if you will, the Alfred Hitchcock of his day. Poe had an uncanny knack of getting into the minds of his tormented characters and describing their intense emotional states. His many stories grip his readers and hold them until the end.

One may wonder what a story like this is doing in a book like this. The answer is that it is a powerful story of how sin can lead to a guilty conscience, which can wreak havoc until the sin is confessed. Written in first person narrative, "The Tell-Tale Heart" deals with how a guilty conscience gets the better of a murderer . . . a killer who took innocent human life simply because he was angrily obsessed over something relatively trivial, his victim's repulsive eye. This is a classic example in literature of what Moses wrote so long ago: "And you may be sure that your sin will find you out" (Num. 32:23). The moral of the story is that a guilty conscience can lead to torment, and, hopefully, confession.

––––––––––

True! Nervous, very, very dreadfully nervous I had been and am; but why *will* you say that I am mad? The disease had sharpened my senses, not destroyed, not dulled them. Above all was the sense of hearing acute. I heard all things in the heaven and in the earth. I heard many in hell. How then am I mad? Hearken! And observe how healthily, how calmly, I can tell you the whole story.

It is impossible to say how first the idea entered my brain, but, once conceived, it haunted me day and night. Object there was none. Passion there was none. I loved the old man. He had never wronged me. He had never given me insult. For his gold I had no desire. I think it was his eye! Yes, it was this! One of his eyes resembled that of a vulture—a pale blue eye with a film over it. Whenever it fell upon me my blood ran cold, and so by degrees, very gradually, I made up my mind to take the life of the old man, and thus rid myself of the eye forever.

Now this is the point. You fancy me mad. Madmen know nothing. But you should have seen *me*. You should have seen how wisely I proceeded—with what caution—with what foresight, with what dissimulation, I went to work! I was never kinder to the old man than during the whole week before I killed him. And every night about midnight I turned the latch of his door and opened it—oh, so gently! And then, when I had made an opening sufficient for my head, I put in a dark lantern all closed, closed so that no light shone out, and then I thrust in my head. Oh, you would have laughed to see how cunningly I thrust it in! I moved it slowly, very, very slowly, so that I might not disturb the old man's sleep. It took me an hour to place my whole head within the opening so far that I could see him as he lay upon his bed. Ha! Would a madman have been so wise as this? And then when my head was well in the room I undid the lantern cautiously—oh, so cautiously—(for the hinges creaked), I undid it just so much that a single thin ray fell upon the vulture eye. And this I did for seven long nights, every night just at midnight, but I found the eye always closed, and so it was impossible to do the work, for it was not the old man who vexed me but his Evil Eye. And every morning, when the day broke, I went boldly into the chamber and spoke courageously to him, calling him by name in a hearty tone, and inquiring how he had passed the night. So you see he would have been a very profound old man, indeed, to suspect that every night, just at twelve, I looked in upon him while he slept.

Upon the eighth night I was more than usually cautious in opening the door. A watch's minute hand moves more quickly than did mine. Never before that night had I felt the extent of my own powers, of my sagacity. I could scarcely contain my feelings of triumph. To think that there I was opening the door little by little, and he not even to dream of my secret deeds or thoughts. I fairly chuckled at the idea, and perhaps he heard me, for he moved on the bed suddenly as if startled. Now you may think that I drew back—but no. His room was as black as pitch with the thick darkness (for the shutters were close fastened through fear of robbers), and so I knew that he could not see the opening of the door, and I kept pushing it on steadily, steadily.

I had my head in, and was about to open the lantern when my thumb slipped upon the tin fastening, and the old man sprang up in the bed, crying out, "Who's there?"

I kept quite still and said nothing. For a whole hour I did not move a muscle, and in the meantime I did not hear him lie down. He was still sitting up in the bed, listening; just as I have done night after night hearkening to the deathwatches in the wall.

Presently, I heard a slight groan, and I knew it was the groan of mortal terror. It was not a groan of pain or of grief—oh no! It was the low stifled sound that arises from the bottom of the soul when over-charged with awe. I knew the sound well. Many a night, just at midnight, when all the world slept, it has welled up from my own bosom, deepening, with its dreadful echo, the terrors that distracted me. I say I knew it well. I knew what the old man felt and pitied him although I chuckled at heart. I knew that he had been lying awake ever since the first slight noise when he had turned in the bed. His fears had been ever since growing upon him. He had been trying to fancy them causeless, but could not. He had been saying to himself, "It is nothing but the wind in the chimney, it is only a mouse crossing the floor," or, "It is merely a cricket which has made a single chirp." Yes, he has been trying to comfort himself with these suppositions; but he had found all in vain. *All in vain*, because Death in approaching him had stalked with his black shadow before him and enveloped the victim. And it was the mournful influence of the unperceived shadow that caused him to feel, although he neither saw nor heard, to *feel* the presence of my head within the room.

When I had waited a long time very patiently without hearing him lie down, I resolved to open a little—a very, very little crevice in the lantern. So I opened it—you cannot imagine how stealthily, stealthily—until at length a single dim ray like the thread of the spider shot out from the crevice and fell upon the vulture eye.

It was open, wide, wide open, and I grew furious as I gazed upon it. I saw it with perfect distinctness—all a dull blue with hideous veil over it that chilled the very marrow in my bones, but I could see nothing else of the old man's face or person, for I had directed the ray as if by instinct precisely upon the d—— spot.

And now have I not told you that what you mistake for madness is but over-acuteness of the senses? Now, I say, there came to my ears a low, dull, quick sound, such as a watch makes when enveloped in cotton. I knew *that* sound well, too. It was the beating of the old man's heart. It increased my fury as the beating of a drum stimulates the soldier into courage.

But even yet I refrained and kept still. I scarcely breathed. I held the lantern motionless. I tried how steadily I could maintain the ray upon the eye. Meantime the hellish tattoo of the heart increased. It grew quicker and quicker, and louder and louder, every instant. The old man's terror *must* have been extreme! It grew louder, I say, louder every moment!—Do you mark me well? I have told you that I am nervous: so I am. And now at the dead hour of the night, amid the dreadful silence of that old house, so strange a noise as this excited me to uncontrollable terror. Yet, for some minutes longer I refrained and stood still. But the beating grew louder, louder! I thought the heart must burst. And now a new anxiety seized me—the sound would be heard by a neighbor! The old man's hour had come! With a loud yell, I threw open the lantern and leaped into the room. He shrieked once—once only. In an instant I dragged him to the floor, and pulled the heavy bed over him. I then smiled gaily, to find the deed so far done. But for many minutes the heart beat on with a muffled sound. This, however, did not vex me; it would not be heard through the wall. At length it ceased. The old man was dead. I removed the bed and examined the corpse. Yes, he was stone, stone dead. I placed my hand upon the heart and held it there many minutes. There was no pulsation. He was stone dead. His eye would trouble me no more.

If still you think me mad, you will think so no longer when I describe the wise precautions I took for the concealment of the body. The night waned, and I worked hastily, but in silence.

I took up three planks from the flooring of the chamber, and deposited all between the scantlings. I then replaced the boards so cleverly, so cunningly, that no human eye—not even *his*—could have detected anything wrong. There was nothing to wash out—no stain of any kind—no blood spot whatever. I had been too wary for that.

When I had made an end of these labors, it was four o'clock—still dark as midnight. As the bell sounded the hour, there came a knocking at the street door. I went down to open it with a light heart—for what had I *now* to fear? There entered three men, who introduced themselves, with perfect suavity, as officers of the police. A shriek had been heard by a neighbor during the night; suspicion of foul play had been aroused; information had been lodged at the police office, and they (the officers) had been deputed to search the premises.

I smiled—for *what* had I to fear? I bade the gentlemen welcome. The shriek, I said, was my own in a dream. The old man, I mentioned, was absent in the country. I took my visitors all over the house. I bade them search—search *well*. I led them, at length, to *his* chamber. I showed them his treasures, secure, undisturbed. In the enthusiasm of my confidence, I brought chairs into the room, and desired them *here* to rest from their fatigues, while I myself, in the wild audacity of my perfect triumph, placed my own seat upon the very spot beneath which reposed the corpse of the victim.

The officers were satisfied. My *manner* had convinced them. I was singularly at ease. They sat, and while I answered cheerily, they chatted of familiar things. But, ere long, I felt myself getting pale and wished them gone. My head ached, and I fancied a ringing in my ears; but still they sat, and still chatted. The ringing became more distinct;—I talked more freely to get rid of the feeling; but it continued and gained definitiveness—until at length, I found that the noise was *not* within my ears.

No doubt I now grew *very* pale; but I talked more fluently, and with a heightened voice. Yet the sound increased—and what could I do? It was *a low, dull, quick sound—much such a sound as a watch makes when enveloped in cotton.* I gasped for breath, and yet the officers heard it not. I talked more quickly, more vehemently; but the noise steadily increased. I arose and argued about trifles, in a high key and with violent gesticulations; but the noise steadily increased. Why *would* they not be gone? I paced the floor to and fro with heavy strides, as if excited to fury by the observations of the men, but the noise steadily increased. O G—! What *could* I do? I foamed—I raved—I swore! I swung the chair upon which I had been sitting, and grated it upon the boards, but the noise arose over all and continually increased. It grew louder—louder—*louder!* And still the men chatted pleasantly, and smiled. Was it possible they heard not? Almighty G—! —no, no? They heard!—they suspected!—they *knew*—they were making a mockery of my horror!—this I thought, and this I think. But anything was better than this agony! Anything was more tolerable than this derision! I could bear those hypocritical smiles no longer! I felt that I must scream or die!—and now—again!—hark! louder! louder! louder! *louder!*—

"Villains!" I shrieked, "dissemble no more! I admit the deed—Tear up the planks—here, here!—it is the beating of his hideous heart!"

---

This story is predicated on the fact that the man has a conscience. A great tragedy of modern America are the millions growing up today who sear theirs, including kids who kill without batting an eyelash. Tim and Beverly LaHaye have covered this well in *A Nation Without a Conscience* (Tyndale, 1994). One other point: this story underscores how little annoyances (in this case, the old man's repulsive eye) can get the better of us, if we let them. So let's not let them!

*This selection is suitable for children.*
*The moral of the story is be rich and generous toward the things of God.*

## "THE FIRST CRECHE"

**from *Through Many Windows*[7]**
by Arthur Gordon

One of the most fascinating characters in the history of the world was St. Francis of Assisi, who lived in thirteenth-century Italy. St. Francis came from a wealthy background, but he chose a simple lifestyle out of homage to Christ. He also organized many priests to pursue a similar lifestyle. During an age when many of the clergy were corrupt and when bishoprics were bought and sold, the Franciscans in their early days stood out as shining examples of authentic piety.

Francis is credited with originating nativity scenes to celebrate the birth of Christ. This imaginative story deals with Francis's very first crèche—a Nativity scene—and his dealings with an embittered and hard merchant whose anger burns against the Lord.

This is another story from Arthur Gordon.

---

More than seven hundred years ago in the village of Greccio in Italy there lived a man who was at war with God. His name was Luigi, and he had his reasons.

He was a strong man, black-eyed, hot-tempered, with wonderful sensitive hands. From childhood, he had had the gift of shaping wood into marvelous imitations of life. And for a long time, he accepted this talent with gratitude, as a sign of God's favor. But the day came when Luigi cursed heaven. It was the day he learned that his daughter—his only child—was blind.

She had seemed perfect when she was born: blonde and blue-eyed like her mother. But when it became apparent that the child would never see, the wood-carver of Greccio seemed to go mad.

He went no more to the little church on the hill. He refused to allow prayers in his house. His child had been called Maria, after the mother of Jesus. He changed her name to Rosa.

---

7.  Gordon, *Through Many Windows*, 139–42.

His wife pleaded in vain; nothing could move him. "I will have nothing to do," he said, "with a God who condemns innocent children to darkness." To an artist, blindness is like a sentence of death.

Then in mid-December, in the year 1207, a mule train came through Greccio. Among the treasures for sale was a magnificent piece of ivory. As soon as he saw it, Luigi had the thought that he would carve it into a doll—a bambino—for his little girl.

In three days it was finished. Life-sized, smiling, with tiny arms outstretched, the ivory bambino seemed almost to breathe. Luigi told no one about it except his wife, and he told her only because he wanted her to make some clothes for the doll.

Meantime, in the village, everyone was talking about the young friar who had come to Greccio from a neighboring town to preach in the little church. No one could say exactly what it was about his preaching, but people who heard him came away with an extraordinary sense of peace, as if all the anger and pain of living had been lifted from their hearts.

Luigi's wife heard the young friar preach, and she begged her husband to come to the church with her. But Luigi shook his head. "When this God of yours shows me that he can cure blindness, then I will believe in him."

He would not let his wife take Rosa, either. But she wanted desperately to bring her child into some sort of contact with the love and warmth that seemed to flow from the young friar. And on Christmas Eve, suddenly, she thought of a way.

When by chance Luigi went into his workshop, his shout of fury brought the servants running. The ivory bambino was gone. From a terrified maid, Luigi learned that his wife had taken it to the church to have it blessed.

Out into the street stalked Luigi, black anger in his heart. Up the hill he went through the pale December sunlight toward the little church. But before he could reach the door, a cavalcade swept up the hill, three young nobles, richly dressed, then half a dozen mounted servants, and finally two carts loaded with farm animals: sheep, goats, oxen, a donkey.

The riders pulled up at the church door with a chorus of shouts. A young man in a purple cloak sprang down.

"Francesco!" he shouted. "Francesco Bernardone! We got your message and we are here!"

Luigi spoke roughly to one of the servants. "Who is this Francesco Bernardone that you seek here in Greccio?"

The servant pointed. "That is he—the friar."

The church door had opened, and a slender, brown-clad figure had come out. "Welcome my friends," he said, smiling, "and God's peace be upon you all."

The young man in the purple cloak swept his arm in a wide gesture. "We've brought the animals, just as you said. But really, Francesco, how much longer are you going to play this farce?"

The servant shrugged despairingly. "In Assisi, until not long ago, he was my master's friend and drinking companion. Now, they say, he preaches the word of God. It is very strange."

Other servants were unloading the carts, where the frightened animals reared and plunged. "A moment, please," the friar said. He walked over to the nearest cart and laid his hand on the donkey's back. "Be calm, there, Brother Ass. And you, Sister Sheep, do not baa so pitifully." And even as he spoke, the animals grew calm and still.

A hush seemed to fall upon the people who had gathered. In this sudden quiet, the friar said to the young man in the purple cloak. "Come into the church, Lorenzo. I want to show you my manger scene."

The young man said in a low voice, "I am not a true believer, Francesco. You know that."

"All the more reason for coming," the little friar said. He turned and went back into the church, and all the animals followed him, and the people, too. Even Luigi.

Inside the church, candles burned dimly. Near the altar was a rude shelter, made of green boughs, and in the shelter was a manger. Luigi could not see into the manger, but he knew what it contained, for a woman was kneeling near it, her face beautiful in the candlelight. The woman was his wife.

Without being led, without being driven, the animals grouped themselves around the manger. Then the little friar stood up on the steps of the altar.

"I was going to read you the Christmas story from the gospel," he said. "But my nativity scene makes me so happy that I am going to sing it to you."

No one who heard it ever forgot the sweetness of his song. He told the ageless story of the angels and the shepherds, of the coming of the Wise Men. Even the animals seemed to be listening, as if they too could understand the words. And Luigi was prepared to believe that they could, because an even greater miracle was taking place within himself. The bitterness and the anger were fading from his heart.

Nor was his the only heart that was being changed, for when at last the music ended, the young man in the purple cloak moved forward. From around his neck he took a chain of gold and put it beside the manger. And after him his companions came and put down gifts, one a ring, the other a jeweled dagger.

Luigi felt a touch on his arm. Looking around, he saw the little friar smiling at him.

"You wondered if God could cure blindness," the friar said. "Well, we are watching him do it, are we not?"

Luigi did not answer, for there was a tightness in his throat. He could see the villagers crowding forward to look into the manger and the awe and wonder in their faces as they gazed upon his handiwork. Afterward, there were those who swore that the ivory bambino stirred and smiled and lifted his arms to them. But this, no doubt, was the flickering candlelight.

Then the friar said, "Please thank your daughter for the loan of her Christmas present. And now you may take it back."

Luigi shook his head, "It is where it belongs. Let it stay."

The friar said, "Tomorrow is Christmas. Your little girl would be disappointed."

"No," said Luigi, "I will make her another bambino. I will work all night. I will carve her a whole nativity scene, just like yours, so that Ro—I mean Maria—will have Christmas at her fingertips whenever she wants it."

So Luigi went home, leaving the ivory bambino with Saint Francis of Assisi in what, according to legend, was the first actual crèche. Hand in hand with his wife, he walked back down the hill. And he worked all night with gratitude in his heart because he knew that in his house blindness had indeed been cured—not his daughter's, but his own.

---

Sometimes life's disappointments can make us angry at God. But such anger should be short-lived and should quickly give way to thankfulness for all His goodness to us. How tragic when people cling to bitterness and anger toward God. They ultimately hurt themselves and block out God's grace and blessings. If you ever feel life is unfair or doubt God's goodness, cling to Romans 8:28: "For all things work together for good for those who love the Lord."

*This selection is NOT suitable for children.*
*The moral of the story is not to let anger, motivated by self-righteous*
*pride, cause you to usurp God's right to judge the wicked.*

# "THE HAMMER OF GOD"

### A Father Brown Mystery
### by G. K. Chesterton

G. K. Chesterton (1874–1936) was a great Christian writer whose work influenced C. S. Lewis. A devout Roman Catholic, Chesterton wrote both nonfiction and fiction.

"The Hammer of God" is one of Chesterton's Father Brown mysteries, short stories featuring a bumbling, roly-poly, umbrella-carrying Catholic priest. The award-winning crime writer, Ross Macdonald, was once asked to list the top ten greatest fictional detectives of all time. He put Father Brown high on the list (close even to Sherlock Holmes).[8]

This Father Brown mystery deals with two brothers. It is a story about anger fueled by pride. It makes the point that an unchecked temper (even if only known to the person himself)—fueled by a pride-filled, self-righteousness—can lead to a downfall. We are not God. It is not up to us, individually, to judge the sin of man. "'Vengeance is Mine,' says the Lord, 'I will repay'" (Rom. 12:19).

---

The little village of Bohun Beacon was perched on a hill so steep that the tall spire of its church seemed only like the peak of a small mountain. At the foot of the church stood a smithy, generally red with fires and always littered with hammers and scraps of iron; opposite to this, over a rude cross of cobbled paths, was "The Blue Boar," the only inn of the place. It was upon this crossways in the lifting of a leaden and silver daybreak, that two brothers met in the street and spoke; though one was beginning the day and the other finishing it. The Rev. and Hon. Wilfred Bohun was very devout, and was making his way to some austere exercises of prayer or contemplation at dawn. Colonel the Hon. Norman Bohun, his elder brother, was by no

---

8.   "Ross Macdonald's Ten Greatest Fictional Detectives of All Time," Irving Wallace, David Wallechinksy, Amy Wallace, Sylvia Wallace, *The People's Almanac Presents the Book of Lists #2* (New York: William Morrow and Company, 1980), 225–26.

means devout, and was sitting in evening-dress on the bench outside "The Blue Boar," drinking what the philosophic observer was free to regard either as his last glass on Tuesday or his first on Wednesday. The colonel was not particular.

The Bohuns were one of the very few aristocratic families really dating from the Middle Ages, and their pennon[9] had actually seen Palestine. But it is a great mistake to suppose that such houses stand high in chivalric traditions. Few except the poor preserve traditions. Aristocrats live not in traditions but in fashions. The Bohuns had been Mohocks[10] under Queen Ann, and Mashers[11] under Queen Victoria. But, like more than one of the really ancient houses, they had rotted in the two centuries into mere drunkards and dandy degenerates, till there had even come a whisper of insanity. Certainly there was something hardly human about the colonel's wolfish pursuit of pleasure, and his chronic resolution not to go home till morning had a touch of the hideous charity of insomnia. He was a tall, fine animal, elderly, but with hair startlingly yellow. He would have looked merely blond and leonine, but his blue eyes were sunk so deep in his face that they looked black. They were a little too close together. He had very long yellow moustaches: on each side of them a fold or furrow from nostril to jaw, so that a sneer seemed to cut into his face. Over his evening clothes he wore a curiously pale yellow coat that looked more like a very light dressing gown than an overcoat, and on the back of his head was stuck an extraordinary broad-brimmed hat of a bright green colour, evidently some oriental curiosity caught up at random. He was proud of appearing in such incongruous attires—proud of the fact that he always made them look congruous.

His brother the curate had also the yellow hair and the elegance, but he was buttoned up to the chin in black, and his face was clean-shaven, cultivated and a little nervous. He seemed to live for nothing but his religion; but there were some who said (notably the blacksmith, who was a Presbyterian) that it was a love of Gothic architecture rather than of God, and that his haunting of the church like a ghost was only another and purer turn of the almost morbid thirst for beauty which sent his brother raging after women and wine. This

---

9. A triangular flag, especially used as the insignia of a knight in the Middle Ages.

10. Ruffians, often aristocrats, who in gangs committed outrages in London in the early eighteenth century.

11. Ibid.

charge was doubtful, while the man's practical piety was indubitable. Indeed, the charge was mostly an ignorant misunderstanding of the love of solitude and secret prayer, and was founded on his being often found kneeling, not before the altar, but in peculiar places, in the crypts or gallery, or even in the belfry. He was at the moment about to enter the church through the yard of the smithy, but stopped and frowned a little as he saw his brother's cavernous eyes staring in the same direction. On the hypothesis that the colonel was interested in the church he did not waste any speculations. There only remained the blacksmith's shop, and though the blacksmith was a Puritan and none of his people, Wilfred Bohun had heard some scandals about a beautiful and rather celebrated wife. He flung a suspicious look across the shed, and the colonel stood up laughing to speak to him.

"Good morning, Wilfred," he said. "Like a good landlord I am watching sleeplessly over my people. I am going to call on the blacksmith."

Wilfred looked at the ground and said: "The blacksmith is out. He is over at Greenford."

"I know," answered the other with silent laughter; "that is why I am calling on him."

"Norman," said the cleric, with his eye on a pebble in the road, "are you ever afraid of thunderbolts?"

"What do you mean?" asked the colonel. "Is your hobby meteorology?"

"I mean," said Wilfred, without looking up, "do you ever think that God might strike you in the street?"

"I beg your pardon," said the colonel; "I see your hobby is folklore."

"I know your hobby is blasphemy," retorted the religious man, stung in the one live place of his nature. "But if you do not fear God, you have good reason to fear man."

The elder raised his eyebrows politely. "Fear man?" he said.

"Barnes the blacksmith is the biggest and strongest man for forty miles round," said the clergyman sternly. "I know you are no coward or weakling, but he could throw you over the wall."

This struck home, being true, and the lowering line by mouth and nostril darkened and deepened. For a moment he stood with the heavy sneer on his face. But in an instant Colonel Bohun had recovered his own cruel good humour and laughed, showing two dog-like front teeth under his yellow moustache. "In that case, my dear Wilfred," he said quite carelessly, "it was wise for the last of the Bohuns to come out partially in armour."

And he took off the queer round hat covered with green, showing that it was lined within with steel. Wilfred recognized it indeed as a light Japanese or Chinese helmet torn down from a trophy that hung in the old family hall.

"It was the first to hand," explained his brother airily; "always the nearest hat—and the nearest woman."

"The blacksmith is away at Greenford," said Wilfred quietly; "the time of his return is unsettled."

And with that he turned and went into the church with bowed head, crossing himself like one who wishes to be quit of an unclean spirit. He was anxious to forget such grossness in the cool twilight of his tall Gothic cloisters; but on that morning it was fated that his still round of religious exercises should be everywhere arrested by small shocks. As he entered the church, hitherto always empty at that hour, a kneeling figure rose hastily to its feet and came towards the full daylight of the doorway. When the curate saw it he stood still with surprise. For the early worshipper was none other than the village idiot, a nephew of the blacksmith, one who neither would nor could care for the church or for anything else. He was always called "Mad Joe," and seemed to have no other name; he was a dark, strong, slouching lad, with a heavy white face, dark straight hair, and a mouth always open. As he passed the priest, his moon-calf countenance gave no hint of what he had been doing or thinking of. He had never been known to pray before. What sort of prayers was he saying now? Extraordinary prayers surely.

Wilfred Bohun stood rooted to the spot long enough to see the idiot go out into the sunshine, and even to see his dissolute brother hail him with a sort of avuncular jocularity. The last thing he saw was the colonel throwing pennies at the open mouth of Joe, with the serious appearance of trying to hit it.

This ugly sunlight picture of the stupidity and cruelty of the earth sent the ascetic finally to his prayers for purification and new thoughts. He went up to a pew in the gallery, which brought him under a coloured window which he loved and which always quieted his spirit; a blue window with an angel carrying lilies. There he began to think less about the half-wit, with his livid face and mouth like a fish. He began to think less of his evil brother, pacing like a lean lion in his horrible hunger. He sank deeper and deeper into those cold and sweet colours of silver blossoms and sapphire sky.

In this place half an hour afterwards he was found by Gibbs, the village Cobbler, who had been sent for him in some haste. He got to his feet with promptitude, for he knew that no small matter would have brought Gibbs into such a place at all. The cobbler was, as in many villages, an atheist, and his appearance in church was a shade more extraordinary than Mad Joe's. It was a morning of theological enigmas.

"What is it?" asked Wilfred Bohun rather stiffly, but putting out a trembling hand for his hat.

The atheist spoke in a tone that, coming from him, was quite startlingly respectful, and even, as it were, huskily sympathetic.

"You must excuse me, Sir," he said in a hoarse whisper, "but we didn't think it right not to let you know at once. I'm afraid a rather dreadful thing has happened, Sir. I'm afraid your brother—"

Wilfred clenched his frail hands. "What devilry has he done now?" he cried in involuntary passion.

"Why, Sir," said the cobbler, coughing, "I'm afraid he's done nothing, and won't do anything. I'm afraid he's done for. You had really better come down, Sir."

The curate followed the cobbler down a short winding stair which brought them out at an entrance rather higher than the street. Bohun saw the tragedy in one glance, flat underneath him like a plan. In the yard of the smithy were standing five or six men, mostly in black, one in an inspector's uniform. They included the doctor, the Presbyterian minister, and the priest from the Roman Catholic chapel to which the blacksmith's wife belonged. The latter was speaking to her, indeed, very rapidly, in an undertone, as she, a magnificent woman with redgold hair, was sobbing blindly on a bench. Between these two groups, and just clear of the main heap of hammers, lay a man in evening dress, spread-eagled and flat on his face. From the height above Wilfred could have sworn to every item of his costume and appearance, down to the Bohun rings upon his fingers; but the skull was only a hideous splash, like a star of blackness and blood.

Wilfred Bohun gave but one glance, and ran down the steps into the yard. The doctor, who was the family physician, saluted him, but he scarcely took any notice. He could only stammer out: "My brother is dead. What does it mean? What is this horrible mystery?" There was an unhappy silence; and then the cobbler, the most outspoken man present, answered: "Plenty of horror, sir," he said, "but not much mystery."

"What do you mean?" asked Wilfred, with a white face.

"It's plain enough," answered Gibbs. "There is only one man for forty miles round that could have struck such a blow as that, and he's the man that had most reason to."

"We must not prejudge anything," put in the doctor, a tall, black-bearded man, rather nervously; "but it is competent for me to corroborate what Mr. Gibbs says about the nature of the blow, sir; it is an incredible blow. Mr. Gibbs says that only one man in this district could have done it. I should have said myself that nobody could have done it."

A shudder of superstition went through the slight figure of the curate. "I can hardly understand," he said.

"Mr. Bohun," said the doctor in a low voice, "metaphors literally fail me. It is inadequate to say that the skull was smashed to bits like an eggshell. Fragments of bone were driven into the body and the ground like bullets into a mud wall. It was the hand of a giant."

He was silent a moment, looking grimly through his glasses; then he added: "The thing has one advantage—that it clears most people of suspicion at one stroke. If you or I or any normally made man in the country were accused of this crime, we should be acquitted as an infant would be acquitted of stealing the Nelson Column."

"That's what I say," repeated the cobbler obstinately, "there's only one man that could have done it, and he's the man that would have done it. Where's Simeon Barnes, the blacksmith?"

"He's over at Greenford," faltered the curate.

"More likely over in France," muttered the cobbler.

"No; he is in neither of those places," said a small and colourless voice, which came from the little Roman priest who had joined the group. "As a matter of fact, he is coming up the road at this moment."

The little priest was not an interesting man to look at, having stubbly brown hair and a round and stolid face. But if he had been as splendid as Apollo no one would have looked at him at that moment. Everyone turned round and peered at the pathway which wound across the plain below, along which was indeed walking, at his own huge stride and with a hammer on his shoulder, Simeon the smith. He was a bony and gigantic man, with deep, dark, sinister eyes and a dark chin beard. He was walking and talking quietly with two other men; and though he was never specially cheerful, he seemed quite at his ease.

"My G—!" cried the atheistic cobbler; "and there's the hammer he did it with."

"No," said the inspector, a sensible-looking man with a sandy moustache, speaking for the first time. "There's the hammer he did it with, over there by the church wall. We have left it and the body exactly as they are."

All glanced round, and the short priest went across and looked down in silence at the tool where it lay. It was one of the smallest and the lightest of the hammers, and would not have caught the eye among the rest; but on the iron edge of it were blood and yellow hair.

After a silence the short priest spoke without looking up, and there was a new note in his dull voice. "Mr. Gibbs was hardly right," he said, "in saying that there is no mystery. There is at least the mystery of why so big a man should attempt so big a blow with so little a hammer."

"Oh, never mind that," cried Gibbs, in a fever. "What are we to do with Simeon Barnes?"

"Leave him alone," said the priest quietly. "He is coming here of himself. I know these two men with him. They are very good fellows from Greenford, and they have come over about the Presbyterian chapel." Even as he spoke the tall smith swung round the corner of the church and strode into his own yard. Then he stood there quite still, and the hammer fell from his hand. The inspector, who had preserved impenetrable propriety, immediately went up to him.

"I won't ask you, Mr. Barnes," he said, "whether you know anything about what has happened here. You are not bound to say. I hope you don't know, and that you will be able to prove it. But I must go through the form of arresting you in the King's name for the murder of Colonel Norman Bohun."

"You are not bound to say anything," said the cobbler in officious excitement. "They've got to prove everything. They haven't proved yet that it is Colonel Bohun, with the head all smashed up like that."

"That won't wash," said the doctor aside to the priest. "That's out of detective stories. I was the colonel's medical man, and I knew his body better than he did. He had very fine hands, but quite peculiar ones. The second and third fingers were the same in length. Oh, that's the colonel right enough."

As he glanced at the brained corpse upon the ground the iron eyes of the motionless blacksmith followed them and rested there also.

"Is Colonel Bohun dead?" said the smith quite calmly. "Then he's damned."

"Don't say anything! Oh, don't say anything," cried the atheist cobbler, dancing about in an ecstasy of admiration of the English legal system. For no man is such a legalist as the good Secularist.

The blacksmith turned on him over his shoulder the august face of a fanatic.

"It is well for you infidels to dodge like foxes because the world's law favours you," he said; "but God guards His own in His pocket, as you shall see this day."

Then he pointed to the colonel and said: "When did this dog die in his sins?"

"Moderate your language," said the doctor.

"Moderate the Bible's language, and I'll moderate mine. When did he die?"

"I saw him alive at six o'clock this morning," stammered Wilfred Bohun.

"God is good," said the smith. "Mr. Inspector, I have not the slightest objection to being arrested. It is you who may object to arresting me. I don't mind leaving the court without a stain on my character. You do mind, perhaps, leaving the court with a bad set-back in your career."

The solid inspector for the first time looked at the blacksmith with a lively eye—as did everybody else, except the short, strange priest, who was still looking down at the little hammer that had dealt the dreadful blow.

"There are two men standing outside this shop," went on the blacksmith with ponderous lucidity, "good tradesmen in Greenford whom you all know, who will swear that they saw me from before midnight till daybreak and long after in the committee-room of our Revival Mission, which sits all night, we save souls so fast. In Greenford itself twenty people could swear to me for all that time. If I were a heathen, Mr. Inspector, I would let you walk on to your downfall; but, as a Christian man, I feel bound to give you your chance and ask you whether you will hear my alibi now or in court."

The inspector seemed for the first time disturbed and said: "Of course I should be glad to clear you altogether now."

The smith walked out of his yard with the same long and easy stride, and returned to his two friends from Greenford, who were indeed friends of nearly everyone present. Each of them said a few words which no one ever thought of disbelieving. When they had spoken, the innocence of Simeon stood up as solid as the great church above them.

One of those silences struck the group which are more strange and insufferable than any speech. Madly, in order to make conversation, the curate said to the Catholic priest:

"You seem very much interested in that hammer, Father Brown."

"Yes, I am," said Father Brown; "why is it such a small hammer?" The doctor swung round on him.

"By George, that's true," he cried; "who would use a little hammer with ten larger hammers lying about?"

Then he lowered his voice in the curate's ear and said: "Only the kind of person that can't lift a large hammer. It is not a question of force or courage between the sexes. It's a question of lifting power in the shoulders. A bold woman could commit ten murders with a light hammer and never turn a hair. She could not kill a beetle with a heavy one."

Wilfred Bohun was staring at him with a sort of hypnotized horror, while Father Brown listened with his head a little on one side, really interested and attentive. The doctor went on with more hissing emphasis:

"Why do those idiots always assume that the only person who hates the wife's lover is the wife's husband? Nine times out of ten the person who most hates the wife's lover is the wife. Who knows what insolence or treachery he had shown her—look there?"

He made a momentary gesture towards the red-haired woman on the bench. She had lifted her head at last and the tears were drying on her splendid face. But the eyes were fixed on the corpse with an electric glare that had in it something of idiocy.

The Rev. William Bohun made a limp gesture as if waving away all desire to know; but Father Brown, dusting off his sleeve some ashes blown from the furnace, spoke in his indifferent way.

"You are like so many doctors," he said; "your mental science is really suggestive. It is your physical science that is utterly impossible.

I agree that the woman wants to kill the co-respondent much more than the petitioner does. And I agree that a woman will always pick up a small hammer instead of a big one. But the difficulty is one of physical impossibility. No woman ever born could have smashed a man's skull out flat like that." Then he added reflectively, after a pause: "These people haven't grasped the whole of it. The man was actually wearing an iron helmet, and the blow scattered it like broken glass. Look at that woman. Look at her arms."

Silence held them all up again, and then the doctor said rather sulkily: "Well, I may be wrong; there are objections to everything. But I stick to the main point. No man but an idiot would pick up that little hammer if he could use a big hammer."

With that the lean and quivering hands of Wilfred Bohun went up to his head and seemed to clutch his scanty yellow hair. After an instant they dropped, and he cried: "That was the word I wanted; you have said the word."

Then he continued, mastering his discomposure: "The words you said were, 'No man but an idiot would pick up the small hammer.'"

"Yes," said the doctor. "Well?"

"Well," said the curate, "no man but an idiot did." The rest stared at him with eyes arrested and riveted, and he went on in a febrile and feminine agitation.

"I am a priest," he cried unsteadily, "and a priest should be no shedder of blood. I—I mean that he should bring no one to the gallows. And I thank God that I see the criminal clearly now—because he is a criminal who cannot be brought to the gallows."

"You will not denounce him?" inquired the doctor.

"He would not be hanged if I did denounce him," answered Wilfred, with a wild but curiously happy smile. "When I went into the church this morning I found a madman praying there—that poor Joe, who has been wrong all his life. God knows what he prayed; but with such strange folk it is not incredible to suppose that their prayers are all upside down. Very likely a lunatic would pray before killing a man. When I last saw poor Joe he was with my brother. My brother was mocking him."

"By Jove!" cried the doctor, "this is talking at last. But how do you explain—"

The Rev. Wilfred was almost trembling with the excitement of his own glimpse of the truth. "Don't you see; don't you see," he cried feverishly, "that is the only theory that covers both the queer things, that answers both the riddles. The two riddles are the little hammer and the big blow. The smith might have struck the big blow, but he would not have chosen the little hammer. His wife would have chosen the little hammer, but she could not have struck the big blow. But the madman might have done both. As for the little hammer—why, he was mad and might have picked up anything. And for the big blow, have you never heard, doctor, that a maniac in his paroxysm may have the strength of ten men?"

The doctor drew a deep breath and then said: "By golly, I believe you've got it."

Father Brown had fixed his eyes on the speaker so long and steadily as to prove that his large grey, ox-like eyes were not quite so insignias as the rest of his face. When silence had fallen he said with marked respect: "Mr. Bohun, yours is the only theory yet propounded which holds water every way and is essentially unassailable. I think, therefore, that you deserve to be told, on my positive knowledge, that it is not the true one." And with that the odd little man walked away and stared again at the hammer.

"That fellow seems to know more than he ought to," whispered the doctor peevishly to Wilfred. "Those popish priests are deucedly sly."

"No, no," said Bohun, with a sort of wild fatigue. "It was the lunatic. It was the lunatic."

The group of the two clerics and the doctor had fallen away from the more official group containing the inspector and the man he had arrested. Now, however, that their own party had broken up, they heard voices from the others. The priest looked up quietly and then looked down again as he heard the blacksmith say in a loud voice:

"I hope I've convinced you, Mr. Inspector. I'm a strong man, as you say, but I couldn't have flung my hammer bang here from Greenford. My hammer hasn't any wings that it should come flying half a mile over hedges and fields."

The inspector laughed amicably and said: "No; I think you can be considered out of it, though it's one of the rummiest coincidences I ever saw. I can only ask you to give us all the assistance you can in finding a man as big and strong as yourself. By George! you might be useful, if only to hold him! I suppose you yourself have no guess at the man?"

"I may have a guess," said the pale smith, "but it is not at a man." Then, seeing the scared eyes turn towards his wife on the bench, he put his huge hand on her shoulder and said: "Nor a woman either."

"What do you mean?" asked the inspector jocularly. "You don't think cows use hammers, do you?"

"I think no thing of flesh held that hammer," said the blacksmith in a stifled voice; "mortally speaking, I think the man died alone."

Wilfred made a sudden forward movement and peered at him with burning eyes.

"Do you mean to say, Barnes," came the sharp voice of the cobbler, "that the hammer jumped up of itself and knocked the man down?"

"Oh, you gentlemen may stare and snigger," cried Simeon; "you clergymen who tell us on Sunday in what a stillness the Lord smote Sennacherib. I believe that One who walks invisible in every house defended the honour of mine, and laid the defiler dead before the door of it. I believe the force in that blow was just the force there is in earthquakes, and no force less."

Wilfred said, with a voice utterly undescribable: "I told Norman myself to beware of the thunderbolt."

"That agent is outside my jurisdiction," said the inspector with a slight smile.

"You are not outside His," answered the smith; "see you to it." And, turning his broad back, he went into the house.

The shaken Wilfred was led away by Father Brown, who had an easy and friendly way with him. "Let us get out of this horrid place, Mr. Bohun," he said. "May I look inside your church? I hear it's one of the oldest in England. We take some interest, you know," he added with a comical grimace, "in old English churches."

Wilfred Bohun did not smile, for humour was never his strong point. But he nodded rather eagerly, being only too ready to explain the Gothic splendours to someone more likely to be sympathetic than the Presbyterian blacksmith or the atheist cobbler.

"By all means," he said; "let us go in at this side." And he led the way into the high side entrance at the top of the flight of steps. Father Brown was mounting the first step to follow him when he felt a hand on his shoulder, and turned to behold the dark, thin figure of the doctor, his face darker yet with suspicion.

"Sir," said the physician harshly, "you appear to know some secrets in this black business. May I ask if you are going to keep them to yourself?"

"Why, doctor," answered the priest, smiling quite pleasantly, "there is one very good reason why a man of my trade would keep things to himself when he is not sure of them, and that is that it is so constantly his duty to keep them to himself when he is sure of them. But if you think I have been discourteously reticent with you or anyone, I will go to the extreme limit of my custom. I will give you two very large hints."

"Well, sir?" said the doctor gloomily.

"First," said Father Brown quietly, "the thing is quite in your own province. It is a matter of physical science. The blacksmith is mistaken, not perhaps in saying that the blow was divine, but certainly in saying that it came by a miracle. It was no miracle, doctor, except in so far as man is himself a miracle, with his strange and wicked and yet halfheroic heart. The force that smashed that skull was a force well known to scientists—one of the most frequently debated of the laws of nature."

The doctor, who was looking at him with frowning intentness, only said: "And the other hint?"

"The other hint is this," said the priest: "Do you remember the blacksmith, though he believes in miracles, talking scornfully of the impossible fairy tale that his hammer had wings and flew half a mile across country?"

"Yes," said the doctor, "I remember that."

"Well," added Father Brown, with a broad smile, "that fairy tale was the nearest thing to the real truth that has been said to-day." And with that he turned his back and stumped up the steps after the curate.

The Reverend Wilfred, who had been waiting for him, pale and impatient, as if this little delay were the last straw for his nerves, led him immediately to his favourite corner of the church, that part of the gallery closest to the carved roof and lit by the wonderful window with the angel. The little Latin priest explored and admired everything exhaustively, talking cheerfully but in a low voice all the time. When in the course of his investigation he found the side exit and the winding stair down which Wilfred had rushed to find his brother dead, Father Brown ran not down but up, with the agility of a monkey, and his clear voice came from an outer platform above.

"Come up here, Mr. Bohun," he called. "The air will do you good."

Bohun followed him, and came out on a kind of stone gallery or balcony outside the building, from which one could see the illimitable plain in which their small hill stood, wooded away to the purple horizon and dotted with villages and farms. Clear and square, but quite small beneath them, was the blacksmith's yard, where the inspector still stood taking notes and the corpse still lay like a smashed fly.

"Might be the map of the world, mightn't it?" said Father Brown.

"Yes," said Bohun very gravely, and nodded his head.

Immediately beneath and about them the lines of the Gothic building plunged outwards into the void with a sickening swiftness akin to suicide. There is that element of Titan energy in the architecture of the Middle Ages that, from whatever aspect it be seen, it always seems to be rushing away, like the strong back of some maddened horse. This church was hewn out of ancient and silent stone, bearded with old fungoids and stained with the nests of birds. And yet, when they saw it from below, it sprang like a fountain at the stars; and when they saw it, as now, from above, it poured like a cataract into a voiceless pit. For these two men on the tower were left alone with the most terrible aspect of the Gothic: the monstrous foreshortening and disproportion, the dizzy perspectives, the glimpses of great things small and small things great; a topsy-turvydom of stone in the mid-air. Details of stone, enormous by their proximity, were relieved against a pattern of fields and farms, pygmy in their distance. A carved bird or beast at a corner seemed like some vast walking or flying dragon wasting the pastures and villages below. The whole atmosphere was dizzy and dangerous, as if men were upheld in air amid the gyrating wings of colossal genii; and the whole of that old church, as tall and rich as a cathedral, seemed to sit upon the sunlit country like a cloudburst.

"I think there is something rather dangerous about standing on these high places even to pray," said Father Brown. "Heights were made to be looked at, not to be looked from."

"Do you mean that one might fall over?" asked Wilfred.

"I mean that one's soul may fall if one's body doesn't," said the other priest.

"I scarcely understand you," remarked Bohun indistinctly.

"Look at that blacksmith, for instance," went on Father Brown calmly; "a good man, but not a Christian—hard, imperious, unforgiving. . . ."[12]

"But he—he didn't do it," said Bohun tremulously.

"No," said the other in an odd voice; "we know he didn't do it."

After a moment he resumed, looking tranquilly out over the plain with his pale grey eyes. "I knew a man," he said, "who began by worshipping with others before the altar, but who grew fond of high and lonely places to pray from, corners or inches in the belfry or the spire. And once in one of those dizzy places, where the whole world seemed to turn under him like a wheel his brain turned also, and he fancied he was God. So that though he was a good man, he committed a great crime."

Wilfred's face was turned away, but his bony hands turned blue and white as they tightened on the parapet of stone.

"He thought it was given to him to judge the world and strike down the sinner. He would never have had such a thought if he had been kneeling with other men upon a floor. But he saw all men walking about like insects. He saw one especially strutting just below him, insolent and evident by a bright green hat—a poisonous insect."

Rooks cawed round the corners of the belfry; but there was no other sound till Father Brown went on.

"This also tempted him, that he had in his hand one of the most awful engines of nature; I mean gravitation, that mad and quickening rush by which all earth's creatures fly back to her heart when released. See, the inspector is strutting just below us in the smithy. If I were to toss a pebble over this parapet it would be something like a bullet by the time it struck him. If I were to drop a hammer—even a small hammer—"

Wilfred Bohun threw one leg over the parapet, and Father Brown had him in a minute by the collar.

"Not by that door," he said quite gently; "that door leads to hell."

Bohun staggered back against the wall, and stared at him with frightful eyes.

"How do you know all this?" he cried. "Are you a devil?"

"I am a man," answered Father Brown gravely; "and therefore have all devils in my heart. Listen to me," he said after a short pause. "I

12. Editor's deletion.

know what you did—at least, I can guess the great part of it. When you left your brother you were racked with no unrighteous rage to the extent even that you snatched up the small hammer, half inclined to kill him with his foulness on his mouth. Recoiling, you thrust it under your buttoned coat instead, and rushed into the church. You pray wildly in many places, under the angel window, upon the platform above, and on a higher platform still, from which you could see the colonel's Eastern hat like the back of a green beetle crawling about. Then something snapped in your soul, and you let God's thunderbolt fall."

Wilfred put a weak hand to his head, and asked in a low voice: "How did you know that his hat looked like a green beetle?"

"Oh, that," said the other with the shadow of a smile, "that was common sense. But hear me further. I say I know all this; but no one else shall know it. The next step is for you; I shall take no more steps; I will seal this with the seal of confession. If you ask me why, there are many reasons, and only one that concerns you. I leave things to you because you have not yet gone very far wrong, as assassins go. You did not help to fix the crime on the smith when it was easy; or on his wife, when that was easy. You tried to fix it on the imbecile, because you knew that he could not suffer. That was one of the gleams that it is my business to find in assassins. And now come down into the village, and go your own way as free as the wind; for I have said my last word."

They went down the winding stairs in utter silence, and came out into the sunlight by the smithy. Wilfred Bohun carefully unlatched the wooden gate of the yard, and going up to the inspector, said: "I wish to give myself up; I have killed my brother."

---

If you're tempted to get angry at someone, count to ten. I remember W. C. Fields saying that to an angry young lady in one of his films. After ten seconds, he told her, "Now throw it, you have a better aim!"

*This selection is NOT suitable for children.*
*The moral of the story is that unregenerate men, without societal restraints, can degenerate into virtual savages.*

# "TROPICAL PARADISE LOST AND FOUND"

## The Story of the Original Settlement on Pitcairn Island

retold by Jerry Newcombe

Sometimes the anger of men can get so out of hand that they end up killing one another. That happened about two hundred years ago in a colony that was set up on a tropical wonderland. The colony was the settlement on the Pacific Ocean island of Pitcairn by some of the surviving mutineers of the *Bounty*, including Fletcher Christian.

This story is based on the third part of the *Mutiny on the Bounty* trilogy by Charles Nordhoff and James Norman Hall. Part 1 is *Mutiny on the Bounty;* part 2 is *Men Against the Sea;* and part 3 is *Pitcairn's Island.*[13] This story is also based on information from the *National Geographic.*[14]

In the brilliant, but disturbing, novel *Lord of the Flies*, William Golding shows what happens when boys from a civilized society become shipwrecked on a remote island. They degenerate into a band of barbaric savages, even engaging in murder, until they are rescued. Take away Christian restraint from people, and—human nature being what it is—this same story could happen to virtually anybody. *Lord of the Flies* is fiction. The account you are about to read is based on fact. The good news is that it had a miraculous outcome thanks to God and the Good Book.

---

Pitcairn Island in the Pacific Ocean was idyllic—lush with beautiful plants and fruits, rich with gorgeous sights, both on the island and off. In short, it was like a new Garden of Eden. But after being settled for a few years by a handful of Europeans and Tahitians, it became a living hell. Men's anger and hostility had transformed the idyllic scene into a hotbed of killing, mistrust, and hatred—reflecting the worst in

---

13. Charles Nordhoff and James Norman Hall, *The Bounty Trilogy* (Boston: Little, Brown and Company, 1962).

14. T. C. Roughley, "*Bounty* Descendants Live on Remote Norfolk Island," *National Geographic* 118, no. 4 (October 1960): 559–84.

human nature. Only the grace of God, working in the human heart, could transform it back to even a semblence of paradise.

Here's the setting. Nine survivors of the *Bounty* mutiny, including their leader Fletcher Christian, settled on this tropical island in 1789. Along with them were their Maori wives of Tahiti and five Tahitian men, including a former tribal chief. (They were called Indians, though not from India.) As the couples settled down, many of them began to have babies.

The Indians set up a heathen place of worship. The Europeans took no such steps. These were blasphemous, crusty men, who were not partakers of the grace of God.

Trouble began almost from the beginning of the settlement. The main cause of the trouble was the godless attitude of a few of the Englishmen[15] who viewed themselves superior to the Indians. They turned some of the Maori men into virtual slaves.

Another bone of contention early on centered around the death of the wife of one of the Europeans. Her husband, the colony's blacksmith, apparently had been committing adultery, somewhat covertly, with one of the Indian's wives. When his wife was found pierced on the jagged rocks below a five-hundred-foot bluff, it was not clear as to whether she had fallen accidentally or jumped. In any event, the blacksmith sought to take his mistress as his wife. Christian was able to block this initially but not ultimately. The wronged Indian tried to get his revenge by slaying the blacksmith, but his former wife ended up poisoning him first! A friend of the Indian shared the same meal and was also thus poisoned to death. Three were dead, and the colony was well on its way to sinking into depravity.

Then the five European troublemakers, of whom Matthew Quintal was the strongest and roughest, came up with a plan that sparked a bloodbath. They decided that they wanted to divide the spacious island into nine parcels of land—one for each European man—and that they would turn the Indians into virtual slaves. Christian didn't agree with this plan, but he was initially prepared to defer to majority rule (of the nine European men), as was his custom.

Meanwhile, word of this unfair plan reached one of the Indians. Immediately, he sought out Fletcher Christian, who half-confirmed

---

15. They weren't all Englishmen. At least one was a Scot.

and half-denied it. The Indian stormed out without waiting for Christian's attempted clarification.

Ironically, Christian had just a little time earlier told his right-hand man, Edward Young, of his plans to have the land divided up into thirteen parcels, not just nine, so that the Maori men would also have their fair share. But the irate Indian didn't stay to listen to what he had to say. Interestingly, Christian had also told Young that he was content to have his two sons reared in the heathen religion of their mother. He felt that there was no advantage to their learning to read or write, a virtual prerequisite of following the Christian religion.

After leaving Fletcher in a huff, the irate Maori man reached the chief, just as the latter was inspecting the remains of what *had* been his new home. It had been burned down, most likely by Quintal, who had claimed the land was his! The Indians were so furious, they met together and decided that the island would not rest till all nine of the European men were dead. They held a pagan service and believed that the gods were pleased with their deadly plan.

The next day, September 22, 1793, the savage butchery began. The Indians beheaded their first victim and crushed to death the skull of their second. Two of them even adorned their belts with the heads of the slain. The colony was sinking quickly into uncivilized depravity.

The chief shot Fletcher Christian with a musket. He didn't die instantly, but he was mortally wounded. He died soon after. Alexander Smith was also shot and left for dead. Eventually, he recovered.

The chief came upon Quintal and could easily have killed him at close range with his musket, but he thought it more honorable to kill him in hand-to-hand combat. That proved to be a mistake. After a bloody and grueling fight, the chief attempted to kick his opponent off the bluff. Instead, the strong white man grabbed the Indian's leg and tossed his whole body off the cliff. He plunged to his death on the sharp rocks some five hundred feet below.

When Quintal returned to his cottage, battered, bruised, and bleeding, he found the three heads of the remaining Indians! They had been beheaded by the widows, who had sworn vengeance for their murdered husbands. But the women feared reprisal from the Indian women, so they begged Quintal to claim credit for the three axe slayings. He agreed and upheld their secret.

The pain from those two days of slaughter was numbing, even for these rough sailors and their women, who had been exposed to much hardship. One of the unsavory men who survived, William McCoy, began to distill gin. And many were glad to imbibe.

For the next several months, the colony sunk into complete debauchery. The four men and three of the women drank all the time, bringing out the worst in them. The other women, concerned about the children, found the situation intolerable. They even tried to escape the island, but providentially their boat was capsized not far from Pitcairn. Smith spotted them, and everybody was rescued. I say providentially because if they had gotten farther, they would most likely have been capsized but would not have been able to have been rescued.

This sobered the men up . . . for a couple of days only. So the debauchery continued. Then, most of the women, led by Christian's widow, took the little children and made a settlement on the other side of the island.

The men kept up with their drinking. McCoy drank so much, he drove himself to insanity. One day, he ran to his death off the high bluff. Quintal also got more and more insane with drink, and he became more and more like a wild savage than a civilized man. Finally, he was put to death by an axe to the head. Everyone sighed in relief.

This left only two of the Englishmen: Young and Smith. They reestablished good relations with the women and children.

One day, as Smith was cleaning out what had been Fletcher Christian's room, he came across the silver-clasped Bible from the *Bounty* and the Prayer Book. They were the only two books on the island. He asked Young to teach him how to read since he didn't know how. Every day for months on end, Young taught him how, using the Bible. Smith suggested they teach the children to read, but Young didn't think that wise because all they had were those two books, and he thought the Bible would just confuse the children. Smith wasn't quite sure, but in any event, Young died soon thereafter (of natural causes)—the first such death on Pitcairn!

Smith now started reading the Bible for himself. This find, coupled with his desire for the children to know a different way of life than that of their fathers, would prove to be the catalysts for a great change on the island.

He began to understand the love of God and the grace of God. In his own words, as he was reading through the whole Bible: "When I came to the Life of Jesus, my heart began to open like doors swingin' apart. Once I was sure God was a loving and merciful Father to them that repent, it seemed to me I could feel His very presence, sir, and I grew more sure every day of His guiding hand." Alexander Smith, former drunken sailor and last adult male survivor of the disaster that was the Pitcairn colony, was converted to Christ!

About a decade later, in 1809, by the time the first ship from the outside managed to reach Pitcairn Island, they found a peaceful and overall blissful colony, led by Alexander Smith (who eventually changed his name to John Adams). Every evening there were public devotions with Smith reading from the open Bible. The colony had been transformed by the application of the Word of God. The anger and hostility that had once soaked the island in blood was gone. The island had become a virtual paradise because it had become a Christ-centered place. In fact, the settlement developed such a level of Christianity that in the nineteenth century "Pitcairn" became a byword for piety! That's a far cry from the murderous hotbed of anger it had once been. Through Christ, the tropical paradise had been restored!

---

This story is truly astounding. What a monument to the grace of God.

I highly recommend the interested reader pick up a copy of *Pitcairn's Island* and devour it, although be forewarned that it gets violent at times. But even the fascinating details of their debauchery point to the love of God and grace of God that was ultimately to take over. What a difference when Jesus Christ reigns supreme in the human heart!

# SECTION 5

# LUST

Ours is a culture saturated with lust, although, I daresay, it's worse in some parts of Western Europe than here. Lust is, according to Webster's, an "intense or unrestrained sexual desire." Advertisers have cashed in on it for quite a while now, using sex to sell anything from soap to cars. Television is often saturated with sex. Sexual images are regular fare on prime-time television.[1] And, of course, movies are constantly showing illicit sex—and often in ways that defy reality. You see the promiscuity but not the effects of it.

Our culture is so saturated with lust that it's hard sometimes for a conscientious parent to shield his or her children from the garbage out there. Recently, a friend took my son and me out on a boat ride. We stopped for lunch at a hotel available by boat. We were all set to order when a lady announced on the loudspeaker that it was time for the bikini fashion show! Before we knew it, well-endowed, scantily clad beauties descended on the crowd and were parading back and forth. We left right away, but what a shame that our society keeps stooping so low. People often sell their souls (and their bodies) just to make a buck.

A classic tale of lust unbridled is Don Giovanni (or Don Juan in other cultures). Here's a brief description of the title character from *Don Giovanni* by E. T. A. Hoffmann (1776–1822). It is a devastating critique of the lust-filled rogue who only cares about himself in his sexual conquests:

> Feverishly the Don rushes from one beautiful woman to another, avidly drinking his fill of their charms until satiated and intoxicated. Per-

---

1. For details of this point, see William Murchison, "TV Is Demolishing Culture," *AFA Journal* (March 1996), 9.

petually disillusioned, yet ever hoping to attain the ideal that will satisfy his longing, he finds life dull and tedious, comes to despise the whole of mankind and revels against the creature who, once the embodiment of his ideal vision, has so bitterly disappointed him. When he takes a woman, it is now no longer an act of sensual gratification but a wanton affront to God and Nature. . . . Each occasion he seduces another man's bride, each time he makes a savage assault on the happiness of two young people, doing their love an irreparable harm, he feels a glorious sense of triumph over that power, a triumph that lifts him out of the suffocating confines of life and sets him above Nature, above the Creator Himself.[2]

The sexual revolution, which has glorified the Don Juan type, has promoted "free love"—only to find out it's not "free." In fact, there's a high price to pay for so-called free love, at least at the back end. There is spiritual damage, emotional damage, and even physical damage (through various diseases) in the wake of promiscuity. More than fifty million Americans now suffer from an incurable (treatable, yes, curable, no) viral sexually transmitted disease, such as herpes or hepatitis B![3]

The following stories, classic and modern, focus on lust. They show how destructive sexual desire can be when not channeled in the proper way.

2.  Heinrich Von Kleist, Ludwig Tieck, E. T. A. Hoffmann, *Six German Romantic Tales*, translated with an introduction by Ronald Taylor (Chester Springs, Pa.: Dufours Editions, 1993), 113–14.

3.  *Miami Herald*, 1 April 1993.

*This selection is NOT suitable for children, or is suitable with caution. The moral of the story is homosexual lust leads to destruction—in this case, literally!*

# THE DESTRUCTION OF SODOM AND GOMORRAH

### from the Book of Genesis (NIV)

What happens when lust gets totally out of hand? That's how it was in Sodom and Gomorrah before it was razed by God. The degree to which lust dominated this wicked city can be seen in the incident when the Sodomite men came to the door and surrounded it, demanding the strangers come out so they could sodomize them.

Homosexuality has made great inroads in our society. The tragedy is that history is strewn with cultures where homosexuality gained ascendancy. But written in stone, as it were, for all time, is what happened in these twin cities near the dawn of recorded history.

This story is found in Genesis 19.

---

The two angels arrived at Sodom in the evening, and Lot was sitting in the gateway of the city. When he saw them, he got up to meet them and bowed down with his face to the ground. "My lords," he said, "please turn aside to your servant's house. You can wash your feet and spend the night and then go on your way early in the morning."

"No," they answered, "we will spend the night in the square."

But he insisted so strongly that they did go with him and entered his house. He prepared a meal for them, baking bread without yeast, and they ate. Before they had gone to bed, all the men from every part of the city of Sodom—both young and old—surrounded the house. They called to Lot, "Where are the men who came to you tonight? Bring them out to us so that we can have sex with them."

Lot went outside to meet them and shut the door behind him and said, "No, my friends. Don't do this wicked thing. Look, I have two daughters who have never slept with a man. Let me bring them out to you, and you can do what you like with them. But don't do anything to these men, for they have come under the protection of my roof."

"Get out of our way," they replied. And they said, "This fellow came here as an alien, and now he wants to play the judge! We'll treat you worse than them." They kept bringing pressure on Lot and moved forward to break down the door.

But the men inside reached out and pulled Lot back into the house and shut the door. Then they struck the men who were at the door of the house, young and old, with blindness so that they could not find the door.

The two men said to Lot, "Do you have anyone else here—sons-in-law, sons or daughters, or anyone else in the city who belongs to you? Get them out of here, because we are going to destroy this place. The outcry to the LORD against its people is so great that he has sent us to destroy it."

So Lot went out and spoke to his sons-in-law, who were pledged to marry his daughters. He said, "Hurry and get out of this place, because the LORD is about to destroy the city!" But his sons-in-law thought he was joking.

With the coming of dawn, the angels urged Lot, saying, "Hurry! Take your wife and your two daughters who are here, or you will be swept away when the city is punished."

When he hesitated, the men grasped his hand and the hands of his wife and of his two daughters and led them safely out of the city, for the Lord was merciful to them. As soon as they had brought them out, one of them said, "Flee for your lives! Don't look back, and don't stop anywhere in the plain! Flee to the mountains or you will be swept away!"

But Lot said to them, "No, my lords, please! Your servant has found favor in your eyes, and you have shown great kindness to me in sparing my life. But I can't flee to the mountains; this disaster will overtake me, and I'll die. Look, here is a town near enough to run to, and it is small. Let me flee to it—it is very small, isn't it? Then my life will be spared."

He said to him, "Very well, I will grant this request too; I will not overthrow the town you speak of. But flee there quickly, because I cannot do anything until you reach it." (That is why the town was called Zoar.)

By the time Lot reached Zoar, the sun had risen over the land. Then the LORD rained down burning sulfur on Sodom and Gomorrah—from the LORD out of the heavens. Thus he overthrew those cities and the entire plain, including all those living in the cities—and also the vegetation in the land. But Lot's wife looked back and she became a pillar of salt.

Early the next morning Abraham got up and returned to the place where he had stood before the LORD. He looked down toward Sodom and Gomorrah, toward all the land of the plain, and he saw dense smoke rising from the land, like smoke from a furnace.

So when God destroyed the cities of the plain, he remembered Abraham, and he brought Lot out of the catastrophe that overthrew the cities where Lot had lived.

---

Notice how warped Lot's thinking had become by being immersed in that culture. He offers his own daughters to those lusting men at the door, as if they were mere objects to appease them. The whole city had degenerated to the degree that even the only godly family there was affected by the sin of Sodom.

As clear as this passage is, believe it or not, there are "homosexual Bible scholars" who claim—with a straight face!—that the sin of Sodom and Gomorrah was not homosexuality, but rather, the sin of inhospitality! Well, they certainly were that too, but clearly from the passage (and Jude 7), their sexual perversions are evident for all to see. The destruction of Sodom and Gomorrah is an eternal reminder that unchecked lust, whether of homosexual or heterosexual nature, leads to death and destruction.

But again, just as there is forgiveness for the repentant heterosexual, there is forgiveness for the repentant homosexual. Thankfully, many former homosexuals have found freedom in Christ.[4]

---

4. If you or someone you know is struggling with this, contact Exodus International for the local group near you. The numbers are 415-454-1017 or 407-629-5770.

*This selection is suitable for children.*
*The moral of the story is to flee sexual temptation.*

# JOSEPH AND POTIPHAR'S WIFE

### from the Book of Genesis (NIV)

Obviously, many of these lust-related stories are negative in nature. They have been written in stone, if you will, so we can see clearly what we are to avoid. Now we come to a story on lust that has a positive ending. Here we have a story with someone whose actions we should emulate. Here is the story in which Potiphar's wife makes repeated advances on Joseph. He in response provides for us the all-time model of what to do when tempted sexually—flee!

Joseph has been sold into slavery in Egypt by his jealous brothers. Now he is in a foreign land, knowing no one, and a mere slave at that. Yet, because God is with him, he has prospered in everything he has done. Now he is about to be tested again.

This story is found in Genesis 39.

———————

Now Joseph had been taken down to Egypt. Potiphar, an Egyptian who was one of Pharaoh's officials, the captain of the guard, bought him from the Ishmaelites who had taken him there.

The LORD was with Joseph and he prospered, and he lived in the house of his Egyptian master. When his master saw that the LORD was with him and that the LORD gave him success in everything he did, Joseph found favor in his eyes and became his attendant. Potiphar put him in charge of his household, and he entrusted to his care everything he owned. From the time he put him in charge of his household and of all that he owned, the LORD blessed the household of the Egyptian because of Joseph. The blessing of the LORD was on everything Potiphar had, both in the house and in the field. So he left in Joseph's care everything he had; with Joseph in charge, he did not concern himself with anything except the food he ate.

Now Joseph was well-built and handsome, and after a while his master's wife took notice of Joseph and said, "Come to bed with me!"

But he refused. "With me in charge," he told her, "my master does not concern himself with anything in the house; everything he owns he has entrusted to my care. No one is greater in this house than I am. My master has withheld nothing from me except you, because you are his wife. How then could I do such a wicked thing and sin against God?" And though she spoke to Joseph day after day, he refused to go to bed with her or even be with her.

One day he went into the house to attend to his duties, and none of the household servants was inside. She caught him by his cloak and said, "Come to bed with me!" But he left his cloak in her hand and ran out of the house.

When she saw that he had left his cloak in her hand and had run out of the house, she called her household servants. "Look," she said to them, "this Hebrew has been brought to us to make sport of us! He came in here to sleep with me, but I screamed. When he heard me scream for help, he left his cloak beside me and ran out of the house."

She kept his cloak beside her until his master came home. Then she told him this story: "That Hebrew slave you brought us came to me to make sport of me. But as soon as I screamed for help, he left his cloak beside me and ran out of the house."

When his master heard the story his wife told him, saying, "This is how your slave treated me," he burned with anger. Joseph's master took him and put him in prison, the place where the king's prisoners were confined.

But while Joseph was there in the prison, the LORD was with him; he showed him kindness and granted him favor in the eyes of the prison warden. So the warden put Joseph in charge of all those held in the prison, and he was made responsible for all that was done there. The warden paid no attention to anything under Joseph's care, because the LORD was with Joseph and gave him success in whatever he did.

---

Note Joseph's unsophisticated method for dealing with temptation. He didn't sit down and write out a "pro" and "con" list as some of us do when weighing a decision. He didn't sit down and try to reason with Potiphar's wife. He didn't even entertain in his own mind whether or not he should sleep with her. To him, it was not an option, so he rebuffed her. When she persisted, he fled.

Obviously, he wasn't instantly rewarded for having fled. (But he did keep his conscience clear.) Instead, he was falsely accused of doing the very thing he carefully avoided. But in the long run, he was richly rewarded by God for his righteous response.

Joseph provides some timeless keys in dealing with sexual temptation. Don't be in the wrong place at the wrong time. And if or when you find yourself in the wrong place at the wrong time, then flee. Get out of there quickly! Don't be like Samson, seeing how far you can go without getting burned. Just leave.

*This selection is suitable for children, with caution.*
*The moral of the story is guard your heart from lust, for lust can lead to devastating consequences.*

# DAVID AND BATHSHEBA

### retold by Jesse Hurlbut

David was at the wrong place at the wrong time. His people were at war, and he should have been with them. But he wasn't.

At this particular phase of life, David was at the top of his career. Earlier in his life, he had undergone immense struggles. He had been promised to be the king long before the realization of this position. Even after he knew he would be king one day, he was chased throughout the countryside and hunted down like a rabbit by King Saul, who was insanely jealous of him. (See "Saul and David" in the Envy section, p. 152). He spent nights in caves. He lived for a time in the nation of the enemy. At one point, he even pretended to be insane to escape with his life! But now all those horrible days were over. Instead, he was the king over Israel at what turned out to be its most prosperous time. And yet, it was precisely at this time that he was proven to be vulnerable to the sin of lust.

This story is taken from 2 Samuel 11.

---

When David first became king, he went with his army upon the wars against the enemies of Israel. But there came a time when the cares of his kingdom were many, and David left Joab, his general, to lead his warriors, while he stayed in his palace on Mount Zion.

One evening, about sunset, David was walking upon the roof of his palace. He looked down into a garden nearby and saw a woman, who was very beautiful. David asked one of his servants who this woman was, and he said to him, "Her name is Bathsheba, and she is the wife of Uriah."

Now Uriah was an officer in David's army, under Joab; and at that time he was fighting in David's war against the Ammonites, at Rabbah, near the desert on the east of Jordan. David sent for Uriah's wife, Bathsheba, and talked with her.[5] He loved her, and greatly longed to

---

5. Editor's note: David not only talked to her; he took her and made her pregnant. Trying to cover it up, he had Uriah come home on leave, and David got him drunk so he would sleep with his wife—even though a soldier was not supposed to during the war season. But David was unable to cover up his sin in this way.

take her as one of his own wives—for in those times it was not thought a sin for a man to have more than one wife. But David could not marry Bathsheba while her husband, Uriah, was living. Then a wicked thought came into David's heart and he formed a plan to have Uriah killed, so that he could then take Bathsheba into his own house.

David wrote a letter to Joab, the commander of his army. And in the letter he said, "When there is to be a fight with the Ammonites, send Uriah into the middle of it, where it will be the hottest; and manage to leave him there, so that he may be slain by the Ammonites."

And Joab did as David had commanded him. He sent Uriah with some brave men to a place near the wall of the city, where he knew that the enemies would rush out of the city upon them; there was a fierce fight beside the wall; Uriah was slain and other brave men with him. Then Joab sent a messenger to tell King David how the war was being carried on, and especially that Uriah, one of his brave officers, had been killed in the fighting.

When David heard this, he said to the messenger, "Say to Joab, 'Do not feel troubled at the loss of the men slain in battle. The sword must strike down some. Keep up the siege; press forward, and you will take the city.'"

And after Bathsheba had mourned for a time over her husband's death, David took her into his palace and she became his wife. And a little child was born to them, whom David loved greatly. Only Joab and David, and perhaps a few others, knew that David had caused the death of Uriah; but God knew it and God was displeased with David for this wicked deed.

Then the Lord sent Nathan, the prophet, to David to tell him that, though men knew not that David had done wickedly, God had seen it, and would surely punish David for his sin. Nathan came to David, and he spoke to him thus:

"There were two men in one city; one was rich, and the other poor. The rich man had great flocks of sheep and herds of cattle; but the poor man had only one little lamb that he had bought. It grew up in his home with his children, and drank out of his cup, and lay upon his lap, and was like a little daughter to him.

"One day a visitor came to the rich man's house to dinner. He did not take one of his own sheep to kill for his guest. He robbed the poor man of his lamb, and killed it, and cooked it for a meal with his friend."

When David heard this, he was very angry. He said to Nathan, "The man who did this thing deserves to die! He shall give back to his poor neighbor fourfold for the lamb taken from him. How cruel to treat a poor man thus, without pity for him!" And Nathan said to David, "You are the man who has done this deed. The Lord made you king in place of Saul, and gave you a kingdom. You have a great house and many wives. Why, then, have you done this wickedness in the sight of the Lord? You have slain Uriah with the sword of the men of Ammon; and you have taken his wife to be your wife. For this there shall be a sword drawn against your house; you shall suffer for it and your wives shall suffer and your children shall suffer, because you have done this."

When David heard all this, he saw, as he had not seen before, how great was his wickedness. He was exceedingly sorry; and said to Nathan, "I have sinned against the Lord."

And David showed such sorrow for his sin that Nathan said to him, "The Lord has forgiven your sin; and you shall not die on account of it. But the child that Uriah's wife has given to you shall surely die."

---

This was the beginning of new problems for David. In judgment for his sins, David faced new threats, mostly from within his own family! The next story is one such example. Note that even though David found mercy with God, he still faced terrible consequences for his sin. Even though God is merciful enough to forgive us our sins, we still are often scarred by their effects. There are millions alive today, scarred by the effects of their uncontrolled lust.

*This selection is NOT suitable for children or is suitable with caution.*
*The moral of the story is that lust takes (as opposed to love, which gives),*
*and lust leads to destruction.*

## AMNON AND TAMAR

### from the Book of 2 Samuel (NIV)

One thing I love about the Bible is that it spells it all out, warts and all. Often Christian biographies paint such glowing pictures of saints from long ago that we are intimidated because we feel we could never be like that. Chances are those Christians weren't nearly as perfect as the biographies would suggest. But the Bible isn't like that. It's realistic. It documents what actually happened. There's no public relations spin to place the characters always in the best possible light. That's even true for the commendable characters in the Scriptures like David.

Here's a big wart—involving one of the sons of David, Israel's all-time greatest king. After David's sin with Bathsheba, David's family life went downhill. God predicted this as a judgment against him for what he did with Bathsheba and Uriah the Hittite.

This story deals with one of the sons of David, Amnon. He confused love with lust, and he thought all the day long about how to fulfill his lust. And so, following his lustful impulses, he brought disaster upon his half-sister, himself and others.

The story also shows the problems fraught with polygamy. The New Testament does away with the plague of multiple marriages by prescribing that the godly man be the husband of but one wife.

The passage is 2 Samuel 13:1–33.

---

In the course of time, Amnon son of David fell in love with Tamar, the beautiful sister of Absalom son of David.

Amnon became frustrated to the point of illness on account of his sister Tamar, for she was a virgin, and it seemed impossible for him to do anything to her.

Now Amnon had a friend named Jonadab son of Shimeah, David's brother. Jonadab was a very shrewd man. He asked Amnon, "Why do you, the king's son, look so haggard morning after morning? Won't you tell me?"

Amnon said to him, "I'm in love with Tamar, my brother Absalom's sister."

"Go to bed and pretend to be ill," Jonadab said. "When your father comes to see you, say to him, 'I would like my sister Tamar to come and give me something to eat. Let her prepare the food in my sight so I may watch her and then eat it from her hand.'"

So Amnon lay down and pretended to be ill. When the king came to see him, Amnon said to him, "I would like my sister Tamar to come and make some special bread in my sight, so I may eat from her hand."

David sent word to Tamar at the palace: "Go to the house of your brother Amnon and prepare some food for him." So Tamar went to the house of her brother Amnon, who was lying down. She took some dough, kneaded it, made the bread in his sight and baked it. Then she took the pan and served him the bread but he refused to eat.

"Send everyone out of here," Amnon said. So everyone left him. Then Amnon said to Tamar, "Bring the food here into my bedroom so I may eat from your hand." And Tamar took the bread she had prepared and brought it to her brother Amnon in his bedroom. But when she took it to him to eat, he grabbed her and said, "Come to bed with me, my sister."

"Don't, my brother!" she said to him. "Don't force me. Such a thing should not be done in Israel! Don't do this wicked thing. What about me? Where could I get rid of my disgrace? And what about you? You would be like one of the wicked fools in Israel. Please speak to the king; he will not keep me from being married to you." But he refused to listen to her, and since he was stronger than she, he raped her.

Then Amnon hated her with intense hatred. In fact, he hated her more than he had loved her. Amnon said to her, "Get up and get out!"

"No!" she said to him. "Sending me away would be a greater wrong than what you have already done to me."

But he refused to listen to her. He called his personal servant and said, "Get this woman out of here and bolt the door after her. So his servant put her out and bolted the door after her. She was wearing a richly ornamented robe, for this was the kind of garment the virgin daughters of the king wore. Tamar put ashes on her head and tore the ornamented robe she was wearing. She put her hand on her head and went away, weeping aloud as she went.

Her brother Absalom said to her, "Has that Amnon, your brother, been with you? Be quiet now, my sister; he is your brother. Don't take this thing to heart." And Tamar lived in her brother Absalom's house, a desolate woman.

When King David heard all this, he was furious. Absalom never said a word to Amnon, either good or bad; he hated Amnon because he had disgraced his sister Tamar.

Two years later, when Absalom's sheepshearers were at Baal Hazor near the border of Ephraim, he invited all the king's sons to come there. Absalom went to the king and said, "Your servant has had shearers come. Will the king and his officials please join me?"

"No, my son," the king replied. "All of us should not go; we would only be a burden to you." Although Absalom urged him, he still refused to go, but gave him his blessing.

Then Absalom said, "If not, please let my brother Amnon come with us."

The king asked him, "Why should he go with you?" But Absalom urged him, so he sent with him Amnon and the rest of the king's sons.

Absalom ordered his men, "Listen! When Amnon is in high spirits from drinking wine and I say to you, 'Strike Amnon down,' then kill him. Don't be afraid. Have not I given you this order? Be strong and brave." So Absalom's men did to Amnon what Absalom had ordered. Then all the king's sons got up, mounted their mules and fled.

While they were on their way, the report came to David: "Absalom has struck down all the king's sons; not one of them is left." The king stood up, tore his clothes and lay down on the ground; and all his servants stood by with their clothes torn.

But Jonadab son of Shimeah, David's brother, said, "My lord should not think that they killed all the princes; only Amnon is dead. This has been Absalom's expressed intention ever since the day Amnon raped his sister Tamar. My lord the king should not be concerned about the report that all the king's sons are dead. Only Amnon is dead."

---

Isn't it fascinating that Amnon "loved" Tamar so much that he raped her and then afterward he "hated" her so much he wanted nothing to do with her? Lust can be like that. Lust must never be confused with love. Josh McDowell points out that lust takes, but love gives. This story underscores that reality.

*The following selection is NOT acceptable for children.*
*The moral of the story is that lust can lead to crazy and destructive actions.*

# THE ROMAN FEAST[6]

### from *Quo Vadis*
#### by Henryk Sienkiewicz, translated by Jeremiah Curtin

If lust is a serious problem in our present culture (and it is), it was also one in antiquity (perhaps even more so!). The following selection will give a taste of just how decadent ancient Rome could be.

This selection consists of a scene from the wonderful Christian novel *Quo Vadis,* written by the Polish writer Henryk Sienkiewicz. Hollywood did a great service by making a film out of this book in the 1950s. In this scene we see how the hero "loves" a beautiful woman he has barely met. At this point in the story his "love" is more of lust than love. At the Roman feast we see how these celebrations catered to man's base nature—sensual, gluttonous, and savage.

Sienkiewicz's *Quo Vadis* was first published in 1895. For three decades after that it became one of the most widely read novels in the world.[7] It is the story of Christians in the early Church struggling with the Roman government under Nero, as he was groping to establish policies on how to deal with them. *Quo Vadis,* writes English professor Clarence Andrews, "has never received great acclaim from the intellectual establishment, nor is it often taught in the universities, but it was acclaimed by the public from the beginning—and remains eminently readable today."[8] *Quo Vadis* is worth Christians' rediscovering; it makes for very enjoyable and edifying reading.

Some background information would be appropriate. A young man, Marcus Vinicius, chief co-protagonist of the book, is madly "in love" with Lygia (also known as Callina), although he has only met her once. (She's the other co-protagonist.) Although she is originally from another country and is even the daughter of a

---

6.   This text has been edited without the use of ellipses.

7.   Clarence A. Andrews, from his Introduction to Henryk Sienkiewicz, *Quo Vadis* (New York: Airmont Publishing Company, 1969), 5.

8.   Ibid., 8.

king, years ago her father gave her over to the Romans to settle a land dispute between his country and the Empire. Basically, the only home she has known is the loving household of Aulus (a pagan) and Pomponia (a Christian). Through Pomponia's influence, Lygia becomes a Christian. But now, Vinicius has managed to get Lygia removed from the home of Aulus and Pomponia. He was able to coordinate that because his conniving uncle, Petronius, has pull with Nero. Initially, Petronius' plan is to get her brought over to Nero's palace (where some ten thousand people dwell), and then a few days later, to quietly get her over to his nephew's house, so Vinicius can take her as his wife. Confused yet? Even if you don't follow all the details of the characters, it doesn't matter, for the lustfulness of the Roman Empire comes through clearly in the passage.

This is the first time Vinicius and Lygia meet since she has been uprooted from her home. She has led a rather sheltered life hitherto, and is therefore shocked at the excesses of the feast. But because she's a guest of Caesar's she cannot just get up and leave, unless she wants to possibly get killed for it. When this scene opens, Marcus Vinicius welcomes Lygia at the banquet.

---

"A greeting, most beautiful of maidens on earth and of stars in heaven. A greeting to thee, divine Callina!"

Lygia, having recovered somewhat, looked up; at her side was Vinicius.

He was without a toga, for convenience and custom had enjoined to cast aside the toga at feasts. His body was covered with only a sleeveless scarlet tunic embroidered in silver palms. His arms were bare, ornamented in Eastern fashion with two broad golden bands fastened above the elbow; below they were carefully stripped of hair. They were smooth, but too muscular,—real arms of a soldier, they were made for the sword and the shield. On his head he wore a garland of roses. With his brows joining above the nose, with splendid eyes and a dark complexion, he was the impersonation of youth and strength, as it were. To Lygia he seemed so beautiful that though her first amazement had passed, she was barely able to answer,—

"A greeting, Marcus."

"Happy," said he, "are my eyes, which see thee; happy my ears, which hear thy voice, dearer to me than the sound of lutes or citharas. Were it commanded to choose who was to rest here by my side at this feast, thou, Lygia, or Venus, I would choose thee, divine one!"

And he looked at the maiden as if he wished to sate himself with the sight of her, to burn her eyes with his eyes. His glance slipped from her face to her neck and bare arms, fondled her shapely out-lines, admired her, embraced her, devoured her; but besides desire, there was gleaming in him happiness, admiration, and ecstasy beyond limit.

"I knew that I should see thee in Caesar's house," continued he; "but still, when I saw thee, such delight shook my whole soul, as if a happiness entirely unexpected had met me."

Lygia, having recovered herself and feeling that in that throng and in that house he was the only being who was near to her, began to converse with him, and ask about everything which she did not understand and which filled her with fear. Whence did he know that he would find her in Caesar's house? Why is she here? Why did Cae-sar take her from Pomponia? She is full of fear where she is and wished to return to Pomponia. She would die from alarm and grief were it not for the hope that Petronius and he will intercede for her before Caesar.

Vinicius explained that he learned from Aulus himself that she had been taken. Why she was there, he does not know.[9] Caesar gives account to no one of his orders and commands. But let her not fear. He, Vinicius, is near her and will stay near her. He would rather lose his eyes than not see her; he would rather lose his life than desert her. She is his soul, and hence he will guard her as his soul. In his house he will build to her, as to a divinity, an altar on which he will offer myrrh and aloes, and in spring saffron and apple-blossoms; and since she has a dread of Caesar's house, he promises that she shall not stay in it.

And though he spoke evasively and at times invented, truth was to be felt in his voice, because his feelings were real. Genuine pity pos-sessed him, too, and her words went to his soul so thoroughly that when she began to thank him and assure him that Pomponia would love him for his goodness, and that she herself would be grateful to him all her life, he could not master his emotion, and it seemed to him that he would never be able in life to resist her prayer. The heart

---

9. This is a bold-faced lie. It was he who arranged for her to be uprooted from her home that he might acquire her. (See introductory remarks.)

began to melt in him. Her beauty intoxicated his senses, and he desired her; but at the same time he felt that she was very dear to him, and that in truth he might do homage to her, as to a divinity; he felt also irresistible need of speaking of her beauty and of his own homage. As the noise at the feast increased, he drew nearer to her, whispered kind, sweet words flowing from the depth of his soul, words as resonant as music and intoxicating as wine.

And he intoxicated her. Amid those strange people he seemed to her ever nearer, ever dearer, altogether true, and devoted with his whole soul. He pacified her; he promised to rescue her from the house of Caesar; he promised not to desert her, and said that he would serve her. Besides, he had spoken before at Aulus's only in general about love and the happiness which it can give; but now he said directly that he loved her, and that she was dear and most precious to him. Lygia heard such words from a man's lips for the first time; and as she heard them it seemed to her that something was wakening in her as from a sleep, that some species of happiness was embracing her in which immense delight was mingled with immense alarm. Her cheeks began to burn, her heart to beat, her mouth opened as if in wonder. She was seized with fear because she was listening to such things, and she did not wish for any cause on earth to lose one word. At moments she dropped her eyes; then again she raised her clear glance to Vinicius, timid and also inquiring, as if she wished to say to him, "Speak on!" The sound of the music, the odor of flowers and of Arabian perfumes, began to daze her. In Rome it was the custom to recline at banquets, but at home Lygia occupied a place between Pomponia and little Aulus. Now Vinicius was reclining near her, youthful, immense, in love, burning; and she, feeling the heat that issued from him, felt both delight and shame. A kind of sweet weakness, a kind of faintness and forgetfulness seized her; it was as if drowsiness tortured her.

But her nearness to him began to act on Vinicius also. His nostrils dilated, like those of an Eastern steed. The beating of his heart with unusual throb was evident under his scarlet tunic; his breathing grew short, and the expressions that fell from his lips were broken. For the first time, too, he was so near her. His thoughts grew disturbed; he felt a flame in his veins which he tried in vain to quench with wine. Not wine, but her marvelous face, her bare arms, her maiden breast heaving under the golden tunic, and her form hidden in the white folds of the peplus,[10] intoxicated him more and more. Finally, he seized her arm above the wrist, as he had done once at Aulus's, and drawing her toward him whispered with trembling lips,—

"I love thee, Callina,—divine one."

"Let me go, Marcus," said Lygia.

But he continued, his eyes mist-covered, "Love me, my goddess!"

But at that moment was heard the voice of Acte,[11] who was reclining on the other side of Lygia.

"Caesar is looking at you both."

Vinicius was carried away by sudden anger at Caesar and at Acte. Her words had broken the charm of his intoxication. To the young man even a friendly voice would have seemed repulsive at such a moment; but he judged that Acte wished purposely to interrupt his conversation with Lygia. So, raising his head and looking over the shoulder of Lygia at the young freedwoman, he said with malice,—

"The hour has passed, Acte, when thou didst rest near Caesar's side at banquets, and they say that blindness is threatening thee; how then canst thou see him?"

But she answered as if in sadness: "Still I see him. He, too, has short sight, and is looking at thee through an emerald."

Everything that Nero did roused attention, even in those nearest him; hence Vinicius was alarmed. He regained self-control, and began imperceptibly to look toward Caesar. Lygia, who, embarrassed at the beginning of the banquet, had seen Nero as in a mist, and afterward, occupied by the presence and conversation of Vinicius, had not looked at him at all, turned to him eyes at once curious and terrified.

Acte spoke truly. Caesar had bent over the table, half closed one eye, and holding before the other a round polished emerald, which he used, was looking at them. For a moment his glance met Lygia's eyes and the heart of the maiden was straitened with terror. When still a child on Aulus's Sicilian estate, an old Egyptian slave had told her of dragons which occupied dens in the mountains, and it seemed to her now that all at once the greenish eye of such a monster was gazing at her. She caught at Vinicius's hand as a frightened child would, and

---

10. A garment like a shawl.

11. Acte lives in the household of Caesar (as do ten thousand others). She is the "former favorite of Nero," but having dropped her, he still lets her live there with some servants of her own. She is beautiful and has a lovely figure, so he likes having her at his banquets. Acte has now become a Christian and exerts a godly influence whenever she can. She protects Lygia from harm during the short time that she remains in Caesar's household.

disconnected, quick impressions pressed into her head: Was not that he, the terrible, the all-powerful? She had not seen him hitherto, and she thought that he looked differently. She had imagined some kind of ghastly face, with malignity petrified in it's features; now she saw a great head, fixed on a thick neck, terrible, it is true, but almost ridiculous, for from a distance, it resembled the head of a child. Under that forehead of a demigod was the face of a monkey, a drunkard, and a comedian,—vain, full of changing desires, swollen with fat, notwithstanding his youthful years; besides, it was sickly and foul. To Lygia he seemed ominous, but above all repulsive.

After a while he laid down the emerald and ceased to look at her. Then she saw his prominent blue eyes, blinking before the excess of light, glassy, without thought, resembling the eyes of the dead.

"Is that the hostage with whom Vinicius is in love?" asked he, turning to Petronius.

"That is she," answered Petronius.

"What are her people called?"

"The Lygians."

"Does Vinicius think her beautiful?"

"Array a rotten olive trunk in the peplus of a woman, and Vinicius will declare it beautiful. But on thy countenance, incomparable judge, I read her sentence already. Thou hast no need to pronounce it! The sentence is true: she is too dry, thin, a mere blossom on a slender stalk; and thou, O divine aesthete, esteem the stalk in a woman. Thrice and four times art thou right! The face alone does not signify. I have learned much in thy company, but even yet I have not a perfect cast of the eye."

The feast grew more animated. Crowds of slaves bore around new courses every moment; from great vases filled with snow and garlanded with ivy, smaller vessels with various kinds of wine were brought forth unceasingly. All drank freely; roses fell on the guests from the ceiling at intervals.

Verses were read or dialogues listened to in which extravagance took the place of wit. After that Paris, the celebrated mime, represented the adventures of Io, the daughter of Inachus. To the guests, and especially to Lygia, unaccustomed to such scenes, it seemed that they were gazing at miracles and enchantment. Paris, with motions of his hands and body, was able to express things apparently impossible in a dance. His hands dimmed the air, creating a cloud, bright, living, quivering, voluptuous, surrounding the half-fainting form of a maiden shaken by a spasm of delight. That was a picture, not a dance; an expressive picture, disclosing the secrets of love, bewitching and shameless; and when at the end of it Corybantes rushed in and began a bacchic dance with girls of Syria to the sounds of cithara, lutes, drums, and cymbals,—a dance filled with wild sounds and wilder license,—it seemed to Lygia that living fire was burning her, and that a thunderbolt ought to strike that house, or the ceiling fall on the heads of those feasting there.

But from the golden net fastened to the ceiling only roses were falling, and the now half-drunken Vinicius said to her,—

"I saw thee in the house of Aulus, at the fountain. It was daylight, and thou didst think that no one saw thee; but I saw thee. And I see thee thus yet, though that peplus conceals thee from me. Cast aside the peplus, like Crispinilla. See, gods and men seek love. There is nothing in the world but love. Lay thy head on my breast and close thy eyes."

The pulse beat oppressively in Lygia's hands and temples. A feeling seized her that she was flying into some abyss, and that Vinicius, who before had seemed so near and so trustworthy, instead of saving was drawing her toward it. And she felt sorry for him. She began again to dread the feast and him and herself. Some voice, like that of Pomponia, was calling yet in her soul, "O Lygia, save thyself!" But something told her also that it was too late. She grew weak. It seemed at moments to her that she would faint, and then something terrible would happen. She knew that, under penalty of Caesar's anger, it was not permitted anyone to rise till Caesar rose; but even were that not the case, she had not strength now to rise.

Meanwhile it was far to the end of the feast yet. Slaves brought more new courses, and filled the goblets unceasingly with wine; but before the table, on a platform open at one side, appeared two athletes to give the guests a spectacle of wrestling.

They began at once, and the powerful bodies, shining from olive oil, formed one mass; bones cracked in their iron arms, and from their set jaws came an ominous gritting of teeth. At moments were heard the quick, dull thump of their feet on the platform strewn with saffron; again they were motionless, silent, and it seemed to the spectators that they had before them a group chiseled out of stone. Roman eyes followed with delight the movement of tremendously

exerted backs, thighs, and arms. But the struggle was not too pro-
longed; for Croton, a master, and the founder of a school of gladiators, did not pass in vain for the strongest man in the empire. His
opponent began to breathe more and more quickly: next there was a
rattle heard in his throat; then his face grew blue; finally he threw
blood from his mouth and fell.

A thunder of applause greeted the end of the struggle, and Croton,
resting his foot on the breast of his opponent, crossed his gigantic
arms on his breast, and cast the eyes of a victor around the hall.

Next appeared men who mimicked beasts and their voices, ball-
players and buffoons. Only few looked at them, however, since wine
had darkened the eyes of the audience. The feast passed by degrees
into a drunken revel and a dissolute orgy. The Syrian damsels, who
appeared at first in the bacchic dance, mingled now with the guests.
The music changed into a disordered and wild outburst of citharas,
lutes, Armenian cymbals, Egyptian sistra, trumpets, and horns. As
some of the guests wished to talk, they shouted at the musicians to
disappear. The air, filled with odor of flowers and the perfume of oils
with which beautiful boys had sprinkled the feet of the guests during
the feast, permeated with saffron and the exhalations of people,
became stifling; lamps burned with a dim flame; the wreaths dropped
sidewise on the heads of guests; faces grew pale and were covered
with sweat. Vitelius rolled under the table. Nigidia, stripping herself to
the waist, dropped her drunken childlike head on the breast of
Lucan, who, drunk in like degree, fell to blowing the golden powder
from her hair, and raising his eyes with immense delight.

Caesar drank himself drunk at last; men were drunk, and women
were drunk. Vinicius was not less drunk than others; and in addition
there was roused in him, besides desire, a wish to quarrel, which
happened always when he passed the measure. His dark face
became paler, and his tongue stuttered when he spoke, in a voice
now loud and commanding,—

"Give me thy lips! To-day, to-morrow, it is all one! Enough of this!
Caesar took thee from Aulus to give thee to me, dost understand? Tomorrow, about dusk, I will send for thee, dost understand? Caesar
promised thee to me before he took thee. Thou must be mine! Give
me thy lips! I will not wait for to-morrow,—give thy lips quickly!"

And he moved to embrace her; but Acte began to defend her, and
she defended herself with the remnant of her strength, for she felt

that she was perishing. But in vain did she struggle with both hands to remove his hairless arm; in vain, with a voice in which terror and grief were quivering, did she implore him not to be what he was, and to have pity on her. Sated with wine, his breath blew around her nearer and nearer, and his face was there near her face. He was no longer the former kind Vinicius, almost dear to her soul; he was a drunken, wicked satyr, who filled her with repulsion and terror. But her strength deserted her more and more. In vain did she bend and turn away her face to escape his kisses. He rose to his feet, caught her in both arms, and, drawing her head to his breast, began, panting, to press her pale lips with his.

But at this instant a tremendous power removed his arms from her neck with as much ease as if they had been the arms of a child, and pushed him aside, like a dried limb or a withered leaf. What had happened? Vinicius rubbed his astonished eyes, and saw before him the gigantic figure of the Lygian, called Ursus,[12] whom he had seen at the house of Aulus.

The Lygian stood calmly, and merely looked at Vinicius so strangely with his blue eyes that the blood stiffened in the veins of the young man; then he took his queen on his arm, and walked out of the triclinium[13] with an even, quiet step.

Acte in that moment went after him.

Vinicius sat for the twinkle of an eye as if petrified; then he sprang up and ran toward the entrance, crying,—

"Lygia! Lygia!"

But desire, astonishment, rage, and wine cut the legs from under him. He staggered once and a second time, seized the naked arm of one of the bacchanals, and began to inquire, with blinking eyes, what had happened. She, taking a goblet of wine, gave it to him with a smile in her mist-covered eyes.

"Drink!" she said.

Vinicius drank, and fell to the floor.

The greater number of the guests were lying under the table; others were walking with tottering tread through the triclinium, while others were sleeping on couches at the table, snoring, or giving forth the excess of wine. Meanwhile, from the golden network, roses were

---

12. Ursus was an exceedingly strong man, who had been a servant of Lygia from her childhood. He went with her when she went to Caesar's household, as did a couple other servants.

13. A dining room.

dropping and dropping continually on those drunken consuls and senators, on those drunken knights, philosophers, and poets, on those drunken dancing damsels and Patrician ladies, on that society all dominant as yet but with the soul gone from it, on that society garlanded and ungirdled but perishing.

Dawn had begun out of doors.

---

*Quo Vadis* goes on to show that that which attracted Marcus Vinicius to Lygia (apart from her beauty) in the first place was her character that resulted from her love of Christ. Ultimately, he too becomes a Christian through her influence.

This selection gives a taste of how decadent and lust-saturated ancient Rome was. Sienkiewicz has made this point through the medium of historical fiction. Meanwhile, in the nonfiction genre, Dr. Kennedy and I have a lot of details on that point in chapter 9 of *What If Jesus Had Never Been Born?* For instance, summing up the historical knowledge of one of the century's greatest historians, Will Durant, we write:

> Durant says that prostitution was so common in ancient Rome that sometimes the votes of politicians had to be collected through the collegium lupanariorum, which was the "guild of brothel-keepers"! Durant adds: "Adultery was so common as to attract little attention unless played up for political purposes, and practically every well-to-do woman had at least one divorce." He writes further: "The Roman, like the Greek, readily condoned the resorts of men to prostitutes. The profession was legalized and restricted . . . The elder Seneca assumed widespread adultery among Roman women."[14]

In short, the ancient pagan world, including Rome, the zenith of culture at that time, was a lust-saturated culture. Historians say, as we show in *What If Jesus Had Never Been Born?,* it was Christianity more than anything else that changed that!

---

14. *What If Jesus Had Never Been Born?*, 128–29.

*Most of this selection is NOT suitable for children or is suitable with caution. The overall moral of the story is to flee youthful lusts.*

# ST. AUGUSTINE'S STRUGGLE WITH LUST

### from *The Confessions of St. Augustine*

Although Augustine—whom we met briefly in the story of the Stolen Fruit—was "*St.* Augustine," the man was anything but a saint in his early life! He had a serious problem with sexual lust; hence, his writings on the subject and his Christian conversion are included in this section of the book. As a young man, Augustine prayed to the effect, "Lord, make me sexually pure—but not yet!" An exact translation of his unorthodox prayer is: "Give me chastity and continence, but not yet!" (book 8, chapter 7).[15]

On the subject of lust, Augustine said (speaking to God): "I broke your laws, but I did not escape your scourges. For what mortal man can do that?"[16] "Then [when he was sixteen years old] it was that the madness of lust, licensed by human shamelessness but forbidden by your laws, took me completely under its scepter, and I clutched it with both hands."[17] He describes himself "a most wicked servant of base lusts."[18] He also told how, as a young man, he "dragged along my chains [of lust] and was fearful of being loosed from them."[19] Here is the true story, albeit from the fourth century, of a "slave to lust" who was set free through the gospel of Christ.

The entire book is a prayer. Therefore, any reference to "you" is a reference to God.

---

In those years [as a young man, pre-conversion] I had a woman companion, not one joined to me in what is named lawful wedlock, but one whom my wandering passion, empty of prudence, had picked up. But I had this one only, and moreover I was faithful to her bed. With her I learned first hand how great a distance lies between the restraint of a conjugal covenant, mutually made for the sake of

---

15. Trans. by John K. Ryan, *The Confessions of St. Augustine*, 194.
16. Ibid., 66.
17. Ibid., 66–67.
18. Ibid., 111.
19. Ibid., 151.

begetting offspring, and the bargain of a lustful love, where a child is born against our will, although once born he forces himself upon our love (book 4, chapter 2).[20]

### The Inner Conflict

The enemy had control of my will, and out of it he fashioned a chain and fettered me with it. For in truth lust is made out of a perverse will, and when lust is served, it becomes habit, and when habit is not resisted, it becomes necessity. By such links, joined one to another, as it were—for this reason I have called it a chain—a harsh bondage held me fast. A new will, which had begun within me, to wish freely to worship you and find joy in you, O God, the sole sure delight, was not yet able to overcome that prior will, grown strong with age. Thus did my two wills, the one old, the other new, the first carnal, and the second spiritual, contend with one another, and by their conflict they laid waste my soul.

Thus I understood from my own experience what I had read, how "the flesh lusts against the spirit, and the spirit against the flesh." I was in both camps, but I was more in that which I approved within myself than in that other which I disapproved within me. . . . Yet I was still bound to the earth, and I refused to become your soldier. I was afraid to be lightened of all my heavy burden, even as I should have feared to be encumbered by it.

Thus by the burdens of this world I was sweetly weighed down, just as a man often is in sleep. Thoughts wherein I meditated upon you were like the efforts of those who want to arouse themselves but, still overcome by deep drowsiness, sink back again. Just as no man would want to sleep forever, and it is the sane judgment of all men that it is better to be awake, yet a man often defers to shake off sleep when a heavy languor pervades all his members, and although the time to get up has come, he yields to it with pleasure even although it now irks him. In like manner, I was sure that it was better for me to give myself up to your love than to give in to my own desires. However, although the one way appealed to me and was gaining mastery, the other still afforded me pleasure and kept me victim. I had no answer to give to you when you said to me, "Rise, you who sleep, and arise from the dead, and Christ will enlighten you." When on all

---

20. Ibid., 94.

sides you showed me that your words were true, and I was overcome by your truth, I had no answer whatsoever to make, but only those slow and drowsy words, "Right away. Yes, right away." "Let me be for a little while." But "Right away—Right away" was never right now, and "Let me be for a little while" stretched out for a long time.

In vain was I delighted with your law according to the inward man, when another law in my members fought against the law of my mind, and led me captive in the law of sin which was in my members. For the law of sin is force of habit, whereby the mind is dragged along and held fast, even against its will, but still deservedly so, since it was by its will that it had slipped into the habit. Unhappy man that I was! Who would deliver me from the body of this death, unless your grace through Jesus Christ our Lord? (Book 8, chapter 5.)[21]

### The Naked Self

Ponticianus told us this story [of the ascetic, self-disciplined Christian monk, Anthony of Egypt], and as he spoke, you, O Lord, turned me back upon myself. You took me from behind my own back, where I had placed myself because I did not wish to look upon myself. You stood me face to face with myself, so that I might see how foul I was, how deformed and defiled, how covered with stains and sores. I looked, and I was filled with horror, but there was no place for me to flee to away from myself. If I tried to turn my gaze from myself, he still went on with the story that he was telling, and once again you placed me in front of myself, and thrust me before my own eyes, so that I might find out my iniquity and hate it. I knew what it was, but I pretended not to; I refused to look at it, and put it out of my memory. . . .

I, a most wretched youth, most wretched from the very start of my youth, had even sought chastity from you, and had said, "Give me chastity and continence [self-restraint, especially sexually], but not yet!" For I feared that you would hear me quickly, and that quickly you would heal me of that disease of lust, which I wished to have satisfied rather than extinguished. . . .

Thus was I gnawed within myself, and I was overwhelmed with shame and horror, while Ponticianus spoke of such things. . . . All arguments were used up, and all had been refuted (book 8, chapter 7).[22]

---

21. Ibid., 189–90.
22. Ibid., 193–94.

### The Voice as of a Child

But when deep reflection had dredged out of the secret recesses of my soul all my misery and heaped it up in full view of my heart, there arose a mighty storm, bringing with it a mighty downpour of tears. That I might pour it all forth with its own proper sounds, I arose from Alypius's side—to be alone seemed more proper to this ordeal of weeping—and went farther apart, so that not even his presence would be a hindrance to me. Such was I at that moment, and he sensed it, for I suppose that I had said something in which the sound of my voice already appeared to be choked with weeping. So I had arisen, while he, in deep wonder, remained there where we were sitting. I flung myself down, how I do not know, under a certain fig tree, and gave free rein to my tears. The floods burst from my eyes, an acceptable sacrifice to you. Not indeed in these very words but to this effect I spoke many things to you: "And you, O Lord, how long? How long, O Lord, will you be angry forever? Remember not our past iniquities." For I felt that I was held by them, and I gasped forth these mournful words, "How long, how long? Tomorrow and tomorrow? Why not now? Why not in this very hour an end to my uncleanness?"

Such words I spoke, and with most bitter contrition I wept within my heart. And lo, I heard from a nearby house, a voice like that of a boy or a girl, I know not which, chanting and repeating over and over, "Take up and read. Take up and read." Instantly, with altered countenance, I began to think most intently whether children made use of any such chant in some kind of game, but I could not recall hearing it anywhere, I checked the flow of my tears and got up, for I interpreted this solely as a command given to me by God to open the book and read the first chapter I should come upon. For I had heard how Anthony had been admonished by a reading from the Gospel at which he chanced to be present, as if the words read were addressed to him: "Go, sell what you have, and give to the poor, and you shall have treasure in heaven, and come, follow me," and that by such a portent he was immediately converted to you.

So I hurried back to the spot where Alypius was sitting, for I had put there the volume of the apostle when I got up and left him. I snatched it up, opened it, and read in silence the chapter on which my eyes first fell: "Not in rioting and drunkenness, not in chambering and impurities, not in strife and envying; but put you on the Lord

Jesus Christ, and make not provision for the flesh in its concupiscences." No further wished I to read, nor was there need to do so. Instantly, in truth, at the end of this sentence, as if before a peaceful light streaming into my heart, all the dark shadows of doubt fled away.

Then, having inserted my finger, or with some other mark, I closed the book, and, with a countenance now calm, I told it all to Alypius. What had taken place in him, which I did not know about, he then made known to me. He asked to see what I had read: I showed it to him, and he looked also at what came after what I had read for I did not know what followed. It was this that followed: "Now him that is weak in the faith take unto you," which he applied to himself and disclosed to me. By this admonition he was strengthened, and by a good resolution and purpose, which were entirely in keeping with his character, wherein both for a long time and for the better he had greatly differed from me, he joined me without any painful hesitation.

Thereupon we went in to my mother; we told her the story, and she rejoiced. We related just how it happened. She was filled with exultation and triumph, and she blessed you, "who are able to do above that which we ask or think." She saw that through me you had given her far more than she had long begged for by her piteous tears and groans. For you had converted me to yourself, so that I would seek neither wife nor ambition in this world, for I would stand on that rule of faith where, so many years before, you had showed me to her. You turned her mourning into a joy far richer than that she had desired, far dearer and purer than that she had sought in grandchildren born of my flesh (book 8, chapter 12).[23]

---

What happened that day was destined to change history! The conversion of St. Augustine, from a self-centered, cult-joining, lustful young man to a pillar of the Western Church, was to have repercussions for centuries, including our own.

Lust can have a powerful, detrimental effect on people's faith. I know of situations where people reject Christianity because they rightfully perceive that they can't make up their own rules about sex. But often instead of being honest and forthright as to why they've rejected the faith, they come up with all sorts of pseudo-intellectual arguments against it. King Solomon was one

---

23. Ibid., 201–203.

man whose heart was led astray by lust and by his many wives, many of whom did not worship the one true God, the God of Israel. He wrote, "I find more bitter than death the woman who is a snare, whose heart is a trap and whose hands are chains. The man who pleases God will escape her, but the sinner she will ensnare" (Eccl. 7:26).

Interestingly, some surveys show that the people with the best sex lives are committed Christians![24] That doesn't surprise me because I find in my own love life with my wife (my one and only partner—we married as virgins) that the more selfish and lustful my approach to the bedroom, the less enjoyable the act is. In contrast, the more I concern myself in pleasing her, the more enjoyable our times are (for me as well). "It is more blessed to give than to receive" applies within the sanctity of the marriage bed as well as the rest of life.

---

24. See D. James Kennedy and Jerry Newcombe, *What If Jesus Had Never Been Born?*, 139.

*This selection is suitable for children.*
*The morals of the story are that the lust for blood is an unhealthy*
*appetite and we must avoid exposure to temptation.*

## "ALYPIUS AND THE GLADIATORS"
### from *The Confessions of St. Augustine*

A different type of lust promoted in our culture today is a
blood lust. When Hollywood churns out movies where they
advertise that "the body count is awesome!" you know there's
something very wrong. People apparently enjoy seeing scenes
where one person mutilates another—complete with blood flowing and body parts flying. Common sense tells you that there's
something sick about all this. Worse yet, there's often a link in
some movies and some pornography of sex and violence. Both
appeal to our lust.

Thankfully, while Hollywood goes to great lengths to make
their violent stunts look real, of course, they aren't. But there was
a time when it was real—as we saw earlier in the story of the
humble monk who stopped the gladiatorial contests once and for
all. (See "In the Arena" by Chuck Colson on p. 66). Here is a
story from fourth-century Rome, from *Confessions of St. Augustine*. He shows here how the lust for blood can even appeal to
people who otherwise should know better.

Alypius is Augustine's friend who ends up watching a gladiatorial contest, at first with loathing. But then he grows to like it.
As Alexander Pope once said,

> Vice is a monster of so frightful mien [appearance],
> As, to be hated, needs but to be seen;
> Yet seen too oft, familiar with her face,
> We first endure, then pity, then embrace.[25]

Since of course he did not plan to give up the worldly career that
had been dinned into him by his parents, he had gone on ahead of
me to Rome to study law, and there he was carried off in an unbelievable way by the unbelievable passion for gladiatorial shows. Although

---

25. Alexander Pope, *Essay on Man,* quoted in Oscar Williams, ed., *Immortal Poems of the
English Language* (New York: Washington Square Press, 1952, 1969), 162.

he would have opposed such shows and detested them, certain of his friends and fellow students whom he chanced to meet as they were returning from dinner, in spite of the fact that he strongly objected and resisted them, dragged him with friendly force into the amphitheater on a day for these cruel and deadly games. All the while he was saying: "Even if you drag my body into this place, can you fasten my mind and my eyes on such shows? I will be absent, though present, and thus I will overcome both you and them."

When they heard this, they nevertheless brought him in with them, perhaps wanting to find out if he would be able to carry it off. When they had entered and taken whatever places they could, the whole scene was ablaze with the most savage passions. He closed his eyes and forbade his mind to have any part in such evil sights. Would that he had been able to close his ears as well! For when one man fell in the combat, a mighty roar went up from the entire crowd and struck him with such force that he was overcome by curiosity. As though he were well prepared to despise the sight and to overcome it, whatever it might be, he opened his eyes and was wounded more deeply in his soul than the man whom he desired to look at was in his body. He fell more miserably than did that gladiator at whose fall the shout was raised. The shout entered into him through his ears and opened up his eyes. The result was that there was wounded and struck down a spirit that was still bold rather than strong, and that was all the weaker because it presumed upon itself whereas it should have relied upon you [God].

As he saw that blood, he drank in savageness at the same time. He did not turn away, but fixed his sight on it, and drank in madness without knowing it. He took delight in that evil struggle, and he became drunk on blood and pleasure. He was no longer the man who entered there, but only one of the crowd that he had joined, and a true comrade of those who brought him there. What more shall I say? He looked, he shouted, he took fire, he bore away with himself a madness that should arouse him to return, not only with those who had drawn him there, but even before them, and dragging others as well.

From all that you rescued him with a hand that was most strong and yet most merciful, and you taught him to put his trust not in himself but in you. But that was long afterwards [book 6, chapter 8].[26]

---

26. St. Augustine, *Confessions of St. Augustine,* 144–45.

If you play with fire, you will get burned. How foolish of Alypius to think he could go into the auditorium but not watch the spectacle. Many times when we succumb to lust, it's because we've allowed ourselves to flirt with it. To conquer lust, some have to take drastic steps, like dropping cable TV or getting rid of the TV altogether. I know one man who won't even go to the beach any more because he doesn't want to be tempted to lust. This may sound extreme and I certainly don't want to be legalistic, but let each reader decide for himself how to keep himself free even from the temptation of lust, inasmuch as it is up to him.

*This selection is suitable for children.*
*The moral of the story is control your natural inclination to lust.*

# BEN FRANKLIN ON LUST
### from *Poor Richard's Almanack*[27]

Ben Franklin didn't always have the reputation of sexual chastity; however, he had much wisdom on the subject of lust. Therefore, I've included his thoughts on the subject as found in *Poor Richard's Almanack*. Even if Franklin didn't necessarily follow his own advice, it's still good advice. ("Do as I say not as I do.")

This selection has been mildly adapted to modern English, for example "whate'er" has been changed to "whatever."

---

- After three days men grow weary of a wench, a guest, and rainy weather.

- He that lieth down with dogs, shall rise up with fleas.

- Where's there's marriage without love, there will be love without marriage.

- Keep your eyes wide open before marriage, half shut afterwards.

- Why does the blind man's wife paint herself?

- 'Tis easier to suppress the first desire, than to satisfy all that follow it.

- He is a governor that governs his passions, and he is a servant that serves them.

- Samson, for all his strong body, had a weak head, or he would not have laid it in a harlot's lap.

---

These observances are tremendously insightful and we would do well to abide by them. Picking up on the last one—Samson let his sexual urges do his thinking for him. (Many a young man falls

27. Ben Franklin, *Poor Richard's Almanack*, 34, 42, 50, 55, 66, 73.

into sexual sins because his testosterone level is higher than his IQ!) Samson accomplished a mere fraction of what he could have, had he exhibited more self-control. He liked to see how close he could get to the fire without getting burned. But this proved to be his downfall. What a tragedy.

*This selection is NOT suitable for children.*
*The moral of the story is although lust may enslave one, Jesus Christ can bring freedom, even from the chains of lust.*

## "FREED FROM LUST"[28]

### by Steve Gallagher

The problems of lust are pervasive in our time. Lust can be so overwhelming and intense because it comes from multiple sources. Films, videos, magazines, and, now, even the computer provide access to pornography. Soft core pornography is sometimes pushed into the mainstream of our culture; thus, it becomes increasingly difficult for people to stay "clean." For anybody who manages, with God's help, to stay pure and monogamous, the blessings are wonderful. But for those who have fallen into the slimy pit of sexual perversion, there is still hope of deliverance, thanks to Jesus Christ, as you will see in the following testimony of Steve Gallagher, the founder and director of Pure Life Ministries. Pure Life Ministries is dedicated to snatching other men from the clutches of uncontrollable lust and having them set free through the power of the gospel of Christ.

---

Although I had a Christian mother who raised me in a Baptist church, my father provided a far different example for me to follow. He was very abusive, but especially to my mother and sister. He also consistently committed adultery throughout their marriage. What I learned from him about women was that they were there to be dominated and manipulated into doing what the man desired.

As a young teenager, I discovered his secret cache of pornography. This further taught me that women were just objects to be used for man's pleasure.

Although my dad was a good provider, he was a poor father. He exhibited all the classic characteristics of a sexual addict: blame shifting, critical, judgmental, manipulative, unapproachable, and living a life in total denial that there was anything wrong with him. One never knew when his vicious verbal attacks would come. He might explode over any trivial thing. Everybody in the house had to walk on eggshells as we didn't know what would set him off. A personable and generous man to his friends, he was far from that to his family.

---

28. Exerpted from Steve Gallagher, *Tearing Down the High Places of Sexual Idolatry* (Fair Oaks, Calif.: Pure Life Ministries, 1986), 7–10.

His consistent verbal attacks on me—the criticism over everything I did, the sarcasm whenever anyone had a different opinion—all left me feeling worthless as a little boy. There were times when he told me that I "would never amount to nothing!" Of course, I grew up believing this. Since this was his opinion of me, I set out to prove it true.

I was quite rebellious in my teenage years, becoming heavily involved with drugs. I was shooting and dealing heroin by the age of sixteen. It was at fifteen when I gave up my virginity. What followed were sexual relationships with dozens of girls throughout my younger years as I sought to "prove myself." My drive was only matched by my recklessness. Often I was caught by girls' mothers, fathers, boyfriends, and husbands.

As I loudly proclaimed to the world what a great womanizer I was, secretly I had a problem with excessive masturbation and pornography. It started with girlie magazines but degenerated from there to hard core pornographic movies.

By the time I met and married my present wife (after ruining my first marriage), this behavior was firmly entrenched in my life. She was a Christian and I really wanted to turn my life over to God but never could quite do it. It wasn't long before I managed to drag her down to my level.

During this time, my career in real estate soured because of the skyrocketing interest rates. Kathy and I went to Los Angeles, and after a lengthy process, I joined the sheriff's department.

I was fairly successful as a deputy, receiving excellent evaluations and two departmental commendations, but my secret sexual life continued. Unknown to my wife, I was frequenting prostitutes and adult bookstores. In there, homosexuals were always available to provide satisfaction for those who wanted it as they viewed pornographic movies in little booths.

My secret life began to become known to my wife. As she scrambled to save the marriage to the man she loved, I gradually got her involved with my secret life. At first it was just watching pornographic movies. While these broke down her resistance and the morality she had grown up with, I began hinting at the involvement of other people in our sex life. It wasn't long before we were involved with orgies and swinging.

Kathy had to use drugs to cover the pain she was experiencing. Finally, she couldn't take it any longer and left me. I spent the next several weeks chasing girls and having fun. One morning though, I woke up at a girl's house really missing my wife.

During the next couple of days, God really started working on my heart. I finally relented and gave my life to Jesus and Kathy came back to me.

It wasn't long after my conversion, though, that those overwhelming compulsions came back over me. I was totally unprepared for it. Before I even knew what happened, I found myself right back to my old habits. I loved God and begged Him to heal me, but I felt powerless to fight those urges. Time and time again I would repent and resolve that I would never, ever do it again, only to find myself overwhelmed later. I listened intently to ministers, talked to counselors and read Christian books, only to get simplistic and "pat" answers from well intentioned men who didn't know any better.

Then one day I happened to get a book called *The Sexual Addiction* by Patrick Carnes, Ph.D. As I read it, I found my life being talked about. After a period of struggling with my addiction, I was finally able to put it down, once and for all. Now, I not only have complete victory in this area of my life, but I am not even tempted to do those things any longer.

After a period of restoration, God allowed me to attend Bible college. As I was searching for direction, I found God closing all of the more "normal" avenues for ministry. I was becoming frustrated as I sought His will for my life. Then slowly, He began unfolding a plan for me that was geared to helping people with the bondages with which I have had to struggle. Pure Life Ministries is the result of that calling.

---

Jesus—who changed the woman of ill-repute in Luke 7:36–50, who cast out seven demons from Mary Magdalene—also changed Steve Gallagher. He can change anybody. Nobody is beyond the reach of Christ, including those caught in the vice-grip of lust.

For those struggling with this sin, as I have in my own life (not anywhere near on the same scale), I highly recommend making yourself accountable to a trusted brother. Be accountable to him. If you have to go on a trip for business, for example, make sure you have to answer to him when you get back as to how you did. Godly accountability has helped many a struggling soul in this area. It is one of the keys that has made Pure Life Ministries so effective in freeing men from lust.[29]

---

29. For more information on Pure Life Ministries, call 800-635-1866.

# SECTION 6

# GLUTTONY

I f the lack of greed means living within your means, then avoiding gluttony means living within your seams! A glutton is defined as "one who consumes immoderate amounts of food and drink."
Gluttony was clearly a problem with the ancient Romans. Some of the wealthy Romans were notorious for their lavish banquets with their many courses, replete with their feathers dipped in olive oil! In *Quo Vadis,* a novel on the early church in ancient Rome, the author describes one of these participants in a banquet as smacking his lips, which were "shining from fat and sauces."[1] And yet Seneca said that a great part of liberty is a well-governed belly.

Gluttony is an interesting sin to zero in on. I've noticed a lot of evangelicals and fundamentalists tend to be fat without frowning on it in the same way they would on smoking. It's a sin that seems to be easily condoned, even though we know the body of the Christian is the temple of the Holy Spirit.

When my son was nine years old, we took him to a Christmas concert at a nearby church. He asked me, "Daddy, how come all these ladies are so fat?" Thankfully, it's rare today to find evangelicals that smoke. But too many Christians seem to think nothing about overeating.

Now, I don't mean to sound self-righteous in this area. I've been struggling with this one for a while. I remember in 1981, I had my wife take a photo of me without my shirt. I was showing off my "spare tire" as the "before" picture. Unfortunately, we haven't gotten around to taking the "after" picture. But we will . . . one of these days . . . er, one of these years.

---

1. Sienkiewicz, *Quo Vadis,* 67.

About eight million Americans struggle with eating disorders, including bulimia and anorexia. Meanwhile, millions more are just plain fat. According to the unofficial census, nearly fifty-two million American adults are reported to be overweight.[2] And we know that Americans spend billions of dollars each year on diet products. So viewing gluttony as a sin and labeling it as such is a helpful start to arrest the problem.

The stories in this section deal with the sin of gluttony. I was a bit hard-pressed to find a lot of tales on the subject, although I pored over many sources. One of them was a whole book filled with testimonials from Overeaters Anonymous. For example, one poor young man was so fat he ended up getting sick in this way: He attended an important meeting, but declined anybody's offer to drive him home. He was too embarrassed to even try and squeeze into their cars. The buses had left, so he called a cab. It was freezing cold, and he was not properly prepared for the weather. He ended up waiting for taxis for two hours in zero-degree temperatures! The first two cabs he had to decline because he couldn't fit into them! Finally, a third one came that he was just barely able to climb into. "This time I managed to squeeze into the front seat. When we got to my house I couldn't get out. The driver had to apply all his strength to pull me out."[3] Fortunately, he found help through Overeaters Anonymous, as have many others.

I hope you benefit from the stories you're about to read as much I have. And I hope something you read might help motivate you to change your eating habits, if they need changing.

---

2.  Tom Heymann, *The Unofficial U.S. Census* (New York: Fawcett Columbine, 1991), 183.
3.  *Lifeline Sampler* (Torrance, Calif.: Overeaters Anonymous, Inc., 1985), 199.

*This selection is suitable for children.*
*The moral of the story is don't let your belly be your god.*

# THE BIBLE ON GLUTTONY

For most of the Seven Deadly Sins, I have looked for relevant short stories from the Scriptures. But when it comes to this subject, one is hard-pressed to find any one story that makes the point.

The Bible doesn't say a lot about gluttony per se. But it does say that God's people are to exhibit self-control. Here are a few points from Scripture that are worth noting related to eating and gluttony. All of these examples are not necessarily examples of gluttony, but they are cases where people fell because of what they ate or because they were driven by their stomachs.

- The first sin man ever committed came through eating that which was prohibited (Gen. 3). Describing Eve's sin, John Milton writes:

Forth reaching to the fruit, she plucked, she eat.
Earth felt the wound, and Nature from her seat
Sighing through all her works gave signs of woe,
That all was lost.

. . . . . . . . . . . . . .

Greedily she engorged without restraint,
And knew not eating death.[4]

- Isaac showed a preference for his son Esau, in part because of the tasty food Esau could prepare (Gen. 27).

- Esau sold his birthright for a single meal (Gen. 27). The New Testament condemns this action sharply: "See that no one is . . . godless like Esau, who for a single meal sold his inheritance rights as the oldest son. Afterward, as you know, when he

---

4.   Douglas Bush, ed., *The Complete Poetical Works of John Milton* (Boston: Houghton Mifflin Company, 1965), 388–89.

wanted to inherit this blessing, he was rejected. He could bring about no change of mind, though he sought the blessing with tears" (Heb. 12:16–17).

- Solomon the Wise points out how overeating (and drunkeness—which are closely related) can bring on drowsiness (Prov. 23:20–21).

- Some people sought out Jesus only for food, as opposed to salvation or something more noble. Their interest in Him was only as deep as their stomachs (John 6:26).

- Paul aptly describes some reprobate people this way: "Their destiny is destruction, their god is their stomach, and their glory is in their shame" (Phil. 3:19). Not just in Paul's day, but in ours as well, there are people whose god is their belly!

- An antidote to gluttony is presented in the biblical practice of fasting. Jesus, Moses, and Elijah are mentioned as having gone for forty days without food so they could pray more intensely.

*This selection is suitable for children.*
*The moral of the story is to be moderate in your food intake.*

# BEN FRANKLIN ON GLUTTONY

### from *Poor Richard's Almanack*[5]

All the pictures of Ben Franklin that I've seen show him as a chubby man. Therefore, his insights on gluttony may seem rather odd, coming from him. However, his insights are still worth heeding, even though it would seem he didn't. Unless he had some sort of physical ailment that kept him overweight of which I'm not aware, this is one of those "Do as I say, not as I do" situations. Also included here are statements on drunkenness, which is a subset of the sin of gluttony.

- Eat few Suppers, and you'll need few Medicines.

- Dine with little, sup with less: Do better still: sleep supperless.

- Hold your council before dinner; the full belly hates thinking as well as acting.

- Eat to live; live not to eat.

- To lengthen thy life, lessen thy meals.

- He that drinks fast, pays slow.

- A fat kitchen, a lean will.

- Many dishes, many diseases.

- Drink water, put the money in your pocket, and leave the dry-bellyache in the punchbowl.

- The excellency of hogs is—fatness; of men—virtue.

- Nice eaters seldom meet with a good dinner.

5.   Ben Franklin, *Poor Richard's Almanack,* 7, 20, 30, 32, 34, 35, 38, 39, 42, 50, 54, 55, 56, 58, 60, 63, 65, 66, 67, 70, 74, 76.

- Drunkenness, that worst of evils, makes some men fools, some beasts, some devils.

- Three good meals a day is bad living.

- Don't go to the doctor with every distemper, nor to the lawyer with every quarrel, nor to the pot for every thirst.

- I saw few die of hunger; of eating—100,000.

- Rather go to bed supperless than run in debt for a breakfast.

- He that would travel much, should eat little.

- When the wine enters, out goes the truth.

- A full belly makes a dull brain.

- The Muses starve in a cook's shop.

- Life with fools consists in drinking; with the wise man, living's thinking.

- He that never eats too much, will never be lazy.

- Eat not to dullness. Drink not to elevation.

---

I remember asking an obese man once how he got to be so heavy. And he told me he had developed the bad habit of eating a lot before he went to bed. I imagine other heavy people would say the same thing. So Franklin's advice on not eating a lot (including at dinner time, at night) is wise. A repeated theme here is to eat less. Imagine, he wrote these things in 1732 at a time we generally don't think of Americans as overweight. Today we need even more to heed "poor Richard's" advice.

*This selection is suitable for children. It is geared toward them.
The moral of the story is that gluttony can get you in trouble.*

# THE DISAPPEARANCE OF AUGUSTUS GLOOP

**from *Charlie and the Chocolate Factory*[6]**

by Roald Dahl

*Charlie and the Chocolate Factory* deals with the sin of gluttony in a very fun and creative way. In the book, which later became a movie, you will recall that many of the children were done in by their gluttony—their greed for food, or in this case, candy. For example, there was one girl named Violet that inflated, like a balloon, from eating too much special candy, despite the warning of the eccentric tour guide, Willy Wonka.

This story of Augustus Gloop comes in the middle of a tour that Wonka is giving of his magical chocolate factory. The tour was limited to a small select number of children, only five, who were lucky enough to have found a special ticket in their chocolate bars. Their parents or guardians were allowed to assist them.

One of the children who got to participate in the coveted tour was Augustus Gloop, an unpleasant and selfish little glutton of a boy. Even his name sounds gluttonous—Augustus Gloop. His gluttony gets him in trouble.

---

## The Chocolate Room

"An important room, this!" cried Mr. Wonka, taking a bunch of keys from his pocket and slipping one into the keyhole of the door. "This is the nerve center of the whole factory, the heart of the whole business! And so *beautiful!* I *insist* upon my rooms being beautiful! I can't *abide* ugliness in factories! *In* we go, then! Don't get overexcited! Keep very calm!"

Mr. Wonka opened the door. Five children and nine grownups pushed their ways in—and *oh*, what an amazing sight it was that now met their eyes!

---

6. Roald Dahl, *Charlie and the Chocolate Factory* (N. Y.: Alfred A. Knopf, Inc., 1964), 68–71, 77–84.

They were looking down upon a lovely valley. There were green meadows on either side of the valley, and along the bottom of it there flowed a great brown river.

What is more, there was a tremendous waterfall halfway along the river—a steep cliff over which the water curled and rolled in a solid sheet, and then went crashing down into a boiling churning whirlpool of froth and spray.

Below the waterfall (and this was the most astonishing sight of all), a whole mass of enormous glass pipes were dangling down into the river from somewhere high up in the ceiling! They really were *enormous*, those pipes. There must have been a dozen of them at least, and they were sucking up the brownish muddy water from the river and carrying it away to goodness knows where. And because they were made of glass, you could see the liquid flowing and bubbling along inside them, and above the noise of the waterfall, you could hear the never-ending suck-suck-sucking sound of the pipes as they did their work. . . .

*"There!"* cried Mr. Wonka, dancing up and down and pointing his gold-topped cane at the great brown river. "It's *all* chocolate! Every drop of that river is hot melted chocolate of the finest quality. The *very* finest quality. There's enough chocolate in there to fill *every* bathtub in the *entire* country! *And* all the swimming pools as well! Isn't it *terrific?* And just look at my pipes! They suck up the chocolate and carry it away to all the other rooms in the factory where it is needed! Thousands of gallons an hour, my dear children! Thousands and thousands of gallons!"

The children and their parents were too flabbergasted to speak. They were staggered. They were dumfounded. They were bewildered and dazzled. They were completely bowled over by the hugeness of the whole thing. They simply stood and stared.

"The waterfall is *most* important!" Mr. Wonka went on. "It mixes the chocolate! It churns it up! It pounds it and beats it! It makes it light and frothy! No other factory in the world mixes its chocolate by waterfall! But it's the *only* way to do it properly! The *only* way! And do you like my trees?" he cried, pointing with his stick. "And my lovely bushes? Don't you think they look pretty? I told you I hated ugliness! And of course they are *all* eatable! All made of something different and delicious! And do you like my meadows? Do you like my grass and my buttercups? The grass you are standing on, my dear little ones, is made of a new kind of soft, minty sugar that I've just invented! I call it swudge! Try a blade! Please do! It's delectable!"

Automatically, everybody bent down and picked one blade of grass—everybody, that is, except Augustus Gloop, who took a big handful. . . .

"Augustus!" shouted Mrs. Gloop. "Augustus, sweetheart, I don't think you had better do *that*." Augustus Gloop, as you might have guessed, had quietly sneaked down to the edge of the river, and he was now kneeling on the riverbank, scooping hot melted chocolate into his mouth as fast as he could.

### Augustus Gloop Goes up the Pipe

When Mr. Wonka turned round and saw what Augustus Gloop was doing, he cried out, "Oh, no! *Please*, Augustus, *please!* I beg of you not to do that. My chocolate must be untouched by human hands!"

"Augustus!" called out Mrs. Gloop. "Didn't you hear what the man said? Come away from that river at once!"

"This stuff is *tee*-riffic!" said Augustus, taking not the slightest notice of his mother or Mr. Wonka. "Oh boy, I need a bucket to drink it properly!"

"Augustus," cried Mr. Wonka, hopping up and down and waggling his stick in the air, "you *must* come away. You are dirtying my chocolate!"

"Augustus!" cried Mrs. Gloop.

"Augustus!" cried Mr. Gloop.

But Augustus was deaf to everything except the call of his enormous stomach. He was now lying full length on the ground with his head far out over the river, lapping up the chocolate like a dog.

"Augustus!" shouted Mrs. Gloop. "You'll be giving that nasty cold of yours to about a million people all over the country!"

"Be careful, Augustus!" shouted Mr. Gloop. "You're leaning too far out!"

Mr. Gloop was absolutely right. For suddenly there was a shriek, and then a splash, and into the river went Augustus Gloop, and in one second he had disappeared under the brown surface.

"Save him!" screamed Mrs. Gloop, going white in the face, and waving her umbrella about. "He'll drown! He can't swim a yard! Save him! Save him!"

"Good heavens, Woman," said Mr. Gloop, "I'm not diving in there! I've got my best suit on!"

Augustus Gloop's face came up again to the surface, painted brown with chocolate. "Help! Help! Help!" he yelled. "Fish me out!"

"Don't just *stand* there!" Mrs. Gloop screamed at Mr. Gloop. "Do something!"

"I *am* doing something!" said Mr. Gloop, who was now taking off his jacket and getting ready to dive into the chocolate. But while he was doing this, the wretched boy was being sucked closer and closer toward the mouth of one of the great pipes that was dangling down into a river. Then all at once, the powerful suction took hold of him completely, and he was pulled under the surface and then into the mouth of the pipe.

The crowd on the riverbank waited breathlessly to see where he would come out.

*"There he goes!"* somebody shouted, pointing upwards. And sure enough, because the pipe was made of glass, Augustus Gloop could be clearly seen shooting up inside it, head first, like a torpedo.

"Help! Murder! Police!" screamed Mrs. Gloop. "Augustus, come back at once! Where are you going?"

"It's a wonder to me," said Mr. Gloop, "how that pipe is big enough for him to go through it."

"It *isn't* big enough!" said Charlie Bucket. "Oh dear, look! He's slowing down!"

"So he is!" said Grandpa Joe.

"By golly, he *has* stuck!" said Charlie.

"It's his stomach that's done it!" said Mrs. Gloop.

"He's blocked the whole pipe!" said Grandpa Joe.

"Smash the pipe!" yelled Mrs. Gloop, still waving her umbrella. "Augustus, come out of there at once!"

The watchers below could see the chocolate swishing around the boy in the pipe, and they could see it building up behind him in a solid mass, pushing against the blockage. The pressure was terrific. Something had to give. Something did give, and that something was Augustus. *Whoof!* Up he shot again like a bullet in the barrel of a gun.

"He's disappeared!" yelled Mrs. Gloop. "Where does that pipe go to? Quick! Call the fire brigade!" "Keep calm!" cried Mr. Wonka. "Keep calm, my dear lady, keep calm. There is no danger! No danger whatsoever! Augustus has gone on a little journey, that's all. A most interesting little journey. But he'll come out of it just fine, you wait and see."

"How can he possibly come out just fine!" snapped Mrs. Gloop. "He'll be made into marshmallows in five seconds!"

"Impossible!" cried Mr. Wonka. "Unthinkable! Inconceivable! Absurd! He could never be made into marshmallows!"

"And why not, may I ask?" shouted Mrs. Gloop.

"Because that pipe doesn't *go* to the Marshmallow Room!" Mr. Wonka answered. "It doesn't go anywhere near it! That pipe—the one Augustus went up—happens to lead directly to the room where I make a most delicious kind of strawberry-flavored chocolate-coated fudge . . ."

"Then he'll be made into strawberry-flavored chocolate-coated fudge!" screamed Mrs. Gloop. "My poor Augustus! They'll be selling him by the pound all over the country tomorrow morning!"

"Quite right," said Mr. Gloop.

"I *know* I'm right," said Mrs. Gloop.

"It's beyond a joke," said Mr. Gloop.

"Mr. Wonka doesn't seem to think so!" cried Mrs. Gloop. "Just look at him! He's laughing his head off! How *dare* you laugh like that when my boy's just gone up the pipe! You monster!" she shrieked, pointing her umbrella at Mr. Wonka as though she were going to run him through. "You think it's a joke, do you? You think that sucking my boy up into your Fudge Room like that is just one great big colossal joke?"

"He'll be perfectly safe," said Mr. Wonka, giggling slightly.

"He'll be chocolate fudge!" shrieked Mrs. Gloop.

"Never!" cried Mr. Wonka.

"Of course he will!" shrieked Mrs. Gloop.

"I wouldn't allow it!" cried Mr. Wonka.

"And why not?" shrieked Mrs. Gloop.

"Because the taste would be terrible," said Mr. Wonka. "Just imagine it! Augustus-flavored chocolate-coated Gloop! No one would buy it."

"They most certainly would!" cried Mr. Gloop indignantly.

"I don't want to think about it!" shrieked Mrs. Gloop.

"Nor do I," said Mr. Wonka. "And I do promise you, madam, that your darling boy is perfectly safe."

"If he's perfectly safe, then where is he?" snapped Mrs. Gloop. "Lead me to him this instant!"

Mr. Wonka turned around and clicked his fingers sharply, *click, click, click,* three times. Immediately, an Oompa-Loompa appeared, as if from nowhere, and stood beside him.

The Oompa-Loompa bowed and smiled, showing beautiful white teeth. His skin was rosy-white, his long hair was golden-brown, and the top of his head came just above the height of Mr. Wonka's knee. He wore the usual deerskin slung over his shoulder.

"Now listen to me!" said Mr. Wonka, looking down at the tiny man, "I want you to take Mr. and Mrs. Gloop up to the Fudge Room and help them to find their son, Augustus. He's just gone up the pipe."

The Oompa-Loompa took one look at Mrs. Gloop and exploded into peals of laughter.

"Oh, do be quiet!" said Mr. Wonka. "Control yourself! Pull yourself together! Mrs. Gloop doesn't think it's at all funny!"

"You can say that again!" said Mrs. Gloop.

"Go straight to the Fudge Room," Mr. Wonka said to the Oompa-Loompa, "and when you get there, take a long stick and start poking around inside the big chocolate-mixing barrel. I'm almost certain you'll find him in there. But you'd better look sharp! You'll have to hurry! If you leave him in the chocolate-mixing barrel too long, he's liable to get poured out into the fudge boiler, and that really *would* be a disaster, wouldn't it? My fudge would become *quite* uneatable."

Mrs. Gloop let out a shriek of fury.

"I'm joking," said Mr. Wonka, giggling madly behind his beard. "I didn't mean it. Forgive me. I'm so sorry. Good-by, Mrs. Gloop! And Mr. Gloop! Good-by! Good-by! I'll see you later. . . ."

As Mr. and Mrs. Gloop and their tiny escort hurried away, the five Oompa-Loompas on the far side of the river suddenly began hopping and dancing about and beating wildly upon a number of very small drums. "Augustus Gloop!" they chanted. "Augustus Gloop! Augustus Gloop! Augustus Gloop!"

"Grandpa!" cried Charlie. "Listen to them, Grandpa! What *are* they doing?"

"Ssshh!" whispered Grandpa Joe. "I think they're going to sing us a song!"

*"Augustus Gloop!"* chanted the Oompa-Loompas.
*"Augustus Gloop! Augustus Gloop!*
*The great big greedy nincompoop!*
*How long could we allow this beast*
*To gorge and guzzle, feed and feast*
*On everything he wanted to?*
*Great Scott! It simply wouldn't do!*
*However long this pig might live,*
*We're positive he'd never give*
*Even the smallest bit of fun*
*Or happiness to anyone."*

---

Augustus Gloop was safe at the other end, but he missed the rest of the tour. Uncontrolled gluttony causes one to miss many things in life. I know a person who's so overweight that it must be his dominant thought in life. It prevents him from things like getting stable employment or meeting Miss Right. The worst, though, was when he was asked by his uncle and aunt not to come in the house during a family reunion on *Christmas Day* no less because the previous year when he attended he "broke the furniture." Our appetite for food must be brought under reasonable control.

*This selection is suitable for children.*
*The moral of the story is that lack of self-control in eating can spill over to other areas of one's life.*

# FORTY-ONE SAUSAGES IN ONE SITTING[7]

## by William Trevor

Success and failure both seem to work on a spiral basis. One success breeds another success. Or one failure leads to another failure. So in the area of personal character, one area of weakness can spill over to another moral failure in a different area of one's life. This story focuses on that in the realm of eating.

Here are the true reflections of William Trevor, the writer of this story, on his former accountant—a man who seemed to be gifted in what he did but who repeatedly ate unto excess. When it comes to overeating, some of us need to learn to "Just Say No." Unfortunately, the man in this story, Mr. Pinkerton, learned this lesson (if he learned it at all) too late.

William Trevor is an author from Ireland and has received many literary awards. Among other books, he's the editor of *The Oxford Book of Irish Short Stories* (1989). This story on Mr. Pinkerton first appeared in *The New York Times Book Review*. Then it was published as the chapter on gluttony in the book *Deadly Sins*, which includes essays by John Updike, Joyce Carol Oates, and others.

---

A few of us meet now and again, not often these days, in the Gran Paradiso or the Cafe Pelican. Once it was downstairs at Bianchi's, but like so much of London, Bianchi's isn't there anymore.

We're of an age now, no longer young yet not entirely old, eating less than we did, drinking a bit less too, though not by much. We have the past in common, and by chance were once clients of Mr. Pinkerton, an accountant who was passed among us in the 1960's, recommended as a miracle worker. In the Gran Paradiso or the Cafe Pelican, we invariably end up talking about Mr. Pinkerton—about his small idiosyncrasies, and the ways in which he was different from

---

7. Retitled by the editor. Originally this was the chapter on gluttony by William Trevor in the book *Deadly Sins*, by eight authors, which originally appeared in *The New York Times Book Review* (New York: William Morrow and Company, 1993), 55–63.

accountants we have subsequently known. We touch upon the subject of gluttony, since it was gluttony that destroyed him, or so we have always assumed. We wonder about its nature and the form it takes, and if St. Thomas Aquinas was fair to designate it a sin when more charitably it might perhaps have been called an eating disorder. We recall other instances of its excesses and other gluttons we have encountered.

I remember them at school—useful boys who would consume our plates of pudding or the cold, stale teatime sausage rolls on Sundays, the porridge that otherwise ended up behind the radiators. There was a man I once accompanied on a railway journey who, having dined in the restaurant car and vexedly complained about the quality of the food, ordered the same meal all over again. Most memorably, though, there was Mr. Pinkerton.

He was in his fifties when we knew him, a cheerful, sandy-haired man of 308 pounds, with small eyes that were puffed away to pinpricks by inflations of the surrounding flesh. With a wife whom none of us ever met, or even saw, but imagined to be small and wiry, forever in a kitchen overall, he occupied a terraced house in Wimbledon in southwest London. The marriage was a late blossoming for both of them, being only a few months old when I placed my modest financial affairs in Mr. Pinkerton's hands. This was one of the first facts he revealed to me and I received the impression, as others did later, that the house was Mrs. Pinkerton's, that her possession of it had even played a part in her husband's decision to relinquish his bachelor status.

"Peckish, old chap?" Mr. Pinkerton inquired in the small, ornament-clad dining room in which all business was conducted. Without waiting for a response, he was already maneuvering his bulk around the table, on which piles of blank ledger pages, pencils, erasers, a pencil sharpener, and pen and ink had been laid out. A few minutes later he returned with two plates of sandwiches—beef, ham, pickle and cheese, sardine, tomato, cucumber—the white bread cut thickly, the plates piled high. On all my visits to the dining room, the procedure never varied. There could be no settling down to the account sheets until the sandwiches were fetched, and when the evening ended there were plates of buttery currant scones to see the stomach through the night.

Mr. Pinkerton belonged to an age long before that of the computer; indeed, he could be said to have predated the typewriter, since his accounts were prepared and submitted to the Inland Revenue in tiny, neat handwriting. Jotting down expenses—meals taken away from home, a proportion of heating and lighting, travel abroad and in the United Kingdom for professional purposes—he estimated rather than recorded. Receipts or other evidence of expenditure didn't feature in his calculations.

"About six hundred, old chap? Say seven? Eight?" There was an entry called "Spare Copies," which had something to do with the purchase of one's own books for promotional purposes. So at least Mr. Pinkerton's literary clients assumed; we never asked, simply agreed to the figures proposed. But born among the china shepherds and shepherdesses, the Highland cattle and flying geese of that small dining room, the term went into the language and to this day appears on accounts annually submitted to various divisions of the British Inland Revenue. "Wife's salary, old chap?" Mr. Pinkerton would inquire, pen poised again, and would suggest an appropriate sum.

Sometimes he visited me rather than I him. He would arrive in the house in the evening, invited to supper because there was hospitality to be returned. He always came on foot, accompanied by a retriever that matched, proportionally, his own great size, and carrying a stout black stick ("for protection, old chap"). On the first of these occasions, when we sat down to eat, he asked for "a couple of slices of bread" to go with the potatoes, vegetables, and meat, and throughout the meal the request was several times repeated. On future occasions my wife anticipated the demand by placing within his reach a sliced loaf that he always managed to finish, chomping his way through it while also consuming whatever else was on offer. "Shouldn't refer to another client, of course," he would say between mouthfuls, and then give us details of a case he was conducting in some northern town, its outcome relevant since he hoped for the establishing of a precedent. "Tax inspector up a gum tree," he would confidently predict, a favorite expression that was always accompanied by a gurgle of mirth. "Friendly cunning" was a favorite also, the weapon of his attack in taxation matters.

By way of further variation as to rendezvous, Mr. Pinkerton occasionally suggested a meeting in a public house, the big, old-fashioned Henekey's in Holborn where, ensconced in a booth, he ate an inordinate number of Scotch eggs and a couple of plates of potato salad. He once told me that these were the only foods he touched in a public house, they being the only barroom dishes that were "safe." I wasn't entirely sure what he meant by that, nor were the clients among whom his gourmandizing eventually became a talking point. We passed on his predilections when, without embarrassment, they were revealed to one or other of us—a particular fondness for a well-roasted parsnip, how he never left the house in Wimbledon without a supply of iced biscuits in his pockets, how he liked to indulge in a midmorning feast of tea and fruitcake, how he had once in someone's presence eaten forty-one sausages.

Gluttony has been numbered among the deadly sins we live with, presumably because it exemplifies an absence of the restraint that dignifies the human condition. Like its six companions, it is at best unattractive. The boys who waded into accumulations of pudding were popular in the dining hall but despised outside it. The two-dinners man in the restaurant car caused revulsion in the features of the waiters. Eyes looked the other way when Mr. Pinkerton reached out for his forty-first sausage.

Even so, in his case we were not censorious. He conducted our affairs with efficiency and was a card as well. We were fond of him because he was mysterious and eccentric, because he enlivened the routine of the work he did for us with the fruits of a prodigious memory, storing away matchbox information and sometimes appearing to know us better than we knew ourselves. "August twenty-sixth, 1952. Day you were married, old chap. A Tuesday, if memory serves." He was always right. If you had to cancel a meeting because of a dentist's appointment, the date and time were recorded forever. "Morning of July fourth, old chap. Upper molar, left, dispatched." All of it, for us, was leaven in the weight of figures and assessments and final demands, and none of us guessed that something was the matter. He was a big man; he ate in order to fill that bulky frame. It never occurred to us that his appetite lay fatally at the heart of his existence, like a cruel tumor.

It is only in retrospect that the bloated figure seems lonely, that the passion that ordered its peculiarities seems in some way sinister. It is only in retrospect that we can speculate with clarity on Mr. Pinkerton's downfall, which for me began as an unheeded intimation on a Sunday morning in 1967 when he tried to borrow 500 pounds. The request came out of the blue, on the telephone, and such was my faith in Mr. Pinkerton's respectability and his professional acumen that I said, of course. I did not yet know that a number of his clients had just been touched for similar sums. Some obliged; others more wisely did not.

As the months went by, the loans remained unpaid and, even worse, the Inland Revenue's Final Notices were now being followed by threats of Immediate Court Action or Distraint on Goods. Men with bowler hats even arrived at some of our houses. "Not to worry, old chap" was Mr. Pinkerton's endless repeated response, followed by soothing promises that he would, that very day, speak to the relevant inspector, who had by the sound of things got himself up a gum tree.

But this time he didn't tramp round to the local tax office with his dog and his stick and his old black briefcase. Instead, all over London, Mr. Pinkerton's clients were in trouble, summoned to the revenue courts, reprimanded, investigated, penalized. Mr. Pinkerton's telephone was cut off; he no longer answered letters. At the behest of a new accountant, I went to see him in Wimbledon one cold winter's morning, hoping to collect some of my papers.

Mr. Pinkerton was in rags. He had been doing the fires, he explained, leading me into the dining room, but there was no sign of anything like that. "Had a burglary, old chap," he said when I asked about my papers, and when I suggested that surely no burglar would steal material as worthless as account sheets, he simply added that he and Mrs. Pinkerton had experienced the misfortune to have had a fire as well. I wanted to ask him what the matter was, why he was talking about events that clearly hadn't occurred, but somewhere in his small eyes there was a warning that this was private territory, so I desisted.

I never saw him again, but from time to time a fragmentary record of his subsequent career was passed about, downstairs in Bianchi's in those days. The house in Wimbledon was seized by a mortgage company; he was struck off as an account; he and Mrs. Pinkerton were in paupers' lodgings. There was a theory that he had destroyed all the papers in his care—a form of symbolic suicide—and a year or so later death was there for real—he died in the streets one day.

Our speculations mourn him. "Peckish, old chap?" comes the echo from his heyday, the question asked of himself after dinner with a client. Tins of peas and beans and meatballs, beetroot in vinegar, cold apple dumplings are laid out to see the stomach through the night.

And later on, in dreams, his table's spread again, with meats and soups and celery in parsley sauce, with cauliflower and leeks and roasted parsnips, potatoes mashed and fried, creme brulee, creme caramel, meringues and brandy snaps, mints and Turkish delight.

If some, we wonder, are selected to be the recipients of the gifts that lift humanity to its heights, can it be said that others are chosen to bear the burdens by which some balance may be struck? And we wonder if the gluttony we knew was a form of disguise or compensation for an inner emptiness, if the burden that is called a sin was more complicated than it seemed to be. We mull uncertainly over that, although we knew the man quite well, and in the end we leave the question unresolved, as somehow it seems meant to be. Blue-suited and courteous, the stout accountant went gratefully to the grave. In the Gran Paradiso or the Cafe Pelican, with his ghost among us, he hints at that.

---

If you have a tendency to eat more and more and to enjoy it more and more, better halt it before it gets out of hand. As Ben Franklin put it: "Eat to live; live not to eat."

*This selection is NOT suitable for children or is suitable with caution.*
*The moral of the story is don't eat to console your hurt feelings and don't*
*eat to the point that it becomes a life-dominating illness!*

## "LENNY'S LAST MEAL"

### by Robert Newcombe

Sometimes we can get jolted to grasp a truth by looking upon the extreme. Hopefully, this next story will do that for some readers. It is a tale that shows how far someone can go when they overindulge their culinary desires without any self-control whatsoever. Here is gluttony taken to its grotesque outer limits.

This story is written by my brother, who is a screenwriter living in Los Angeles, and who once sold a movie script to Walt Disney. I commissioned him to write this story.

———————

"Mama?" Lenny called out. "Are you home already? I wasn't expecting you for another hour. What's that smell? Did you leave the oven on again? Mama?"

Lenny tried to get out of bed, but his weak muscles could no longer support his body. He listened quietly, hoping for an answer. A soft, "tho, tho, tho, tho," was the only sound he heard. He couldn't tell what it was. Footsteps? An animal? A dripping faucet? He wasn't sure.

"Who's there?" he cried. No one answered. "Who's in the house?" he demanded. Lenny listened for a response but heard only the same sound, "tho, tho, tho," getting louder.

"Please answer me," Lenny begged, but the intruder said nothing.

Lenny struggled to sit up, using the wall for support. He could see his reflection in the beveled mirror on the opposite wall. How pathetic I look, he thought. His brown hair was dirty and greasy; it hadn't been washed in two weeks. His skin was ghostly pale, but his cheeks were flushed bright pink from this exertion. His blue eyes looked black in the dim light. His pajamas were yellowed and stained with spaghetti sauce and grape juice from last night's dinner.

Lenny hated what he saw in the mirror. He had asked his mother to take it down many times because he didn't like looking at himself, but she left it up. "Every proper living room has to have a mirror," she insisted.

The noise grew louder, and Lenny became more nervous. He was so worried that he forced himself to do something he hadn't done in three months: put his feet on the floor. To him this effort was equivalent to a normal person walking up the Empire State Building.

His left foot wasn't too hard since it was near the edge of the bed to begin with. He just wiggled until it fell off the bed. The right leg, however, was much more difficult.

The extra foot and a half felt like miles. Lenny pulled with what little thigh muscle he had left and pushed with his arms until that leg finally fell over the edge, too. It took him over twenty minutes according to the grandfather clock in the corner. Lenny couldn't place his feet next to each other, though. The rolls of fat on his legs kept them apart.

Lenny wasn't weak from disease. He was weak from fat. His body carried more flab than his muscles could support. The last time he weighed himself was at a meat house in Chicago, where he hung from the scale like a slab of beef. He was astounded to find he weighed 512 pounds—over a quarter of a ton. (His home scale only went to 350 pounds, which he had long since outgrown.) Lenny knew he had "put on a few pounds" since the meat house weighing, but he never felt the need to know just how many. Fifty? A hundred? Two hundred pounds? It could have been more. He didn't care.

"Tho, tho, tho," repeated the noise. It was a constant noise, and Lenny decided it was probably not an intruder after all.

*It's probably a leaky faucet,* he thought. *What a relief! I don't think I could stand up anyway.* Nor could he sit up without the wall to support him. He lay there with his back on the bed, his feet on the floor, and his head staring straight up at the light fixture hanging from the ceiling.

Reflecting off the translucent globe, Lenny thought he saw an orange flicker. *What's that?* he wondered.

*Keeerack* went the door from the basement. The loud, sharp unmistakable sound of wood splitting. Lenny turned his head—that was about all he could move—and saw flames consuming the door.

"Fire!" he yelled. "Help! Mama, are you here?" He was sure she hadn't come home from grocery shopping, but he called for her just in case. He angrily turned to the flames and asked, "Where did you come from?" He remembered his mother saying something about the furnace needing to be cleaned; *maybe that's what started the fire*, he thought.

Lenny looked across the room at the cordless phone, still plugged into the recharging unit. The telephone jack wasn't close enough to Lenny's bed for a normal phone cord, and his mother refused to drape a long cord across the room. She considered it a dangerous nuisance. So every morning she'd give him the cordless phone to use, and every night, she'd plug it back into the base to recharge. This morning she had forgotten to give him the phone.

Lenny attempted to sit up, but he had no strength left after using what little he had to expend putting his feet on the floor. He lay on the bed, with his legs hanging down, looking disgustedly at his enormous, helpless body in the mirror. *A normal person would get up and walk away, but I can't even stand up.*

Lenny had not been a particularly big baby. Nine pounds, three ounces. The record is over twice that. But Lenny was always near the top of his pediatrician's weight bracket, and as he grew older, he was usually the heaviest kid in his class. Only Scott Anderson weighed more, but when Lenny was in fifth grade, Scott's father was transferred to Minneapolis, and from then on, Lenny was the heaviest kid in every class he took.

Lenny's mother, Agnes, loved to cook, and whenever she got the chance, she would try a new recipe. More like a new creation. Agnes never used cookbooks. She always seemed to know just the right amount of which ingredients to make almost anything taste delicious.

Lenny loved his mother's cooking so much that eating it became his favorite activity. While other kids were learning piano or playing baseball, Lenny was inhaling his mother's chateaubriand or double-fudge cookies. Agnes knew her son was "putting on a few pounds" (a phrase they both used often) but the food made him so content she didn't care. She enjoyed the cooking, and he enjoyed the eating. A perfect mix, especially since neither Lenny's older brother nor his father liked this fancy food. A lifetime of hamburgers and french fries would have been fine with them.

When Lenny went away to college, he missed his mother's cooking more than anything else. More than her company. More than his brother. More than his father. Agnes sent him recipes she created, but Lenny couldn't cook anywhere near as well as his mother, so every week Agnes sent her son "care packages," loaded with pineapple upside down cakes, oatmeal raisin bars, apple crisps, or whatever homemade pastries inspired her that week. Normally a boy with those kinds of goodies would be the most popular kid in the dorm, but Lenny coveted those packages and never shared the contents with anyone. His roommates considered him selfish and refused to associate with him after months of being tantalized by the smells of the wonderful foods but denied the opportunity to eat them.

By the time Lenny was a sophomore, he weighed nearly two hundred and twenty-five pounds. The school doctor insisted that Lenny lose some weight; he even put together a strict diet and exercise plan for the boy. Lenny hated exercising, partly because he found it "boring," but mostly because he was carrying around so much fat that exercising was hard work. He didn't have enough time to study and exercise so he chose to study. At least, that's how he rationalized it.

Lenny never told his mother about the doctor's plan, and she continued to send her son the weekly packages, which he continued to keep for himself. After a year, the doctor gave up trying to help Lenny, who was so pleased to hear this that he celebrated with a double banana split and two hot fudge sundaes.

In spite of his weight and the taunting of classmates, Lenny did well in school and was lucky enough to get a job with an accounting firm that had a policy against discrimination based on sex, race, religion, or size. Lenny had originally hoped to find something close to home in Milwaukee, but Chicago wasn't so far that he couldn't drive home on weekends for home-cooked meals.

Lenny found a first-floor apartment on the north side of the city, right next to an "el" stop. He didn't mind the noise of the trains as they rounded the curved tracks, metal wheels grating against metal rails, since he could easily walk the fifty-five feet to the station and catch a train downtown to the office. Even though Lenny was a full-grown (and then some) man, his mother continued to send him care packages.

In the office, there was a woman five years older than Lenny, Mary Anne Kozlowski, who was barely five feet tall and weighed two hundred and ten pounds. Like Lenny's mother, she loved to cook. Every day she brought in her homemade goodies. Peanut butter fudge. Lemon cakes. Chocolate peanut candies. Blueberry muffins.

In an office with over 150 employees, any kind of free food would be gobbled up quickly, but Mary Anne's gourmet treats were so treasured by her co-workers that they would line up next to her desk before she even arrived in the morning.

Lenny was the first in line each morning until his new supervisor refused to let Lenny leave his desk until break time. By then, Mary Anne's goodies were long gone. So Mary Anne started saving a piece for Lenny. She knew how much he loved her cooking.

Their romance took a long time to blossom. Both were extremely shy around the opposite sex. Mary Anne asked Lenny to lunch first, and after three months finally got up the nerve to invite Lenny over for dinner. But once they broke bread at her house, they were inseparable. Lenny had dinner at Mary Anne's house almost every night, and she started making double batches of her goodies after dinner. One batch for Lenny and one for the office.

Even though Lenny was in love for the first time in his life, he didn't tell his mother about Mary Anne. He was afraid Agnes might stop sending him the care packages if she knew. Lenny did not share these with Mary Anne, though. He continued to keep them for himself.

The rich dinners combined with entire batches of Mary Anne's pastries and Agnes's care packages added more pounds to Lenny's already large girth. He had to move up to new sizes of clothes almost every two months. At first he could buy his clothes off the rack at large-and-tall clothing shops, but after his weight passed the 350 mark, Lenny had to have his clothes custom made. He didn't care, though, because he was happy. He loved his job. He loved Mary Anne. He loved her cooking. And he loved his mother's care packages.

Mary Anne's sister Francine was an even better cook than Mary Anne, and Lenny loved Tuesday nights because that's when they went to Francine's house for dinner. Francine made cream sauces that rivaled anything Agnes could make. She loaded everything with butter. She marinated thick, fatty steaks with hunks of blue cheese. Francine and Mary Anne ignored everything they read about low-fat diets. They intended to enjoy themselves, and they couldn't imagine life without lots of butter, lard, and cream. Lenny agreed with them completely.

When Francine dropped dead from a heart attack—she fell onto the deep fryer, spilling three-hundred-degree oil all over her body and forcing a closed-casket funeral—Mary Anne immediately changed her thinking. Before this, neither she nor Francine thought this could happen to them. They thought the doctors who wrote and spoke of low-fat diets were nothing more than crackpots. After the funeral, the doctor told Mary Anne that Francine's heart was so covered in fat that he didn't even recognize it as being her heart. He warned Mary Anne that the same fate was awaiting her if she didn't change her eating habits.

Some people have trouble taking advice like this, but not Mary Anne. She went on a low-fat diet immediately. She threw out every fatty thing in her home, from the cartons of butter to her dozens of cookbooks. She started exercising, and the weight came off immediately. She lost twenty-three pounds the first month and a half. "That's too fast," the doctor warned.

Lenny was worried. Not because Mary Anne was losing weight too fast, but because she wanted him to lose weight too. She tried to convince him to change his ways, but he couldn't stand the taste of skinless chicken. Lentil soup. Broccoli with no cheese or butter. Lenny stopped for a second dinner on the way home every night. And of course he continued to devour his mother's care packages.

As Mary Anne became more devout in her low-fat lifestyle, she could no longer tolerate Lenny's obesity. She nagged him about it and finally gave up when she caught him eating a dozen jelly doughnuts during his coffee break.

The end of their romance was hard on both of them. Mary Anne used the anguish to push herself physically harder, while Lenny comforted himself the only way he knew how. With food. Lots of it. More than he had ever eaten before in his life. He ate four, five, six, sometimes even seven meals a day, plus his mother's care packages. Lenny got so big that he could feel both sides of the door jamb rub against his stomach as he passed through. When he stepped into an elevator, it would drop at least two inches. He broke three seat backs at the movies when he tried to use them for support as he stood up. He went through six chairs at work.

Lenny's rolls of fat repelled everyone who saw him, and he became increasingly aware that people were staring at him. He could hear kids calling him names behind his back. He was hurt, of course, but he couldn't help himself. He could not stop eating. The more he felt sorry for himself, the more he ate.

When a large accounting firm bought out the company he worked for, Lenny was laid off. Lenny had a fine work record, but no one would hire him because of his size. He had trouble fitting through doors, and he accidentally broke chairs during interviews. After he spent his entire savings while trying to find a new job, Lenny moved back home with his mother.

Agnes was glad for the company. Lenny's father had died when Lenny was in college, and Lenny's older brother was living in London. Agnes spoiled Lenny even more than she had with her care packages.

Since Lenny was depressed about not being able to get a job, Agnes would try to cheer him up with great feasts, and he would eat in one sitting meals meant for ten people. Entire chickens. Dozens of eggs. Four foot-long-submarine sandwiches. And that would be just one meal.

Lenny got so fat that he could no longer fit through the doors without having to shove the rolls of flab through the jambs. In March he decided moving around was so painful that he was just going to stay in the living room. Agnes agreed to let him move his bed in, and from that point on Lenny watched TV from bed. Read from bed. Ate from bed. Relieved himself from bed, into a bed-pan.

Lenny looked at himself in the mirror as the flames lept to his sheets. He beat the encroaching blaze out with his hands, but as soon as he put that one out, another started by the footboard. He was surrounded by flames, and he knew he would not survive unless he got out of bed. Lenny lifted his head and once again tried to sit up, but his muscles refused to help.

Lenny noticed the crumbs from this morning's breakfast next to his pillow. *My last meal,* he thought. Then he licked up the tiny morsels as the burning house collapsed onto his immovable body.

---

Interestingly, I've tended to gain weight during the work on two previous books. But while working on this book, specifically after I was gathering up stories on gluttony, I was challenged not to let myself go. I was challenged to alter my eating habits, not my belt notches! This story in particular was one of those that helped me make that decision. I hope it does for others as well.

*This selection is suitable and is geared for children.*
*The moral of the story is don't be a little pig when it comes to your food*
*. . . share with others.*

## "BETTY AND THE PIGS"

### by Lily Guzman

It's hard to get children to share things. A child may own a toy that he never plays with, but when a neighbor child expresses an interest in the item, suddenly this seems to be the kid's favorite possession! The same holds for food. Children, in their natural state, are often reticent to share their food with others.

I remember years ago my sister was wearing a big button that declared "I'm for Sharing." My dad saw the button and saw the big candy bar she was eating. He asked her for a little bite, but she wouldn't give him any. He then told her, "Well, Margo, you shouldn't wear that button if you don't mean it!" (Thankfully, she has grown up to be quite a generous adult.)

This is a story in the mode of a fairy tale that a friend of mine wrote to warn her own children on the evils of gluttony. My friend, Lily Guzman, has worked in television production for more than twenty years, beginning in her native land of the Dominican Republic. I think the story worked—her children are all thin!

––––––––––

Betty's parents loved her too much, they thought, to ever discipline her. They didn't want to lose her love. Instead, they ended up losing her altogether. Here's what happened. . . .

Betty lived with her family on a farm not too far from the center of town. Every morning before going off to school, she helped feed the chickens and the little pigs—a task which she found quite fun. On the farm, Betty learned many things about the animals and was able to tell her friends many stories based on her morning job.

Betty and her family planted a beautiful orchard with many different fruits and vegetables. Betty was lucky, because unlike many children who lived in the city, she never had to go hungry. Although they were not rich, all the goodies she could *possibly* want were right there in her own backyard! Betty could pick and eat any fruit any time. She was allowed and encouraged to take anything she wanted from the farm. Her parents always told her how hard they had worked for many years to provide her with a home and a secure future. She was their only child.

Depending on the season, Betty would pick apples, pears, strawberries, and blueberries. Her mother would then turn these fruits into delicious desserts. Every day, Betty would pack baskets full of goodies from the farm to take to school, but she would never share those goodies with other children.

Regardless of how plenty her bounty was, Betty believed that somehow she was going to run out of food; she had a real problem letting others enjoy what she considered hers. Betty was very selfish: when her mother prepared the baskets for her to share with friends, she would eat all she could on her way, before she got to school, so she did not have to share as much. Sometimes, when she could eat no more, she would take a bite out each of the cakes and fruits, so no one else would feel like eating them!

When Betty's friends asked about her farm, she would tell them how nice it was to live in the country. She would talk about her little chicks, rabbits and all the other animals she had in the barn. Betty's parents often invited other children to visit, perhaps because they were concerned that Betty was spending too much time by herself. But, instead of enjoying their company, she would complain about "those people" using up everything and eating up all her goodies (which wasn't true).

Betty's parents didn't seem to understand the meaning of discipline. Or perhaps, because they loved her so much, they were afraid to hurt her feelings and, therefore, somehow lose her love. They were so dedicated to pleasing her, that she simply interpreted this to mean that she *deserved* everything she had. She truly believed she was the center of the universe.

But the lack of discipline and proper guidelines affected Betty deeply. She could only think of pleasing herself. She did not know how to relate to others, and above all she was obsessed with food.

Something had to be done about those table manners! The more she ate, the more she wanted. When a plate of any food was in front of Betty, she turned into a monster. She served herself big portions regardless of how many guests were at the dinner table. She could not care less about others.

It hadn't always been like that. It was not clear how and when she started to become, well . . . how can I say it? . . . like a pig! . . . completely insatiable.

First, it was the pies her mother baked that she gobbled down as fast as she could. "Betty, you do not have to eat the entire pie in one serving!" her mother used to say.

"But it tastes soooo good. Mom, your pies are the best pies in the world! Besides, it will not taste the same when it cools down. Let me have another one!" she would reply. Receiving flattery about her cooking, her mother would give in and let Betty eat without control.

At the school cafeteria, it was hot dogs and fries that she could not stop eating. She'd tell her friends, "My mom only cooks things from the farm . . . but I love hot dogs, and here is the only place I can eat my favorite food. I better serve myself another hot dog." She used the same excuse to eat more pizzas and hamburgers. Later, Betty would not even attempt to make up an excuse to overeat; she would simply eat all the time.

During classes, she would stuff her pockets with food to munch on, even though the teacher had said many times that no food was allowed in the classroom. But Betty could not wait for a recess to eat; she had to have food, and she needed it now! Betty was getting big and fat, and the bigger she got, the more she ate.

Children were starting to get cruel, shouting ugly names at her; they would even recite little songs calling her a fat cow, making Betty angry and sad. The sadder she got the more she ate.

After school, she would hide in the barn and eat whatever she had just found around the house. In the house, there were crumbs all over—on her bed, under the furniture, empty food bags stuffed under the couch or in between the pillows. To make matters worse, Betty's parents would not confront her about her behavior. If they did, she would cry and tell them, "You don't want me to eat at all. You don't want to feed me anymore. You think I am big and fat." Her parents would end up apologizing or saying something like, "Oh no, honey. You are not fat. You are just a little bit chubby." But the reality was far different. Her parents even resorted to hiding food to keep it from their daughter.

During the state fair some kids jokingly said the biggest pig's award should go to Betty! She began to eat as much as she could to drown out the painful words with the sound of her munching.

But that was the last time Betty was ever seen. She's been missing ever since . . . oh, and by the way, no one can explain why there was an extra pig in her parents' barn!

---

Speaking of taking a bite out of goodies so no one else would want them . . . . When I was young, a friend used to spit in his Cracker Jacks just so no one would ask him for any! We didn't.

It's sad to see the vicious cycle described here—Betty feels so bad that she's fat, that she eats more to stuff her feelings. In reading many testimonials from Overeaters Anonymous, I've seen that trend. A key solution then is to break that cycle—to substitute some other activity when you want to overeat.

# SECTION 7

# SLOTH

S loth, which is defined as an "aversion to exertion or work: laziness," is a spiritual problem, as is the case with all the seven deadly sins. It is a root attitude of apathy.

Sloth is an extreme form of procrastination. Many people who are lazy by nature are not necessarily slothful. It depends on whether they give in to their lazy inclinations or whether they roll up their sleeves and get to work on the task at hand, despite their natural proclivity to forget about it.

The Bible, in particular Proverbs, has a lot to say about sloth. "How long will you lie there, you sluggard? When will you get up from your sleep? A little sleep, a little slumber, a little folding of the hands to rest—and poverty will come on you like a bandit and scarcity like an armed man" (Prov. 6:9–11). It also says, "Go to the ant, you sluggard; consider its ways and be wise!" (Prov. 6:6). The diligence of the ant has much to teach the slothful. In his book *Patience, My Foot!* Michael LeFan tells a great story about a powerful lesson a man learned from nature's tiniest instructors:

> It happened in Southwest Asia in the fourteenth century. The army of the conqueror Emperor Tamerlane (a descendant of Ghengis Khan) had been thrashed, scattered by a powerful enemy. Tamerlane himself was hiding in a deserted stable while enemy troops combed the countryside looking for him.
>
> As he lay there, desperate and defeated, Tamerlane watched an ant try to carry a grain of corn over a perpendicular wall. The kernel was larger than the ant itself. The emperor counted the attempts—sixty-nine times the ant tried to carry it up the wall. Sixty-nine times it fell back. On the seventieth effort the ant pushed the grain of corn over the top.
>
> Tamerlane jumped to his feet with a shout. He could see that he, too, would prevail in the end. And he did, reorganizing his army and putting the enemy to flight. Big lessons sometimes come from small teachers.[1]

---

1. LeFan, *Patience, My Foot!*, 91.

The ant is not slothful and neither should we be. It stores for the winter while it's still the summer. The sluggard, on the other hand, just wants to put off till the day after tomorrow that which he could put off till tomorrow!

In Jesus' parable of the talents, the man who was judged severely was guilty of what? Sloth! He had been entrusted with a talent, but he did nothing with it. He didn't even squander it; he just buried it. There's a snapshot of the type of sloth we should avoid like the plague.

When Christian and Faithful were plodding along in Bunyan's *The Pilgrim's Progress,* they came to a town that was built to appeal to man's sense of sloth. The goal of the town that the devil and his minions constructed was to sidetrack pilgrims, to keep them from continuing their journey to the Celestial City. Here's the background on why that town was built up: "Almost five thousand years [ago], there were pilgrims walking to the Celestial City, as these two honest persons are [Christian and Faithful]; and Beelzebub, Apollyon, and Legion, with their companions, perceiving by the path that the pilgrims made, that their way to the city lay through this town of Vanity, they contrived here to set up a fair."[2]

The name of that town is, therefore, Vanity Fair. It's *raison d'etre* is to keep pilgrims from continuing their all-important journey. Therefore, it is full of baubles to distract souls from their spiritual pursuits. Bunyan writes that in this town there is: "a fair wherein should be sold all sorts of vanity, and that it should last all the year long. Therefore at this fair are all such merchandise sold, as . . . lusts, pleasures and delights of all sorts, as whores, bawds, wives, husbands, children, masters, servants, lives, blood, bodies, souls, silver, gold, pearls, precious stones, and what not. . . . And moreover, at this fair there is at all times to be seen jugglings, cheats, games, plays, fools, apes, knaves, and rogues, and that of every kind. Here are to be seen too, and that for nothing, thefts, murders, adulteries, false-swearers, and that of a blood-red colour."[3]

In short, spiritual sloth keeps us from pursuing God's goals for us. Even when we may be *busy* or *diligent* in pursuing this world's agenda, we could still be spiritually slothful! We must be aware of the devil's schemes.

---

2. John Bunyan, *The Pilgrim's Progress* (Springdale, Pa.: Whittaker House, 1973), 105.
3. Ibid.

To combat spiritual sloth, we should engage in those spiritual disciplines already well known, but not always well practiced, such as Bible reading, meditation and memorization of Scripture, prayer, fasting, witnessing, worshiping, fellowshiping. What Mark Twain once quipped applies here: it's not the parts of the Bible I don't understand that disturb me; it's the parts I do understand.

The following stories are geared either toward sloth or its opposite: diligence. I hope you find some of them helpful to avert the last of the seven deadly sins.

*While this selection is suitable for children, on occasion they may have difficulty with the words.*
*The moral of the story is not to be lazy, but rather industrious.*

# BEN FRANKLIN ON SLOTH

from *Poor Richard's Almanack*[4]

Ben Franklin was the model of the industrious American. He was anything but lazy, and he accomplished a lot in his lifetime. *Ripley's Believe it or Not* writes of Franklin:

He was the first American philosopher.[5]
He was the first American ambassador.
He invented the harmonica.
He invented the rocking chair.
He invented the street lamp.
He was the first political cartoonist.
He was the best swimmer of his time.
He originated the first circulating library.
He discovered the Gulf Stream.
He invented the lightning conductor.
He is the originator of Daylight Saving Time.
He was four times President of Pennsylvania.
He introduced newspaper-carrying by mail.
He first charted the course of the northeast storms.
He originated the first street-cleaning department.[6]

So, Franklin has a lot of credibility on the subject of industry and its negative flipside, sloth. Here are some of his gems on the subject from *Poor Richard's Almanack*. Here are clear articulations of a secularized version of the Protestant work ethic.

- Have you somewhat to do to-morrow, do it today.

- Sloth (like Rust) consumes faster than Labour wears: the used Key is always bright.

---

4. Franklin, *Poor Richard's Almanack*, 13, 15, 18, 19, 20, 27, 28, 31, 38, 41, 42, 43, 46, 48, 54, 56, 58, 60, 62, 66, 67, 69, 70, 73, 75, 76.

5. However, I have heard from other sources that that distinction goes to theologian and colonial minister Jonathan Edwards.

6. *Ripley's Believe It or Not Wonder Book of Strange Facts: An Encyclopedia of Fascinating Events and Curious Facts—in Words and Dramatic Pictures—Gathered Together from the Four Corners of the World* (New York: The Universal Guild, 1957), 203–204.

- There are lazy minds as well as lazy bodies.
- Little Strokes, Fell great Oaks.
- Fear to do ill, and you need fear nought else.
- O Lazy bones! Dost thou think God would have given thee arms and legs, if he had not design'd thou should'st use them?
- No gains without pains.
- Be always ashamed to catch thyself idle.
- He that waits upon fortune, is never sure of a dinner.
- You may delay, but time will not.
- Lost time is never found again.
- All things are easy to industry, all things difficult to sloth.
- By diligence and patience, the mouse bit in two the cable.
- Diligence is the mother of good luck.
- Idleness is the greatest prodigality.
- The busy man has few idle visitors; to the boiling pot the flies come not.
- The sleeping fox catches no poultry. Up! Up!
- Look before, or you'll find yourself behind.
- God gives all things to industry.
- Diligence overcomes difficulties, sloth makes them.
- Dost thou love life? Then do not squander time; for that's the stuff life is made of.
- Prodigality of time produces poverty of mind as well as of estate.
- Employ thy time well, if thou meanest to gain leisure.
- He that has a trade has an office of profit and honour.
- The diligent spinner has a large shift.
- Plough deep while sluggards sleep; and you shall have corn to sell and to keep.
- Laziness travels so slowly that poverty soon overtakes him.
- He that by the plough would thrive, himself must either hold or drive.

- The honest man takes pains, and then enjoys pleasures; the knave takes pleasure, and then suffers pains.
- One today is worth two tomorrows.
- Work as if you were to live 100 years, pray as if you were to die tomorrow.
- Idleness is the Dead Sea, that swallows all virtues: Be active in business, that temptation may miss her aim; the bird that sits, is easily shot.
- A life of leisure and a life of laziness are two things.

---

Surely, if we would take and apply some of these principles in our daily lives, our productivity would increase. If we would apply most of them, sloth would be a thing of the past. The final thing Franklin lists in his book are "the thirteen virtues." In that list he mentions "industry," and he writes: "Lose no time. Be always employed in something useful. Cut off all unnecessary actions."[7] As the Bible says, "Be redeeming the time, because the days are evil" (Eph. 5:16 KJV).

---

7.   Ibid., 76.

*This selection is suitable for children.*
*The moral of the story is not to neglect the Bible, but (implied) to read it*
*daily. Also, spend your time diligently in God's service.*

# A TALE OF TWO DIARIES

I came across two short diary accounts that make for an interesting contrast. The first (a fictional account, based on true practices) shows sloth in full force. The other (a true report) shows
spiritual diligence in full force. The first diary passage is the fictional journal of a Bible, as if a Bible could talk and explain
where it has been. The second diary passage is a selection from
John Wesley of eighteenth-century England. Wesley was the
founder of the Methodist Church. He worked hard for the Lord,
even in the face of great opposition, as the journal entries reveal.
The moral of the story in the case of the Bible diary is to read the
Word of God daily; with Wesley's journal, it is this: Blessed are
the persistent.

---

## The Diary of a Bible

If *your* copy of the Word of God could speak and tell of its usage,
what would it say? What would you learn of your "devotional habits"?
The following brief story was originally an article in the *Churchman
Magazine,* entitled "The Diary of a Bible." I'm not sure of the date of
the article, but I know it appeared in the 1938 book *Christ and the
Fine Arts,* edited by Cynthia Pearl Maus.

January 15:      "I've been resting quietly for a week. The first few
                 nights after the first of the year my owner read me
                 regularly; but now he has forgotten me, I guess."

February 2:      "Cleaned up. I was dusted today, along with other
                 things, and put back in my place."

February 22:     "My owner used me for a short time after dinner.
                 Looked up a few references.

                 Going to Sunday school tomorrow."

| | |
|---|---|
| March 7: | "Cleaned up. Dusted, and in my old place again. Have been down in the lower hall since my trip to Sunday school." |
| April 2: | "Busy day. My owner led a Christian Endeavor meeting and had to look up references. He had an awful time finding me, although I was right there in my place all the time." |
| May 5: | "In Grandma's lap. She is here on a visit. Today she let a tear drop on Colossians 2:5–7." |
| May 6: | "In Grandma's lap again this afternoon. She spent most of her time on 1 Corinthians 13, and the last four verses of the fifteenth chapter." |
| May 7- 9: | "In Grandma's lap every afternoon now. It's a comfortable spot. Sometimes she reads me, and sometimes she talks to me." |
| May 10: | "Grandma's gone. Back in my old place again. She kissed me goodbye." |
| June 4: | "Had a couple of four-leaf clovers stuck in me today." |
| July 1: | "Packed in a suitcase[8] with clothes and other things. Off on a vacation, I guess." |
| July 7: | "Still in the suitcase." |
| July 10: | "Still in the suitcase, although nearly everything else has been taken out." |
| July 15: | "Home again and in my old place. Quite a journey, although I don't see why I went, for I was never taken out of the suitcase." |
| August 1: | "Rather stuffy and hot. Have two magazines, a novel and an old hat on top of me. Wish they would take them off." |
| September 10: | "Cleaned up. Dusted and set right again." |
| September 22: | "Used by Mary a few minutes today. She was writing a letter to a friend whose brother died and wanted an appropriate verse." |

---

8. I use the word "suitcase" where they originally said "old trunk."

October 1:          "Back in my old place again. Not even dusted this
                    week. I seem to be used only for emergencies.
                    Wonder why they bother with me at all?"

---

I trust that if your Bible could speak, it would communicate
something very different. In the last two decades, I've tried to
make it a habit to read the Bible daily. I don't always succeed,
but thankfully I do more times than not. I view reading and
studying the Bible and meditating on it as spiritual food. In the
same way we eat food every day, it's worthwhile to read the
Bible every day. It is spiritual food that nourishes the soul.

---

## A Page from the Diary of John Wesley[9]

- Sunday morning, May 5, preached in St. Ann's, was asked not to
  come back anymore.

- Sunday p.m., May 5, preached at St. John's, deacons said, "Get
  out and stay out."

- Sunday a.m., May 12, preached at St. Jude's, can't go back there
  either.

- Sunday p.m., May 12, preached at St. George's, kicked out again.

- Sunday a.m., May 19, preached at St. somebody else's, deacons
  called special meeting and said I couldn't return.

- Sunday p.m., May 19, preached on the street, kicked off the
  street.

- Sunday a.m., May 26, preached in meadow, chased out of
  meadow as a bull was turned loose during the services.

- Sunday a.m., June 2, preached out at the edge of town, kicked
  off the highway.

- Sunday p.m., June 2, afternoon service, preached in a pasture,
  10,000 people came to hear me.

---

9.    Quoted in LeFan, *Patience, My Foot!*, 80. Unfortunately, the year of Wesley's journal
entry is not listed, but the point still comes across.

Wow! Can you imagine that perseverance? Here we can barely crack open our Bibles or get on our knees to spend some time in prayer, and this man goes out to preach the gospel faithfully despite great opposition! It reminds me of what John Stuart Mill once said: "One person with a belief is equal to a force of 99 who only have interest."[10] Wesley truly believed in the urgency of getting the gospel out. His life was the antithesis of sloth.

10. Quoted in Paul Lee Tan, *Encyclopedia of 7,700 Illustrations* (Rockville, Md.: Assurance Publishers, 1984), 1675.

*This selection is suitable for children with caution.*
*The moral of the story is that sloth does not stand still.*

# "HOW STONEWALL JACKSON GOT HIS NAME"
## An Account of Dooley Thomas Hudson
### by Robert Folsom

One of the finest soldiers America ever produced was Lt. General Thomas Jonathan Jackson (1824–63), affectionately known as "Stonewall" Jackson. This story is the tale of how he earned that nickname. Jackson was the opposite of slothful. Incredibly, he could take on an army virtually ten times the size of his own and win! He was a very hardworking and dedicated man who pushed himself and his men to the uttermost limits. One time he was so tired from having gone through a few days and nights in a row without any sleep that he fell asleep while eating biscuits at supper!

Military historians have examined Jackson's Civil War battles for 130 years. Studies of his character have inspired people of faith for just as long. He fought for the Confederacy, so some readers will find it difficult to embrace General Jackson as a hero. Yet hindsight offers its most rewarding lessons to its most humble students. No one issue defines the Civil War, any more than one attribute defines an individual. Be humble, therefore, as you consider Thomas "Stonewall" Jackson's life, and what you learn will reward you indeed.

Robert Folsom is a writer in Gainesville, Georgia. He has carefully researched many aspects of the life of Stonewall Jackson, and he wrote this story as if it were the eyewitness account of one of Jackson's own men. Robert hopes one day to own a house in the Shenandoah Valley and find a genuine historical eyewitness account from the Civil War up in the attic!

---

I came to know many things as a soldier in the Stonewall Brigade, but I tell you that sloth was not one of them. In these pages I will explain that Stonewall Jackson always prevailed in battle mainly because he never kept his army standing still; any pause in our movement was simply a tactic in his strategy to act. That a man of action earned the name of an object that will not yield is an irony for the reader to ponder.

General Jackson required the utmost from his men, it is true. No activity is more vital to an army's life than the routine drill and marching that readies a soldier for battle; nor will anything occasion louder protests from a body of men. Yet our commander knew that no matter how hard he was, war is less merciful still. Sloth had no role in Stonewall Jackson's conduct: he allowed it no place in ours.

I am from the Valley of Virginia, the mention of which all citizens of the state would know to be the Shenandoah; in this region also was Virginia's first clash in the great conflict. It happened in the village of Harper's Ferry, on April 18, 1861, one day after Old Dominion seceded from the United States. Our governor dispatched the state militia to occupy the Federal arsenal in Harper's Ferry, the very location where the murderous fanatic John Brown had commenced his insurrection plot eighteen months before.

My militia company, the Winchester Rifles, was one of the first to arrive in response to the governor's order. The small number of Federal troops guarding the arsenal withdrew in the face of our greater numbers, though not before destroying by fire much of what they could not defend. Hindsight obliges me to say that this incident was not even a skirmish, for not a shot was fired. Yet there was much excitement amongst all the men: we knew this was our entry into the war, and we had accomplished our purpose.

Harper's Ferry was a place of vital importance for the defense of Virginia, so the governor presently had men and militia converge there in a general call to arms. Within one month eight thousand patriots from all over the commonwealth answered, including then-Colonel Thomas J. Jackson. He arrived to take command on April 29, amidst little discipline and much frolic; he issued his first orders the next day. None of us knew of Colonel Jackson, though word spread that he had graduated from West Point, and fought with distinction in Mexico; he taught artillery tactics at the Virginia Military Institute, whence he came at the behest of the governor. It was also reported that he was a singularly religious man.

The men in our "camp," such as it was, were all citizen-soldier volunteers with no conception of military life. The several days prior to Colonel Jackson's arrival saw less attention paid to the soldierly arts than to recreating the comforts of home: Valley men were in the great majority, and since none of our families had too far to travel, we enjoyed constant visits from our mothers, sisters, and dear ones. Some brought wagons packed full of supplies. During these few days of plenty, no one could have anticipated the deprivations which the next four years would visit on our army, our families, and the Valley we loved.

This sense of an escapade was fleeting, for Colonel Jackson changed the camp from top to bottom. He had reveille sound at five o'clock in the morning, for us the start of a seventeen-hour day; no fewer than seven of those hours were spent marching. He had guards on picket twenty-four hours a day, established cavalry patrols, and positioned artillery batteries on the heights surrounding Harper's Ferry. We saw these changes and felt them in every muscle, though he kept us too tired to grumble. Colonel Jackson also imposed strict obedience to orders, and swiftly punished transgressors. He even examined men who reported for sick call, deterring those with lesser ills.

These things and more he accomplished in three weeks. Most importantly Colonel Jackson increased the endurance of every soldier, while fashioning the whole into a fighting unit that would so bravely meet the test of battle. At the time it made no sense to us that we should learn the manual of arms, or even practice such military courtesies as a proper salute. Nor were many of the men there familiar with menial labor: in our camp were rank privates with the family names of Randolph, Mason, Beverly, Harrison, and Lee; whereas these and other gentlemen had from childhood given orders to Negroes, slop-carrying duty did not come so easily to them. Only in army service could the heirs of Virginia's wealthiest families and her most humble sons come together, to share duty as equals.

This is not to say Colonel Jackson could extinguish every trace of mischief from spirited young men. When he learned that some of his soldiers had volumes of whiskey stored in town, he had it searched out and dumped into the street. Yet these men did not surrender their occasion for a dram so easily; they scrambled to the foot of the gutters to gather up what they could. Our commander then ordered the remaining whiskey thrown from the steep bluffs over the Potomac River, where the most committed drinkers waited on the riverbank with buckets in hand. For his discipline our Colonel was soon called "Old Man Jackson," and then "Old Jack." The latter name grew to become the favorite and most endearing name given by the men to General Jackson; yet it was not spoken with affection in the early days.

General Joseph E. Johnston arrived in our camp on May 24: Colonel Jackson formally transferred the post at Harper's Ferry to Confederate authority, though he retained command of our brigade. General Johnston was a strong-willed officer, and concluded that we should retire from Harper's Ferry south to Winchester.

Our brigade bivouacked north of Winchester, standing as the van against a Union attack. We still had our daily routine of drill, though the presence of Yankees in the area had us responding to constant "false alarms," sometimes several in a day. The first true engagement came on July 2. It was a morning battle, fought mainly by the men in our fifth Regiment. They thoroughly whipped a force much larger than their own, work that made our entire brigade swell with pride. My regiment stood nearby in reserve, where we could all hear the clatter of muskets and the artillery rounds exploding. It was an insignificant fight, compared to what the future had for us. Yet for the first time I saw the dead and wounded of battle, as the ambulance wagon later passed through our ranks; several dozen captured Federal soldiers trailed behind. I shall never forget my thoughts as I gazed upon the bloodied limbs bouncing past in the wagons, for I felt very grim indeed. I reflected on what is worth dying for, and whether some greater purpose could sustain me in my duty.

Old Jack was presently promoted to brigadier general, which somehow increased talk in the brigade of our taking part in a full-scale battle: all of us had heard that a large Yankee army was gathering to our east, with General P.T.G. Beauregard's Southern force nearby to meet it. Such talk reflected an eagerness to fight that can be found only in men who have not yet charged a line of soldiers with muskets aimed in their direction.

The circulation of rumors is a daily feature of the soldier's life. All soldiers would affirm this, though "Madame Rumor" was especially well-known to the men in our brigade, because Stonewall Jackson was arguably the most secretive man in the history of warfare. He kept his purposes from his most intimate staff and even generals of his own rank; all were left to speculate about "where next" and "what then." As speculation is fuel for the fire of rumor, what sounds sensible too quickly becomes "fact." Time and truth usually betray gossip for what it is, of course. Relief from the hearsay about our next movement ended at twelve o'clock noon on July 18. We were ordered to leave Winchester, headed east.

The entire army was moving by three o'clock, with our brigade in the advance. No large cavalry accompanied us, for Stuart and Ashby employed an effective screen of our movement, leaving General Patterson unawares. Shortly after our march began we were halted; we heard wild cheering erupt down the column amongst the other brigades. Presently an officer read us General Johnston's orders aloud:

"Our gallant army under General Beauregard is now attacked by overwhelming numbers. The commanding general hopes that his troops will step out like men, and make a forced march to save the country."

My voice joined the joyful cheering and shouting. With this motivation we began our forced march toward the Blue Ridge, on a dusty road under the July sun.

At dark we reached the Shenandoah River, which was waist-deep at the crossing. We marched up the Blue Ridge toward Ashby's Gap, and did not halt for the night until our brigade was on the eastern slope, around two o'clock. I note the time to help portray the exhaustion all the men felt; most simply lay down and slept in the very place they stopped marching. Yet my anxiety about our purpose did not allow me even to close my eyes; nor was I alone in my restlessness. Twice that night I saw General Jackson walk slowly past, standing himself as guard for the camp. I saw the lips on his peaceful countenance moving both times, as I lay still on the ground; for the first time I discerned the spiritual resolve which sustained him. It was a strength I did not know.

Near daylight our columns raised the dust cloud again, marching four-abreast. In a short time we arrived at the rail station in the village of Piedmont, to meet with an unexpected yet most pleasant surprise. People from the village and surrounding areas assembled to feed us, and to encourage us to drive away the Yankees; many enthusiastic young ladies were among them. For a short time we all enjoyed the atmosphere of a picnic. Presently we boarded the trains for Manassas Junction, and pulled away amidst waving and shouts on behalf of Virginia.

Our brigade was transported quickly enough, though the field at Manassas appeared very confused. We did have to march right past fresh graves, a solemn evidence that the two armies had already skirmished. Trainloads of our soldiers continued to arrive that day and the next.

We were stationed in reserve, near the strong positions General Beauregard's army already held along Bull Run creek. That night we lay on our arms, and no one doubted what was going to happen in the morning. By the tens of thousands the opposing armies were now gathered, separated by a small creek, each side ready with their tools of war to inflict death on the other. Trepidation led many men to make woeful promises that night: to each other, in writing to loved ones, and to Heaven. That is the least that fear will do, though it can make a man do much worse. Early in the night I heard a gunshot down the line, so I walked over to see that a fellow in a nearby regiment had deliberately fired into his own foot. Unfortunately he aimed too high and blew it half off; the doctor chose to amputate. This man's fear cost him more than the battle might have.

Artillery guns awakened the sleepers at 4:30 that morning; the sharpshooters began their work at daylight. It was a Sunday, July 21. None of the racket was coming from our front, where all was quiet. We heard it on the distant left, far up Bull Run, and presently General Jackson had us marching double-quick toward the sound. We covered three miles, and as the exchange of cannon and musketry grew, our brigade marched past many score of wounded and unnerved soldiers who limped or ran from the field.

We were ordered into position just below the crest of a widely plateaued rise known as "Henry Hill." My regiment formed along the edge of a pine thicket, which offered both a cover and a peril all its own; Federal shells were now flying directly above us, exploding in the trees and dismembering them onto our heads. I do not speak with shame about how wrenched my own insides were, for there is no fear like that of the first battle. We had to crouch and lay in position for more than two hours under the hateful cannon fire. Men cried out in fear during the bombardment, while others, myself included, shook hands and bade farewell all around; some of us were sure to die that afternoon.

The moment which gave General Jackson his immortal name came during this episode. Men from other Valley regiments were streaming back from the direction of the artillery fire, saying our lines beyond the hill were broken. Their commander, General Bernard Bee, rode up to General Jackson and shouted, "They are beating us back!" Calmly Old Jack replied, "Then, sir, we will give them the bayonet." Bee turned his horse, dashed toward his retreating men and with his sword raised cried, "Look! There is Jackson standing like a stone wall! Rally behind the Virginians!" At this time General Beauregard also appeared, who likewise helped to rally the men; he shouted for resistance against invaders who would defile the homes of a free people. The retreat was halted, though General Bee fell within the hour, mortally wounded.

Our own brigade's artillery batteries worked furiously from the front of our line, but seemed only to add to the cacophony. In the distance, moving up the far side of the plateau, we could see thousands of the cheering Federals forming a line of attack, though our own position remained disguised. General Jackson had been fearlessly riding along our lines since we first took our position on the hill, calling upon us to be "Steady," saying "All's well!" Now the Yankees were close enough to aim at, and that is what our officers ordered us to do.

We waited until they reached the crest of Henry Hill and were profiled against the sky. Four regiments simultaneously opened fire, and the advancing Union soldiers must have imagined the earth itself was exploding into their faces. At that time also Jeb Stuart charged his cavalry against the companies supporting their cannon, allowing the fifth of our regiments, the 33rd Virginia, to attack the batteries and chase off the gunners.

The Federals fell back, but they did not retreat; the struggle had favored them all day. We could see their courageous officers reforming the lines for another attack. General Jackson told the brigade to wait until they were upon us, then to "fire and give them the bayonet!" On they came, and into their surging blue line we delivered a tremendous volley: as they staggered, Old Jack gave the order to charge and "yell like furies!" At 3:30 that afternoon the Stonewall Brigade introduced the Yankees to the Rebel yell.

Our charge broke the center of their line, though for an hour we remained locked in murderous up-close fighting. Men who emptied their rifles used the bayonet; men losing a race to re-load threw rocks; men with only their fists left to fight used those. During the charge my company came upon a battery of Federal guns, one of which I helped drag back to our original line. Our attempt to go grab a second of their guns earned us a wrathful barrage of musketry and shell; the Union men were not relinquishing.

Yet our brigade-strength attack, the only one on Henry Hill that day, gave General Beauregard time to bring forward his reserves. He ordered a general counterattack, which collapsed the Union's will to fight. At first their retreat showed order; we loudly pursued, and our reserves also took up the Rebel yell. Presently the Yankees panicked, many dropping their rifles to flee, the threatenings of their officers shouted in vain.

At the last it resembled nothing but one mob chasing another. Soon we were ordered to fall back, and it was just as well. Soldiers by the thousands, Union and Confederate, were stray on the field, separated from their commands. President Jefferson Davis himself, up from Richmond, arrived late to the battlefield and passed many stragglers; their foreboding tales left him in fear of the true outcome. At the sight of our president we offered a resonant cheer, though he did not grasp the decisive victory of the Southern Army until he reached headquarters after dark.

Stonewall Jackson earned his name when the men he led held steadfast at the telling moment: the fortitude shown on Henry Hill that day bestowed victory on the South in the first great battle of the war. There we learned what it meant to have a great commander present to give orders while we were under fire. We did not know why we should lie still on the ground as artillery shells exploded all about us, and not a few men had cursed General Jackson's name at the time   but never again in battle. By following him we would know when to stay put, when to shoot, and when to get up and charge the enemy. He had won our confidence with victory: our brigade never lost its trust in him, nor did we lose any battle we fought as long as he was alive.

---

Although Stonewall Jackson may be a controversial figure, even more than a century after his death, he provides an incredible example of diligence and hard work. Whatever faults he may have had, sloth was not one of them!

*This selection is suitable for children.*
*The moral of the story is that it may take hard work to achieve your goals, even if your aim is as simple as getting an education, but it's worth it to make the effort.*

# MY INTENSE LONGING TO LEARN TO READ
### from *Up from Slavery*[11]
### by Booker T. Washington

If you enjoy inspirational and motivational reading, you would enjoy the autobiography of Booker T. Washington (1856–1915), a portion of which is excerpted here. *Up from Slavery,* first published in 1900 and 1901, is the true account of a great American who was born into slavery and worked his way up. As you'll read in this story, even a simple education was not anything provided to him that he could take for granted. He struggled to get one at great personal sacrifice.

Booker T. Washington's life was the antithesis of sloth. Reared in one of the most backward, impoverished backgrounds imaginable, he knew he could make his life count for something. It all began with the right attitude: "I have begun everything with the idea that I could succeed, and I never had much patience with the multitudes of people who are always ready to explain why one cannot succeed."[12] Sloth looks for excuses; diligence looks for what steps to take next.

Washington founded and presided over for more than twenty years the Tuskegee Institute in Alabama. He worked tirelessly and selflessly to build up the school, providing all sorts of opportunities for African Americans in his day—so much so that he was the "most outstanding Black leader of his day."[13] He was also a most gifted speaker who received invitations to speak from around the country.

Initially, the Tuskegee Institute began in the most humble of circumstances: "in a broken-down shanty and an old hen-house, without owning a dollar's worth of property, and with but one teacher and thirty students."[14] And yet within two decades it was

---

11. (Williamstown, Mass.: Corner House Publishers, 1978; originally published, 1900, 1901), 1–2, 6–7, 27–37.

12. Ibid., 66.

13. Ibid., inside jacket.

14. Ibid., 311.

so significant in helping to improve the lives of blacks that it was visited by an American president, William McKinley, in 1898—the first such school to enjoy such a prestigious honor.

Booker T. Washington was also a committed Christian, who said that probably the most valuable lesson he learned in his second year of college was "an understanding of the use and value of the Bible . . . I learned to love to read the Bible."[15] He says in his autobiography that he was impressed with the witness of the Church in terms of helping his race: "If no other consideration had convinced me of the value of the Christian life, the Christlike work which the Church of all denominations in America has done during the last thirty-five years for the elevation of the black man would have made me a Christian."[16] Under his direction, Tuskegee was "thoroughly Christian," while at the same time being "strictly undenominational."[17]

Unfortunately, the respect for Washington has waned a bit in the latter half of the twentieth century, at least in the black community. This is due in part to a disagreement that he had with W. E. DuBois, a younger black leader, as to what was the best way for the black community in America to rise out of its poverty; since the end of World War II, DuBois's view has gained prominence over Washington's. Nonetheless, Booker T. Washington was a great American and the first black American to achieve many honors for his hard work to make life better for his people. No matter one's socio-economic background, one can learn a lot from Booker T. Washington, especially when he considers the many obstacles the man had to overcome—even in his goal to learn how to *read*.

---

My life had its beginning in the midst of the most miserable, desolate, and discouraging surroundings. This was so, however, not because my owners were especially cruel, for they were not, as compared with many others. I was born in a typical log cabin, about fourteen by sixteen feet square. In this cabin I lived with my mother and a brother and sister till after the Civil War, when we were all declared free. . . .

I was asked not long ago to tell something about the sports and pastimes that I engaged in during my youth. Until that question was

15. Ibid., 67.
16. Ibid., 193.
17. Ibid., 198.

asked it had never occurred to me that there was no period of my life that was devoted to play. From the time that I can remember anything, almost every day of my life has been occupied in some kind of labour; though I think I would now be a more useful man if I had had time for sports. . . .

I had no schooling whatever while I was a slave, though I remember on several occasions I went as far as the schoolhouse door with one of my young mistresses to carry her books. The picture of several dozen boys and girls in a schoolroom engaged in study made a deep impression upon me, and I had the feeling that to get into a schoolhouse and study in this way would be about the same as getting into paradise.

So far as I can now recall, the first knowledge that I got of the fact that we were slaves, and that freedom of the slaves was being discussed, was early one morning before day, when I was awakened by my mother kneeling over her children and fervently praying that Lincoln and his armies might be successful, and that one day she and her children might be free. . . .

From the time that I can remember having any thoughts about anything, I recall that I had an intense longing to learn to read. I determined, when quite a small child, that, if I accomplished nothing else in life, I would in some way get enough education to enable me to read common books and newspapers. Soon after we got settled in some manner in our new cabin in West Virginia, I induced my mother to get hold of a book for me. How or where she got it I do not know, but in some way she procured an old copy of Webster's "blue-back" spelling-book, which contained the alphabet, followed by such meaningless words as "ab," "ba," "ca," "da." I began at once to devour this book, and I think that it was the first one I ever had in my hands. I had learned from somebody that the way to begin to read was to learn the alphabet, so I tried in all the ways I could think of to learn it,—all of course without a teacher, for I could find no one to teach me. At that time there was not a single member of my race anywhere near us who could read, and I was too timid to approach any of the white people. In some way, within a few weeks, I mastered the greater portion of the alphabet. In all my efforts to learn to read my mother shared fully my ambition, and sympathized with me and aided me in every way that she could. Though she was totally ignorant, so far as mere book knowledge was concerned, she had high ambitions for her children, and a large fund of good, hard, common sense which seemed to enable her to meet and master every situation. If I have done anything in life worth attention, I feel sure that I inherited the disposition from my mother.

In the midst of my struggles and longing for an education, a young coloured boy who had learned to read in the state of Ohio came to Malden [West Virginia]. As soon as the coloured people found out that he could read, a newspaper was secured, and at the close of nearly every day's work this young man would be surrounded by a group of men and women who were anxious to hear him read the news contained in the papers. How I used to envy this man! He seemed to me to be the one young man in all the world who ought to be satisfied with his attainments.

About this time the question of having some kind of a school opened for the coloured children in the village began to be discussed by members of the race. As it would be the first school for Negro children that had ever been opened in that part of Virginia, it was, of course, to be a great event, and the discussion excited the widest interest. The most perplexing question was where to find a teacher. The young man from Ohio who had learned to read the papers was considered, but his age was against him. In the midst of the discussion about a teacher, another young coloured man from Ohio, who had been a soldier, in some way found his way into town. It was soon learned that he possessed considerable education, and he was engaged by the coloured people to teach their first school. As yet no free schools had been started for coloured people in that section, hence each family agreed to pay a certain amount per month, with the understanding that the teacher was to "board 'round"—that is, spend a day with each family. This was not bad for the teacher, for each family tried to provide the very best on the day the teacher was to be its guest. I recall that I looked forward with an anxious appetite to the "teacher's day" at our little cabin.

This experience of a whole race beginning to go to school for the first time, presents one of the most interesting studies that has ever occurred in connection with the development of any race. Few people who were not right in the midst of the scenes can form any exact idea of the intense desire which the people of my race showed for an education. As I have stated, it was a whole race trying to go to school. Few were too young, and none too old, to make the attempt to learn.

As fast as any kind of teachers could be secured, not only were day-schools filled, but night-schools as well. The great ambition of the older people was to try to learn to read the Bible before they died. With this end in view, men and women who were fifty or seventy-five years old would often be found in the night-school. Sunday-schools were formed soon after freedom, but the principal book studied in the Sunday-school was the spelling-book. Day-school, night-school, Sunday-school, were always crowded, and often many had to be turned away for want of room.

The opening of the school in the Kanawha Valley, however, brought to me one of the keenest disappointments that I ever experienced. I had been working in a salt-furnace for several months, and my stepfather had discovered that I had financial value, and so, when the school opened, he decided that he could not spare me from my work. This decision seemed to cloud my every ambition. The disappointment was made all the more severe by reason of the fact that my place of work was where I could see the happy children passing to and from school, mornings and afternoons. Despite this disappointment, however, I determined that I would learn something, anyway. I applied myself with greater earnestness than ever to the mastering of what was in the "blue-book" speller.

My mother sympathized with me in my disappointment, and sought to comfort me in all the ways she could, and to help me find a way to learn. After a while I succeeded in making arrangements with the teacher to give me some lessons at night, after the day's work was done. These night lessons were so welcome that I think I learned more at night than the other children did during the day. My own experiences in the night-school gave me faith in the night-school idea, with which, in after years, I had to do both at Hampton and Tuskegee. But my boyish heart was still set upon going to the day-school, and I let no opportunity slip to push my case. Finally I won, and was permitted to go to the school in the day for a few months, with the understanding that I was to rise early in the morning and work in the furnace till nine o'clock, and return immediately after school closed in the afternoon for at least two more hours of work.

The schoolhouse was some distance from the furnace, and as I had to work till nine o'clock, and the school opened at nine, I found myself in a difficulty. School would always be begun before I reached it, and sometimes my class had recited. To get around this difficulty I yielded to a temptation for which most people, I suppose, will condemn me; but since it is a fact, I might as well state it. I have great faith in the power and influence of facts. It is seldom that anything is permanently gained by holding back a fact. There was a large clock in a little office in the furnace. This clock, of course, all the hundred or more workmen depended upon to regulate their hours of beginning and ending the day's work. I got the idea that the way for me to reach school on time was to move the clock hands from half-past eight up to the nine o'clock mark. This I found myself doing morning after morning, till the furnace "boss" discovered that something was wrong, and locked the clock in a case. I did not mean to inconvenience anybody. I simply meant to reach that schoolhouse in time.

When, however, I found myself at the school for the first time, I also found myself confronted with two other difficulties. In the first place, I found that all of the other children wore hats or caps on their heads, and I had neither hat nor cap. In fact, I do not remember that up to that time of going to school I had ever worn any kind of covering upon my head, nor do I recall that either I or anybody else had even thought anything about the need of covering for my head. But, of course, when I saw how all the other boys were dressed, I began to feel quite uncomfortable. As usual, I put the case before my mother, and she explained to me that she had no money with which to buy a "store hat," which was a rather new institution at that time among the members of my race and was considered quite the thing for young and old to own, but that she would find a way to help me out of the difficulty. She accordingly got two pieces of "homespun" (jeans) and sewed them together, and I was soon the proud possessor of my first cap.

The lesson that my mother taught me in this has always remained with me, and I have tried as best I could to teach it to others. I have always felt proud, whenever I think of the incident, that my mother had strength of character enough not to be led into the temptation of seeming to be that which she was not—of trying to impress my schoolmates and others with the fact that she was able to buy me a "store hat" when she was not. I have always felt proud that she refused to go into debt for that which she did not have the money to pay for. Since that time I have owned many kinds of caps and hats, but never one of which I have felt so proud as of the cap made of the two pieces of cloth sewed together by my mother. I have noted the fact, but without satisfaction, I need not add, that several of the boys who began their careers with "store hats" and who were my school-mates and used to join in the sport that was made of me because I had only a "homespun" cap, have ended their careers in the peniten-tiary, while others are not able now to buy any kind of hat.

My second difficulty was with regard to my name, or rather *a* name. From the time when I could remember anything, I had been called simply "Booker." Before going to school it had never occurred to me that it was needful or appropriate to have an additional name. When I heard the school-roll called, I noticed that all of the children had at least two names, and some of them indulged in what seemed to me the extravagance of having three. I was in deep perplexity, because I knew that the teacher would demand of me at least two names, and I had only one. By the time the occasion came for the enrolling of my name, an idea occurred to me which I thought would make me equal to the situation; and so, when the teacher asked me what my full name was, I calmly told him "Booker Washington," as if I had been called by that name all my life; and by that name I have since been known. Later in my life I found that my mother had given me the name of "Booker Taliaferro" soon after I was born, but in some way that part of my name seemed to disappear, and for a long while was forgotten, but as soon as I found out about it I revived it, and made my full name "Booker Taliaferro Washington." I think there are not many men in our country who have had the privilege of nam-ing themselves in the way that I have.

More than once I have tried to picture myself in the position of a boy or man with an honoured and distinguished ancestry which I could trace back through a period of hundreds of years, and who not only inherited a name, but fortune and a proud family homestead; and yet I have sometimes had the feeling that if I had inherited these, and had been a member of a more popular race, I should have been inclined to yield to the temptation of depending upon my ancestry and my colour to do that for me which I should do for myself. Years ago I resolved that because I had no ancestry myself I would leave a record of which my children would be proud, and which might encourage them to still higher effort.

The world should not pass judgment upon the Negro, and espe-cially the Negro youth, too quickly or too harshly. The Negro boy has obstacles, discouragements, and temptations to battle with that are little known to those not situated as he is. When a white boy undertakes a task, it is taken for granted that he will succeed. On the other hand, people are usually surprised if the Negro boy does not fail. In a word, the Negro youth starts out with the presumption against him.

The influence of ancestry, however, is important in helping forward any individual or race, if too much reliance is not placed upon it. Those who constantly direct attention to the Negro youth's moral weaknesses, and compare his advancement with that of white youths, do not consider the influence of the memories which cling about the old family homesteads. I have no idea, as I have stated elsewhere, who my grandmother was. I have, or have had, uncles and aunts and cousins, but I have no knowledge as to where most of them are. My case will illustrate that of hundreds of thousands of black people in every part of our country. The very fact that the white boy is conscious that, if he fails in life, he will disgrace the whole family record, extending back through many generations, is of tremendous value in helping him to resist temptations. The fact that the individual has behind and surrounding him proud family history and connection serves as a stimulus to help him to overcome obstacles when striving for success.

The time that I was permitted to attend school during the day was short, and my attendance was irregular. It was not long before I had to stop attending day-school altogether, and devote all of my time again to work. I resorted to the night-school again. In fact, the greater part of the education I secured in my boyhood was gathered through the night-school after my day's work was done. I had difficulty often in securing a satisfactory teacher. Sometimes, after I had secured someone to teach me at night, I would find, much to my disappointment, that the teacher knew but little more than I did. Often I would have to walk several miles at night in order to recite my night-school lessons. There was never a time in my youth, no matter how dark and discouraging the days might be, when one resolve did not continually remain with me, and that was a determination to secure an education at any cost.

---

When Booker T. Washington went on to higher levels of education, he had to work his way through college as a janitor at the school. At no time did the man reflect the sloth that too often characterizes too many young people in America today. He tells us, "I have learned that success is to be measured not so much by the position that one has reached in life as by the obstacles which he has overcome while trying to succeed."[18]

All his hard work paid off. He helped found an important school that continues to operate to this day. He helped open up many opportunities to black people that had earlier been denied them. He was the first black person to speak at Harvard University. He addressed that august body in 1896 after being the first black to receive an honorary degree (a Master's) from any New England college. He recalls for us the poignant day when the invitation came in a letter: "This was a recognition that had never in the slightest manner entered into my mind, and it was hard for me to realize that I was to be honoured by a degree from the oldest and most renowned university in America. As I sat upon my veranda, with this letter in my hand, tears came into my eyes. My whole former life—my life as a slave on the plantation, my work in the coal-mine, the times when I was without food and clothing, when I made my bed under a sidewalk, my struggles for an education, the trying days I had had at Tuskegee, days when I did not know where to turn for a dollar to continue the work there, the ostracism and sometimes oppression of my race,—all this passed before me and nearly overcame me."[19]

All his diligence and service to the Lord had paid off in ways beyond what he could have imagined!

---

18.  Ibid., 39.
19.  Ibid., 296.

*This selection is suitable for children.*
*The moral of the story is to diligently pursue whatever opportunities you*
*have, no matter how small they may seem.*

# THE ACTOR WHO GAVE HIS ALL

from *Tapping Your Secret Source of Power*[20]
by Lee Buck with Dick Schneider

The following story is an inspirational antidote to sloth. It drives home the point that we should give our all, even when it may seem fruitless to do so. If you really believed deep down that it didn't matter how hard you tried, then you wouldn't try very hard, would you?

Sometimes people think, *if only I had such and such a job, then I'd really work hard and be successful.* Meanwhile, they're not successful with the little they do have! Why, then, should they be given more? Jesus pointed out that if you're faithful with little, then you'll be given more. But if you're faithless even with the little you do have, then even the little you have will be taken away from you! (Matt. 25:14–30). Therefore, we should make the most of what we do have rather than worrying about what we don't have.

Lee Buck is a successful businessman, who at one time served as the international director-at-large of the Full Gospel Business Men's Fellowship International. Lee and his wife have four daughters and ten foster daughters.

---

There once was a little-known actor who was barely making a living back in 1930. His future looked bleak. In fact, the Broadway play in which he had a role was about to fold. It was called *The Up and Up.* One of its scenes left the young man completely exhausted after he played it. That was because the scene called for him to argue with two angry men, one perched on the edge of his desk and the other on the phone. Afterward, he was soaked with perspiration from putting so much of himself into it. Despite everything, the play itself got

---

20. Lee Buck with Dick Schneider, *Tapping Your Secret Source of Power* (Old Tappan, N.J.: Fleming H. Revell, 1985), 25–26. Note that the first sentence in their version of the story, which reads: "Take the case of a little-known actor who was barely making a living back in 1930," has been slightly changed here since it is no longer in its original context.

mixed reviews. It moved to a less prestigious theater, the actors accepted less pay, but the handwriting was on the wall.

Under these doleful circumstances, the young actor was tempted to coast through the scene. After all, he reasoned, why knock himself out on something that was hopeless?

Then something he'd heard ever since his boyhood days came back to him: "Whatever task lies to your hand, do it with all your might. . . ." (Eccl. 9:10a). So the young actor stuck with it. He continued to put everything he had into that scene. And almost every time he did it he found himself wondering, *What's the use? Nobody cares that much anyway.*

Finally the play folded and the young man moved on to other small plays. Then one winter day, over a year later, he got a surprising phone call. It was from a representative of Howard Hughes, who was making movies at the time.

"Mr. Hughes is filming the play *The Front Page,*" said the caller, "and he wants you in it."

At first the young man thought someone was pulling his leg. But finally he was convinced and within a few days was aboard the Twentieth Century Limited heading for Hollywood. His role in the film *The Front Page* launched him to stardom. But why he had been selected to play that part was a mystery to him. It was Lewis Milestone, director of *The Front Page,* who finally revealed to him how it all came about.

"I was in New York last year and some friends and I had a block of seats for a hit Broadway show," Milestone explained. "We were one seat short so I volunteered to step across the street to another theater. It was presenting *The Up and Up* and plenty of seats were available. *The Up and Up* wasn't much of a play but one scene really impressed me. It was the one with the big argument and I could see you put everything you had into it. When we started doing this movie, it called for a similar scene but we couldn't get anybody to do it right. Then I remembered the night I saw you in *The Up and Up* and that's why we called."

*The Front Page* launched that young actor on a fabulous movie career, but Pat O'Brien always remembered that what really got him started was what kept him going back when he had a role in a play that was a flop. O'Brien practiced the simple secret of doing his best, even when it didn't seem to matter.

This story powerfully brings home the point that we should make as much as we can with the limited opportunities we do have, instead of worrying about those opportunities we don't have. Pat O'Brien had a small opportunity, but he was not slothful. He made the most of it. So should we, regardless of the outcome.

*This selection is suitable for children.*
*The moral of the story is use diligently what you do have and don't worry about what you don't have.*

# THE DILIGENCE OF A POLIO VICTIM

from *Patience, My Foot!*[21]
by Michael LeFan

We live in a "nation of victims," where people are constantly blaming others for their problems. They're denouncing their parents for having reared them improperly. They're decrying their fourth-grade teacher for some nasty incident that has now warped them forever. Turn on just about any TV talk show during the day and you'll see many victims singing the blues.

Michael LeFan is one of the biggest true victims I've ever met. But he doesn't complain about it. We heard from him earlier. He is a victim of polio. Here is the description of the victimization process and how he and his family chose to respond to it. I include this story under Sloth because the man has proven to be extremely hard working with what little he has.

His polio left him incapable of using his arms or his hands. But nobody said he couldn't use his foot. He discovered he had dexterity enough with his left foot to do all sorts of things. He has painted beautiful pictures with a brush between his toes; he's served as president of the local ham radio club, operating the radio with just his foot; and he's written books by tapping a computer keyboard with the eraser end of a pencil between the toes. In fact, the story you're about to read was written by Michael in just that way! Tapped out, stroke by stroke, with his left foot! He's learned patience the hard way, as he describes in his book, *Patience, My Foot!*

Michael could easily have an excuse for sloth since he has so little to work with. He has chosen to be diligent instead with the little he does have.

---

In the long hot August of 1954, polio was still a summer-time dread all across the U.S. The Salk vaccine wouldn't be available until 1955. Since nobody was certain about how polio was transmitted from per-

---

21. LeFan, *Patience, My Foot!*, 11–15.

son to person, folks lived in a sort of general fear—especially through the summers, which seemed to be the disease's favorite season. Parents kept children at home, while swimming pools, movie theaters, and other public places closed, and drinking fountains were dismantled in order to curb the spread of polio. Special polio treatment centers around the nation were full of children and adults who had been infected by this virus. Many patients required iron lung machines to do their breathing for them, since polio had destroyed the nerves which control normal respiration. And in many cases, a new patient had to be placed on an iron lung waiting list—until some other patient died and no longer needed the machine.

I was eight years old and getting ready for the third grade in August of 1954 when my mother and father learned that what the doctor first diagnosed as "tonsillitis" was actually severe paralytic polio with full respiratory involvement, meningitis, and possibly encephalitis. There was no guarantee that I would live, and if I did it was certain that I'd be almost totally paralyzed. I would be able to breathe only with the aid of one of those iron lungs. Nothing could stop the inroads of the disease which was attacking me. Undoubtedly that was the worst case of "tonsillitis" in medical history. Everyone felt deep compassion for my folks, my four-year-old sister, my two-month-old brother, and for me, as our family faced this heartbreaking crisis. My dad was minister at what was then the Avenue G Church of Christ in Temple, Texas. The congregation rallied with support, allowing him time away to be with me in the Southwest Poliomyelitis Institute in Houston. Church members helped care for my brother and sister while my parents were frequently away over the following six months of my first hospitalization.

In the intervening years, I've talked about this period and the years of subsequent rehabilitation. As my dad, James, once said, "It seemed as though we had three choices. We could curse God for letting this happen to us and look for ways to vent our rage. We could grit our teeth and bear it. Or we could accept what life had brought our way."

The first choice is fruitless and self-destructive. The second is unproductive and debilitating. The third is the only reasonable way. . . .

We must learn to face life's jolting experiences, accepting them patiently as a challenge—and not in supine resignation. . . .

My polio left me totally paralyzed—almost. I needed someone else's help to eat, bathe, dress, and take care of all personal necessities. And I still need that. But as months and years passed, I found that my left leg and foot had movement, even dexterity. It began as a way to entertain myself, but over time I learned to pick up a pencil in my toes and eventually even to scribble with it. The rehabilitation professionals ignored this small capability and focused instead on teaching me to use my arms with the aid of special overhead slings. All of this required that I sit up straight, which was demanding because of my deficient breathing ability (then aided by a chest respirator device called a "shell") and because my back was weak and soon fatigued. I was more comfortable in a reclining position about halfway between sitting up and lying down. This was also the angle at which I could most effectively use my toes. So this tug-of-war went on, my occupational and physical therapists determined that I'd sit up and learn to feed myself with special utensils strapped to my useless hands, and with me equally determined to do things my way using my left foot.

How the decision was made, I don't know. Nobody that I recall ever said to me, "Accept it." But at some point it must have dawned on me that my two rehab options each carried advantages and drawbacks. To sit up and use the arm slings was more "natural," but my abilities would be severely limited. On the other hand, concentrating on the dexterity of my toes offered a fuller range of possibilities even though it was not so "normal."

At some point I accepted myself as I was, for what I was, even if that didn't fit the therapists' vision of a rehabilitated person. But that was their problem. From that time on, I began developing whatever skills I could get my left foot to perform. I write with the toes of my left foot—I earned a degree in English at the University of Mary Hardin-Baylor in Belton, Texas. And I took all class notes, tests, and did other work using my toes. The choice to concentrate on using my foot has been a happy one. Ability came only when I accepted my disability. . . .

When we accept ourselves with patience, without feeling envy or anger toward others (including God), we are set free to begin the joyful business of living.

Michael is truly an inspiration. Too often we fret about things we can't control, instead of concentrating on that which we do have power over. He has learned to focus on that which he *can* do, and that's what makes him so effective.

# PART III

Faith,
Hope,
and Love

The previous section dealt
with sins to avoid.
Now we return our focus
to the right thing to do.
These stories focus on faith, hope, and love.

# SECTION 1

# FAITH

**66** F aith" said the child to the Sunday school teacher, "is believing what you know isn't true." NOT! Faith may be beyond reason, but it is not unreasonable.

Faith is one of the human characteristics that separates us from the animals. Without faith, it is impossible to please God. The Bible says that "Faith is being sure of what we hope for and certain of what we do not see" (Heb. 11:1).

Above all, the most important aspect of faith is the *object* of one's faith. If you put your trust in the wrong person or the wrong belief, you will be disappointed. There are conflicts every day because of misplaced faith, trusting someone who proved untrustworthy. Our courts are clogged with conflicts of this sort.

Suppose we have a lot of faith that a particular boat will keep us afloat. It really is of little consequence. The important factor is whether the boat is seaworthy! Thus, the object of our faith is the most important factor in the equation and not the faith itself.

That's the great thing about Jesus Christ. He will never disappoint you. The Church might. Christians might let you down. But Jesus never will. Faith in Jesus will never disappoint.

The stories that follow deal with faith in one aspect or another. The goal is to build up our faith.

*This selection is suitable for children.*
*The moral of the story is that faith (even faith to do the impossible)*
*comes when we keep our eyes focused on Jesus.*

# PETER WALKS ON THE WATER
### from the Gospel According to Matthew (NIV)

Here is one of my favorite stories, short as it is, on faith. This comes from the Gospels. This story shows that through faith we can do even the impossible, if we keep our eyes focused on Jesus.

It's so easy to lose focus today. There are many things that vie for our attention. Even if we have the best of intentions, we can easily let our minds (and affections) wander. The attention span of today seems to lessen with each year because of the influence of television. Watch MTV for a minute (if you can stomach it). Notice how frequently the shots change. It's hard for books, parents, teachers, preachers, and Sunday school teachers to compete with the pace of modern television. Thus, the average attention span continues to shrink.

But here's a timeless story showing us the need to stay focused on Christ—not the "wind and the waves" but on Christ alone. I remember when my wife was in labor, how it made such a difference for her to stay calm and focused on some object as she did her Lamaze exercises. In the same way, with the eyes of faith, let us keep our eyes on Jesus Christ.

This passage is from Matthew 14:22–32.

---

Immediately Jesus made the disciples get into the boat and go on ahead of him to the other side, while he dismissed the crowd. After he had dismissed them, he went up on a mountainside by himself to pray. When evening came, he was there alone, but the boat was already a considerable distance from land, buffeted by the waves because the wind was against it.

During the fourth watch of the night Jesus went out to them, walking on the lake. When the disciples saw him walking on the lake, they were terrified. "It's a ghost," they said, and cried out in fear.

But Jesus immediately said to them: "Take courage! It is I. Don't be afraid."

"Lord, if it's you," Peter replied, "tell me to come to you on the water."

"Come," he said.

Then Peter got down out of the boat, walked on the water and came toward Jesus. But when he saw the wind, he was afraid and, beginning to sink, cried out, "Lord, save me!"

Immediately Jesus reached out his hand and caught him. "You of little faith," he said, "why did you doubt?"

And when they climbed into the boat, the wind died down. Then those who were in the boat worshiped him, saying, "Truly you are the Son of God."

---

Frank Slaughter, in his novel on Simon Peter, *Upon This Rock*, gives us an idea of what Peter might have felt when undergoing this experience:

> It was a strange and exhilarating feeling to take first one and then another step upon the surface of the raging sea without sinking beneath it. Simon's eyes were fixed upon Jesus, who had stopped a few paces from the boat and was waiting for him with a warm smile upon his face. But suddenly a backwash of the old fears, dredged up from the depths of his childhood memories, assailed Simon, and yielding to them momentarily, he glanced down at his feet to reassure himself that they were indeed treading upon the water. In an instant the thread of strength he had found in Jesus's eyes was broken and the faith which had supported him upon the water suddenly left him.[1]

However accurate these details may or may not be, this whole incident provides a crystal clear object lesson: When Peter kept his eyes focused on Jesus, he could literally walk on water! But when he focused on the problems, the wind and the waves— that's when he sank. And so it is with us, if we fix our eyes on Jesus (which we do through Bible reading, meditating on the Bible, singing psalms, hymns, and spiritual songs, worship, and praying to our Lord), we can weather any storm. But if we fix our eyes on the problems, then the problems overwhelm us.

---

1.   Frank Slaughter, *Upon This Rock* (New York: Pocket Books, 1964), 112.

*This selection is suitable for children.*
*The moral of the story is that God's promises in His Word can overcome our doubts and despair.*

# CAPTURED BY GIANT DESPAIR

from *The Pilgrim's Progress*
by John Bunyan

One of the greatest masterpieces in all of literature is *The Pilgrim's Progress* by John Bunyan (1628–88). Bunyan was a Puritan writer and preacher who lived in England during the tumultuous seventeenth century, a century racked by Civil War and numerous conflicts, many related to religion. Bunyan was a member of an independent church, and he was imprisoned on and off for twelve years for the crime of preaching without proper license. While in prison, he wrote *The Pilgrim's Progress*, the story of one man's journey from damnation to salvation—from the City of Destruction to the Celestial City. The path along the way is fraught with many perils, and they comprise the substance of the book.

*The Pilgrim's Progress* has proven to be one of the best-selling books of all time. It is reported that just about no Victorian home was without a copy of this spiritually rich novel. Many common terms in English come from this classic work, such as "Vanity Fair," "Slough of Despond," and "Celestial City."

The portion of *The Pilgrim's Progress* included here is when Christian, the main character of the book, gets off track with fellow pilgrim, Hopeful. Being off course, they end up in the clutches of Giant Despair. Yet they learn that they had the key to escape all along in the promises of God. The moral of the story is that when we apply them to our lives, the promises of God will melt away our doubts and despair.

---

Now I beheld in my dream, that they had not journeyed far, but the river and the way, for a time, parted; at which they were not a little sorry, yet they durst[2] not go out of the way. Now the way from the river was rough, and their feet tender by reason of their travels; so the souls of the pilgrims were much discouraged because of the way

---

2. Dared.

(Num. 21:24). Wherefore still as they went on, they wished for a better way. Now a little before them, there was on the left hand of the road a meadow, and a stile[3] to go over into it, and that meadow is called By-path Meadow. Then said Christian to his fellow, "if this meadow lieth along by our way-side, let's go over into it." Then he went to the stile to see, and behold a path lay along by the way on the other side of the fence. "'Tis according to my wish," said Christian. "Here is the easiest going; come, good Hopeful, and let us go over."

HOPEFUL: "But how if this path should lead us out of the way?"

CHRISTIAN: "That's not likely; Look, doth it not go along by the way-side?"

So Hopeful, being persuaded by his fellow, went after him over the stile. When they were gone over, and were got into the path, they found it very easy for their feet: and withal, they looking before them, espied a man walking as they did, and his name was Vain-confidence: so they called after him, and asked him whither that way led? He said, "To the Celestial Gate." "Look," said Christian, "did I not tell you so? By this you may see we are right." So they followed, and he went before them. But behold the night came on, and it grew very dark, so that they that were behind lost sight of him that went before.

He therefore that went before (Vain-confidence by name) not seeing the way before him, fell into a deep pit, which was on purpose made by the Prince of the grounds, to catch vainglorious fools withal, and was dashed in pieces with his fall.

Now Christian and his fellow heard him fall. So they called, to know the matter, but there was none to answer, only they heard a groaning. Then said Hopeful, "Where are we now?" Then was his fellow silent, as mistrusting that he had led him out of the way; and now it began to rain, and thunder, and lighten in a very dreadful manner, and the water rose amain.[4]

Then Hopeful groaned in himself, saying, "Oh, that I had kept on my way!"

CHRISTIAN: "Who would have thought that this path should have led us out of the way?"

HOPEFUL: "I was afraid on't at the very first, and therefore gave you that gentle caution. I would have spoke plainer, but that you are older than I."

---

3. A set of steps for passing over a fence or wall.
4. At full speed.

CHRISTIAN: "Good brother, be not offended; I am sorry I have brought thee out of thy way, and that I have put thee into such imminent danger; pray, my brother, forgive me, I did not do it of evil intent."

HOPEFUL: "Be comforted, my brother, for I forgive thee; and believe too that this shall be for our good."

CHRISTIAN: "I am glad I have with me a merciful brother; But we must not stand thus, let's try to go back again."

HOPEFUL: "But, good brother, let me go before."

CHRISTIAN: "No, if you please, let me go first; that, if there be any danger, I may be first therein, because by my means we are both gone out of the way."

HOPEFUL: "No, you shall not go first; for your mind being troubled, may lead you out of the way again."

Then for their encouragement, they heard the voice of one saying, "Set thine heart towards the highway, even the way that thou wentest; turn again" (Jer. 31:21). But by this time the waters were greatly risen, by reason of which the way of going back was very dangerous. (Then I thought that it is easier going out of the way when we are in, than going in when we are out.) Yet they adventured to go back; but it was so dark, and the flood was so high, that in their going back, they had like to have been drowned nine or ten times.

Neither could they, with all the skill they had, get again to the stile that night. Wherefore, at last, lighting under a little shelter, they sat down there until daybreak; but, being weary, they fell asleep. Now there was, not far from the place where they lay, a castle, called Doubting Castle, the owner whereof was Giant Despair, and it was in his grounds they now were sleeping: wherefore he, getting up in the morning early, and walking up and down in his fields, caught Christian and Hopeful asleep in his grounds. They told him they were pilgrims, and that they had lost their way. Then said the giant, "You have this night trespassed on me, by trampling in and lying on my grounds, and therefore you must go along with me." So they were forced to go, because he was stronger than they. They also had but little to say; for they knew themselves in a fault. The giant therefore drove them before him, and put them into his castle, into a very dark dungeon, nasty and stinking to the spirits of these two men. Here then they lay, from Wednesday morning till Saturday night, without one bit of bread, or drop of drink, or light, or any to ask how they did. They were therefore here in evil case, and were far from friends and acquaintance (Psalm 88:18). Now in this place, Christian had double sorrow, because 'twas through his unadvised counsel that they were brought into this distress.

Now Giant Despair had a wife, and her name was Diffidence. So when he was gone to bed, he told his wife what he had done, to wit, that he had taken a couple of prisoners, and cast them into his dungeon, for trespassing on his grounds. Then he asked her also what he had best to do further to them. So she asked him what they were, whence they came, and whither they were bound; and he told her. Then she counselled him, that when he arose in the morning he should beat them, without mercy. So when he arose, he getteth him a grievous crab-tree cudgel, and goes down into the dungeon to them, and there first falls to rating[5] of them as if they were dogs, although they gave him never a word of distaste. Then he falls upon them, and beats them fearfully, in such sort, that they were not able to help themselves, or to turn them upon the floor. This done, he withdraws and leaves them, there to condole their misery, and to mourn under their distress. So all that day they spent the time in nothing but sighs and bitter lamentations. The next night, she, talking with her husband about them further, and understanding that they were yet alive, did advise him to counsel them to make away themselves. So when morning was come, he goes to them in a surly manner as before and perceiving them to be very sore with the stripes that he had given them the day before, he told them, that since they were never like[ly] to come out of that place, their only way would be, forthwith to make an end of themselves, either with knife, halter,[6] or poison: "For why," said he, "should you choose life, seeing it is attended with so much bitterness?" But they desired him to let them go. With that he looked ugly upon them, and rushing to them had doubtless made an end of them himself, but that he fell into one of his fits (for he sometimes in sunshiny weather fell into fits), and lost for a time the use of his hand; wherefore he withdrew and left them as before, to consider what to do. Then did the prisoners consult between themselves, whether 'twas best to take his counsel or no; and thus they began to discourse:

CHRISTIAN: "Brother, what shall we do? The life that we now live is miserable. For my part I know not whether is best, to live thus, or

5.  Vehement chiding.
6.  A rope for hanging a malefactor.

to die out of hand. 'My soul chooseth strangling rather than life,' and the grave is more easy for me than this dungeon (Job 7:15). Shall we be ruled by the giant?"

HOPEFUL: "Indeed our present condition is dreadful, and death would be far more welcome to me than thus for ever to abide: But yet let us consider, the Lord of the country to which we are going hath said, Thou shalt do no murder, no, not to another man's person; much more then are we forbidden to take his counsel to kill ourselves. Besides, he that kills another, can but commit murder upon his body; but for one to kill himself, is to kill body and soul at once. And moreover, my brother, thou talkest of ease in the grave; but hast thou forgotten the hell, whither for certain the murderers go? for 'no murderer hath eternal life,' etc. And, let us consider, again, that all the law is not in the hand of Giant Despair: Others, so far as I can understand, have been taken by him as well as we; and yet have escaped out of his hand: Who knows, but that God that made the world, may cause that Giant Despair may die; or that at some time or other he may forget to lock us in; or but he may in a short time have another of his fits before us, and may lose the use of his limbs; and if ever that should come to pass again, for my part I am resolved to pluck up the heart of a man, and to try my utmost to get from under his hand. I was a fool that I did not try to do it before; but however, my brother, let's be patient, and endure a while: the time may come that may give us a happy release; but let us not be our own murderers." With these words Hopeful at present did moderate the mind of his brother; so they continued together (in the dark) that day, in their sad and doleful condition.

Well, towards evening the giant goes down into the dungeon again, to see if his prisoners had taken his counsel; but when he came there, he found them alive, and truly, alive was all; for now, what for want of bread and water, and by reason of the wounds they received when he beat them, they could do little but breathe: But, I say, he found them alive; at which he fell into a grievous rage, and told them, that seeing they had disobeyed his counsel, it should be worse with them than if they had never been born.

At this they trembled greatly, and I think that Christian fell into a swoon; but coming a little to himself again, they renewed their discourse about the giant's counsel, and whether yet they had best to take it or no. Now Christian again seemed to be for doing it, but Hopeful made his second reply as followeth:

HOPEFUL: "My brother, rememberest thou not how valiant thou hast been heretofore? Apollyon could not crush thee, nor could all that thou didst hear, or see, or feel in the Valley of the Shadow of Death. What hardship, terror, and amazement hast thou already gone through, and art now nothing but fear? Thou seest that I am in the dungeon with thee, a far weaker man by nature than thou art: Also this giant had wounded me as well as thee, and hath also cut off the bread and water from my mouth; and with thee I mourn without the light. But let's exercise a little more patience. Remember how thou playest the man at Vanity Fair, and wast neither afraid of the chain nor cage; not yet of bloody death. Wherefore let us (at least to avoid the shame that becomes not a Christian to be found in) bear up with patience as well as we can."

Now night being come again, and the giant and his wife being in bed, she asked him concerning the prisoners, and if they had taken his counsel. To which he replied, "They are sturdy rogues, they choose rather to bear all hardship, than to make away themselves." Then said she, "Take them into the castle-yard to-morrow, and show them the bones and skulls of those that thou hast already despatched, and make them believe, ere a week comes to an end, thou also wilt tear them in pieces, as thou hast done their fellows before them."

So when the morning was come, the giant goes to them again, and takes them into the castle-yard, and shows them as his wife had bidden him. "These," said he, "were pilgrims as you are, once, and they trespassed in my grounds, as you have done; and when I thought fit, I tore them in pieces, and so within ten days I will do you. Go, get you down to your den again." And with that he beat them all the way thither. They lay therefore all day on Saturday in lamentable case, as before. Now when night was come, and when Mrs. Diffidence and her husband the giant were got to bed, they began to renew their discourse of their prisoners; and withal, the old giant wondered, that he could neither by his blows, nor counsel, bring them to an end. And with that his wife replied, "I fear," said she, "that they live in hope that some will come to relieve them, or that they have pick-locks about them, by the means of which they hope to escape." "And, sayest thou so, my dear?" said the giant, "I will therefore search them in the morning."

Well, on Saturday about midnight they began to pray, and continued in prayer till almost break of day.

Now a little before it was day, good Christian, as one half amazed, brake out in this passionate speech: "What a fool," quoth he, "am I thus to lie in a stinking dungeon, when I may as well walk at liberty! I have a key in my bosom called Promise, that will, I am persuaded, open any lock in Doubting Castle." Then said Hopeful, "That's good news; good brother, pluck it out of thy bosom and try."

Then Christian pulled it out of his bosom, and began to try at the dungeon door, whose bolt (as he turned the key) gave back, and the door flew open with ease, and Christian and Hopeful both came out. Then he went to the outward door that leads into the castle-yard, and with his key opened that door also. After he went to the iron gate, for that must be opened too, but that lock went damnable hard, yet the key did open it. Then they thrust open the gate, as it opened, made such a creaking, that it waked Giant Despair, who hastily rising to pursue his prisoners, felt his limbs to fail, for his fits took him again, so that he could by no means go after them. Then they went on, and came to the King's highway, and so were safe, because they were out of his jurisdiction.

Now when they were gone over the stile, they began to contrive with themselves what they should do at that stile, to prevent those that should come after from falling into the hands of Giant Despair. So they consented to erect there a pillar, and to engrave upon the side thereof this sentence, "Over this stile is the way to Doubting Castle, which is kept by Giant Despair, who despiseth the King of the Celestial Country, and seeks to destroy his holy pilgrims." Many therefore that followed after, read what was written, and escaped the danger. This done, they sang as follows:

"Out of the way we went, and then we found
What 'twas to tread upon forbidden ground;
And let them that come after have a care,
Lest heedlessness makes them, as we, to fare;
Lest they, for trespassing, his prisoners are,
Whose Castle's Doubting, and whose name's Despair."

There are some eight thousand promises to be found in the Bible. They have been rightly compared to blank checks waiting for us to use. Need strength? "I can do everything through him who gives me strength" (Phil. 4:13). Need faith? "Faith cometh by hearing, and hearing by the word of God" (Rom. 10:17 KJV). Need wisdom? "If any of you lacks wisdom, he should ask God, who gives generously to all without finding fault" (James 1:5). Need financial help? "My God shall supply all your need, according to his riches in glory by Christ Jesus" (Phil. 4:19 KJV). And on and on it goes. In the Bible, we already have the keys that will open the doors that lead us out of our despair. We only need to use the keys.

*This story is suitable for children, although it may go over the heads of many.*

*The moral of this clever piece of satire is that the way that leads to heaven is still narrow, despite the false teaching of the modernists. A further moral of this story is not to compromise with the devil.*

# "THE CELESTIAL RAILROAD"[7]

### by Nathaniel Hawthorne

Generally, I'm not a fan of the writings of Nathaniel Hawthorne (1804–64). It was fashionable in early nineteenth century New England to dump on the Puritans, and Hawthorne seems to be among those who engaged in "Puritan bashing." The best known example of that is *The Scarlet Letter*, which, by the way, is not as anti-Christian as often thought. Furthermore, Hawthorne is often cited for his insights into the sin nature of man—a natural outgrowth of the biblical worldview of his Puritan forebears.

This story, *The Celestial Railroad,* is a satire that assumes its readers' familiarity with Bunyan's *Pilgrim's Progress*. At the time it was written (1843), many homes had only two books: the Bible and *Pilgrim's Progress*. The point of the satire is that the fuzzy-minded theological liberals of his day were wrong and that Bunyan was right after all: the way that leads to heaven is narrow.

In her book *A Reader's Guide to Religious Literature,* English professor Beatrice Batson points out that in his day, while Transcendental thought was quite popular, Hawthorne opposed it. She pens, "Satirizing the optimistic, utopian ideals of the Transcendental reformers, Hawthorne contended that their superficial ideals would come to nothing if man himself remained unregenerate."[8] The Celestial Railroad does just that!

---

Not a great while ago, passing through the gate of dreams, I visited that region of the earth in which lies the famous City of Destruction. It interested me much to learn that by the public spirit of some of the inhabitants a railroad has recently been established between this populous and flourishing town and the Celestial City. Having a little time

---

7. The text has been slightly edited without the use of ellipses.
8. Beatrice Batson, *A Reader's Guide to Religious Literature* (Chicago: Moody Press, 1968), 129.

upon my hands, I resolved to gratify a liberal curiosity by making a trip thither. Accordingly, one fine morning after paying my bill at the hotel, and directing the porter to stow my luggage behind a coach, I took my seat in the vehicle and set out for the station-house. It was my good fortune to enjoy the company of a gentleman—one Mr. Smooth-it-away—who, though he had never actually visited the Celestial City, yet seemed as well acquainted with its laws, customs, policy, and statistics, as with those of the City of Destruction, of which he was a native townsman. Being, moreover, a director of the railroad corporation and one of its largest stockholders, he had it in his power to give me all desirable information respecting that praise-worthy enterprise.

Our coach rattled out of the city, and at a short distance from its outskirts passed over a bridge of elegant construction, but somewhat too slight, as I imagined, to sustain any considerable weight. On both sides lay an extensive quagmire, which could not have been more disagreeable, either to sight or smell, had all the kennels of the earth emptied their pollution there.

"This," remarked Mr. Smooth-it-away, "is the famous Slough of Despond—a disgrace to all the neighborhood; and the greater that it might so easily be converted into firm ground."

"I have understood," said I, "that efforts have been made for that purpose from time immemorial. Bunyan mentions that above twenty thousand cartloads of wholesome instructions had been thrown in here without effect."

"Very probably! And what effect could be anticipated from such unsubstantial stuff?" cried Mr. Smooth-it-away. "You observe this convenient bridge. We obtained a sufficient foundation for it by throwing into the slough some editions of books of morality; volumes of French philosophy and German rationalism; tracts, sermons, and essays of modern clergymen; extracts from Plato, Confucius, and various Hindoo sages, together with a few ingenious commentaries upon texts of scripture,—all of which by some scientific process, have been converted into a mass like granite. The whole bog might be filled up with similar matter."

It really seemed to me, however, that the bridge vibrated and heaved up and down in a very formidable manner; and, [in] spite of Mr. Smooth-it-away's testimony to the solidity of its foundation, I should be loath to cross it in a crowded omnibus, especially if each passenger were encumbered with as heavy luggage as that gentleman and myself. Nevertheless we got over without accident, and soon found ourselves at the station-house. This very neat and spacious edifice is erected on the site of the little wicket gate, which formerly, as all old pilgrims will recollect, stood directly across the highway, and, by its inconvenient narrowness, was a great obstruction to the traveler of liberal mind and expansive stomach. The reader of John Bunyan will be glad to know that Christian's old friend Evangelist, who was accustomed to supply each pilgrim with a mystic roll, now presides at the ticket office. Some malicious persons it is true deny the identity of this reputable character with the Evangelist of old times, and even pretend to bring competent evidence of an imposture. Without involving myself in a dispute I shall merely observe that, so far as my experience goes, the square pieces of pasteboard now delivered to passengers are much more convenient and useful along the road than the antique roll of parchment. Whether they will be as readily received at the gate of the Celestial City I decline giving an opinion.

A large number of passengers were already at the station-house awaiting the departure of the cars. By the aspect and demeanor of these persons it was easy to judge that the feelings of the community had undergone a very favorable change in reference to the celestial pilgrimage. It would have done Bunyan's heart good to see it. Instead of a lowly and ragged man with a huge burden on his back, plodding along sorrowfully on foot while the whole city hooted after him, here were parties of the first gentry and most respectable people in the neighborhood setting forth towards the Celestial City as cheerfully as if the pilgrimage were merely a summer tour. Among the gentlemen were characters of deserved eminence—magistrates, politicians, and men of wealth, by whose example religion could not but be greatly recommended to their meaner brethren. In the ladies' apartment, too, I rejoiced to distinguish some of those flowers of fashionable society who are so well fitted to adorn the most elevated circles of the Celestial City. There was much pleasant conversation about the news of the day, topics of business and politics, or the lighter matters of amusement; while religion, though indubitably the main thing at heart, was thrown tastefully into the background. Even an infidel would have heard little or nothing to shock his sensibility.

One great convenience of the new method of going on pilgrimage I must not forget to mention. Our enormous burdens, instead of being carried on our shoulders as had been the custom of old, were all snugly deposited in the baggage car, and, as I was assured, would be delivered to their respective owners at the journey's end. Another thing, likewise, the benevolent reader will be delighted to understand. It may be remembered that there was an ancient feud between Prince Beelzebub and the keeper of the wicket gate, and that the adherents of the former distinguished personage were accustomed to shoot deadly arrows at honest pilgrims while knocking at the door. This dispute, much to the credit as well of the illustrious potentate above mentioned as of the worthy and enlightened directors of the railroad, has been pacifically arranged on the principle of mutual compromise. The prince's subjects are now pretty numerously employed about the station-house, some in taking care of the baggage, others in collecting fuel, feeding the engines, and such congenial occupations; and I can conscientiously affirm that persons more attentive to their business, more willing to accommodate, or more generally agreeable to the passengers, are not to be found on any railroad. Every good heart must surely exult at so satisfactory an arrangement of an immemorial difficulty.

"Where is Mr. Greatheart?" inquired I. "Beyond a doubt the directors have engaged that famous old champion to be chief conductor on the railroad?"

"Why, no," said Mr. Smooth-it-away, with a dry cough. "He was offered the situation of brakeman; but, to tell you the truth, our friend Greatheart has grown preposterously stiff and narrow in his old age. He has so often guided the pilgrims over the road on foot that he considers it a sin to travel in any other fashion. Besides, the old fellow had entered so heartily into the ancient feud with Prince Beelzebub that he would have been perpetually at blows or ill language with some of the prince's subjects, and thus have embroiled us anew. So, on the whole, we were not sorry when honest Greatheart went off to the Celestial City in a huff and left us at liberty to choose a more suitable and accommodating man. Yonder comes the engineer of the train. You will probably recognize him at once."

The engine at this moment took its station in advance of the cars, looking, I must confess, much more like a sort of mechanical demon that would hurry us to the infernal regions than a laudable contrivance for smoothing our way to the Celestial City. On its top sat a personage almost enveloped in smoke and flame, which, not to startle the reader, appeared to gush from his own mouth and stomach as well as from the engine's brazen abdomen.

"Do my eyes deceive me?" cried I. "What on earth is this?! A living creature? If so, he is the brother of the engine he rides upon!"

"Come, Come, you are obtuse!" said Mr. Smooth-it-away, with a hearty laugh. "Don't you know Apollyon, Christian's old enemy, with whom he fought so fierce a battle in the Valley of Humiliation? He was the very fellow to manage the engine; and so we have reconciled him to the custom of going on pilgrimage, and engaged him as chief engineer."

"Bravo, bravo!" exclaimed I, with irrepressible enthusiasm; "this shows the liberality of the age; this proves, if anything can, that all musty prejudices are in a fair way to be obliterated. And how will Christian rejoice to hear of this happy transformation of his old antagonist! I promise myself great pleasure in informing him of it when we reach the Celestial City."

The passengers being all comfortably seated, we now rattled away merrily, accomplishing a greater distance in ten minutes than Christian probably trudged over in a day. It was laughable, while we glanced along, as it were, at the tail of a thunderbolt, to observe two dusty foot travelers in the old pilgrim guise, with cockle shell[9] and staff, their mystic rolls of parchment in their hands and their intolerable burdens on their backs. The preposterous obstinacy of these honest people in persisting to groan and stumble along the difficult pathway rather than take advantage of modern improvements, excited great mirth among our wiser brotherhood. We greeted the two pilgrims with many pleasant gibes[10] and a roar of laughter; whereupon they gazed at us with such woeful and absurdly compassionate visages that our merriment grew tenfold more obstreperous.[11] Apollyon also entered heartily into the fun, and contrived to flirt the smoke and flame of the engine, or of his own breath, into their faces, and envelop them in an atmosphere of scalding steam. These little practical jokes amused us mightily, and doubtless afforded the pilgrims the gratification of considering themselves martyrs.

At some distance from the railroad Mr. Smooth-it-away pointed to a large, antique edifice, which, he observed, was a tavern of long

---

9. A cockle shell is one that looks like the logo used by Shell Oil.
10. Taunts.
11. Unruly.

standing, and had formerly been a noted stopping-place for pilgrims. In Bunyan's road-book it is mentioned as the Interpreter's House.

"I have long had a curiosity to visit that old mansion," remarked I.

"It is not one of our stations, as you perceive," said my companion. "The keeper was violently opposed to the railroad; and well he might be, as the track left his house of entertainment on one side, and thus was pretty certain to deprive him of all his reputable customers. But the footpath still passes his door, and the old gentleman now and then receives a call from some simple traveler, and entertains him with fare as old-fashioned as himself."

Before our talk on this subject came to a conclusion we were rushing by the place where Christian's burden fell from his shoulders at the sight of the Cross. This served as a theme for Mr. Smooth-it-away, Mr. Live-for-the-world, Mr. Hide-sin-in-the-heart, Mr. Scaly-conscience, and a knot of gentlemen from the town of Shun-repentance, to descant upon the inestimable advantages resulting from the safety of our baggage. Myself, and all the passengers indeed, joined with great unanimity in this view of the matter; for our burdens were rich in many things esteemed precious throughout the world; and, especially, we each of us possessed a great variety of favorite Habits, which we trusted would not be out of fashion even in the polite circles of the Celestial City. It would have been a sad spectacle to see such an assortment of valuable articles tumbling into the sepulchre. Thus pleasantly conversing on the favorable circumstances of our position as compared with those of past pilgrims and of narrow-minded ones at the present day, we soon found ourselves at the foot of the Hill Difficulty. Through the very heart of this rocky mountain a tunnel has been constructed of most admirable architecture, with a lofty arch and a spacious double track; so that, unless the earth and rocks should chance to crumble down, it will remain an eternal monument of the builder's skill and enterprise. It is a great though incidental advantage that the materials from the heart of the Hill Difficulty have been employed in filling up the Valley of Humiliation, thus obviating the necessity of descending into that disagreeable and unwholesome hollow.

"This is a wonderful improvement, indeed," said I. "Yet I should have been glad of an opportunity to visit the Palace Beautiful and be introduced to the charming young ladies—Miss Prudence, Miss Piety,

Miss Charity, and the rest—who have the kindness to entertain pilgrims there."

"Young ladies!" cried Mr. Smooth-it-away, as soon as he could speak for laughing. "And charming young ladies! Why, my dear fellow, they are old maids, every soul of them—prim, starched, dry, and angular;[12] and not one of them, I will venture to say, has altered so much as the fashion of her gown since the days of Christian's pilgrimage."

"Ah, well," said I, much comforted, "then I can very readily dispense with their acquaintance."

The respectable Apollyon was now putting on the steam at a prodigious rate, anxious, perhaps, to get rid of the unpleasant reminiscences connected with the spot where he had so disastrously encountered Christian. Consulting Mr. Bunyan's road-book, I perceived that we must now be within a few miles of the Valley of the Shadow of Death, into which doleful region, at our present speed, we should plunge much sooner than seemed at all desirable. In truth, I expected nothing better than to find myself in the ditch on one side or the quag[13] on the other; but on communicating my apprehensions to Mr. Smooth-it-away, he assured me that the difficulties of this passage, even in its worst condition, had been vastly exaggerated, and that, in its present state of improvement, I might consider myself as safe as on any railroad in Christendom.

Even while we were speaking the train shot into the entrance of this dreaded Valley. Though I plead guilty to some foolish palpitations of the heart during our headlong rush over the causeway here constructed, yet it were unjust to withhold the highest encomiums[14] on the boldness of its original conception and the ingenuity of those who executed it. It was gratifying, likewise, to observe how much care had been taken to dispel the everlasting gloom and supply the defect of cheerful sunshine, not a ray of which has ever penetrated among these awful shadows. For this purpose, the inflammable gas which exudes plentifully from the soil is collected by means of pipes, and thence communicated to a quadruple row of lamps along the whole extent of the passage. Thus a radiance has been created even out of the fiery and sulphurous curse that rests forever upon the

12. Stiff in character or manner.
13. Marsh.
14. Glowing words of praise.

valley—a radiance hurtful, however, to the eyes, and somewhat bewildering, as I discovered by the changes which it wrought in the visages of my companions. In this respect, as compared with natural daylight, there is the same difference as between truth and falsehood; but if the reader has ever traveled through the dark Valley, he will have learned to be thankful for any light that he could get—if not from the sky above, then from the blasted soil beneath. Such was the red brilliancy of these lamps that they appeared to build walls of fire on both sides of the track, between which we held our course at lightning speed, while a reverberating thunder filled the Valley with its echoes. Had the engine run off the track,—a catastrophe, it is whispered, by no means unprecedented,—the bottomless pit, if there be any such place, would undoubtedly have received us. Just as some dismal fooleries of this nature had made my heart quake there came a tremendous shriek, careering along the valley as if a thousand devils had burst their lungs to utter it, but which proved to be merely the whistle of the engine on arriving at a stopping-place.

The spot where we had now paused is the same that our friend Bunyan—a truthful man, but infected with many fantastic notions— has designated, in terms plainer than I like to repeat, as the mouth of the infernal region. This, however, must be a mistake, inasmuch as Mr. Smooth-it-away, while we remained in the smoky and lurid cavern, took occasion to prove that Tophet[15] has not even a metaphorical existence. The place, he assured us, is no other than the crater of a half-extinct volcano, in which the directors had caused forges[16] to be set up for the manufacture of railroad iron. Hence, also, is obtained a plentiful supply of fuel for the use of the engines. Whoever had gazed into the dismal obscurity of the broad cavern mouth, whence darted huge tongues of dusky flame, and had seen the strange, half-shaped monsters, and visions of faces horribly grotesque, into which the smoke seemed to wreathe itself, and had heard the awful murmurs, and shrieks, and deep, shuddering whispers of the blast, sometimes forming themselves into words almost articulate, would have seized upon Mr. Smooth-it-away's comfortable explanation as greedily as we did. The inhabitants of the cavern, moreover, were unlovely personages, dark, smoke-begrimed, generally deformed, with misshapen feet, and a glow of dusky redness in

---

15. Hell; Gehenna.
16. Blacksmith workshops.

their eyes as if their hearts had caught fire and were blazing out of the upper windows. It struck me as a peculiarity that the laborers at the forge and those who brought fuel to the engine, when they began to draw short breath, positively emitted smoke from their mouth and nostrils.

Among the idlers about the train, most of whom were puffing cigars which they had lighted at the flame of the crater, I was perplexed to notice several who, to my certain knowledge, had heretofore set forth by railroad for the Celestial City. They looked dark, wild, and smoky, with a singular resemblance, indeed, to the native inhabitants, like whom, also, they had a disagreeable propensity to ill-natured gibes and sneers, the habit of which had wrought a settled contortion of their visages. Having been on speaking terms with one of these persons,—an indolent, good-for-nothing fellow, who went by the name of Take-it-easy,—I called him, and inquired what was his business there.

"Did you not start," said I, "for the Celestial City?"

"That's a fact," said Mr. Take-it-easy, carelessly puffing some smoke into my eyes. "But I heard such bad accounts that I never took pains to climb the hill on which the city stands. No business doing, no fun going on, nothing to drink, and no smoking allowed, and a thrumming of church music from morning till night. I would not stay in such a place if they offered me house room and living free."

"But, my good Mr. Take-it-easy," cried I, "why take up your residence here, of all places in the world?"

"Oh," said the loafer, with a grin, "it is very warm hereabouts, and I meet with plenty of old acquaintances, and altogether the place suits me. I hope to see you back again some day soon. A pleasant journey to you."

While he was speaking the bell of the engine rang, and we dashed away after dropping a few passengers, but receiving no new ones. Rattling onward through the Valley, we were dazzled with the fiercely gleaming gas lamps, as before. But sometimes, in the dark of intense brightness, grim faces, that bore the aspect and expression of individual sins, or evil passions, seemed to thrust themselves through the veil of light, glaring upon us, and stretching forth a great, dusky hand, as if to impede our progress. I almost thought that they were my own sins that appalled me there. These were freaks of imagination—nothing more, certainly—mere delusions, which I ought to be heartily ashamed of; but all through the Dark Valley I was tormented, and pestered, and dolefully bewildered with the same kind of waking dreams. The mephitic[17] gases of that region intoxicate the brain. As the light of natural day, however, began to struggle with the glow of the lanterns, these vain imaginations lost their vividness, and finally vanished with the first ray of sunshine that greeted our escape from the Valley of the Shadow of Death. Ere we had gone a mile beyond it I could wellnigh have taken my oath that this whole gloomy passage was a dream.

At the end of the valley, as John Bunyan mentions, is a cavern, where, in his days, dwelt two cruel giants, Pope and Pagan, who had strewn the ground about their residence with the bones of slaughtered pilgrims. These vile old troglodytes[18] are no longer there; but into their deserted cave another terrible giant has thrust himself, and makes it his business to seize upon honest travelers and fatten them for his table with plentiful meals of smoke, mist, moonshine, raw potatoes, and sawdust. He is a German by birth, and is called Giant Transcendentalist; but as to his form, his features, his substance, and his nature generally, it is the chief peculiarity of this huge miscreant that neither he for himself, nor anybody for him, has ever been able to describe them. As we rushed by the cavern's mouth we caught a hasty glimpse of him, looking somewhat like an ill-proportioned figure, but considerably more like a heap of fog and duskiness. He shouted after us, but in so strange a phraseology that we knew not what he meant, nor whether to be encouraged or affrighted.

It was late in the day when the train thundered into the ancient city of Vanity, where Vanity Fair is still at the height of prosperity, and exhibits an epitome of whatever is brilliant, gay, and fascinating beneath the sun. As I purposed to make a considerable stay here, it gratified me to learn that there is no longer the want of harmony between the town's-people and pilgrims, which impelled the former to such lamentably mistaken measures as the persecution of Christian and the fiery martyrdom of Faithful. On the contrary, as the new railroad brings with it great trade and a constant influx of strangers, the lord of Vanity Fair is its chief patron, and the capitalists of the city are among the largest stockholders. Many passengers stop to take their pleasure or make their profit in the Fair, instead of going onward to

---

17. Foul-smelling.
18. Primitive cave-dwellers.

the Celestial City. Indeed, such are the charms of the place that people often affirm it to be the true and only heaven; stoutly contending that there is no other, that those who seek further are mere dreamers, and that, if the fabled brightness of the Celestial City lay but a bare mile beyond the gates of Vanity, they would not be fools enough to go thither. Without subscribing to these perhaps exaggerated encomiums, I can truly say that my abode in the city was mainly agreeable, and my intercourse with the inhabitants productive of much amusement and instruction.

Being naturally of a serious turn, my attention was directed to the solid advantages derivable from a residence here, rather than to the effervescent pleasures which are the grand object with too many visitants. The Christian reader, if he has had no accounts of the city later than Bunyan's time, will be surprised to hear that almost every street has its church, and that the reverend clergy are nowhere held in higher respect than at Vanity Fair. And well do they deserve such honorable estimation; for the maxims of wisdom and virtue which fall from their lips come from as deep a spiritual source, and tend to as lofty a religious aim, as those of the sagest philosophers of old. In justification of this high praise I need only mention the names of the Rev. Mr. Shallow-deep, the Rev. Mr. Stumble-at-truth, that fine old clerical character the Rev. Mr. This-to-day, who expects shortly to resign his pulpit to the Rev. Mr. That-to-morrow; together with the Rev. Mr. Bewilderment, the Rev. Mr. Clog-the-spirit, and, last and greatest, the Rev. Dr. Wind-of-doctrine. The labors of these eminent divines are aided by those of innumerable lecturers, who diffuse such a various profundity, in all subjects of human or celestial science, that any man may acquire an omnigenous[19] erudition without the trouble of even learning to read. Thus literature is etherealized by assuming for its medium the human voice; and knowledge, depositing all its heavier particles, except, doubtless, its gold, becomes exhaled into a sound, which forthwith steals into the ever-open ear of the community. These ingenious methods constitute a sort of machinery, by which thought and study are done to every person's hand without him putting himself to the slightest inconvenience in the matter.[20] There is another species of machine for the wholesale manufacture of

---

19. Consisting of all kinds.

20. Editor's Note: consider radio, television, and tape recordings in the light of this machinery he describes here!

individual morality. This excellent result is effected by societies for all manner of virtuous purposes, with which a man has merely to connect himself, throwing, as it were, his quota of virtue into the common stock, and the president and directors will take care that the aggregate amount be well applied. All these, and other wonderful improvements in ethics, religion, and literature, being made plain to my comprehension by the ingenious Mr. Smooth-it-away, inspired me with a vast admiration of Vanity Fair.

It would fill a volume, in an age of pamphlets, were I to record all my observations in this great capital of human business and pleasure. There was an unlimited range of society—the powerful, the wise, the witty, and the famous in every walk of life; princes, presidents, poets, generals, artists, actors, and philanthropists,—all making their own market at the fair, and deeming no price too exorbitant for such commodities as hit their fancy. It was well worth one's while, even if he had no idea of buying or selling, to loiter through the bazaars and observe the various sorts of traffic that were going forward.

Some of the purchasers, I thought, made very foolish bargains. For instance, a young man having inherited a splendid fortune, laid out a considerable portion of it in the purchase of diseases, and finally spent all the rest for a heavy lot of repentance and a suit of rags. A very pretty girl bartered a heart as clear as crystal, and which seemed her most valuable possession, for another jewel of the same kind, but so worn and defaced as to be utterly worthless. In one shop there were a great many crowns of laurel and myrtle, which soldiers, authors, statesmen, and various other people pressed eagerly to buy; some purchased these paltry wreaths with their lives, others by a toilsome servitude of years, and many sacrificed whatever was most valuable, yet finally slunk away without the crown. There was a sort of stock or scrip,[21] called Conscience, which seemed to be in great demand, and would purchase almost anything. Indeed, few rich commodities were to be obtained without paying a heavy sum in this particular stock, and a man's business was seldom very lucrative unless he knew precisely when and how to throw his hoard of conscience into the market. Yet as this stock was the only thing of permanent value, whoever parted with it was sure to find himself a loser in the long run. Several of the speculations were of questionable character.

---

21. A document which gives evidence that the bearer is entitled to receive something.

Occasionally a member of Congress recruited his pocket by the sale of his constituents; and I was assured that public officers have often sold their country at very moderate prices. Thousands sold their happiness for a whim. Gilded chains were in great demand, and purchased with almost any sacrifice. In truth, those who desired, according to the old adage, to sell anything valuable for a song, might find customers all over the Fair; and there were innumerable messes of pottage, piping hot, for such as chose to buy them with their birthrights. A few articles, however, could not be found genuine at Vanity Fair. If a customer wished to renew his stock of youth the dealers offered him a set of false teeth and an auburn wig; if he demanded peace of mind, they recommended opium or a brandy bottle.

Tracts of land and golden mansions, situated in the Celestial City, were often exchanged, at very disadvantageous rates, for a few years' lease of small, dismal, inconvenient tenements in Vanity Fair. Prince Beelzebub himself took great interest in this sort of traffic, and sometimes condescended to meddle with smaller matters. I once had the pleasure to see him bargaining with a miser for his soul, which, after much ingenious skirmishing on both sides, his highness succeeded in obtaining at about the value of sixpence. The prince remarked with a smile, that he was a loser by the transaction.

Day after day, as I walked the streets of Vanity, my manners and deportment[22] became more and more like those of the inhabitants. The place began to seem like home; the idea of pursuing my travels to the Celestial City was almost obliterated from my mind. I was reminded of it, however, by the sight of the same pair of simple pilgrims at whom we had laughed so heartily when Apollyon puffed smoke and steam into their faces at the commencement of our journey. There they stood amidst the densest bustle of Vanity; the dealers offering them their purple and fine linen and jewels, the men of wit and humor gibing at them, a pair of buxom ladies ogling them askance, while the benevolent Mr. Smooth-it-away whispered some of his wisdom at their elbows, and pointed to a newly-erected temple; but there were these worthy simpletons, making the scene look wild and monstrous, merely by their sturdy repudiation of all part in its business or pleasures.

---

22. Behavior.

One of them—his name was Stick-to-the-right—perceived in my face, I suppose, a species of sympathy and almost admiration, which, to my own great surprise, I could not help feeling for this pragmatic couple. It prompted him to address me.

"Sir," inquired he, with a sad, yet mild and kindly voice, "do you call yourself a pilgrim?"

"Yes," I replied, "my right to that appellation is indubitable. I am merely a sojourner here in Vanity Fair, being bound to the Celestial City by the new railroad."

"Alas, friend," rejoined Mr. Stick-to-the-right, "I do assure you, and beseech you to receive the truth of my words, that that whole concern is a bubble. You may travel on it all your lifetime, were you to live thousands of years, and yet never get beyond the limits of Vanity Fair. Yea, though you should deem yourself entering the gates of the blessed city, it will be nothing but a miserable delusion."

"The Lord of the Celestial City," began the other pilgrim, whose name was Mr. Foot-it-to-heaven, "has refused, and will ever refuse, to grant an act of incorporation for this railroad; and unless that be obtained, no passenger can ever hope to enter his dominions. Wherefore every man who buys a ticket must lay his account with losing the purchase money, which is the value of his own soul."

"Nonsense!" said Mr. Smooth-it-away, taking my arm and leading me off, "these fellows ought to be indicted for a libel. If the law stood as it once did in Vanity Fair we should see them grinning through the iron bars of the prison window."

This incident made a considerable impression on my mind, and contributed with other circumstances to indispose me to a permanent residence in the city of Vanity; although, of course, I was not simple enough to give up my original plan of gliding along easily and commodiously by railroad. Still, I grew anxious to be gone. There was one strange thing that troubled me. Amid the occupations or amusements of the Fair, nothing was more common than for a person—whether at feast, theatre, or church, or trafficking for wealth and honors, or whatever he might be doing, and however unseasonable the interruption—suddenly to vanish like a soap bubble, and be never more seen of his fellows; and so accustomed were the latter to such little accidents that they went on with their business as quietly as if nothing had happened. But it was otherwise with me.

Finally, after a pretty long residence at the Fair, I resumed my journey towards the Celestial City, still with Mr. Smooth-it-away at my side. At a short distance beyond the suburbs of Vanity we passed the ancient silver mine, of which Demas was the first discoverer, and which is now wrought to great advantage, supplying nearly all the coined currency of the world. A little further onward was the spot where Lot's wife had stood forever under the semblance of a pillar of salt. Curious travelers have long since carried it away piecemeal. Had all regrets been punished as rigorously as this poor dame's were, my yearning for the relinquished delights of Vanity Fair might have produced a similar change in my own corporeal substance, and left me a warning to future pilgrims.

The next remarkable object was a large edifice, constructed of mossgrown[23] stone, but in a modern and airy style of architecture. The engine came to a pause in its vicinity, with the usual tremendous shriek.

"This was formerly the castle of the redoubted giant Despair," observed Mr. Smooth-it-away; "but since his death Mr. Flimsy-faith has repaired it, and keeps an excellent house of entertainment here. It is one of our stopping-places."

"It seems but slightly put together," remarked I, looking at the frail yet ponderous walls. "I do not envy Mr. Flimsy-faith his habitation. Some day it will thunder down upon the heads of the occupants."

"We shall escape at all events," said Mr. Smooth-it-away, "for Apollyon is putting on the steam again."

The road now plunged into a gorge of the Delectable Mountains, and traversed the field where in former ages the blind men wandered and stumbled among the tombs. One of these ancient tombstones had been thrust across the track by some malicious person, and gave the train of cars a terrible jolt. Far up the rugged side of a mountain I perceived a rusty iron door, half overgrown with bushes and creeping plants, but with smoke issuing from its crevices.

"Is that," inquired I, "the very door in the hill-side which the shepherds assured Christian was a by-way to hell?"

"That was a joke on the part of the shepherds," said Mr. Smooth-it-away, with a smile. "It is neither more nor less than the door of a

---

23. Moss-covered.

cavern which they use as a smoke-house for the preparation of mutton hams."

My recollections of the journey are now, for a little space, dim and confused, inasmuch as a singular drowsiness here overcame me, owing to the fact that we were passing over the enchanted ground, the air of which encourages a disposition to sleep. I awoke, however, as soon as we crossed the borders of the pleasant land of Beulah. All the passengers were rubbing their eyes, comparing watches, and congratulating one another on the prospect of arriving so seasonably at the journey's end. The sweet breezes of this happy climb came refreshingly to our nostrils; we beheld the glimmering gush of silver fountains, overhung by trees of beautiful foliage and delicious fruit, which were propagated by grafts from the celestial gardens. Once, as we dashed onward like a hurricane, there was a flutter of wings and the bright appearance of an angel in the air, speeding forth on some heavenly mission. The engine now announced the close vicinity of the final station-house by one last and horrible scream, in which there seemed to be distinguishable every kind of wailing and woe, and bitter fierceness of wrath, all mixed up with the wild laughter of a devil or a madman. Throughout our journey, at every stopping-place, Apollyon had exercised his ingenuity in screwing the most abominable sounds out of the whistle of the steam-engine; but in this closing effort he outdid himself and created an infernal uproar, which, besides disturbing the peaceful inhabitants of Beulah, must have sent its discord even through the celestial gates.

While the horrid clamor was still ringing in our ears we heard an exulting strain, as if a thousand instruments of music, with height and depth and sweetness in their tones, at once tender and triumphant, were struck in unison, to greet the approach of some illustrious hero, who had fought the good fight and won a glorious victory, and was come to lay aside his battered arms forever. Looking to ascertain what might be the occasion of this glad harmony, I perceived, on alighting from the cars, that a multitude of shining ones had assembled on the other side of the river, to welcome two poor pilgrims, who were just emerging from its depths. They were the same whom Apollyon and ourselves had persecuted with taunts, and gibes, and scalding steam, at the commencement of our journey—the same whose unworldly aspect and impressive words had stirred my conscience amid the wild revelers of Vanity Fair.

"How amazingly well those men have got on," cried I to Mr. Smooth-it-away. "I wish we were secure of as good a reception."

"Never fear, never fear!" answered my friend. "Come, make haste; the ferry boat will be off directly, and in three minutes you will be on the other side of the river. No doubt you will find coaches to carry you up to the city gates."

A steam ferry boat, the last improvement on this important route, lay at the river side, puffing, snorting, and emitting all those other disagreeable utterances which betoken the departure to be immediate. I hurried on board with the rest of the passengers, most of whom were in great perturbation: some bawling out for their baggage; some tearing their hair and exclaiming that the boat would explode or sink; some already pale with the heaving of the steam; some gazing affrighted at the ugly aspect of the steersman; and some still dizzy with the slumberous influences of the Enchanted Ground. Looking back to the shore, I was amazed to discern Mr. Smooth-it-away waving his hand in token of farewell.

"Don't you go over to the Celestial City?" exclaimed I.

"Oh, no!" answered he with a queer smile, and that same disagreeable contortion of visage which I had remarked in the inhabitants of the Dark Valley. "Oh, no! I have come thus far only for the sake of your pleasant company. Good-bye! We shall meet again."

And then did my excellent friend Mr. Smooth-it-away laugh outright, in the midst of which cachinnation[24] a smoke-wreath issued from his mouth and nostrils, while a twinkle of lurid flame darted out of either eye, proving indubitably that his heart was all of a red blaze. The impudent fiend! To deny the existence of Tophet, when he felt its fiery tortures raging within his breast. I rushed to the side of the boat, intending to fling myself on shore; but the wheels, as they began their revolutions, threw a dash of spray over me so cold—so deadly cold, with the chill that will never leave those waters until Death be drowned in his own river—that with a shiver and a heartquake I awoke. Thank Heaven it was a dream!

---

What a brilliant story! Unfortunately, the theological liberals and radicals of our day are surely greater in number and in percentage than those of Hawthorne's day. (I'm referring to those who deny such basics as the deity, the atonement, and the

---

24. Loud laughter.

resurrection of Christ.) Many of them preach in the pulpit. Many of them have tenure, teaching religion classes in our universities and divinity schools. But they are just as deceived by "Mr. Smooth-it-away" and his kind as the man in this story was. And they in turn lead others astray.

What a rude awakening for them when they receive their eternal reward, and it won't be a dream, as found in Hawthorne's story, but the beginning of an endless nightmare! The way that leads to heaven, said Jesus, is straight and narrow. Thankfully, they can find forgiveness—at the present time, before it's too late—through the very atonement of Christ they now mock as antiquated.

All I can say is: Give me that old-time religion!

*This selection is suitable for children.*
*The moral of the story is that an outlook of faith lifts our depression.*

# "GOD LIVES"

by Hans Christian Andersen
translated by Kirsti Saebo Newcombe

It's so nice to read the faith-building fairy tales of Hans Christian Andersen. This one shows the difference applied faith can have in our outlook on life (and how doubts can impair that outlook).

Francis Schaeffer once pointed out that a lot of professing Christians are "practical atheists." They may say with their lips that they trust God, but really they just trust in themselves and what they can see. But the believer with true faith has a clear vision and an optimistic, yet still realistic, outlook on life.

---

It was a Sunday morning. The sun was shining brightly, bringing warmth into the living room. Outside under God's blue sky, where the meadow was green and fragrant with flowers, the birds were rejoicing. But while there was joy and happiness outside, inside there was sorrow and gloom. Even the wife who usually was such a cheerful person, sat this morning at the breakfast table and looked down sadly. She got up without hardly touching her food. She dried her eyes and slowly headed for the door.

It was as if a curse lay over the house as a black cloud. There was an economic depression in the land; industry was down. Everything in the country seemed to be going down, except the taxes. In fact, the taxes were becoming more and more pressing. The crops always seemed to be worse than the year before. Now, there was nothing to look forward to but poverty and misery. All of this lay heavy on the man of the house. He was usually such a hard-working and upright citizen, but now he despaired at the thought of the future.

He even said on several occasions that he might just do himself in and end this miserable and dreary life. Whatever his cheerful wife said could not console him; neither could the secular and spiritual comfort of his friends. It made him even more silent and depressed. It was no wonder that his poor wife would lose hope also. But her sorrow had a different reason as we shall soon discover.

When the husband saw his wife so unhappy that she was about to go out, by herself, he stopped her and said, "I will not let you go before you tell me what's wrong!"

She was quiet for a while, then she sighed deeply and said, "Oh, my dear husband, last night I dreamt that God was dead, and that all the angels followed Him to His grave!"

"How can you imagine and believe such nonsense?" said the man. "Don't you know that God can never die?"

Suddenly the face of his dear wife shone with happiness, and as she lovingly squeezed his hands, she said, "You mean, the good God is still alive then?"

"Of course," answered the man. "Who could ever doubt that?"

She embraced him and looked up at him with eyes shining with faith, peace and pure joy, and she said, "Oh, my dear husband. Since God is alive, why should we then not believe in Him and trust Him? He who has counted each hair on our heads . . . He who will not let one fall outside His will . . . He who clothes the lilies of the field and gives the sparrows and the ravens their food."

As she spoke, it was as if scales fell from his eyes, as if all the heavy bands around his heart loosened. For the first time in ages, he smiled and thanked his dear, godly wife for the scheme she had used to rekindle his faith and give him back his trust in God.

Then the sun shone brighter into their living room. It shone on happy faces. The air blew more refreshingly about them, and the birds rejoiced even more, giving their heartful thanks to God.

---

This reminds me of a true incident from the life of Luther. He went through a period of depression, and nothing his wife could say snapped him out of it. So one day, she dressed in black as if mourning. When he asked her why, she replied that God had died. And he asked her if she was crazy. She countered that if he really believed God wasn't dead then why did he act if He were? Luther got the point, and his depression lifted.

*This selection is suitable for children.*
*The moral of the story is that God can and sometimes does the miraculous to call people to Himself.*

# THE CONVERSION OF ADONIRAM JUDSON

from *Heroes of Faith on Pioneer Trails*[25]

by E. Myers Harrison

Adoniram Judson (1788–1850) was one of the finest missionaries America ever produced. He initiated a very fruitful pioneering mission in the Far East, especially Burma, despite the dangers. Most evangelicals are aware of his fame, but few are aware of the fact that as a young man he rejected the faith. Here is the true story of his odyssey from a childhood faith to atheism to a true and imperishable faith in Jesus who loved us and gave Himself up for us all.

---

Judson was a precocious boy. When only three years of age he learned to read under the tutelage of his mother while his father was absent on a journey. Great was the father's astonishment and delight upon his return, to hear his young son read to him a chapter from the Bible!

He grew up in a devout Christian home. His father, a Congregational minister, cherished the fond hope that his son would follow in his footsteps. But Adoniram was enamored of his brilliance and could not think of wasting his superb talents in so dull a calling as the ministry. Having vanquished all rivals in intellectual contests, he graduated at nineteen from Providence College (now Brown University) as valedictorian. He pictured himself as an orator, greater than Demosthenes, swaying the multitudes with his eloquence; as a second Homer, writing immortal poems; as a second Alexander the Great, weeping because there were no more worlds to conquer.

Judson was not only inordinately ambitious; he was also openly atheistic. It was during the early years of the nineteenth century, while Judson was in college, that French infidelity swept over the country. With only three or four exceptions, all the students of Yale were

---

25. E. Myers Harrison, *Heroes of Faith on Pioneer Trails* (Chicago: Moody Press, 1945), 87–90.

avowed infidels and preferred to call each other by the names of leading infidels such as Tom Paine or Voltaire, instead of their own names.

Providence College did not escape the contaminations of this vile
flood of skepticism. In the class just above that of Judson was a
young man by the name of Ernest, who was exceptionally gifted,
witty and clever, and an outspoken atheist. An intimate friendship
developed between these two brilliant young men, with the result
that Judson also became a bold exponent of infidelity, to the extreme
mortification of his father and mother. When his father sought to
argue with him, he quickly demonstrated his intellectual superiority,
but he had no answer to his mother's tears and solemn warnings.

Shortly thereafter he set out on horseback on a tour of adventure
through several states. He joined a band of strolling players, and lived,
as he himself related later, "a wild, reckless life." Leaving the troupe
after a few weeks, he continued his trip on horseback, stopping on a
certain historic night at a country inn. Apologetically, the landlord
explained that, only one room being vacant, he would be obliged to
put him next door to a young man who was extremely ill; in fact, probably dying. Judson assured him that, aside from a natural feeling of pity,
he would in no wise be affected, since death meant nothing to him.

Judson retired, but sleep eluded him. The partition was very thin,
and for long hours he listened to the groans of the dying man—groans
of agony, groans of despair. "The poor fellow is evidently dying in terror. I suppose I should go to his assistance, but what could I say that
would help him?" thought Judson to himself; and he shivered at the
very thought of going into the presence of the dying man. He felt a
blush of shame steal over him. What would his late unbelieving companions think if they knew of his weakness? Above all, what would
witty, brilliant Ernest say, if he knew? As he tried to compose himself,
the dreadful cries from the next room continued. He pulled the blan-
kets over his head but still he heard the awful sounds—and shuddered! Finally, all became quiet in the next room. At dawn Judson rose
and inquired of the innkeeper concerning his fellow-lodger.

"He is dead!"

"Dead!" replied Judson. "And do you know who he was?"

"Yes," the innkeeper answered, "he was a graduate of Providence
College, a fine young fellow named Ernest."

Judson was overwhelmed by the news that the young man who
died the previous night in the adjoining room in evident terror of

death was his skeptical college friend, Ernest. For many hours the words "Dead! Lost! *Lost!*" kept ringing in his ears. There was now just one place that beckoned him. Turning his horse's direction, he went home and begged his father and mother to help him find a faith that would stand the test of life and of death, of time and eternity.

The brilliant young skeptic realized at last that he needed:

*A faith for the testings of life!*
*A faith for the exigencies of death!*
*A faith for time and eternity!*

At this time of acute spiritual struggle, when his mind was filled with the dark clouds of skepticism and his soul enveloped with the black darkness of sin, the voice of God spoke and "there was light." When he became penitent and submissive, he learned that "the voice of the Lord is powerful and full of majesty"—abundantly able to save. He not only heard a *Voice*; he saw a *Face*, surpassingly sweet, and fell in love with a *Person*, the dear Son of God. Henceforth the quenchless song of his heart was, "The love of Christ! His sufferings! His forgiveness! His world-wide compassion! His abiding presence! O to know the love of Christ—in its breadth and length, its depth and height!"

The *depth* of love: the sufferings of Christ!
The *height* of love: the forgiveness of Christ!
The *breadth* of love: the world-wide compassion of Christ!
The *length* of love: the ever abiding presence of Christ!

---

And now, as Paul Harvey would put it, you know the rest of the story! What are the odds that, of all men, Judson would share a room that fateful night with Ernest Ames? (We know from other sources that Ames was his last name.) It's a tragedy when young people from Christian homes fall into the wrong crowd and lose their faith. In this situation, that problem was short-lived, thanks to divine intervention.

# SECTION 2

# HOPE

H ope is the ability to imagine ourselves in a good and better situation in the future. Without hope, life would be rather bleak. At the entrance to hell in Dante's *Divine Comedy* are the ominous words, "Abandon all hope, ye who enter here!" Note that hell begins where hope ends.

"Bright hope for tomorrow"—That is what Christ gives us. Hope for a better tomorrow is what sees us through a thousand "everydays." The hope of a nice weekend sees us through the weekdays. The hope of a wonderful holiday can see us through weeks of much busyness and stress. Above all, the hope of heaven sees us through life.

Hope is another of those human qualities that makes us different from the animals. The ability to believe in a better future and picture it in our minds drives us forward. In a small way, the hope of that special cup of coffee may help us finish an unpleasant task. And the hope of a great reward may help us finish a large project.

Hope is the basis for advertising—the ability of people to picture themselves enjoying the merchandise is what makes them go buy it. And the hope that "this time I'll win" is the basis for all gambling, from the lottery to the casinos. But much more often than not, these are false hopes.

Because we know that Jesus will triumph over evil in the end, just as He triumphed over the devil on the cross, we have a sure hope about the future. God has put eternity into our hearts, and that is why hope springs eternal in the human heart.

The following stories illustrate hope in one way or another.

*This selection is suitable for children.*
*The moral of the story is that Jesus Christ, the Lord of life, can do the impossible; therefore, we should have hope for a positive future, come what may.*

# "THE IMPOTENT MAN OF BETHESDA"
### from *The Glorious Galilean*
### by J. W. G. Ward

How can you have hope when you keep experiencing failure? If you visit people in the ghetto, as I do on occasion to assist a food ministry, perhaps the biggest problem you see is the hopelessness. Many people don't even want to bother to try anymore; they've been beaten down so much by life. They've lost all hope.

But Jesus Christ can do the impossible. He is the Lord of life and the King of the universe. The forces of nature must yield to His command. Therefore, we can and should have hope. Furthermore, He cares for us. (It is one thing for the God of the universe to be able to do anything He wanted; it would be another if He were malignant, as some people think because of the evil in the world.)

The Gospels say that Jesus went about doing good. Here is one of those episodes. In this situation the man He helped seemed to be beyond hope, for he had tried so many times before in vain. What a difference it made that Jesus Christ entered his life!

This selection is the third and final selection from Dr. J. W. G. Ward's *The Glorious Galilean*, a book with several stories of lives touched by their encounters with Christ. The book was published in 1936. Although the story is based on true incidents and real characters, Dr. Ward takes obvious poetic license here.

---

As we walked down the narrow, sun-baked streets of Jerusalem, we found ourselves in the craftsmen's quarter. Beneath faded and tattered awnings were the shops of the potters, the smiths, the makers of harness for the beasts of the caravan, and the workers in brass. But we wanted none of these. We were in search of a certain man who was a carpenter. At last, guided by the sound of the saw, we discovered him busy at his bench.

"Greetings, Joshua," we began. "How fare you today?"

He laid down his saw and, straightening his back as though weary, returned our salutations warmly. The preliminaries disposed of, he inquired what he could do for us, and without more ado we told him why we had come in quest of him.

"You once met with Jesus of Nazareth," we said. "Will you, out of the goodness of your heart, favor us with the story of that day and its happenings?"

"Assuredly," he replied, "and right gladly. But doubtless you are tired with the heat. Sit here."

He brushed the shavings from a log and, leaning against the bench, began.

"You are surprised to find me here, hale and hearty, and engaged in laborious toil? I read it in your glance as you entered."

"It is even so," we answered. "We had been led to believe that for long years you were afflicted, and even though the Master had compassion on you—"

His laughter left the sentence uncompleted.

"You were right, but, my friend, I have discovered the joy of honest work. To think how poor life was, and how much I have missed! But that is not what you want to hear. I will commence at the beginning."

We settled ourselves as comfortably as the unyielding log would permit, and waited for his story with avid interest.

"First of all, the days of my youth were made weary by recurring sickness. My good father did all in his power to secure for me the priceless boon of health. He was but a craftsman, however, working in this same shop where you found me. And he impoverished himself on my behalf. One after another skilled in the art of healing, did he bring to my side. All their remedies and their efforts were unavailing. So it seemed as though I were doomed to a life of continued misery and suffering. Then some of our neighbors urged my father to bear me to the pool called Bethesda. This was held in high repute by certain of our people. It stands near the sheep gate which is, as you perhaps know, at the north of the Temple area.

"Many resorted thither, for it was commonly reported that an angel troubled the waters at given intervals. And the tradition ran that he who stepped in first, after the angel's touch, would be cured. Accordingly, although my father had little faith in the story, he carried me there, laying me in the most advantageous position he could find. Still that amounted to little. As I have said, many, afflicted with divers diseases, were there. Some had waited for weary months, even years, in the hope of being cured. A few were still sanguine; most had become embittered by repeated disappointments. Yet I soon learned that there were compensations. Pilgrims coming from afar, and others returning from the Temple, were stirred to pity by the sight of these people in such an unhappy plight. And with the object of securing some blessing, or in gratitude for the good bestowed, these pious folk gave us freely of their bounty.

"As the days passed, I confess that I found myself more resigned to my fate than I had ever been before. The money thus obtained procured for me many a little luxury to which I had hitherto been stranger. Moreover, as one after another was cured and went away, I was able to gain a better position. I do not mean better as being nearer to the steps of the pool, but where I was among the first to catch the notice of pilgrims passing through the gate. This brought me a large increase in the amount of alms, and I found not without some inner misgiving, that I was now much more concerned about these returns than about recovery. I had become a professional mendicant! My affliction and the piteous look I was able to assume, together with a certain whining voice I had acquired, were my stock-in-trade. While my companions and I cumbering the gate still retained some belief in the miraculous powers of the pool, I fear that our chief interest now centered upon the money which our piteous appeals brought forth.

"As I have already said, I was therefore, resigned to my condition. Yet, more, as I looked at the care-lined faces of the merchants who came and went, or watched those who toiled, carrying their heavy loads along the street in the blazing heat of the sun while I was seated in the shade of the wall, I began to thank the Powers that I had escaped a lot so arduous. When my father remonstrated with me, as he did—for as an honest craftsman it was horrible to him to see his son consorting with common beggars—I bade him begone. What had life to offer me? It were surely better to be an object of public sympathy, and to be well paid for it, than to lie at home, a drag upon my parents' industry. And so, bitter as life was, it had some recompense to offer.

"It had, until—But this is what you want to know. Through that same gate of which I have spoken, mingling with the jostling crowd of passers by—pilgrims, traders, men of business, and human beasts of burden—came Jesus of Nazareth. I had already heard of him, for he had created a great stir in the capital by reason of his wondrous words, and also his compassion for the afflicted. Yet, I had not seen him before, nor did I even know it was he to whom I stretched out my hand for alms. Yet as I did so, I felt instinctively that this was no ordinary pilgrim coming to the city. There was a dignity of bearing to which his peasant robes seemed ill suited. But more, there was a kindliness in his face as he stopped, regarding me earnestly. It may have been merely my fancy, but I had the feeling that he was looking right into my very heart, reading there the record of a forfeited manhood.

"He spoke, and as he did so something awakened in my soul. It seemed to me almost the same as when, at the touch of the angel, the waters of the pool bubbled and boiled. He asked me how long I had been stricken with this infirmity. I replied, 'Thirty and eight years.' He looked at me with his discerning eyes, and a light irradiated his face as though he had fully probed the actual reason for my being there. Then he asked, 'Wilt thou be made whole?' I did not intend to lower my defenses, nor to have my means of livelihood snatched away from me by an idle question. I replied instantly, and, I fear, not without a flash of anger, 'Sir, I have no man, when the water is troubled, to put me into the pool, but while I am coming another steppeth down before me.'

"Even while I spoke, I knew that was only an excuse. Nor is that all: I was sure that he knew it also. By some strange chance it flitted across my mind at that very instant that I, in common with people around me, had limited the possible blessing through sheer lack of faith. This was a curative spring. It certainly possessed beneficial qualities. But just as certainly its benefits might have been enjoyed by all who made the effort to immerse themselves in the waters. Those benefits were not confined merely to the first one who made the venture of faith. But that is by the way. I am turning aside from my story.

"As I looked up at him, still with some measure of insolence, I noticed that a look almost of sternness sat enthroned there. He had detected my insincerity, and saw that my futile excuse was meant to cover my acquiescence in my lot. More, that I greatly preferred a life of remunerative, if enforced, idleness, rather than assume the obligations of health and robust manhood. Jesus stretched out his hand commandingly, saying unto me, 'Rise, take up thy bed, and walk.'

"My first impulse was to sneer defiantly, and bid him not to jest at the affliction of a poor sufferer. But, almost in spite of myself, I was compelled to obey. Like the sudden gleaming of the lightning's scimitar, cleaving the dark curtains of night, I saw a vision, the like of which these eyes had never beheld up to that hour. I saw myself, Joshua the mendicant, taking what fortune might fling into my lap, or cursing any who passed by unmoved by my doleful appeals, now no longer a cripple, no longer a parasite, but a man! A swift accession of strength came to me, and obeying his word, I leaped to my feet. I could have laughed outright at the astonished faces around about me. I could have struck the pompous figure of a merchant who had frequently declined my pleas for money as he nodded his head as much as to say, 'It is even as I thought—an imposter.' But my mind was dominated by the picture I had seen. Henceforth, I was to be a man, filling a man's place, and making the days rich with honorable labor.

"As you will understand, I was so excited by these new sensations that immediately I left the place both of my bondage and my shame. My feet and legs, unaccustomed to bear my weight, caused me at first to stagger like a drunken man, but I made my way as quickly as I could toward the Temple. I felt strangely prompted first to offer my gratitude to Jehovah. Only after I had done this did I remember that I had uttered no words of thanks to my unknown benefactor. I retraced my steps to the pool, hoping to find him still in the cloisters, but it was in vain.

"But I must tell you this. All days had become much alike to me. They were distinguished only by whether returns were good or bad. I had completely forgotten that it was the Sabbath. As I hunted for the Master, I walked again toward the Temple. There I was stopped by some of the elders. 'It is the Sabbath day,' said one, pointing to the padded rug upon which I had lain so long. 'It is not lawful for thee to carry thy bed.' I was wrathful at such petty quibbling, considering the cure that had been wrought, and I said indignantly, 'He that made me whole, the same said unto me, "Take up thy bed and walk."'

"But they were plainly not to be silenced so easily. Another turned upon me demanding, 'What man is that which said unto thee, "Take up thy bed and walk?"' I stared at them abashed. I knew not what to answer. It came to me then, only for the first time, that I did not even know the name of him to whom I owed so much. It was possibly a foolish and irreverent thing for me to do, but angrily I flung the rug at their feet, and went my way.

"There was a great multitude in the Temple courts, and I was soon lost in the crowd. But so was he whom I sought. I felt that I could not leave the precincts of the sanctuary until I had voiced my thankfulness to him. Then, after a time, although I had looked for him in vain, he found me. Surrounded by a group of people, and talking earnestly with them, he saw me. He left the charmed circle. I began to pour forth my gratitude, as I fell upon my knees. But taking me firmly by the arm, he lifted me up and said, 'Behold, thou art made whole—sin no more, lest a worse thing come unto thee.'

"It seemed a hard saying, but not harder than I merited. It was true, then! He knew me for a man full of hypocrisy—one who had gone aside from seeking deliverance in order to live upon the honest efforts of others. My sin had been unbelief.

"My parents were now dead. I had no home, no friends but the beggars with whom I had consorted. But the next day I came to the shop of the carpenter where my father had labored so long. I saw there the deserted bench. And all about me was the joyous hum of men, industrious and God-fearing, who found daily happiness in the labor of their hands. This is not recorded by those who set down the story of our Lord's life, for it was a matter between myself and him. At any rate, it could not be of interest to the world at large. But before another day had passed, I again went to him. I told him that I wanted to be the man he would desire, and that I would work for my bread if I only knew how. I acquainted him with my story, and that my father had acquired the name of an honest worker of wood. And to my surprise, Jesus said that he also had toiled in a carpenter's shop. Therefore it was he who, with his own hands, taught me how to handle the plane and saw. It was he who set my feet in the path in which a man may live not only by his own exertions, but also to the glory of God, even though his tasks be commonplace.

"It was only after many days, when he again returned to Jerusalem, that I heard the gracious words that proceeded out of his mouth. And then I discovered that he was indeed the Christ of God. I had no gifts to offer him. I had no wealth to lay at his feet. My days were too full, battling for bread, to render him any service. But I gave him what, perchance, is the gift he desires most. By that I mean, the love and devotion of a man who realizes his indebtedness to the divine Lord, and who would express his love, not in high-sounding words, but in the daily doing of his will. And if, as I have since learned, he magnified the name of God in all he wrought in the workshop of Nazareth, then at least my service shall be so inspired, and dedicated to an aim so great."

As we walked homeward, we could not help feeling that not only had this onetime mendicant discovered life's meaning, but also he had laid bare this significant truth impinging with irresistible force upon our mind. We had scarcely grasped it before. The life acceptable to the Almighty is not one spent idly waiting for some hoped-for blessing. It is one of faith which goes on its way trustfully, but which also works toward the realization of the heart's desire. It is not in mute and ignoble acquiescence in circumstances, but rather in obedience to the promptings of his Spirit. It is not even in pious resignation, but in utilizing spiritual forces about us that we please him. Nor is it in following minutely the demands of religious ritual, but, instead, seeking to do our daily duty with the divine approval upon us that we glorify his name. The common service of the day, in the place of business or the home, is thus a means by which the faith within us finds expression. And the service we render to one another, for love's sweet sake, becomes a sacrament unto God.

---

Can you imagine ill health (in the prime of one's life) for *thirty-eight years?* But God can change situations; He can do the impossible. And in fact, that's just what He did for this man. His plan may be different for different people, but because of His goodness and His sovereignty, we need never lose hope.

*This selection is suitable for children.*
*The moral of the story is that, thanks to Jesus, we can have hope, even in the face of what seems incurable.*

# THE HEALING OF THE LEPER WOMEN

from *Ben-Hur: A Tale of the Christ*
by Lew Wallace

In the latter half of the last century, one of America's best-known infidels, Robert Ingersoll, was talking with a friend, Lew Wallace, about theology. They both agreed Christianity was nonsense. Ingersoll encouraged Wallace, since he was a writer, to take up the pen and debunk Christianity once and for all by showing it rested on a weak foundation and by showing the fallibility of Jesus Himself. Wallace agreed to take up the challenge.

But his research into the historicity of Christianity led him to see that he and Ingersoll had been wrong and that indeed the faith was based on solid historical fact. He wrote a book, all right, but it wasn't the kind he initially set out to write. Along the way, he had become a Christian and wrote one of the all-time great Christian novels, *Ben-Hur*, which was later made into a blockbuster movie.

This story is an excerpt from the book, and it's about the mother and sister of the main character, Judah Ben-Hur. The two women had contacted leprosy while wasting away unjustly in a Roman prison. Only through Christ—who can do the impossible—are they freed from their horrible plight. Note that the movie differs a bit from the book as to when the healing takes place in this. After Wallace's description of leprosy comes the story, which begins on Palm Sunday, the day of Christ's triumphal entrance into Jerusalem. The two leper women see His public appearance as their only chance to reach Him for healing.

---

To be a leper was to be treated as dead—to be excluded from the city as a corpse; to be spoken to by the best beloved and most loving only at a distance; to dwell with none but lepers; to be utterly unprivileged; to be denied the rites of the Temple and the synagogue; to go about in rent garments and with covered mouth, except when crying, "Unclean, unclean!"; to find home in the wilderness or in abandoned tombs; to become a materialized spectre of Hinnom and Gehenna; to be at all times less a living offence to others than a breathing torment to self; afraid to die, yet without hope except in death. . . .

Meanwhile, the people in the east came up slowly. When at length the foremost of them were in sight, the gaze of the lepers fixed upon a man riding in the midst of what seemed a chosen company which sang and danced about him in extravagance of joy. The rider was bareheaded and clad all in white. When he was in distance to be more clearly observed, these, looking anxiously, saw an olive-hued face shaded by long chestnut hair slightly sunburned and parted in the middle. He looked neither to the right nor left. In the noisy *abandon* of his followers he appeared to have no part; nor did their favor disturb him in the least, or raise him out of the profound melancholy into which, as his countenance showed, he was plunged. The sun beat upon the back of his head, and lighting up the floating hair gave it a delicate likeness to a golden nimbus. Behind him the irregular procession, pouring forward with continuous singing and shouting, extended out of view. There was no need of any one to tell the lepers that this was he—the wonderful Nazarene!

"He is here, Tirzah," the mother said; "he is here. Come, my child."

As she spoke she glided in front of the white rock and fell upon her knees.

Directly the daughter and servant were by her side. Then at sight of the procession in the west, the thousands from the city halted, and began to wave their green branches, shouting, or rather chanting (for it was all in one voice), "Blessed is the King of Israel that cometh in the name of the Lord!"

And all the thousands who were of the rider's company, both those near and those afar, replied so the air shook with the sound, which was as a great wind threshing the side of the hill. Amidst the din, the cries of the poor lepers were not more than the twittering of dazed sparrows.

The moment of the meeting of the hosts was come, and with it the opportunity the sufferers were seeking; if not taken, it would be lost forever, and they would be lost as well.

"Nearer, my child—let us get nearer. He cannot hear us," said the mother.

She arose, and staggered forward. Her ghastly hands were up, and she screamed with horrible shrillness. The people saw her—saw her hideous face, and stopped awestruck—an effect for which extreme human misery, visible as in this instance, is as potent as majesty in purple and gold. Tirzah, behind her a little way, fell down too faint and frightened to follow farther.

"The lepers! the lepers!"

"Stone them!"

"The accursed of God! Kill them!"

These, with other yells of like import, broke in upon the hosannas of the part of the multitude too far removed to see and understand the cause of the interruption. Some there were, however, near by familiar with the nature of the man to whom the unfortunates were appealing—some who, by long intercourse with him, had caught somewhat of his divine compassion: they gazed at him, and were silent while, in far view, he rode up and stopped in front of the woman. She also beheld his face—calm, pitiful, and of exceeding beauty, the large eyes tender with benignant purpose.

And this was the colloquy that ensued:

"O Master, Master! Thou seest our need; thou canst make us clean. Have mercy upon us—mercy!"

"Believest thou I am able to do this?" he asked.

"Thou art he of whom the prophets spake—thou art the Messiah!" she replied.

His eyes grew radiant, his manner confident.

"Woman," he said, "great is thy faith; be it unto thee even as thou wilt."

He lingered an instant after, apparently unconscious of the presence of the throng—and instant—then he rode away.

To the heart divinely original, yet so human in all the better elements of humanity, going with sure prevision to a death of all the inventions of men the foulest and most cruel, breathing even then in the forecast shadow of the awful event, and still as hungry and thirsty for love and faith as in the beginning, how precious and ineffably soothing the farewell exclamation of the grateful woman:

"To God in the highest, glory! Blessed, thrice blessed, the Son whom he hath given us!"

Immediately both the hosts, that from the city and that from Bethphage, closed around him with their joyous demonstrations, with hosannas and waving of palms, and so he passed from the lepers forever. Covering her head, the elder hastened to Tirzah, and folded her in her arms, crying, "Daughter, look up! I have his promise; he is indeed the Messiah. We are saved—saved!" And the two remained kneeling while the procession, slowly going, disappeared over the mount. When the noise of its singing afar was a sound scarcely heard the miracle began.

There was first in the hearts of the lepers a freshening of the blood; then it flowed faster and stronger, thrilling their wasted bodies with an infinitely sweet sense of painless healing. Each felt the scourge going from her; their strength revived; they were returning to be themselves. Directly, as if to make the purification complete, from body to spirit the quickening ran, exalting them to a very fervor of ecstasy. The power possessing them to this good end was most nearly that of a draught of swift and happy effect; yet it was unlike and superior in that its healing and cleansing were absolute, and not merely a delicious consciousness while in progress, but the planting, growing, and maturing all at once of a recollection so singular and so holy that the simple thought of it should be of itself ever after a form-less yet perfect thanksgiving.

---

Only Jesus can effect a change like that. Granted, these two are fictional characters, but the novel is based on fact.

The 1959 film *Ben-Hur* became one of the greatest movies of all time. In fact, to date, *Ben-Hur,* directed by William Wyler and starring Charlton Heston, still holds the record for the number of Oscars—eleven—for any one movie. That's quite an honor when you consider that the film so clearly glorifies Jesus Christ.

# "I HEARD THE BELLS ON CHRISTMAS DAY"

by Henry Wadsworth Longfellow

The best loved American poet of the nineteenth century was Henry Wadsworth Longfellow of Massachusetts (1807–82). He was the first American poet to focus on American themes—the landscapes, Indians, American history. Some of his best known poems include "The Courtship of Miles Standish," "Hiawatha," "The Midnight Ride of Paul Revere," and "Evangeline."

The following selection is not a story, but there's a story behind it. It is a hymn, specifically a Christmas carol. And the story behind it is that the U.S. Civil War raged while this song was being written. How could we talk about "peace on Earth" when brother was killing brother in the most bloody fighting Americans have ever engaged in as a nation? Surely, the realities of war made a mockery of the message of Christmas, didn't they, thinks the poet? But when Longfellow meditates on God's justice, he regains his hope.

I heard the bells on Christmas day
Their old familiar carols play,
And wild and sweet the words repeat
Of peace on earth, good-will to men.

I thought how, as the day had come,
The belfries of all Christendom
Had rolled a-long th'unbroken song
Of peace on earth, good-will to men.

And in despair I bowed my head,
"There is no peace on earth," I said,
"For hate is strong, and mocks the song
Of peace on earth, good-will to men."

Then pealed the bells more loud and deep:
"God is not dead: nor doth He sleep;
The wrong shall fail, the right prevail,
With peace on earth, good-will to men."

Till, ringing, singing on its way,
The world revolved from night to day,
A voice, a chime, a chant sublime,
Of peace on earth, good-will to men!

---

It gives us great hope to know that God will one day make right all that is wrong in the world. Longfellow says it so well:

God is not dead: nor doth He sleep;
The wrong shall fail, the right prevail.

Dr. D. James Kennedy tells a story that makes the point that God's judgment may seem slow in coming, but it's still coming:

There was a farmer who lived in New England a few generations ago. He was a complete unbeliever and skeptic. He believed in nothing at all. He mocked his Christian friends, especially in their efforts to try to observe the Sabbath. This skeptic wrote a letter to the editor of his newspaper: "I purchased my seed on the Sabbath. I planted it on the Sabbath. I harvested it on the Sabbath, and now it is the middle of October and I have the largest harvest in the valley. What do you think of that?"

The editor, apparently a wise and godly man, appended this one simple sentence to the letter. He said: "God does not always settle His accounts in October."[1]

---

1. Kennedy with Newcombe, *The Gates of Hell Shall Not Prevail,* 91–92.

*This selection is suitable for children.*
*The moral of the story is to have faith and wait on the Lord because His*
*timing is different from ours. Don't doubt in the darkness what God has*
*shown us in the light.*

# THE CAVE SCENE

### from *Prince Caspian,* book 2 of *The Chronicles of Narnia*
### by C. S. Lewis

C. S. Lewis (1898–1963) was probably this century's greatest Christian writer. Lewis was a professor of English literature at Oxford and, later, Cambridge. He was a great original thinker, whose books are still widely read.

One of Lewis's greatest works is his children's series, *The Chronicles of Narnia.* The books are entertaining and they teach many biblical truths. To understand the backdrop to this story, more background information than normal is required.

Narnia is a magical place that some British schoolchildren have found quite accidentally. Those children are brothers and sisters—Peter, Susan, Edmund, and Lucy. They even become kings and queens in the first book of Narnia, *The Lion, the Witch, and the Wardrobe,* with Peter becoming "the High King."

Time is different in Narnia than here. In Narnia several years could elapse, where back on earth only a few minutes or so would have passed.

Aslan the lion is the overall king of Narnia. C. S. Lewis unmistakably wants us to know that Aslan is a symbolic Jesus Christ.

In book 2 of Narnia, *Prince Caspian,* the title character, is the rightful king. But his uncle, Miraz, is trying to usurp the throne by force. So Caspian blows "the magical horn" to summon Aslan's servants, Peter and Edmund (who, again, had been kings in Narnia in a previous visit, many generations ago). Now, summoned by the horn, they come as soon as called; but, to the Narnians (who have a different time frame), they have been slow in their return. Their delay has caused some to doubt if they'll ever come back. Those who don't trust in their return decide to resort to the old, evil magic, even though that means essentially turning things over to the White Witch, who is a personification of the devil. In the previous book, the White Witch had all of Narnia under a spell. It was she who made it "always winter, but never Christmas." Only Aslan could break the spell. He destroyed her power and ended her reign.

Just before they make their presence known, Peter and Edmund overhear this great debate between those who will side with good versus those who will side with evil. The debate comprises the bulk of this story.

The characters in this scene can be classed into one of two categories: pro-Aslan or anti-Aslan. To make things simple, all the pro-Aslan names will be **bold**. All the names of the anti-Aslan characters will be *italicized*.

In this scene, here are the characters that are *pro*-Aslan:

- **Peter** and **Edmund**

- **Trumpkin**, a Dwarf (**D.L.F.**, Dear Little Friend)

- the sentinel **Badgers**, standing guard

- **Caspian**, the current King of Narnia

- **Master Cornelius**, a good magician, advisor to Caspian

- **Trufflehunter**, the Badger

Here are the characters who are *anti*-Aslan:

- *Nikabrik*, the Dwarf

- a *Hag*

- a *Wer-wolf*

- *Miraz*, the evil prince (not present)

- the *White Witch*, who is present, but in a state of helplessness without magical input, which *Nikabrik* seeks for her.

The moral of the story is that while God's timing may be different than ours, we are to have hope, to trust in God, even when the circumstances look bleak. Often the solution is just around the corner if we persist in hope a little bit more. And whatever happens, don't turn to the devil. His solution to problems only worsens everything and has fatal consequences.

Another moral of the story relates to the Second Coming of Christ. There are many who scoff that Jesus will ever return—it's been so long since His first advent. But to the Lord, a day is like a thousand years and a thousand years is like a day. This story gives a good analogy to those who will wait and trust in the Lord versus those who will turn to the evil one since Christ seems so slow to return.

---

Meanwhile **Trumpkin** and the two boys arrived at the dark little stone archway which led into the inside of the Mound, and two sentinel **Badgers** (the white patches on their cheeks were all **Edmund** could see of them) leaped up with bared teeth and asked them in snarling voices, "Who goes there?"

"**Trumpkin**," said the Dwarf. "Bring the **High King of Narnia** out of the far past."

The **Badgers** nosed at the boys' hands. "At last," they said. "At last."

"Give us a light, friends," said **Trumpkin**.

The **Badgers** found a torch just inside the arch and **Peter** lit it and handed it to **Trumpkin**. "The **D.L.F.** had better lead," he said. "We don't know our way about this place."

**Trumpkin** took the torch and went ahead into the dark tunnel. It was a cold, black, musty place, with an occasional bat fluttering in the torchlight, and plenty of cobwebs. The boys, who had been in the open air ever since that morning at the railway station, felt as if they were going into a trap or a prison.

"I say, **Peter**," whispered **Edmund**. "Look at those carvings on the walls. Don't they look old? And yet we're older than that. When we were last here, they hadn't been made."

"Yes," said **Peter**. "That makes one think."

The Dwarf went on ahead and then turned to the right, and then to the left, and then down some steps, and then to the left again. Then at last they saw a light ahead—light from under a door. And now for the first time they heard voices, for they had come to the door of the central chamber. The voices inside were angry ones. Someone was talking so loudly that the approach of the boys and the Dwarf had not been heard.

"Don't like the sound of that," whispered **Trumpkin** to **Peter**. "Let's listen for a moment." All three stood perfectly still on the outside of the door.

"You know well enough," said a voice ("That's the King [**Caspian**]," whispered **Trumpkin**, "why the Horn was not blown at sunrise that morning. Have you forgotten that *Miraz* fell upon us almost before **Trumpkin** had gone, and we were fighting for our lives for the space of three hours and more? I blew it when first I had a breathing space."

"I'm not likely to forget it," came the angry voice, "when my Dwarfs bore the brunt of the attack and one in five of them fell." ("That's *Nikabrik*," whispered **Trumpkin**.)

"For shame, Dwarf," came a thick voice ("**Trufflehunter'S**," said **Trumpkin**.) "We all did as much as the Dwarfs and none more than the King [**Caspian**]."

"Tell that tale your own way for all I care," answered *Nikabrik*. "But whether it was that the Horn was blown too late, or whether there was no magic in it, no help has come. You, you great clerk, you master magician, you know-all; are you still asking us to hang our hopes on Aslan and **King Peter** and all the rest of it?"

"I must confess—I cannot deny it—that I am deeply disappointed in the result of the operation," came the answer. ("That'll be **Master Cornelius**," said **Trumpkin**.)

"To speak plainly," said *Nikabrik*, "your wallet's empty, your eggs addled, your fish uncaught, your promises broken. Stand aside then and let others work. And that is why—"

"The help will come," said **Trufflehunter**. "I stand by Aslan. Have patience, like us beasts. The help will come. It may be even now at the door."

"Pah!" snarled *Nikabrik*. "You badgers would have us wait till the sky falls and we can all catch larks. I tell you we can't wait. Food is running short; we lose more than we can afford at every encounter; our followers are slipping away."

"And why?" asked **Trufflehunter**. "I'll tell you why. Because it is noised among them that we have called on the Kings of old and the Kings of old have not answered. The last words **Trumpkin** spoke before he went (and went, most likely, to his death) were 'If you must blow the Horn, do not let the army know why you blow it or what you hope from it.' But that same evening everyone seemed to know."

"You'd better have shoved your grey snout in a hornets' nest, badger, than suggest that I am the blab," said *Nikabrik*. "Take it back, or—"

"Oh stop it, both of you," said **King Caspian**. "I want to know what it is that *Nikabrik* keeps on hinting we should do. But before that, I want to know who those two strangers are whom he has brought into our council and who stand there with their ears open and their mouths shut."

"They are friends of mine," said *Nikabrik*. "And what better right have you yourself to be here than that you are a friend of **Trumpkin's**, and the badger's? And what right has that old dotard in the black gown [**Master Cornelius**] to be here except that he is your friend? Why am I to be the only one who can't bring in his friends?"

"His Majesty is the King to whom you have sworn allegiance," said **Trufflehunter** sternly.

"Court manners, court manners," sneered *Nikabrik*. "But in this hole we may talk plainly. You know—and he knows—that this Telmarine boy will be king of nowhere and nobody in a week unless we can help him out of the trap in which he sits."

"Perhaps," said **Cornelius**, "your new friends would like to speak for themselves. You there, who and what are you?"

"Worshipful master doctor," came a thin, whining voice. "So please you, I'm only a poor old woman, I am, and very obliged to his Worshipful Dwarfship for his friendship, I'm sure. His Majesty, bless his handsome face, has no need to be afraid of the old woman, that's nearly doubled up with the rheumatics and hasn't two sticks to put under her kettle. I have some poor little skill—not like yours, master doctor, of course—in small spells and cantrips that I'd be glad to use against our enemies if it was agreeable to all concerned. For I hate 'em. Oh yes. No one hates better than me."

"That is all most interesting and—er—satisfactory," said **Master Cornelius**. "I think I now know what you are madam. Perhaps your other friend, *Nikabrik*, would give some account of himself?"

A dull, grey voice at which Peter's flesh crept replied, "I'm hunger. I'm thirst. Where I bite, I hold till I die, and even after death they must cut out my mouthful from my enemy's body and bury it with me. I can fast a hundred years and not die. I can lie a hundred nights on the ice and not freeze. I can drink a river of blood and not burst. Show me your enemies."

"And it is in the presence of these two that you wish to disclose your plan?" said **Caspian**.

"Yes," said *Nikabrik*. "And by their help that I mean to execute it."

There was a minute or two during which his two friends speaking in low voices but could not make out what they were saying. Then **Caspian** spoke aloud.

"Well, *Nikabrik*," he said, "we will hear your plan."

There was a pause so long that the boys began to wonder if *Nikabrik* were ever going to begin; when he did, it was in a lower voice, as if he himself did not much like what he was saying.

"All said and done," he muttered, "none of us knows the truth about the ancient days in Narnia. **Trumpkin** believed none of the stories. I was ready to put them to the trial. We tried first the Horn and it has failed. If there ever was a **High King Peter** and a **Queen Susan** and a **King Edmund** and a **Queen Lucy**, then either they have not heard us, or they cannot come, or they are our enemies—"

"Or they are on the way," put in **Trufflehunter**.

"You can go on saying that till *Miraz* has fed us all to his dogs. As I was saying, we have tried one link in the chain of old legends, and it has done us no good. Well. But when your sword breaks, you draw your dagger. The stories tell of other powers beside the ancient Kings and Queens. How if we could call them up?"

"If you mean Aslan," said **Trufflehunter**, "it's all one calling on him and on the Kings. They were his servants. If he will not send them (but I make no doubt he will), is he more likely to come himself?"

"No, you're right there," said *Nikabrik*. "Aslan and the Kings go together. Either Aslan is dead, or he is not on our side. Or else something stronger than himself keeps him back. And if he did come—how do we know he'd be our friend? He was not always a good friend to Dwarfs by all that's told. Not even to all beasts. Ask the *Wolves*. And anyway, he was in Narnia only once that I ever heard of, and he didn't stay long. You may drop Aslan out of the reckoning. I was thinking of someone else."

There was no answer, and for a few minutes it was so still that **Edmund** could hear the wheezy and snuffling breath of the badger.

"Whom do you mean?" said **Caspian** at last.

"I mean a power so much greater than Aslan's that it held Narnia spellbound for years and years, if the stories are true."

"*The White Witch!*" cried three voices all at once, and from the noise **Peter** guessed that three people had leaped to their feet.

"Yes," said *Nikabrik* very slowly and distinctly, "I mean the *Witch*. Sit down again. Don't all take fright at a name as if you were children. We want power: and we want a power that will be on our side. As for power, do not the stories say that the *Witch* defeated Aslan, and bound him, and killed him on that very stone which is over there, just beyond the light?"

"But they also say that he came to life again," said the badger sharply.

"Yes, they *say*," answered *Nikabrik*, "But you'll notice that we hear precious little about anything he did afterwards. He just fades out of the story. How do you explain that, if he really came to life? Isn't it much more likely that he didn't, and that the stories say nothing more about him because there was nothing more to say?"

"A King who has just won a great battle can usually establish himself without the help of a performing lion," said *Nikabrik*. There was a fierce growl, probably from **Trufflehunter**.

"And anyway," *Nikabrik* continued, "what came of the Kings and their reign? They faded too. But it's very different with the *Witch*. They say she ruled for a hundred years: a hundred years of winter. There's power, if you like. There's something practical."

"But, heaven and earth!" said the **King**, "haven't we always been told that she was the worst enemy of all? Wasn't she a tyrant ten times worse than *Miraz?*"

"Perhaps," said *Nikabrik* in a cold voice. "Perhaps she was for you humans, if there were any of you in those days. Perhaps she was for some of the beasts. She stamped out the Beavers, I daresay; at least there are none of them in Narnia now. But she got on all right with us Dwarfs. I'm a Dwarf and I stand by my own people. We're not afraid of the *Witch*."

"But you've joined with us," said **Trufflehunter**.

"Yes, and a lot of good it has done my people so far," snapped *Nikabrik*. "Who is sent on all the dangerous raids? The Dwarfs. Who goes short when the rations fail? The Dwarfs. Who——"

"Lies! All lies!" said the Badger.

"And so," said *Nikabrik*, whose voice now rose to a scream, "if you can't help my people, I'll go to someone who can."

"Is this open treason, Dwarf?" asked the king.

"Put that sword back in its sheath, **Caspian**," said *Nikabrik*. "Murder at council, eh? Is that your game? Don't be fool enough to try it. Do you think I'm afraid of you? There's three on my side, and three on yours."

"Come on, then," snarled **Trufflehunter**, but he was immediately interrupted.

"Stop, stop, stop," said **Master Cornelius**. "You go on too fast. The *Witch* is dead. All the stories agree on that. What does *Nikabrik* mean by calling on the *Witch?*"

That grey and terrible *voice* which had spoken only once before said, "Oh is she?"

And then the shrill, whining *voice* began, "Oh, bless his heart, his dear little Majesty needn't mind about the White Lady—that's what we call her—being dead. The Worshipful Master Doctor is only making game of a poor old woman like me when he says that. Sweet master doctor, learned master doctor, who ever heard of a witch that really died? You can always get them back."

"Call her up," said the grey *voice*. "We are all ready. Draw the circle. Prepare the blue fire."

Above the steadily increasing growl of the badger and **Cornelius's** sharp "What?" rose the voice of **King Caspian** like thunder.

"So that is your plan, *Nikabrik!* Black sorcery and the calling up of an accursed spirit. And I see who your companions are—a *Hag* and a *Wer-Wolf!*"

The next minute or so was very confused. There was an animal roaring, a clash of steel; the boys and **Trumpkin** rushed in; **Peter** had a glimpse of a horrible, grey gaunt creature, half man and half wolf, in the very act of leaping upon a boy about his own age, and **Edmund** saw a badger and a Dwarf rolling on the floor in a sort of cat fight. **Trumpkin** found himself face to face with the *Hag*. Her nose and chin stuck out like a pair of nut-crackers, her dirty grey hair was flying about her face and she had just got **Master Cornelius** by the throat. At one slash of **Trumpkin's** sword her head rolled on the floor. Then the light was knocked over and it was all swords, teeth, claws, fists and boots for about sixty seconds. Then silence.

"Are you all right, **Ed**?"

"I—I think so," panted **Edmund**. "I've got that brute *Nikabrik*, but he's still alive."

"Weights and water bottles!" came an angry voice. "It's me you're sitting on. Get off. You're like a young elephant."

"Sorry, **D.L.F.**," said **Edmund**. "Is that better?"

"Ow! No!" bellowed **Trumpkin**. "You're putting your boot in my mouth. Go away."

"Is **King Caspian** anywhere?" asked **Peter**.

"I'm here," said a rather faint voice. "Something bit me."

They all heard the noise of someone striking a match. It was **Edmund**. The little flame showed his face, looking pale and dirty. He blundered about for a little, found a candle (they were no longer using the lamp, for they had run out of oil), set it on the table and lit it. When the flame rose clear, several people scrambled to their feet. Six faces blinked at one another in the candlelight.

"We don't seem to have any enemies left," said **Peter**. "There's the *Hag*, dead." (He turned his eyes quickly away from her.) And *Nikabrik*, dead too. And I suppose this thing is a *Wer-Wolf*. It's so long since I've seen one. Wolf's head and man's body. That means he was just turning from man into wolf at the moment he was killed. And you, I suppose, are **King Caspian**?"

"Yes," said the other boy. "But I've no idea who you are."

"It's the High King, **King Peter**," said **Trumpkin**.

"Your Majesty is very welcome," said **Caspian**.

"And so is your Majesty," said **Peter**. "I haven't come to take your place, you know, but to put you into it."

"Your Majesty," said another voice at **Peter**'s elbow. He turned and found himself face to face with the Badger. **Peter** leaned forward, put his arms round the beast and kissed the furry head: it wasn't a girlish thing for him to do, because he was the High King.

"Best of badgers," he said. ""You never doubted us all through."

"No credit to me, your Majesty," said **Trufflehunter**. "I'm a beast and we don't change. I'm a badger, what's more, and we hold on."

"I am sorry for *Nikabrik*," said **Caspian**, "though he hated me from the first moment he saw me. He had gone sour from long suffering and hating. If we had won quickly he might have become a good Dwarf in the days of peace. I don't know which of us killed him. I'm glad of that."

"You're bleeding," said **Peter**.

"Yes, I'm bitten," said **Caspian**. "It was that—that wolf thing." Cleaning and bandaging the wound took a little time, and when it was done **Trumpkin** said, "Now. Before everything else we want some breakfast."

"But not here," said **Peter**.

"No," said **Caspian** with a shudder. "And we must send someone to take away the bodies."

"Let the vermin be flung into a pit," said **Peter**. "But the Dwarf we will give to his people to buried in their own fashion."

They breakfasted at last in another of the dark cellars of Alsan's How. It was not such a breakfast as they would have chosen, for **Caspian** and **Cornelius** were thinking of venison pastries, and **Peter** and **Edmund** of buttered eggs and hot coffee, but what everyone got was a little bit of cold bear-meat (out of the boy's pockets), a lump of hard cheese, an onion, and a mug of water. But, from the way they fell to, anyone would have supposed it was delicious.

---

So help was on the way after all. It was right at the door ready to barge in at the right time. So it is with our lives. God is willing and able to help in *His* time. So we should never lose hope.

It's interesting to see the parallels between the choices of some in our day to the choices of some of the characters in that cave. The Bible predicts a time will come when people will give up on the return of Christ—"where is this 'coming' he promised?" they ask (2 Pet. 3:4). Just as some of the characters in the cave gave up waiting for the rightful king and instead turned to the old sorcery, so too many today have given up on Christianity and are turning to the devil's power through the occult, although they wouldn't necessarily recognize it as such. I read a disturbing article in 1996 that said that in France there were fifty thousand people who earned their living as mediums, stargazers, or the like, in contrast to thirty-six thousand Roman Catholic priests (and far less protestant ministers)! But the rightful King is coming one day, and then those who have turned to the devil's power, through the occult, will see the fatal consequence of that decision. Mercifully, before that time, there is forgiveness for those who repent.

*This selection is suitable for children.*
*The moral of the story is that the Christian has a real and solid hope in the face of life's biggest threat: death.*

## "GO DOWN DEATH—A FUNERAL SERMON"
### from *God's Trombones*
by James Weldon Johnson

In New Orleans, some funerals in the black community are more like celebrations than they are times of mourning—complete with jazz music and a joyous march. When you think about it, that's biblical in one sense. If you're a true Christian, you know you're on your way to heaven, and so death is a welcome friend in that it brings you to Him. Not that we should ever do anything foolish to hasten our death; that's prohibited in His Word. But when death comes, we don't need to fear it since it means we come into His glorious presence. Paraphrasing the apostle Paul: "To be absent from the body, is to be present with the Lord" (Phil. 1:2–3; 2 Cor. 5:8).

This story, in poetic form, makes that point. One specific sister in Christ has died, and those who know her should weep not, for she has finally gone to her true home. This is a beautiful poem from James Weldon Johnson.[2] It's contained in his book of Christian poems, *God's Trombones*.

---

Weep not, weep not,
She is not dead;
She's resting in the bosom of Jesus.
Heart-broken husband—weep no more;
Grief-stricken son—weep no more;

Left-lonesome daughter—weep no more;
She's only just gone home.

Day before yesterday morning,
God was looking down from his great, high heaven,
Looking down on all his children,

---

2.   For information on James Weldon Johnson, see 36.

And his eye fell on Sister Caroline,
Tossing on her bed of pain.
And God's big heart was touched with pity,
With the everlasting pity.

And God sat back on his throne,
And he commanded that tall, bright angel standing at
    his right hand:
Call me Death!
And that tall, bright angel cried in a voice
That broke like a clap of thunder:
Call Death!—Call Death!
And the echo sounded down the streets of heaven
Till it reached away back to that shadowy place,
Where Death waits with his pale, white horses.
And Death heard the summons,
And he leaped on his fastest horse,
Pale as a sheet in the moonlight.
Up the golden street Death galloped,
And the hoofs of his horse struck fire from the gold,
But they didn't make no sound.
Up Death rode to the Great White Throne,
And waited for God's command.

And God said: Go down, Death, go down,
Go down to Savannah, Georgia,
Down in Yamacraw,
And find Sister Caroline.
She's borne the burden and heat of the day,
She's labored long in my vineyard,
And she's tired —
She's weary —
Go down, Death, and bring her to me.

And Death didn't say a word,
But he loosed the reins on his pale, white horse,
And he clamped the spurs to his bloodless sides,
And out and down he rode,
Through heaven's pearly gates,
Past suns and moons and stars;

On Death rode,
And the foam from his horse was like a comet in the
    sky;
On Death rode,
Leaving the lightning's flash behind;
Straight on down he came.

While we were watching round her bed,
She turned her eyes and looked away,
She saw what we couldn't see;
She saw Old Death. She saw Old Death
Coming like a falling star.
But Death didn't frighten Sister Caroline;
He looked to her like a welcome friend.
And she whispered to us: I'm going home,
And she smiled and closed her eyes.

And Death took her up like a baby,
And she lay in his icy arms,
But she didn't feel no chill.
And Death began to ride again —
Up beyond the evening star,
Out beyond the morning star,
Into the glittering light of glory,
On to the Great White Throne.

And there he laid Sister Caroline
On the loving breast of Jesus.

And Jesus took his own hand and wiped away her tears,
And he smoothed the furrows from her face,
And the angels sang a little song,
And Jesus rocked her in his arms,
And kept a-saying: Take your rest,
Take your rest, take your rest.

Weep not—weep not,
She is not dead;
She's resting in the bosom of Jesus.

This is a beautiful word picture that drives home the point that Jesus Christ is the only one who has conquered the grave. Throughout human history, the biggest fear is the fear of death. The grave is inescapable. Death is the greatest problem we've ever faced or we ever will face as human beings. But Jesus Christ conquered the grave! He conquered death in His own resurrection. He is alive today and has been since that first Easter morning. There's no one else about whom that can be said!

The hope that a Christian has in the face of death does not exist for everybody. Nor should it. Those who reject Christ reject His free gift of eternal life.[3]

Different accounts of the last moments of atheists often reveal a horrible scene, e.g., at the deaths of Voltaire or of Stalin. The woman who nursed the infidel Professor J. H. Huxley during his final illness reported that, as he was dying, he abruptly looked up at something she couldn't see. Then, after a while, he said softly, "So it *is* true" and then died. What a contrast is death for those who know the Savior vs. those who don't.

The promise that Jesus is the "resurrection and the life" (John 11:25) has comforted hundreds of millions of people worldwide, since the day He first spoke those words when He raised Lazarus from the dead, down through the centuries, and up to the present moment. In the classic ending of Charles Dickens' *A Tale of Two Cities,* Sidney Carton, the man who chooses to die so that another man may live, finds great comfort in Christ's promise. In the very last chapter, as he and a girl whom he comforts are about to face the guillotine, Carton recites the words of Christ: "I am the resurrection and the life, saith the Lord: he that believeth in me, though he were dead, yet shall he live: and whosoever liveth and believeth in me, shall never die!" And so he declares just moments later in one of literature's classic statements: "It is a far, far better thing that I do, than I have ever done; it is a far, far better rest that I go to, than I have ever known." How does he know? Because he has Christ's own word on it, and we do too!

---

3. For more details on this, see the appendix.

*This story is NOT suitable for children. (It may plant doubts that have not arisen yet.)*
*The moral of the story is no darkness is too dark for God, and hope can spring out of the darkest circumstances.*

# THOUGH HE SLAY ME

### from *Song of the Silent Harp*
### by B. J. Hoff

It is encouraging to see the rise of quality historical fiction being written by Christians. This next selection is a short excerpt from one such novel, *Song of the Silent Harp* by B. J. Hoff. *Song of the Silent Harp* is one of the novels in *The Emerald Ballad* series, which deals with Irish immigrants to America.

The story here deals with a Christian's struggle with a great personal loss and his frustration over it. He trusts God, yet he continues to have his doubts. Hope wins out because faith wins out.

Here is the context in which this story appears. A ship is sailing to the New World. At the helm is the evil Captain Schell. Gold is his goal, and his cargo is Chinese girls, destined for the whorehouses in New York. His passengers are two hundred poor Irish immigrants, locked in the stern with rotting corpses and no cooked food and no fresh air. Among these lay Evan Whittaker, an Englishman who has just lost an arm because a wound he incurred had become infected and the ship's surgeon was forced to amputate it. Evan had been injured when he was helping a poor Irish family, Nora and her children, escape into this ship.

Dealing with the loss of an arm would be a calamity for anyone, especially one on his way to starting a new life in a new world. This story captures the struggle between faith and unbelief . . . between hope and despair.

---

Evan was trying to wake up. He thought he heard music . . . a harp . . . the bright sound of children. He wanted to listen, but the sounds swelled and died away into silence.

He fought to open his eyes, but they were too heavy, and he was too weak. It didn't matter. Whether he was awake or asleep, the days and nights remained the same.

He passed the time in a twilight world induced by the laudanum, drifting through the slow-rolling hours in a haze of pain and macabre dreams. He never quite slept, but simply hung suspended in a drug-induced web, where his nightmares were the only reality.

Tonight was no different. He was awake, yet not awake, aware but without any real sensations—except for the pain. Even that was easier now, almost bearable. He was healing, that much was certain. Even the sullen Dr. Leary had made a grudging snarl of approval the last time he'd examined his . . .

*Stump. Say the word. Say it!*

He tried to force the word from leaden lips, but it remained only a hateful thought.

*You no longer have an arm. You have a stump. . . .*

For days now, he had struggled to face the reality of his circumstances. Between the ebb and flow of an opium stupor, he tried out a number of words and descriptions, searching for one that did not sound quite so grisly.

He was a man with one arm. A one-armed man. He'd had an arm surgically removed. Amputated.

*He was a cripple . . . he had a stump. He would never be whole again . . .*

There. That was further than he had gone before. And as far as he would ever need to go. There was nothing else to be said.

*Lord . . . oh, Lord, why did you allow this to happen to me? Didn't I do what you asked? Didn't I go where you sent me? I was obedient, I even managed to put aside my cowardice, to trust your guidance, your power. . . . Why, Lord?*

The pain that seized him now was far worse than all the physical agony he had endured so far, a pain that went beyond bodily suffering. Indeed, the distress of body was nothing compared to the anguish of soul that now closed over him, weighing him down like a sodden grave blanket.

From somewhere . . . a dark, shadowy place he had not known existed within him . . . came a whispering, an ugly hiss of accusation:

*God betrayed you, didn't He? He let you down completely, after everything you went through to obey Him! He let you down . . . He failed you . . . failed you . . .*

Evan shuddered, stiffened in horrified denial. Again the dark pit in his spirit gaped open, and the whisper grew more insistent:

*You trusted Him . . . you've always trusted Him. Well, just see how He's rewarded your trust. Look at yourself . . . look at your ugly self . . .*

His Bible . . . where had he put his Bible? Desperate, he pushed himself up on his right arm, looked around, but all was a blur. Where were his eyeglasses? His heart thudding madly with the effort, he patted the bunk around him, stretching to peer down at the floor. There was no sign of the eyeglasses or the Bible.

He tried to squirm to the edge of the bunk to feel beneath it, but was overwhelmed by a dizzying surge of nausea.

Sinking back onto the bunk, he threw his arm over his eyes and waited for his head to stop spinning.

*Why did God allow this to happen? You were only doing what was expected of you, just as you always have. You've always done your best, you've been a good man, a decent man, lived an honorable life. But does God care about any of that? Does He care about what you're going through right now, at this moment . . . does He even know?*

Something cold and depraved was breathing on Evan's soul, struggling to suffocate his faith.

"Jesus . . . Savior . . . Jesus . . . "

Over and over he mumbled his Shepherd's name, clinging to it like a shield.

Finally, out of his memory, the words came, light exploding in the darkness:

"The Lord gave, and the Lord has taken away; blessed be the name of the Lord."

*He has failed you . . .*

"Shall we receive good from the hand of God and not trouble?"

*He allowed it to happen . . .*

"He wounds, but He binds up . . . He smites, but He also heals."

*If He's really as powerful as you seem to believe, why didn't He keep you from this dread thing? Why didn't He save your arm? Where was His power when you needed it? Where was He then?*

"In his hand is the life of every living thing and the breath of all mankind."

*He took your arm . . . He made you ugly and repulsive . . . He made you a joke, a caricature of a man . . .*

"But the Lord sees not as man sees . . . He looks on the heart."

*He has deserted you, you fool! Why shouldn't you deny Him and start anew?*

"I know that my Redeemer lives . . . though He slay me, yet will I trust in Him . . . "

When you cling to what you know about God, it can lift you out of the worst darkness. Clearly, Evan had done himself a great service by memorizing a lot of Scripture, which he now drew upon during this time of doubt. It brought him hope where there could have been despair. C. S. Lewis once wrote in his *Chronicles of Narnia* series, "Never doubt in the darkness what Aslan [Jesus] has shown you in the light."

# SECTION 3

# LOVE

I t has been said that the greatest thing in the world is love. In the famous "love chapter," the Bible says, "Now these three remain: Faith, hope and love. But the greatest of these is love" (1 Cor. 13:13).

The source of love is God Himself. That's why the first story in this collection of stories on love is a story about the love of God for us.

God is love. We love because He first loved us.

Love means putting others ahead of us. That's not easy to do in such a selfish culture as ours. When a mother picks up her first-born baby, she generally puts the welfare of the child before her own. When a young couple falls in love, they start to consider their potential mate's needs as well as their own.

God showed us what love is in Jesus Christ, who died for us when we were unlovable, ugly, and mean. He laid down His life for us. He gave up all His rights, forgave us, and made us perfect in Christ when we hadn't done a thing to deserve it.

The following stories illustrate love, both divine and human (which is a reflection of God's love).

*This selection is suitable for children.*
*The moral of the story is that God loves us and welcomes us back no*
*matter how far we may have strayed.*

## "THE PRODIGAL SON"

### from *The Life of Our Lord*
### retold by Charles Dickens

Charles Dickens (1812–70) was the author of many classics, including *Oliver Twist, A Tale of Two Cities, A Christmas Carol, David Copperfield,* and *Great Expectations.* Most people don't realize that his last published book was one about Jesus Christ. Dickens retold many aspects of the life of Christ in *The Life of Our Lord.* He wrote the book to teach his children about the Savior, about whom he said: "No one ever lived, who was so good, so kind, so gentle, and so sorry for all people who did wrong, or were in any way ill or miserable, as he was."

Dickens, a good judge of the merits of a story, said that the greatest story ever crafted in the history of the world was the parable of the prodigal son. This was one of the parables Jesus told in order to explain the love of God to His hearers. It can be found in the original in Luke 15.

There was once a Man, he told them, who had two sons: and the younger of them said one day, "Father, give me my share of your riches now, and let me do with it what I please." The father granting his request, he traveled away with his money into a distant country, and soon spent it in riotous living.

When he had spent all, there came a time, through all the country, of great public distress and famine, when there was no bread, and when the corn, and the grass, and all the things that grow in the ground were all dried up and blighted. The Prodigal Son fell into such distress and hunger, that he hired himself out as a servant to feed swine in the fields. And he would have been glad to eat, even the poor coarse husks that the swine were fed with, but his Master gave him none. In this distress, he said to himself, "How many of my father's servants have bread enough, and to spare, while I perish with hunger! I will arise and go to my father, and will say unto him,

'Father! I have sinned against Heaven, and before thee, and am no more worthy to be called Thy Son!'"

And so he traveled back again, in great pain and sorrow and difficulty, to his father's house. When he was yet a great way off, his father saw him, and knew him in the midst of all his rags and misery, and ran towards him, and wept, and fell upon his neck, and kissed him. And he told his servants to clothe this poor repentant Son in the best robes, and to make a great feast to celebrate his return. Which was done; and they began to be merry.

But the eldest Son, who had been in the field and knew nothing of his brother's return, coming to the house and hearing the music and dancing, called to one of the servants, and asked him what it meant. To this the servant made answer that his brother had come home, and that his father was joyful because of his return. At this, the elder brother was angry and would not go into the house; so the father, hearing of it, came out to persuade him.

"Father," said the elder brother, "you do not treat me justly, to show so much joy for my younger brother's return. For these many years I have remained with you constantly, and have been true to you, yet you have never made a feast for me. But when my younger brother returns, who has been prodigal, and riotous, and spent his money in many bad ways, you are full of delight, and the whole house makes merry!" "Son," returned the father, "you have always been with me, and all I have is yours. But we thought your brother dead, and he is alive. He was lost, and he is found; and it is natural and right that we should be merry for his unexpected return to his old home."

By this, our Saviour meant to teach, that those who have done wrong and forgotten God, are always welcome to him and will always receive his mercy, if they will only return to Him in sorrow for the sin of which they have been guilty.

---

One of my favorite aspects of this story is that phrase, "when he was yet a great way off." That speaks volumes, that our Heavenly Father wants so much for us to come back home to Him.

In short, He awaits our return, even if we have badly strayed! God's love for us is the greatest love there is.

*This selection is suitable for children.*
*The moral of the story is that love includes forgiving others, even one's enemies.*

# "TERJE VIGEN"

by Henrik Ibsen, translated by Kirsti Saebo Newcombe

Here is an amazing story of forgiveness told in poetic form. In our time of "make my day"—in which "revenge is sweet"—Hollywood gives us many violent movies built on the theme of vengeance, and getting even supersedes the Christian ideal of forgiveness—here is a true story from the last century that is a breath of fresh air.

Here is the backdrop of the story: During the Napoleonic Wars, Norway's coast was blocked by the British Navy. Since many had to depend on food from overseas, famine was claiming the lives of many. Terje Vigen (TEAR-yah VEEK-uhn), the main character of this poem, was a young man who decided to risk breaking through the blockade to get grain to save his family. Vigen rowed his little boat through Skagerak (SKA-guh-rock), which is an arm of the North Sea between Norway and Denmark. A pilot boat, which comes later in the story, is a boat that purposefully helps other boats in their time of distress. The captain of such a vessel is well-experienced at sea.

"Terje Vigen" was written by Henrik Ibsen (1828–1906), the Norwegian playwright and author. He took a true story and set it to poetic verse. This poem has been translated by the editor's wife. Kirsti Saebo Newcombe, a native of Norway, grew up in Kristiansand, which is less than an hour from Ibsen's orginal home. Ultimately, Terje Vigen was able to show a great deal of love through the forgiveness he was able to display.

---

There lived a strange and graying man
    on the uttermost naked shoal.
He did not harm anyone neither on land nor sea.
But sometimes his eyes held an ugly gleam,
    especially when the weather turned bad.
Then people believed him to be mad

and few there were who, without fear,
    came near Terje Vigen.

I will tell you what I have heard
    of Terje from first to last,
    and if it isn't from his own mouth,
    it's from those who stood near him—
Those who closed his eyes and laid him to rest
    when he died well past three scores of age.

In his youth he was a wild and adventuresome chap; he
    signed on as cabin boy and left home without looking
    back.
He longed for home as seamen do,
    but when he finally got back
    his mother and father were dead,
    and not a kinsman was to be found.
He grieved for a day, maybe two,
    then he threw his sorrow off.

He married in haste;
    some said, to his regret,
    but he spent a winter under his own roof.
The windows shone
    and there were flowers seen
    behind the laced curtains in the little red house.

As the spring winds were blowing
    the sea was calling,
    and a captain always needs a crew.
A year was well past before he approached
    the little red house by the sea.
He lifted the curtain the summer wind blew
    and there in his home—he saw two!

His wife was spinning, and in a cradle by her side
    lay a little girl glowing with laughter and smiles.
Terje now worked his plot of land.
No longer did he send a longing glance

to the adventuresome sea.
On his knee he bounced Anna, his girl.
She pulled his hair and laughed.

But soon came hard times:
   war broke out, and laughter and smiles would die.
In 1809, English vessels were blockading each harbor.
Death and sorrow and pestilence and tears were the
   bread the Norwegians ate.
Terje then remembered his old friend, the sea.
He selected the smallest rowboat around,
   and when the wind died down,
     he rowed over Skagerack for wife and child.

Three nights and three days he rowed to Denmark
   and picked up in Fladstrand his precious cargo.
It was three barrels of grain,
   and that would save the lives of his beloved wife and
   child.
Three days and three nights again he rowed
   and when the fourth morning dawned
   he saw the hills of Norway!
His heart lifted up in fierce joy and strengthened belief
   and a thanksgiving prayer to God.
But the words froze on his lips,
   because out of the lifting fog, an English Corvette
   headed right for his little boat.

A sign was given, a dinghy lowered,
   and as the sailors sang
Terje rowed for his life, like an arrow through the waves.
The sea foamed and the blood dripped from his nails.
The fifteen-man dingy caught up with him,
   and at a sunken rock, so near his home,
   he ran his boat aground.
Terje cried in his uttermost distress:
"There on the shore in my impoverished house
   are my wife and child waiting for bread!"

But the officer lifted an ore
    and struck it through the bottom of the boat.
The wood splintered, and the sea poured in
    and there on two feet of water
    sank his precious cargo.
Terje swam between bullets and ores
    and they caught him at last
    and brought him before the captain—
    a mere boy of eighteen.
His first battle was Terje Vigen, and he had won.
The strong Norwegian knelt,
    begging and crying, on the deck of an English Corvette.

He spent five years in an English prison,
    and when he came home,
    all he found of his wife and child
    was a common grave for the poor
    where the wildflowers grow.

The years went by and he worked as a pilot
    living on the uttermost naked shoal.
He did not hurt anyone, neither on land nor sea.
But sometimes his eyes held an ugly gleam
    especially when the weather turned bad.
Then, people believed he was mad,
    and few there were who, without fear,
    came near Terje Vigen.

One night a storm was raging,
    and an English yacht was drifting helplessly
    with torn sails, towards the ragged coast.
Her red distress signal was a silent scream for help.
The pilot boat was on its way
    with the sturdy pilot on-board.
He looked so sure and safe,
    that gray haired giant, as he stood by the wheel.
Soon the yacht was safely in tow
    and the lord with his lady and child,

bowed before the pilot and said:
"I'll make you as rich as you now are poor. . . ."

The pilot let go of his wheel—
    his cheeks paled, as a slow smile grew on his lips.
He ordered them down in a dinghy
    and took them to the fateful spot
    where the little boat had sunk.
The lord with his lady and child were standing
    up to their knees in water,
    not on a sunken rock,
    but on a sunken boat with three barrels of grain.
Yes, that is what they were standing on.

The lord now remembered well the man who had bowed
    his knees on the deck of his Corvette,
And Terje Vigen screamed above the storm:
"All that was mine you held in your hand
    and you let it go for praise.
Now is the time for revenge."

The English lord bent his knee for the Norwegian pilot
    while Terje's eyes burned with a terrible force.
"You sailed your Corvette, I rowed my boat.
I slaved for mine unto death,
    and you took their bread.
How easy it was for you to scoff at my bitter tears.
My wife's hands were not soft like your wife's,
    but she was mine.
My daughter did not look like an angel;
    she was pale and thin like poor folks' children are.
But they were my treasure on earth.
It was for me riches—and for you so little.
Now, I'll have revenge for the long years
    which bent my neck, and paled my hair
    and sank my happiness."

He grabbed the child with his right hand,
    his left around the lady's waist.

"Stand back, my lord, a single step
    will cost you your wife and child."
The lord's hair became gray that night.
When Terje swung the child high, the lady cried:
"Anna, my child!"

Terje's eyes cleared, and in his face was peace.
Carefully, he set the child down
    and kissed her hands.
He straightened, as loosed from a prison,
    and his voice was calm as he said:
"Now, Terje Vigen is himself again.
Until now, my blood ran like a stone river—
I had to—I had to—have revenge!
The long years in prison made my heart sick
    while I looked down into that awful abyss."

As the new day dawned, everybody was safe
    and the yacht laid in harbor.
Terje's mind was free and his neck was now straight
    which had been bent on the deck of an English Corvette,
    so many years before.

The lord and the lady came to his simple house
    to bid farewell and God's peace.
As they thanked him for their salvation,
he stroked the child's hair and said:
"The one who saved you when things were the worst—
    it was the little one here.
For the name of my own daughter was also *Anna!*"

When the yacht sailed out from the rugged coast,
    they ran up a Norwegian flag.
A tear trickled down a weatherworn cheek
    as the pilot watched them leave.
"Great was my loss, but much have I gained;
    maybe it was best after all
    that everything happened like this.
So thanks and praise then, to you, O God!"

I saw him every now and then;
he came to the dock with fish.
His hair was white, but he sang and laughed,
healthy and glad like a youth.
He teased the girls, and played with the children;
then he would wave his sou'wester,
and jump on board his boat,
    hoist his sail and head for home,
In sunshine he traveled that old eagle.

By Fjaere Church, I saw a grave,
    on a weatherbeaten spot.
It was not cared for,
    but the white-lettered inscription was clear:
"Terje Vigen," it read.
Here he found a resting place
    with sun and wind and stiff rough grass,
    where the wildflowers grow.

---

Alexander Pope was right when he penned, "To err is human; to forgive divine." Love, the Bible tells us, forgives all things. It keeps no record of wrongs. It turns the other cheek when struck. It's not easy stuff to put into practice, but it certainly is rewarding. How can we not forgive others for their small offenses (when viewed in the light of eternity) when our Heavenly Father has forgiven our huge one (when viewed by the same criterion)?

*This selection is suitable for children.*
*The moral of the story is to do your good deeds in a way that you don't get the credit for them.*

# "THE MANSION"[1]

### by Henry Van Dyke

I must confess . . . I don't mean to play favorites . . . but this is one of my favorite stories in this book. It is a powerful story that kind of grabs your heart and makes you think about why we do so much of what we do, especially our works of love.

When we give to charity, how often do we do it for the mere recognition of others? How often do we just do it in secret so that no one but God knows? This wonderful story addresses this point.

During the course of his life, Henry Van Dyke (1852–1933) served as a Presbyterian minister, an author, and a professor of English literature at Princeton. Not all at the same time, mind you!

"The Mansion," which was first published in 1911, is one half of a two-part book, the other half of which is "The Story of the Other Wise Man."[2] One reader said this of Van Dyke's book:

> I can truthfully say that this miniature masterpiece is one of the few books that has actually changed my life. Before I read it, I still contributed money or gifts with an eye to the response of the recipient. But the book shamed me into a realization that most of my giving was ego-centric and self-gratifying. Since that time my life has radically changed, thanks in no small part, to the Van Dyke message.[3]

---

1. This text has been partially edited without the use of ellipses.

2. You can find a copy of "The Story of the Other Wise Man" by Henry Van Dyke in Dr. Joe Wheeler's *Christmas in My Heart*, volume 3 (Hagerstown, Md.: Review and Herald Publishing Association, 1994).

3. Testimonial written in the preface of Henry Van Dyke's "The Mansion," appearing in an unpublished handout with this information listed at the end of the tale: "Christmas Story #4. A gift to those who attended the Fifth Annual Community Lycenn Series Advisory Board Banquet on December 3, 1981, Keene, Texas."

There was an air of calm and reserved opulence about the Weightman mansion that spoke not of money squandered, but of wealth prudently applied. Standing on a corner of the Avenue no longer fashionable for residence, it looked upon the swelling tide of business with an expression of complacency and half-disdain.

The house was not beautiful. There was nothing in its straight front of chocolate-colored stone, its heavy cornices, its broad, staring windows of plate glass, its carved and bronze-bedecked mahogany doors at the top of the wide stoop, to charm the eye or fascinate the imagination. But it was eminently respectable, and in its way imposing. It seemed to say that the glittering shops of the jewelers, the muliners, the confectioners, the florists, the picture-dealers, the furriers, the makers of rare and costly antiques, retail traders in luxuries of life, were beneath the notice of a house that had its foundations in the high finance, and was built literally and figuratively in the shadow of St. Petronius' Church.

John Weightman was like the house into which he had built himself thirty years ago, and in which his ideals and ambitions were incrusted. He was a self-made man. But in making himself he had chosen a highly esteemed pattern and worked according to the approved rules. There was nothing irregular, questionable, flamboyant about him. He was solid, correct, and justly successful.

Harold Weightman had often listened to his father discoursing in this fashion on the fundamental principles of life, and always with a divided mind. He admired immensely his father's talents and the single-minded energy with which he improved them. But in the paternal philosophy there was something that disquieted and oppressed the young man, and made him gasp inwardly for fresh air and free action.

At times, during his college course and his years at the law school, he had yielded to this impulse and broken away—now toward extravagance and dissipation, and then, when the reaction came, toward a romantic devotion to work among the poor. He had felt his father's disapproval for both of these forms of imprudence; but it was never expressed in a harsh or violent way, always with a certain tolerant patience, such as one might show for the mistakes and vagaries of the very young.

"Father plays us," said Harold, in a moment of irritation, to his mother, "like pieces in a game of chess."

"My dear," said that lady, whose faith in her husband was religious, "you ought not to speak so impatiently. At least he wins the game. He is one of the most respected men in New York. And he is very generous, too."

"I wish he would be more generous in letting us be ourselves," said the young man. "He always has something in view for us and expects to move us up to it."

"But isn't it always for our benefit?" replied his mother. "Look what a position we have. No one can say there is any taint on our money. There are no rumors about your father. He has kept the laws of God and of man. He has never made any mistakes."

Harold got up from his chair and poked the fire. Then he came back to the ample, well-gowned, firm-looking lady, and sat beside her on the sofa.

"I feel like a hired man, in the service of this magnificent mansion—say in training for father's place as majordomo. I'd like to get out some way, to feel free—perhaps to do something for others."

The young man's voice hesitated a little. "Yes, it sounds like cant, I know, but sometimes I feel as if I'd like to do some good in the world, if father only wouldn't insist upon God's putting it into the ledger."

His mother moved uneasily, and a slight look of bewilderment came into her face.

"Isn't that almost irreverent?" she asked. "Surely the righteous must have their reward. And your father is good. See how much he gives to all the established charities, how many things he has founded. He's always thinking of others, and planning for them. And surely, for us, he does everything. How well he has planned this trip to Europe for me and the girls—the court-presentation at Berlin, the season on the Riviera, the visits in England with the Plumptons and the Halverstones. He says Lord Halverstone has the finest old house in Sussex, pure Elizabethan, and all the old customs are kept up, too—family prayers every morning for all the domestics. By-the-way, you know his son Bertie, I believe."

Harold smiled a little to himself as he answered: "Yes, I fished at Catalina Island last June with the Honorable Ethelbert; he's rather a decent chap, in spite of his ingrowing mind. But you?—mother, you are simply magnificent! You are father's masterpiece." The young man leaned over to kiss her, and went up to the Riding Club for his after-noon canter in the Park.

So it came to pass, early in December, that Mrs. Weightman and her two daughters sailed for Europe, on their serious pleasure trip, even as it had been written in the book of Providence; and John Weightman, who had made the entry, was left to pass the rest of the winter with his son and heir in the brownstone mansion.

They were comfortable enough. The machinery of the massive establishment ran as smoothly as a great electric dynamo. They were busy enough, too. John Weightman's plans and enterprises were com-plicated, though his principle of action was always simple—to get good value for every expenditure and effort. The banking-house of which he was the chief, the brain, the will, the absolutely controlling hand, was so admirably organized that the details of its direction took but little time. But there were board meetings of corporations and hospitals, conferences in Wall Street and at Albany, consultations and committee meetings in the brownstone mansion.

For a share in all this business and its adjuncts John Weightman had his son in training in one of the famous law firms of the city; for he held that banking itself is a simple affair, the only real difficulties of finance are on its legal side. Meantime he wished the young man to meet and know the men with whom he would have to deal when he became a partner in the house. So a couple of dinners were given in the mansion during December, after which the father called the son's attention to the fact that over a hundred million dollars had sat around the board.

But on Christmas Eve father and son were dining together without guests, and their talk across the broad table, glittering with silver and cut glass, and softly lit by shaded candles, was intimate, though a little slow at times. The elder man was in rather a rare mood, more expan-sive and confidential than usual; and, when the coffee was brought in and they were left alone, he talked more freely of his personal plans and hopes than he had ever done before.

"I feel very grateful tonight," said he, at last; "it must be something in the air of Christmas that gives me this feeling of thankfulness for the many divine mercies that have been bestowed upon me. All the principles by which I have tried to guide my life have been justified. I have never made the value of this salted almond by anything that the courts would not uphold, at least in the long run, and yet—or wouldn't it be truer to say and therefore?—my affairs have been wonderfully prospered. There's a great deal in that text 'Honesty is the best'—but no, that's not from the Bible, after all, is it? Wait a moment; there is something of that kind, I know."

"May I light a cigar, father," said Harold, turning away to hide a smile, "while you are remembering the text?"

"Yes, certainly," answered the elder man, rather shortly; "you know I don't dislike the smell. But it is a wasteful, useless habit, and therefore I have never practiced it. Nothing useless is worthwhile, that's my motto—nothing that does not bring the reward. Oh, now I recall the text, 'Verily I say unto you they have their reward.' I shall ask Doctor Snodgrass to preach a sermon on that verse some day."

"Using you as an illustration?"

"Well, not exactly that; but I could give him some good material from my own experience to prove the truth of Scripture. I can honestly say that there is not one of my charities that has not brought me in a good return, either in the increase of influence, the building up of credit, or the association with substantial people. Of course you have to be careful how you give, in order to secure the best results—no indiscriminate giving—no pennies in beggars' hats! It has been one of my principles always to use the same kind of judgment in charities that I use in my other affairs, and they have not disappointed me."

"Even the check that you put in the plate when you take the offertory up the aisle on Sunday morning?"

"Certainly; though there the influence is less direct; and I must confess that I have my doubts in regard to the collection for Foreign Missions. That always seems to me romantic and wasteful. You never hear from it in any definite way. They say the missionaries have done a good deal to open the way for trade; perhaps—but they have also gotten us into commercial and political difficulties. Yet I give to them—a little—it is a matter of conscience with me to identify myself with all the enterprises of the Church; it is the mainstay of social order and a prosperous civilization. But the best forms of benevolence are the well-established organized ones here at home, where people can see them and know what they are doing."

"You mean the ones that have a local habitation and a name."

"Yes; they offer by far the safest return, though of course there is something gained by contributing to general funds. A public man can't afford to be without public spirit. But on the whole I prefer a building, or an endowment. There is a mutual advantage to a good name and a good institution in their connection in the public mind. It helps them both. Remember that, my boy. Of course at the beginning you will have to practice it in a small way; later, you will have larger opportunities. But try to put your gifts where they can be identified and do good all around. You'll see the wisdom of it in the long run."

"I can see it already, sir, and the way you describe it looks amazingly wise and prudent. In other words, we must cast our bread on the waters in large loaves, carried by sound ships marked with the owner's name, so that the return freight will be sure to come back to us."

The father laughed, but his eyes were frowning a little as if he suspected something irreverent under the respectful reply.

"You put it humorously, but there's sense in what you say. Why not? God rules the sea; but He expects us to follow the laws of navigation and commerce. Why not take good care of your bread, even when you give it away?"

"It's not for me to say why not—and yet I can think of cases—" The young man hesitated for a moment. His half-finished cigar had gone out. He rose and tossed it into the fire, in front of which he remained standing—a slender, eager, restless young figure, with a touch of hunger in the fine face, strangely like and unlike the father, at whom he looked with half-wistful curiosity.

"The fact is, sir," he continued, "there is such a case in my mind now, and it is a good deal on my heart, too. So I thought of speaking to you about it tonight. You remember Tom Rollins, the Junior who was so good to me when I entered college?"

The father nodded. He remembered very well indeed the annoying incidents of his son's first escapade, and how Rollins had stood by him and helped to avoid a public disgrace, and how a close friendship had grown between the two boys, so different in their fortunes.

"Yes," he said, "I remember him. He was a promising young man. Has he succeeded?"

"Not exactly—that is, not yet. His business has been going rather badly. He has a wife and little baby, you know. And now he has broken down,—something wrong with his lungs. The doctor says his only chance is a year or eighteen months in Colorado. I wish we could help him."

"How much would it cost?"

"Three or four thousand, perhaps, as a loan."

"Does the doctor say he will get well?"

"A fighting chance—the doctor says."

The face of the older man changed subtly. Not a line was altered, but it seemed to have a different substance, as if it were carved out of some firm, imperishable stuff.

"A fighting chance," he said, "may do for a speculation, but it is not a good investment. You owe something to young Rollins. Your grateful feeling does you credit. But don't overwork it. Send him three or four hundred, if you like. You'll never hear from it again, except in the letter of thanks. But for Heaven's sake don't be sentimental. Religion is not a matter of sentiment; it's a matter of principle."

The face of the younger man changed now. But instead of becoming fixed and graven, it seemed to melt into life by the heat of an inward fire. His nostrils quivered with quick breath, his lips curled.

"Principle!" he said. "You mean principal—and interest too. Well, sir, you know best whether that is religion or not. But if it is, count me out, please. Tom saved me from going to the devil, six years ago; and I'll be d—— if I don't help him to the best of my ability now."

John Weightman looked at his son steadily. "Harold," he said at last, "you know I dislike violent language, and it never has any influence with me. If I could honestly approve of this proposition of yours, I'd let you have the money; but I can't; it's extravagant and useless. But you have your Christmas check for a thousand dollars coming to you tomorrow. You can use it as you please. I never interfere with your private affairs."

"Thank you," said Harold. "Thank you very much! But there's another private affair. I want to get away from this life, this town, this house. It stifles me. You refused last summer when I asked you to let me go up to Grenfell's Mission on the Labrador. I could go now, at least as far as the Newfoundland Station. Have you changed your mind?"

"Not at all. I think it is an exceedingly foolish enterprise. It would interrupt the career that I have marked out for you."

"Well, then, here's a cheaper proposition. Algy Vanderhoof wants me to join him on his yacht with—well, with a little party—to cruise in the West Indies. Would you prefer that?"

"Certainly not! The Vanderhoof set is wild and godless—I do not wish to see you keeping company with fools who walk in the broad and easy way that leads to perdition."

"It is rather a hard choice," said the young man, with a short laugh, turning toward the door. "According to you there's very little difference—a fool's paradise or a fool's hell! Well, it's one or the other for me, and I'll toss up for it tonight: heads, I lose; tails, the devil wins. Anyway, I'm sick of this, and I'm out of it."

"Harold," said the older man (and there was a slight tremor in his voice), "don't let us quarrel on Christmas Eve. All I want is to persuade you to think seriously of the duties and responsibilities to which God has called you—don't speak lightly of heaven and hell—remember, there is another life."

The young man came back and laid his hand upon his father's shoulder.

"Father," he said, "I want to remember it. I try to believe in it. But somehow or other, in this house, it all seems unreal to me. No doubt all you say is perfectly right and wise. I don't venture to argue against it, but I can't feel it—that's all. If I'm to have a soul, either to lose or to save, I must really live. Just now neither the present nor the future means anything to me. But surely we won't quarrel. I'm very grateful to you, and we'll part friends. Goodnight, sir."

The father held out his hand in silence. The heavy portiere dropped noiselessly behind the son, and he went up the wide, curving stairway to his own room.

Meantime John Weightman sat in his carved chair in the Jacobean dining room. He felt strangely old and dull. The portraits of beautiful women by Lawrence and Reynolds and Raeburn, which had often seemed like real company to him, looked remote and uninteresting. He fancied something cold and almost unfriendly in their expression, as if they were staring through him or beyond him. They cared nothing for his principles, his hopes, his disappointments, his successes; they belonged to another world, in which he had no place. At this he felt a vague resentment, a sense of discomfort that he could not have defined or explained. He was used to being considered, respected, appreciated at his full value in every region, even in that of his own dreams.

Presently he rang for the butler, telling him to close the house and not to sit up, and walked with lagging steps into the long library, where the shaded lamps were burning. His eye fell upon the low shelves full of costly books, but he had no desire to open them.

He dropped into the revolving chair before his big library table. It was covered with pamphlets and reports of the various enterprises in which he was interested. There was a pile of newspaper clippings in which his name was mentioned with praise for his sustaining power as a pillar of finance, for his judicious benevolence, for his support of wise and prudent reform movements, for his discretion in making permanent public gifts—"the Weightman Charities," one very complaisant editor called them, as if they deserved classification as a distinct species.

He turned the papers over listlessly. There was a description and a picture of the "Weightman Wing of the Hospital for Cripples," of which he was president; and an article on the new professor in the "Weightman Chair of Political Jurisprudence" in Jackson University, of which he was a trustee; and an illustrated account of the opening of the "Weightman Grammar School" at Dulwich-on-the-Sound, where he had his legal residence for purposes of taxation.

This last was perhaps the most carefully planned of all the Weightman Charities. He desired to win the confidence and support of his rural neighbors. It had pleased him much when the local newspaper had spoken of him as an ideal citizen and the logical candidate for the Governorship of the State; but upon the whole it seemed to him wiser to keep out of active politics. It would be easier and better to put Harold into the running, to have him sent to the Legislature from the Dulwich district, then to the national House, then to the Senate. Why not? The Weightman interests were large enough to need a direct representative and guardian at Washington.

But tonight all these plans came back to him with dust upon them. They were dry and crumbling like forsaken habitations. The son upon whom his complacent ambition had rested had turned his back upon the mansion of his father's hopes. The break might not be final; and in any event there would be much to live for; the fortunes of the family would be secure. But the zest of it all would be gone if John Weightman had to give up the assurance of perpetuating his name and his principles in his son. It was a bitter disappointment, and he felt that he had not deserved it.

He rose from the chair and paced the room with leaden feet. For the first time in his life his age was visibly upon him. His head was heavy and hot, and the thoughts that rolled in it were confused and depressing. Could it be that he had made a mistake in the principles of his existence? There was no argument in what Harold had said—it was almost childish—and yet it had shaken the elder man more deeply than he cared to show. It held a silent attack which touched him more than open criticism.

Suppose the end of his life were nearer than he thought—the end must come some time—what if it were now? Had he not founded his house upon a rock? Had he not kept the Commandments? Was he not, "touching the law, blameless"? And beyond this, even if there were some faults in his character—and all men are sinners—yet he surely believed in the saving doctrines of religion—the forgiveness of sins, the resurrection of the body, the life everlasting. Yes, that was the true source of comfort, after all. He would read a bit in the Bible, as he did every night, and go to bed and to sleep.

He went back to his chair at the library table. A strange weight of weariness rested upon him, but he opened the book at a familiar place, and his eyes fell upon the verse at the bottom of the page.

"Lay not up for yourselves treasures upon earth."

That had been the text of the sermon a few weeks before. Sleepily, heavily, he tried to fix his mind upon it and recall it. What was it that Doctor Snodgrass had said? Ah, yes—that it was a mistake to pause here in reading the verse. We must read on without a pause—Lay not up treasures upon earth where moth and rust do corrupt and where thieves break through and steal—that was the true doctrine. We may have treasures upon earth, but they must not be put into unsafe places, but into safe places. A most comforting doctrine! He had always followed it. Moths and rust and thieves had done no harm to his investments.

John Weightman's drooping eyes turned to the next verse, at the top of the second column.

"But lay up for yourselves treasures in heaven."

Now what had the Doctor said about that? How was it to be understood—in what sense—treasures—in heaven?

The book seemed to float away from him. The light vanished. He wondered dimly if this could be Death, coming so suddenly, so quietly, so irresistibly. He struggled for a moment to hold himself up, and then sank slowly forward upon the table. His head rested upon his folded hands. He slipped into the unknown.

How long afterward conscious life returned to him he did not know. The blank might have been an hour or a century. He knew only that something had happened in the interval. What it was he could not tell. He found great difficulty in catching the thread of his identity again. He felt that he was himself; but the trouble was to make his connections, to verify and place himself, to know who and where he was.

At last it grew clear. John Weightman was sitting on a stone, not far from a road in a strange land.

The road was not a formal highway, fenced and graded. It was more like a great travel-trace, worn by thousands of feet passing across the open country in the same direction.

From the edge of the hill, where John Weightman sat, he could see travelers, in little groups or larger companies, gathering from time to time by the different paths, and making the ascent. They were all clothed in white, and the form of their garments was strange to him; it was like some old picture. They passed him, group after group, talking quietly together or singing; not moving in haste, but with a certain air of eagerness and joy as if they were glad to be on their way to an appointed place. They did not stay to speak to him, but they looked at him often and spoke to one another as they looked; and now and then one of them would smile and beckon him a friendly greeting, so that he felt they would like him to be with them.

There was quite an interval between the groups; and he followed each of them with his eyes after it had passed.

For a long time he sat there watching and wondering. It was a very different world from that in which his mansion on the Avenue was built; and it looked strange to him, but most real—as real as anything he had ever seen. Presently he felt a strong desire to know what country it was and where the people were going. He had a faint premonition of what it must be, but he wished to be sure. So he rose from the stone where he was sitting, and came down through the short grass and the lavender flowers, toward a passing group of people. One of them turned to meet him, and held out his hand. It was an old man, under whose white beard and brows John Weightman thought he saw a suggestion of the face of the village doctor who had cared for him years ago, when he was a boy in the country.

"Welcome," said the old man. "Will you come with us?"

"Where are you going?"

"To the heavenly city, to see our mansions there."

"And who are these with you?"

"Strangers to me, until a little while ago; I know them better now. But you I have known for a long time, John Weightman. Don't you remember your old doctor?"

"Yes," he cried—"yes; your voice has not changed at all. I'm glad indeed to see you, Doctor McLean, especially now. All this seems very strange to me, almost oppressive. I wonder if—but may I go with you, do you suppose?"

"Surely," answered the doctor, with his familiar smile, "it will do you good. And you also must have a mansion in the city waiting for you—a fine one, too—are you not looking forward to it?"

"Yes," replied the other, hesitating a moment; "yes—I believe it must be so, although I had not expected to see it so soon. But I will go with you, and we can talk by the way."

The two men quickly caught up with the other people, and all went forward together along the road. The doctor had little to tell of his experience, for it had been a plain, hard life, uneventfully spent for others, and the story of the village was very simple. John Weightman's adventures and triumphs would have made a far richer, more imposing history, full of contacts with the great events and personages of the time. But somehow or other he did not care to speak much about it, walking on that wide heavenly moorland, under that tranquil, sunless arch of blue, in that free air of perfect peace, where the light was diffused without a shadow, as if the spirit of life in all things was luminous.

There was only one person besides the doctor in that little company whom John Weightman had known before—an old bookkeeper who had spent his life over a desk, carefully keeping accounts—a rusty, dull little man, patient and narrow, whose wife had been in the insane asylum for twenty years and whose only child was a crippled daughter, for whose comfort and happiness he had toiled and sacrificed himself without stint. It was a surprise to find him here—as care-free and joyful as the rest.

The lives of others in the company were revealed in brief glimpses as they talked together—a mother, early widowed, who had kept her little flock of children together and labored through hard and heavy years to bring them up in purity and knowledge—a Sister of Charity who had devoted herself to the nursing of poor folk who were being eaten to death by cancer—a schoolmaster whose heart and life had been poured into his quiet work of training boys for a clean and thoughtful manhood—a medical missionary who had given up a brilliant career in science to take the charge of a hospital in darkest Africa—a beautiful woman with silver hair who had resigned her dreams of love and marriage to care for an invalid father, and after his death had made her life a long, steady search for ways of doing kindnesses to others—a poet who had walked among the crowded tenements of the great city, bringing cheer and comfort not only by his songs, but by his wise and patient works of practical aid—a paralyzed woman who had lain for thirty years upon her bed, helpless but not hopeless, succeeding by a miracle of courage in her single aim, never to complain, but always to impart a bit of her joy and peace to every one who came near her. All these, and other persons like them, people of little consideration in the world, but now seemingly all full of great contentment and an inward gladness that made their steps light, were in the company that passed along the road, talking together of things past and things to come, and singing now and then with clear voices from which the veil of age and sorrow was lifted.

So they came to the summit of the moorland and looked over into the world beyond. It was a vast, green plain, softly rounded like a shallow vase, and circled with hills of amethyst. A broad, shining river flowed through it, and many silver threads of water were woven across the green; and there were borders of tall trees on the banks of the river, and orchards full of roses abloom along the little streams, and in the midst of all stood the city, white and wonderful and radiant.

When the travelers saw it they were filled with awe and joy. They passed over the little streams and among the orchards quickly and silently, as if they feared to speak lest the city should vanish.

The wall of the city was very low, a child could see over it, for it was made only of precious stones, which are never large. The gate of the city was not like a gate at all, for it was not barred with iron or wood, but only a single pearl, softly gleaming, marked the place where the wall ended and the entrance lay open.

A person stood there whose face was bright and grave, and whose robe was like the flower of the lily, not a woven fabric, but a living texture. "Come in," he said to the company of travelers; "you are at your journey's end, and your mansions are ready for you."

They passed from street to street among fair and spacious dwellings, set in amaranthine gardens, and adorned with an infinitely varied beauty of divine simplicity. The mansions differed in size, in shape, in charm; each one seemed to have its own personal look of loveliness; yet all were alike in fitness to their place, in harmony with one another, in the addition which each made to the singular and tranquil splendor of the city.

As the little company came, one by one, to the mansions which were prepared for them, and their Guide beckoned to the happy inhabitant to enter in and take possession, there was a soft murmur of joy, half wonder and half recognition; as if the new and immortal dwelling were crowned with the beauty of surprise, lovelier and nobler than all the dreams of it had been; and yet also as if it were touched with the beauty of the familiar, the remembered, the long-loved. One after another the travelers were led to their own mansions, and went in gladly; and from within, through the open doorways, came sweet voices of welcome, and low laughter, and song.

At last there was no one left with the Guide but the two old friends, Doctor McLean and John Weightman. They were standing in front of one of the largest and fairest of the houses, whose garden glowed softly with radiant flowers. The Guide laid his hand upon the doctor's shoulder.

"This is for you," he said. "Go in; there is no more pain here, no more death, nor sorrow, nor tears; for your old enemies are all conquered. But all the good that you have done for others, all the help that you have given, all the comfort that you have brought, all the strength and love that you have bestowed upon the suffering, are here; for we have built them all into this mansion for you."

The good man's face was lighted with a still joy. He clasped his old friend's hand closely, and whispered: "How wonderful it is! Go on, you will come to your mansion next, it is not far away, and we shall see each other again soon, very soon."

So he went through the garden, and into the music within. The Keeper of the Gate turned to John Weightman with level, quiet, searching eyes. Then he asked, gravely:

"Where do you wish me to lead you now?"

"To see my own mansion," answered the man, with half-concealed excitement. "Is there not one here for me? You may not let me enter it yet, perhaps, for I must confess to you that I am only—"

"I know," said the Keeper of the Gate—"I know it all. You are John Weightman."

"Yes," said the man, more firmly than he had spoken at first, for it gratified him that his name was known. "Yes, I am John Weightman, Senior Warden of St. Petronius' Church. I wish very much to see my mansion here, if only for a moment. I believe that you have one for me. Will you take me to it?"

The Keeper of the Gate drew a little book from the breast of his robe and turned over the pages.

"Certainly," he said, with a curious look at the man, "your name is here; and you shall see your mansion if you will follow me."

It seemed as if they must have walked miles and miles, through the vast city, passing street after street of houses larger and smaller, of gardens richer and poorer, but all full of beauty and delight. They came into a kind of suburb, where there were many small cottages, with plots of flowers, very lowly, but bright and fragrant. Finally they reached an open field, bare and lonely-looking. There were two or three little bushes in it, without flowers, and the grass was sparse and thin. In the center of the field was a tiny hut, hardly big enough for a shepherd's shelter. It looked as if it had been built of discarded things, scraps and fragments of other buildings, put together with care and pains, by some one who had tried to make the most of cast-off material. There was something pitiful and shamefaced about the hut. It shrank and drooped and faded in its barren field, and seemed to cling only by sufferance to the edge of the splendid city.

"This," said the Keeper of the Gate, standing still and speaking with a low, distinct voice—"this is your mansion, John Weightman."

An almost intolerable shock of grieved wonder and indignation choked the man for a moment so that he could not say a word. Then he turned his face away from the poor little hut and began to remonstrate eagerly with his companion.

"Surely, sir," he stammered, "you must be in error about this. There is something wrong—some other John Weightman—a confusion of names—the book must be mistaken."

"There is no mistake," said the Keeper of the Gate, very calmly; "here is your name, the record of your title and your possessions in this place."

"But how could such a house be prepared for me," cried the man, with a resentful tremor in his voice—"for me, after my long and faithful service? Is this a suitable mansion for one so well known and devoted? Why is it so pitifully small and mean? Why have you not built it large and fair, like the others?"

"That is all the material you sent us."

"What!"

"We have used all the material that you sent us," repeated the Keeper of the Gate.

"Now I know that you are mistaken," cried the man, with growing earnestness, "for all my life long I have been doing things that must have supplied you with material. Have you not heard that I have built a school-house; the wing of a hospital; two—yes, three—small churches, and the greater part of a large one, the spire of St. Petro—"

The Keeper of the Gate lifted his hand.

"Wait," he said; "we know all these things. They were not ill done. But they were all marked and used as foundation for the name and mansion of John Weightman in the world. Did you not plan them for that?"

"Yes," answered the man, confused and taken aback, "I confess that I thought often of them in that way. Perhaps my heart was set upon that too much. But there are other things—my endowment for the college—my steady and liberal contributions to all the established charities—my support of every respectable—"

"Wait," said the Keeper of the Gate again. "Were not all these carefully recorded on earth where they would add to your credit? They were not foolishly done. Verily, you have had your reward for them. Would you be paid twice?"

"No," cried the man, with deepening dismay, "I dare not claim that. I acknowledge that I considered my own interest too much. But surely not altogether. You have said that these things were not foolishly done. They accomplished some good in the world. Does not that count for something?"

"Yes," answered the Keeper of the Gate, "it counts in the world—where you counted it. But it does not belong to you here. We have saved and used everything that you sent us. This is the mansion prepared for you."

As he spoke, his look grew deeper and more searching, like a flame of fire. John Weightman could not endure it. It seemed to strip him naked and wither him. He sank to the ground under a crushing weight of shame, covering his eyes with his hands and cowering face downward upon the stones. Dimly through the trouble of his mind he felt their hardness and coldness.

"Tell me, then," he cried, brokenly, "since my life has been so little worth, how came I here at all?"

"Through the mercy of the King"—the answer was like the soft tolling of a bell.

"And how have I earned it?" he murmured.

"It is never earned; it is only given," came the clear, low reply.

"But how have I failed so wretchedly," he asked, "in all the purpose of my life? What could I have done better? What is it that counts here?"

"Only that which is truly given," answered the bell like voice. "Only that good which is done for the love of doing it. Only those plans in which the welfare of others is the master thought. Only those labors in which the sacrifice is greater than the reward. Only those gifts in which the giver forgets himself."

The man lay silent. A great weakness, an unspeakable despondency and humiliation were upon him. But the face of the Keeper of the Gate was infinitely tender as he bent over him.

"Think again, John Weightman. Has there been nothing like that in your life?"

"Nothing," he sighed. "If there ever were such things, it must have been long ago—they were all crowded out—I have forgotten them."

There was an ineffable smile on the face of the Keeper of the Gate, and his hand made the sign of the cross over the bowed head as he spoke gently:

"These are the things that the King never forgets; and because there were a few of them in your life, you have a little place here."

The sense of coldness and hardness under John Weightman's hands grew sharper and more distinct. The feeling of bodily weariness and lassitude weighed upon him, but there was a calm, almost a lightness, in his heart as he listened to the fading vibrations of the silvery bell-tones. The chimney clock on the mantel had just ended the last stroke of seven as he lifted his head from the table. Thin, pale strips of the city morning were falling into the room through the narrow partings of the heavy curtains.

What was it that had happened to him? Had he been ill? Had he died and come to life again? Or had he only slept, and had his soul gone visiting in dreams? He sat for some time, motionless, not lost, but finding himself in thought. Then he took a narrow book from the table drawer, wrote a check, and tore it out.

He went slowly up the stairs, knocked very softly at his son's door, and, hearing no answer, entered without noise. Harold was asleep, his bare arm thrown above his head, and his eager face relaxed in peace. His father looked at him a moment with strangely shining eyes, and then tiptoed quietly to the writing-desk, found a pencil and a sheet of paper, and wrote rapidly:

"My dear boy, here is what you asked me for; do what you like with it, and ask for more if you need it. If you are still thinking of that work with Grenfell, we'll talk it over today after church. I want to know your heart better; and if I have made mistakes—"

A slight noise made him turn his head. Harold was sitting up in bed with wide open eyes.

"Father!" he cried, "is that you?"

"Yes, my son," answered John Weightman; "I've come back—I mean I've come up—no, I mean come in—well, here I am, and God give us a good Christmas together."

---

It's easy to do our good deeds in such a way that people know all about it. Even if we just drop hints as to what we did, we want everyone to know how charitable we are. But we have it from the highest source that that's not the way to do it. Jesus said: "Be careful not to do your 'acts of righteousness' before men, to be seen by them. If you do, you will have no reward from your Father in heaven. So when you give to the needy, do not announce it with trumpets, as the hypocrites do in the synagogues and on the streets, to be honored by men. I tell you the truth, they have received their reward in full. But when you give to the needy, do not let your left hand know what your right hand is doing, so that your giving may be in secret. Then your Father, who sees what is done in secret, will reward you" (Matt. 6:1–4).

*This selection is suitable for children.*
*The moral of the story is that love means to be interested in what others are interested in.*

# "FIRST HUNT"

### by Arthur Gordon

A lot of parents assume that what *they're* interested in is automatically what their children should be interested in. They often don't take into consideration that the child may have completely different hobbies and interests. Love means looking out for the other's best interest, not your own.

This is a touching story of a sensitive father who showed such love. If more parents showed the type of love exhibited by this father, there would be a lot less strife among families. This is another story by Arthur Gordon, whom we introduced on page 121.

---

His father said, "All set, boy?" and Jeremy nodded quickly, picking up his gun with awkward mittened hands. His father pushed open the door and they went out into the freezing dawn together, leaving the snug security of the shack, the warmth of the kerosene stove, the companionable smell of bacon and coffee.

Not that Jeremy had eaten much breakfast. It had stuck in his throat, and his father, noticing this, had said, "Just a touch of duck fever, son; don't let it bother you." And he added, almost wistfully, "Wish I were fourteen again, getting ready to shoot my first duck. You're luckier than you realize, Jerry boy."

They stood for a moment in front of the shack, their breaths white in the icy air. Ahead of them was only flatness; not a house, not a tree, nothing but the vast expanse of marsh and water and sky. Ordinarily Jeremy would have been pleased by the bleak arrangements of black and gray and silver that met his eye. Ordinarily he would have asked his father to wait while he fussed around with his camera, trying to record these impressions on film. But not this morning. This was the morning, solemn and sacred, when he was to be initiated at last into the mystic rites of duck shooting.

This was the morning. And he hated it, had hated the whole idea ever since his father had bought him a gun, had taught him to shoot clay pigeons, had promised him a trip to this island in the bay where the point shooting was the finest in the state.

He hated it, but he was determined to go through with it. He loved his father, wanted more than anything in the world his approval and admiration. If only he could conduct himself properly this morning, he knew that he would get it.

Plodding now across the marshland, he remembered what his father had said to his mother after the first shotgun lesson: "You know, Martha, Jerry's got the makings of a fine wing shot. He's got coordination and timing. And—the kind of nerve it takes, too."

They came to the blind, a narrow, camouflaged pit facing the bay. In it was a bench, a shelf for shotgun shells, nothing else. Jeremy sat down tensely, waited while his father waded out with an armful of decoys. Light was pouring into the sky, now. Far down the bay a string of ducks went by, etched against the sunrise. Watching them, Jeremy felt his stomach contract.

To ease the sense of dread that was oppressing him, he picked up his camera and took a picture of his father silhouetted blackly against the quicksilver water. Then it occurred to him that this might not be the thing to do. He put the camera hastily on the shelf in front of him, picked up his gun again.

His father came back and dropped down beside him, boots dripping, hands blue with cold. "Better load up. Sometimes they're on top of you before you know it." He watched Jeremy break his gun, insert the shells, close it again. "I'll let you shoot first," he said, "and back you up if necessary." He loaded his own gun, closed it with a metallic snap. "You know," he said, happily, "I've been waiting a long time for this day. Just the two of us, out here on the marshes. We—"

He broke off, leaning forward, eyes narrowed. "There's a small flight now, headed this way. Four, no, five. Blacks, I think. They'll come in from left to right, against the wind, if they give us a shot at all. Keep your head down. I'll give you the word."

Jeremy kept his head down. Behind them the sun had cleared the horizon, now, flooding the marshes with tawny light. He could see everything with an almost unbearable clarity: his father's face, tense and eager, the faint white rime of frost on the gun barrels. His heart was thudding wildly. *No,* he prayed, *don't let them come. Make them stay away, please!*

But they kept coming. "Four blacks," his father said in a whisper. "One mallard. Keep still!"

Jeremy kept still. High above them, thin and sweet, he heard the pulsing whistle of the wings as the flight went over, swung wide, began to circle. "Get set," Jeremy's father breathed. "They're coming."

In they came, gliding down the sunlit aisles of space, heads raised alertly, wings set in a proud curve. The mallard was leading; light flashed from the iridescent feathers around his neck and glinted on his ruddy breast. Down dropped his bright orange feet, reaching for the steel-colored water. Closer, closer . . .

"Now!" cried Jeremy's father in an explosive roar. He was on his feet, gun ready. "Take him! Take the leader!"

Jeremy felt his body obey. He stood up, leaned into the gun the way his father had taught him. He felt the stock cold against his cheek, saw the twin muzzles rise. Under his finger the trigger curved, smooth and final and deadly.

In the same instant, the ducks saw the gunners and flared wildly. Up went the mallard as if jerked by an invisible string. For a fraction of a second he hung there, poised against the wide and sun, balanced between life and death. *Now*, said something sharply in Jeremy's brain, *now!* And he waited for the slam of the explosion.

But it didn't come. Up went the mallard, higher still, until suddenly he tipped a wing, caught the full force of the wind and whirled away, out of range, out of danger, out of sight.

There was no sound, then, except the faint rustle of the grasses. Jeremy stood there, gripping his gun.

"Well," his father said at last, "what happened?"

The boy did not answer. His lips were trembling.

His father said, in the same controlled voice, "Why didn't you shoot?"

Jeremy thumbed back the safety catch. He stood the gun carefully in the corner of the blind. "Because they were so alive," he said, and burst into tears.

He sat on the rough bench, face buried in his hands, and wept. All hope he had had of pleasing his father was gone. He had had his chance, and he had failed.

Beside him his father crouched suddenly. "Here comes a single. Looks like a pintail. Let's try again."

Jeremy did not lower his hands. "It's no use, Dad, I can't."

"Hurry," his father said roughly. "You'll miss him altogether. Here!"

Cold metal touched Jeremy. He looked up, unbelieving. His father had taken the camera out of its case, was offering it to him. "Quick, here he comes. He won't hang around all day!"

In swept the single, a big pintail drake driving low across the water, skidding right into the decoys. Jeremy's father clapped his hands together, a sound like a pistol shot. The splendid bird soared up; the pressure of his wings sent him twelve feet. One instant he was there, not thirty yards away, feet retracted, head raised, wings flailing, white breast gleaming. The next he was gone, whistling like a feathered bullet downwind.

Jeremy lowered the camera. "I got him!" His face was radiant. "I *got* him!"

"Did you?" His father's hand touched his shoulder briefly. "That's good. There'll be others along soon; you can get all sorts of shots." He hesitated, looking at his son, and Jeremy saw that there was no disappointment in his eyes, only pride and sympathy and love. "It's okay, son. I'll always love shooting. But that doesn't mean you have to. Sometimes, it takes just as much courage not to do a thing as to do it. Think you could teach me how to work that gadget?"

"Teach you?" Jeremy felt as if his heart would burst with happiness. "Gosh, Dad, there's nothing to it. It's easy, really it is. Look here, let me show you . . . "

----

The bonding that can occur in the hunt between father and son is strong, I'm sure, as I know it is with my son and me in fishing. But in this story, Gordon cleverly shows that the bonding can continue even though the son doesn't have a stomach for hunting.

So many children get intimidated by their parents for the "crime" of not liking what the parents like. Of course, I'm talking about differences in taste and preferences—not differences in morality. We as Christian parents would do well to let our children pursue the hobbies and interests they choose—if they don't violate God's moral code.

# PART IV

# Just
# for Fun

The final section of this book includes
stories that are light in nature.
While the morals of these stories are not
necessarily as profound as other works
in this book, they still make a point that fits
within a biblical framework.

*This selection is suitable for children.*
*The moral of the story here is that you need to know where you want to go, if you're ever going to get there.*

# ALICE AND THE CHESHIRE-CAT

**from *Alice in Wonderland***
by Lewis Carroll

*Alice in Wonderland* has captured the imagination of millions of people ever since it was first published in 1865 (*Alice's Adventures in Wonderland*) and 1871 (*Through the Looking Glass and What Alice Found There*). Those two books combined comprise what we know today as *Alice in Wonderland*. The author, Charles Lutwidge Dodgson (1832–98), used the pen name of Lewis Carroll.

Because, I am such a literalist, it's hard for me to always understand *Alice in Wonderland*. But I like the short excerpt here because its points are lucid. For example, how can you get where you want to go, if you don't know where you want to go? Similarly, how can you achieve a goal if you don't know what it is?

A moment before this scene takes place, Alice has been in a kitchen where she notices a large cat "grinning from ear to ear." She asks why the cat does so and is told that it's a Cheshire-cat. A couple of pages later, she's out of the kitchen and walking in the woods when she notices the Cheshire-cat sitting in the branches of a tree a few yards ahead of her. That's where our short excerpt begins.

---

The Cat only grinned when it saw Alice. It looked good-natured, she thought: still it did have *very* long claws and a great many teeth, so she felt it ought to be treated with respect.

"Cheshire-Puss," she began, rather timidly, as she did not at all know whether it would like the name; however, it only grinned a little wider. "Come, it's pleased so far," thought Alice, and she went on. "Would you tell me, please, which way I ought to go from here?"

"That depends a good deal on where you want to get to," said the Cat.

"I don't much care where—" said Alice.

"Then it doesn't matter which way you go," said the Cat.

"—so long as I get *somewhere*," Alice added as an explanation.

"Oh, you're sure to do that," said the Cat, "if you only walk long enough."

Alice felt that this could not be denied, so she tried another question. "What sort of people live about here?"

"In *that* direction," the Cat said, waving its right paw round, "lives a Hatter: and in *that* direction," waving the other paw, "lives a March Hare. Visit either you like: they're both mad."

"But I don't want to go among mad people," Alice remarked.

"Oh, you can't help that," said the Cat: "we're all mad here. I'm mad. You're mad."

"How do you know I'm mad?" said Alice.

"You must be," said the Cat, "or you wouldn't have come here."

Alice didn't think that proved it at all: however, she went on: "And how do you know that you're mad?"

"To begin with," said the Cat, "a dog's not mad. You grant that?"

"I suppose so," said Alice.

"Well, then," the Cat went on, "you see a dog growls when it's angry, and wags its tail when it's pleased. Now *I* growl when I'm pleased, and wag my tail when I'm angry. Therefore I'm mad."

"*I* call it purring, not growling," said Alice.

"Call it what you like," said the Cat.

[The Cat then disappears and suddenly reappears to ask a quick question. After receiving Alice's answer, it vanishes only to reappear yet again. So Alice said:]

"I wish you wouldn't keep appearing and vanishing so suddenly: you make one quite giddy."

"All right," said the Cat; and this time it vanished quite slowly, beginning with the end of the tail, and ending with the grin, which remained some time after the rest of it had gone.

"Well! I've often seen a cat without a grin," thought Alice; "but a grin without a cat! It's the most curious thing I ever saw in all my life!"

---

The grin of the Cheshire-cat reminds me of the false smiles of certain individuals who have an agenda. They may grin to your face but stab you in the back. "Let love be without hypocrisy" (Rom. 12:9, NASB).

*This selection is suitable for children.*
*The moral of the story is be as creative as you can as you serve God.*

# "PETER DASS OUTWITS THE DEVIL"

### Traditional Norwegian Folktale
retold by Kirsti Saebo Newcombe

In many folktales from many lands, there is a theme of people trying to outwit the devil or demons. There is also another theme of people making pacts with the devil, which, of course, is always wrong. The following is a traditional Norwegian folktale utilizing these themes. The title character really lived, and the incident of his challenging pulpit assignment is reported to be real. But everything else is fanciful.

There lived a priest in the north of Norway in the 1600s. His name was Peter Dass. The stories and legends about him and his work spread quickly. He was a poet and a hymn writer as well as a good speaker. His sermons were widely known.

During this time Norway was under Danish rule, and the king in Copenhagen heard the rumors about this Norwegian priest. He sent an invitation for Peter Dass to come and speak to the Court of the Palace Chapel. Because of the great distance and the lack of transportation, by the time Peter Dass received the invitation, it was too late for him to travel all the way to Copenhagen and be there on time. So the devil came to him and said, "I'll make you a deal. I will get you there on time if you will give me all the souls that fall asleep during your sermon in Copenhagen." Peter Dass agreed and off they went. Over seas and land, through storms and quiet, Peter Dass made it to Copenhagen just on time.

In the invitation, it said that a sheet of paper would be lying on the pulpit and the topic for his sermon would be stated there. When he reached the pulpit, he found the sheet, but there was nothing written on it. He turned the sheet over and the other side was also blank. He looked puzzled, but then he started speaking, "Out of nothing, God created the heavens and the earth." And he went on to give a most excellent sermon on creation. The king was pleased, but the devil was not because not one person fell asleep during that sermon.

This story illustrates being creative for God. When we rely on Him, He has promised to give us not only wisdom, but even the very words we need.

*This selection is suitable for children.*
*The moral of the story is use your head when you're in hot water.*


## "REINERT MEETS THE CANNIBALS"
**Traditional Norwegian Folktale**
retold by Kirsti Saebo Newcombe

Norway has been known as a seafaring nation since the time of the Vikings. Many are the stories of Norsemen on the sea. Some are tall tales and some are more or less true. This story, "Reinert Meets the Cannibals," is a tale of overcoming evil with brains. The self-mocking humor is quite typical for the southern part of Norway. The story would have taken place in the early 1800s. It is told from the perspective of a sea mate of Reinert (RINE-ert).

---

There was an old Norwegian sea hawk named Reinert, who had sailed the Seven Seas for as long as anyone could remember. He and I had had many an adventure together, but none as terrifying as the one you are about to hear.

We were sailing in the Pacific Ocean, and of all the bad storms we'd ever been in, this one was out to get us. Sure enough, the ship went down, and only Reinert and I and the boat chef floated ashore on a little island. It was wonderful to be safe and dry again, but the wonder didn't last. There were natives there, and we discovered it when we were rudely awakened by someone poking us and tying us up and dragging us along. Or maybe we should say, "they discovered us."

We were brought to a little village—at least there were huts and a big fire and people who were more or less (especially less) dressed. We were tied to a pole and the people started some sort of preparations. They put a big iron pot with water in it over a fire. They put different roots and greens in it. Then our chef started to lose his normal coloring and his teeth started chattering. I understood it too. We were among cannibals! They were preparing the pot for us; we were dinner!

We couldn't communicate with them, and I had to think quickly. I whispered, "Your wooden leg, screw it off and throw it over to them!"

Reinert understood, and it was sure worth a try. We managed to get the leg loose, and we threw it over to the natives. The crowd screamed in excitement. But all of a sudden the crowd grew extremely quiet. I can only imagine that they started thinking something like, *What kind of people is this who can divide themselves in pieces as they wish?* Then they tasted the leg!

After that, they let us go *very* quickly, and the rumor spread among all the islands and on all the Seven Seas. "You can't eat people from Norway—they are totally unpalatable."

---

Here again we see rewarded in a folktale the idea of being clever, using your head, being quick on your feet. I've noticed that same moral in a lot of the fairy tales from all sorts of different cultures and countries. There is no premium on dullness.

*This selection is suitable for children.*
*The moral of the story is be careful what you choose to pursue—you just might get it!*

## "THE COP AND THE ANTHEM"

### by O. Henry

O. Henry (1862–1910), whose real name was William Sydney Porter, was a master of the short story. He has sometimes been described as "America's most popular short-story writer." He wrote a lot of his short stories while living in New York City. He seemed to have a fascination with the vagrants sleeping on park benches. Note what O. Henry says in the following story about charity that is unloving—how's that for an oxymoron! (But note also there are some proud homeless people who would rather receive no help than receive help from those who require a few common sense rules.)

By way of introduction, I wouldn't read too much into the story in terms of it making some profound cynical statement against true reformation of the human soul. There are some cynics who don't believe in real change and real conversion of the likes of Soapy. But the annals of every rescue mission and Salvation Army base are full of genuine stories of true conversion and regeneration (as well as many stories of those who fell away, unfortunately). Be that as it may, I think "The Cop and the Anthem" is a charming story.

---

On his bench in Madison Square Soapy moved uneasily. When wild geese honk high of nights, and when women without sealskin coats grow kind to their husbands, and when Soapy moves uneasily on his bench in the park, you may know that winter is near at hand.

A dead leaf fell in Soapy's lap. That was Jack Frost's card. Jack is kind to the regular denizens of Madison Square, and gives fair warning of his annual call. At the corners of four streets he hands his pasteboard to the North Wind, footman of the mansion of All Outdoors, so that the inhabitants thereof may make ready.

Soapy's mind became cognizant of the fact that the time had come for him to resolve himself into a singular Committee of Ways and

Means to provide against the coming rigor. And therefore he moved uneasily on his bench.

The hibernatorial ambitions of Soapy were not of the highest. In them were no considerations of Mediterranean cruises, of soporific Southern skies, of drifting in the Vesuvian Bay. Three months on the Island was what his soul craved. Three months of assured board and bed and congenial company, safe from Boreas and bluecoats, seemed to Soapy the essence of things desirable.

For years the hospitable Blackwell's had been his winter quarters. Just as his more fortunate fellow New Yorkers had bought their tickets to Palm Beach and the Riviera each winter, so Soapy had made his humble arrangements for his annual hegira to the Island. And now the time was come. On the previous night three Sabbath newspapers, distributed beneath his coat, about his ankles and over his lap, had failed to repulse the cold as he slept on his bench near the spurting fountain in the ancient square. So the Island loomed big and timely in Soapy's mind. He scorned the provisions made in the name of charity for the city's dependents. In Soapy's opinion the Law was more benign than Philanthropy. There was an endless round of institutions, municipal and eleemosynary, on which he might set out and receive lodging and food accordant with the simple life. But to one of Soapy's proud spirit the gifts of charity are encumbered. If not in coin you must pay in humiliation of spirit for every benefit received at the hands of philanthropy. As Caesar had his Brutus, every bed of charity must have its toll of a bath, every loaf of bread its compensation of a private and personal inquisition. Wherefore it is better to be a guest of the law, which, though conducted by rules, does not meddle unduly with a gentleman's private affairs.

Soapy, having decided to go to the Island, at once set about accomplishing his desire. There were many easy ways of doing this. The pleasantest was to dine luxuriously at some expensive restaurant; and then, after declaring insolvency, be handed over quietly and without uproar to a policeman. An accommodating magistrate would do the rest.

Soapy left his bench and strolled out of the square and across the level sea of asphalt, where Broadway and Fifth Avenue flow together. Up Broadway, he turned, and halted at a glittering cafe, where are gathered together nightly the choicest products of the grape, the silkworm, and the protoplasm.

Soapy had confidence in himself from the lowest button of his vest upward. He was shaven, and his coat was decent and his neat black, ready-tied four-in-hand had been presented to him by a lady missionary on Thanksgiving Day. If he could reach a table in the restaurant unsuspected success would be his. The portion of him that would show above the table would raise no doubt in the waiter's mind. A roasted mallard duck, thought Soapy, would be about the thing— with a bottle of Chablis, and then Camembert, a demi-tasse and a cigar. One dollar for the cigar would be enough. The total would not be so high as to call forth any supreme manifestation of revenge from the cafe management; and yet the meat would leave him filled and happy for the journey to his winter refuge.

But as Soapy set foot inside the restaurant door the head waiter's eye fell upon his frayed trousers and decadent shoes. Strong and ready hands turned him about and conveyed him in silence and haste to the sidewalk and averted the ignoble fate of the menaced mallard.

Soapy turned off Broadway. It seemed that his route to the coveted Island was not to be an epicurean one. Some other way of entering limbo must be thought of.

At a corner of Sixth Avenue electric lights and cunningly displayed wares behind plate-glass made a shop window conspicuous. Soapy took a cobblestone and dashed it through the glass. People came running around the corner, a policeman in the lead. Soapy stood still, with his hands in his pockets, and smiled at the sight of brass buttons.

"Where's the man that done that?" inquired the officer, excitedly.

"Don't you figure out that I might have had something to do with it?" said Soapy, not without sarcasm, but friendly, as one greets good fortune.

The policeman's mind refused to accept Soapy even as a clue. Men who smash windows do not remain to parley with the law's minions. They take to their heels. The policeman saw a man halfway down the block running to catch a car. With drawn club he joined in the pursuit. Soapy, with disgust in his heart, loafed along, twice unsuccessful.

On the opposite side of the street was a restaurant of no great pretensions. It catered to large appetites and modest purses. Its crockery and atmosphere were thick; its soup and napery thin. Into this place Soapy took his accusive shoes and telltale trousers without challenge. At a table he sat and consumed beefsteak, flapjacks, doughnuts and pie. And then to the waiter he betrayed the fact that the minutest coin and himself were strangers.

"Now, get busy and call a cop," said Soapy. "And don't keep a gentleman waiting."

"No cop for youse," said the waiter, with a voice like butter cakes and an eye like the cherry in a Manhattan cocktail. "Hey, Con!"

Neatly upon his left ear on the callous pavement two waiters pitched Soapy. He arose joint by joint, as a carpenter's rule opens, and beat the dust from his clothes. Arrest seemed but a rosy dream. The Island seemed very far away. A policeman who stood before a drug store two doors away laughed and walked down the street.

Five blocks Soapy traveled before his courage permitted him to woo capture again. This time the opportunity presented what he fatuously termed to himself a "cinch." A young woman of a modest and pleasing guise was standing before a show window gazing with sprightly interest at its display of shaving mugs and inkstands, and two yards from the window a large policeman of severe demeanor leaned against a water plug.

It was Soapy's design to assume the role of the despicable and execrated "masher." The refined and elegant appearance of his victim and the contiguity of the conscientious cop encouraged him to believe that he would soon feel the pleasant official clutch upon his arm that would insure his winter quarters on the right little, tight little isle.

Soapy straightened the lady missionary's ready-made tie, dragged his shrinking cuffs into the open, set his hat at a killing cant and sidled toward the young woman. He made eyes at her, was taken with sudden coughs and "hems," smiled, smirked and went brazenly through the impudent and contemptible litany of the "masher." With half an eye Soapy saw that the policeman was watching him fixedly. The young woman moved away a few steps, and again bestowed her absorbed attention upon the shaving mugs. Soapy followed, boldly stepping to her side, raised his hat and said:

"Ah there, Bedelia! Don't you want to come and play in my yard?"

The policeman was still looking. The persecuted young woman had but to beckon a finger and Soapy would be practically en route for his insular haven. Already he imagined he could feel the cozy warmth of the station-house. The young woman faced him and, stretching out a hand, caught Soapy's coat sleeve.

"Sure, Mike," she said, joyfully, "if you'll blow me to a pail of suds. I'd have spoken to you sooner, but the cop was watching."

With the young woman playing the clinging ivy to his oak Soapy walked past the policeman overcome with gloom. He seemed doomed to liberty.

At the next corner he shook off his companion and ran. He halted in the district where by night are found the lightest streets, hearts, vows, and librettos. Women in furs and men in greatcoats moved gaily in the wintry. A sudden fear seized Soapy that some dreadful enchantment had rendered him immune to arrest. The thought brought little of panic upon it, and when he came upon another policeman lounging grandly in front of a transplendent theater he caught at the immediate straw of "disorderly conduct."

On the sidewalk Soapy began to yell drunken gibberish at the top of his harsh voice. He danced, howled, raved, and otherwise disturbed the welkin.

The policeman twirled his club, turned his back to Soapy and remarked to a citizen.

"'Tis one of them Yale lads celebratin' the goose egg they give to the Hartford College. Noisy; but no harm. We've instructions to lave them be."

Disconsolate, Soapy ceased his unavailing racket. Would never a policeman lay hands on him? In his fancy the Island seemed an unattainable Arcadia. He buttoned his thin coat against the chilling wind.

In a cigar store he saw a well-dressed man lighting a cigar at a swinging light. His silk umbrella he had set by the door on entering. Soapy stepped inside, secured the umbrella and sauntered off with it slowly. The man at the cigar light followed hastily.

"My umbrella," he said, sternly.

"Oh, is it?" sneered Soapy, adding insult to petit larceny. "Well, why don't you call a policeman? I took it. Your umbrella! Why don't you call a cop? There stands one on the corner."

The umbrella owner slowed his steps. Soapy did likewise, with a presentiment that luck would again run against him. The policeman looked at the two curiously.

"Of course," said the umbrella man—"that is—well, you know how these mistakes occur—I—if it's your umbrella I hope you'll excuse me—I picked it up this morning in a restaurant—If you recognize it as yours, why—I hope you'll—"

"Of course it's mine," said Soapy, viciously.

The ex-umbrella man retreated. The policeman hurried to assist a tall blonde in an opera cloak across the street in front of a street car that was approaching two blocks away.

Soapy walked eastward through a street damaged by improvements. He hurled the umbrella wrathfully into an excavation. He muttered against the men who wear helmets and carry clubs. Because he wanted to fall into their clutches, they seemed to regard him as a king who could do no wrong.

At length Soapy reached one of the avenues to the east where the glitter and turmoil was but faint. He set his face down this toward Madison Square, for the homing instinct survives even when the home is a park bench.

But on an unusually quiet corner Soapy came to a standstill. Here was an old church, quaint and rambling and gabled. Through one violet-stained window a soft light glowed, where, no doubt, the organist loitered over the keys, making sure of his mastery of the coming Sabbath anthem. For there drifted out to Soapy's ears sweet music that caught and held him transfixed against the convolutions of the iron fence.

The moon was above, lustrous and serene; vehicles and pedestrians were few; sparrows twittered sleepily in the eaves—for a little while the scene might have been a country churchyard. And the anthem that the organist played cemented Soapy to the iron fence, for he had known it well in the days when his life contained such things as mothers and roses and ambitions and friends and immaculate thoughts and collars.

The conjunction of Soapy's receptive state of mind and the influences about the old church wrought a sudden and wonderful change in his soul. He viewed with swift horror the pit into which he had tumbled, the degraded days, unworthy desires, dead hopes, wrecked faculties and base motives that made up his existence.

And also in a moment his heart responded thrillingly to this novel mood. An instantaneous and strong impulse moved him to battle with his desperate fate. He would pull himself out of the mire; he would make a man of himself again; he would conquer the evil that had taken possession of him. There was time; he was comparatively young yet: he would resurrect his old eager ambitions and pursue them without faltering. Those solemn but sweet organ notes had set up a revolution in him. Tomorrow he would go into the roaring downtown district and find work. A fur importer had once offered him a place as driver. He would find him tomorrow and ask for the position. He would be somebody in the world. He would—

Soapy felt a hand laid on his arm. He looked quickly around into the broad face of a policeman.

"What are you doin' here?" asked the officer.

"Nothin'," said Soapy.

"Then come along," said the policeman.

"Three months on the Island," said the Magistrate in the Police Court the next morning.

---

It's hard to picture a time when loitering could land you three months in jail! Nowadays, murderers sometimes serve less time.

O. Henry, as we can see, was a master of the ironic ending. The story underscores (indirectly) that we should be careful choosing what to pursue. We just might get it, though not always when or how we want it.

*This selection is suitable for children.*
*The moral of the story is to be wise.*

## "THE INNKEEPER'S WISE DAUGHTER"

by Peninnah Schram

There is a great reward in having wisdom. While we live in the Information Age, there are many who may have lots of *knowledge* but who lack *wisdom*. They may do well playing "Trivial Pursuit," but they are not wise in how they live their lives!

The Bible talks a lot about the value of having wisdom. The fear (or reverence) of the Lord is the beginning of wisdom. It even says that wisdom is better than gold, silver, or rubies (Prov. 8:10–11).

Here is a folktale from Jewish oral tradition that playfully deals with the subject of wisdom. In some ways it takes the idea of being wise to absurd proportions. Nonetheless, the point still stands that it is good to use your head and be clever, but not in a way that manipulates or takes advantage of other people. The heroine of this story is wise, but she also treats others as she would want to be treated.

This story has been retold by Peninnah Schram, an associate professor of speech and drama at Stern College of Yeshiva University. The founding director of the Jewish Storytelling Center in New York City, Ms. Schram is the author of many books, including *Jewish Stories One Generation Tells Another, Tales of Elijah the Prophet,* and *Chosen Tales.*

---

Many years ago in a small village in Russia, there were two friends—a tailor and an innkeeper. One day as they were drinking glasses of tea, they began to talk about their philosophies of life. As their discussion went on, they began to argue more and more intensely, each one claiming to know more about life than the other, and they almost came to blows. They realized that neither one would win the argument, so they decided to bring the matter to the local nobleman, who was respected for his wisdom and honesty and who often served as a judge in disputes. The two friends finished their tea in silence and set out to see the nobleman.

When the nobleman had heard the case, he said to the two men, "Whoever answers these three questions correctly will be the one who knows more about life: What is the quickest thing in the world? What is the fattest thing in the world? And what is the sweetest? Return in three days' time with your answers, and I will settle your disagreement."

The tailor returned home and spent the three days thinking about these riddles, but found no answers to them. When the innkeeper returned to his home, he sat down, holding his head in his hands. Just then, his daughter saw him and cried out, "What's wrong, Father?" The innkeeper told her about the three questions. She answered, "Father, when you go back to the nobleman, give him these answers: The quickest thing in the world is thought. The fattest thing is the earth itself. The sweetest is sleep."

When three days had passed, the tailor and the innkeeper came before the nobleman. "Have you found answers to my questions?" he asked. The tailor stood there silently.

But when the innkeeper gave his answers, the nobleman exclaimed, "Wonderful! Those are wonderful answers! But tell me, how did you think of those answers?"

"I must tell you truthfully that those answers were told to me by my daughter," replied the innkeeper.

"Since your daughter knows so much about life," said the nobleman, "I will test her further. Give her this dozen eggs, and see if she can hatch them all in three days. If she does so, she will have a great reward."

The innkeeper carefully took the eggs and returned home. When his daughter saw him carrying a large basket, and she also saw how he trembled, she asked him, "What is wrong, Father?" He showed her the eggs and told her what she must do in order to receive a reward and prove her wisdom again.

The daughter took the eggs, and she weighed them, each one, in her hands. "Dear Father, how can these eggs be hatched when they are cooked? Boiled eggs indeed! But wait, Father, I have a plan as to how to answer the riddle." The daughter boiled some beans and waited three days. Then she instructed her father to go to the nobleman's house and ask permission to plant some special beans.

"Beans?" asked the nobleman. "What sort of special beans?" Taking the beans from his pocket, the innkeeper showed them to the nobleman and said, "These are boiled beans, Your Honor, that I want to plant."

The nobleman burst out laughing and said, "Well, you certainly are not wise to the ways of the world if you don't even know that beans can't grow from boiled beans—only from seeds."

"Well, then," replied the innkeeper, "neither can chickens hatch from boiled eggs!"

The nobleman immediately sensed the clever mind of the innkeeper's daughter in the answer. So he said to the innkeeper, "Tell your daughter to come here in three days. And she must come neither dressed nor undressed, neither walking nor riding, neither hungry nor overfed, and she must bring me a gift that is not a gift."

The innkeeper returned home even more perplexed than before. When his daughter heard what she had to do in three days' time, she laughed and said, "Father, tomorrow I will tell you what to do."

The next day the daughter said to her father, "Go to the marketplace, and buy these things: a large net, some almonds, a goat, and a pair of pigeons." The father was puzzled by these requests, but as he loved his daughter and knew her to be wise, he did not question her. Instead, he went to the marketplace and bought all that she had requested.

On the third day the innkeeper's daughter prepared for her visit to the nobleman. She did not eat her usual morning meal. Instead, she got undressed and wrapped herself in the transparent net, so she was neither dressed nor undressed.

Then she took two almonds in one hand and the pair of pigeons in the other. Leaning on the goat, she held on so that one foot dragged on the ground while she hopped on the other one. In this way, she was neither walking nor riding.

As she approached the nobleman's house, he saw her and came out to greet her.

At the gate, she ate the two almonds to show that she was neither hungry nor overfed.

Then the innkeeper's daughter extended her hand, showing the pigeons she intended to give as a gift. The nobleman reached out to take them, but just at that moment the young woman opened her hand to release the pigeons—and they flew away. So she had brought a gift that was not a gift.

The nobleman gave a laugh of approval and called out, "You are a clever woman! I want to marry you, but on one condition. You must promise never to interfere with any of my judgments."

"I will marry you," said the innkeeper's daughter, "but I also have one condition: If I do anything that will cause you to send me away, you must promise to give me whatever I treasure most in your house." They each agreed to the other's condition, and they were married.

Some time passed, and one day a man came to speak with the young wife, who had become known for her wisdom. "Help me, please," the man begged, "for I know you are wise and understand things in ways your husband does not."

"Tell me what is wrong, for you look very troubled, sir," she answered. And the man told her his story.

"Last year," said the man, "my partner and I bought a barn that we now share. He keeps his wagon there, and I keep my horse there. Well, last night my horse gave birth to a foal under the wagon. So my partner says the foal belongs to him. We began to argue and fight, so we brought our dispute to the nobleman. The nobleman judged that my partner was right. I protested but to no avail. What can I do?"

The young woman gave him certain advice and instructions to follow. As she told him to do, he took a fishing pole, went over to the nobleman's well, and pretended he was fishing there. The nobleman rode by the well, just as his wife had predicted, and when he saw the man, he stopped and asked, "What are you doing?" The man replied, "I am fishing in the well." The nobleman started to laugh and said, "Are you really so stupid that you do not know that you can't catch a fish in a well?" "No, sir," said the man, "not any more than I know that a wagon cannot give birth to a foal."

At this answer, the nobleman stopped laughing. Understanding that his wife must be involved in the case, he got out of his carriage and went looking for her. When he found his wife, he said, "You did not keep your promise not to interfere with my judgments, so I must send you back to your father's home."

"You are right, my husband," she said. "But before I leave, let us dine together one last time." The nobleman agreed to this request.

At dinner the nobleman drank a great deal of wine, for his wife kept refilling his cup, and as a result he soon became very sleepy. As soon as he was asleep, the wife signaled to the servants to pick him up and put him in the carriage next to her, and they returned to her father's home.

The next morning when the nobleman woke up, he looked around and realized where he was. "But how did I get here? What is the meaning of this?" he shouted.

"You may remember, dear husband, that you also made an agreement with me," she answered. "You promised that if you sent me away, I would be able to pick whatever I treasured most in your house to take with me. There is nothing I treasure more than you. So that is how you came to be here with me."

The nobleman laughed, embraced his wife, and said, "Knowing how much you love me, I now realize how much I love you. Let us return to our home."

And they did go home, where they lived with love and respect for many happy years.

---

Wisdom, says the Bible, is to be desired more than wealth, more than silver or gold.

# APPENDIX

## THE MOST WONDERFUL STORY

Of all the wonderful stories in the world, there is one that surpasses them all. It is the story of how God Himself built a bridge between heaven and earth.

We humans had messed up everything. We had made ourselves totally unfit for God's heaven. Have we not all sinned? Not only have we broken the Ten Commandments; but the underlying conditions of the heart—spelled out in the seven deadly sins—are present in us all. Pride and anger, envy and greed, lust, gluttony, and laziness are sins that touch us all.

We're all sinners. Although some may be better than others, in God's eyes, no one is perfect. Suppose we likened reaching heaven in our natural state to a swimming contest from Hawaii to California, and the better a person you were, the farther you'd be able to swim. Let's say, Mother Teresa then would be able to swim perhaps hundreds of miles toward the goal. You and I might swim between five to ten miles. Al Capone might dog-paddle for a few hundred feet before he goes under, while Hitler and Stalin would drown in the first foot off shore! So compared with each other, there are great differences in how good we are. But compared to God's standard, we all drown. No one can make it to California.[1] In the same way, no one can make it to heaven on his own by his own good deeds. Because God is perfect and He will accept no less than perfection into His heaven, then who can make it to heaven?

D. James Kennedy tells a wonderful story that drives home this same point:

--------

I remember twenty-five years or so ago, my wife and I were invited to a dinner at the home of one of our families. There must have been about ten or fifteen people present. There was a long table. I was invited to sit down near one end of the table; my wife was seated near the other end. Across from me was the mother of the hostess—a lady about sixty-five or seventy, and she said to me, "Oh,

--------

1. I'm indebted to Paul Little for the gist of this analogy.

Rev. Kennedy, I am so happy to be seated across from you because I've always wanted to ask a minister a question."

And I said, "Well, fine, I'll be glad to try and answer it. Don't make it too hard or I'll have to get up and go ask my wife. But what is it?"

She said, "How good does a person have to be to be good enough to get into Heaven?"

Well, now, that's a question that so many people ought to ask themselves. So many do not even bother to do so, but at least this woman had the intelligence to realize that if one was going to get into Heaven by being good, then one should intelligently ask how good is good enough. What is the passing grade in this course? Is it 70 or 75 or 80 or 60 or 50 or what is it?

And I said, "Oh, is that your question? Well, that's easy."

And her face just broke out in a huge smile. She said, "Do you mean you *know?*"

And I said, "Of course. That's the simplest possible question."

She said, "You'll never know how relieved I am. I have been worrying about that for years."

I said, "Well, you'll never need to worry about the answer to that question ever again, because from this day forward, you will know."

She said, "Oh, I'm so glad I came." She said, "What is it?"

I said, "Jesus said it very clearly, very understandably. He said, 'Be ye therefore perfect, even as your Father which is in Heaven is perfect.'"

The smile left her face. She looked like one of those cartoon characters that had been hit by a skillet. Her face just sort of fell onto the table and she sat there silently for a long time, and then she said, "I think I'm going to worry about that more than ever."

And I said, "Well, dear lady, I did not go into the ministry to make people worry, but far from it—to deliver them from their worries." And I was happy to share with her the Gospel of Jesus Christ, that while none of us is perfect, and none of us has lived up to God's standard, and all of us have fallen short, Jesus Christ came to do what we have been unable to do.[2]

2.   D. James Kennedy, "Law and Gospel" (Ft. Lauderdale, Fla.: Coral Ridge Ministries, 1989).

Christianity is indeed good news. Jesus Christ died for us in our place in order that we might be saved, in order that we might be acceptable to the Father.

There is an ancient law proclaiming that only blood can atone for sin. People throughout all the centuries of human history, and in all kinds of different societies and cultures have known this. They have tried the blood of animals and of humans. They have tried and tried, but they always come up short.

God saw our pitiful attempts, and He had mercy on us. The blood of lambs and of bulls couldn't make us clean before God. So God Himself became the Lamb. That is what Christmas is all about—God becoming human. And God Himself became the sacrifice that was indeed good enough. That is what Easter is all about—Jesus dying on the cross to atone for our sins and rising from the dead three days later. That cross became the bridge spanning the unassailable chasm between heaven and earth, between God and man.

The way to heaven is not closed any more. This is the time of mercy. This is the time of grace. God freely offers us His salvation. He offers us the protection of His blood—good enough and clean enough for all eternity.

Some people think that we are saved by doing good works. But the truth is rather that we are saved *unto* good works. Good works are a natural by-product of a soul that is saved. Since the beginning of the Church, good works have followed the believers, not only the keeping of the Ten Commandments but acts of mercy. Jesus told us to feed the hungry, clothe the naked, visit the prisoner, care for the sick, and do good to strangers in His name. Christians do this in obedience to Jesus and in gratitude for our salvation. But in no way can good works make us right with God because even our best work is contaminated by sin. But if we confess our sins to God, which means that we name the specific sin(s) we have committed and reject them in all their ugliness. It also means that we reject the devil and all his ways. When we come to the Lord with sorrow in our hearts, then He will forgive us.

So if we turn away from our sins, and promise to try to stay away from sin, and with God's help live after His commandments, then we have "repented." To be sorry for what we have done is the first step to get right with God. The most important step is giving our life to God. If we give up the rights to our own life and give God the right to rule and decide, then we belong to Him—for time and eternity.

The words we use can be simple, like this:

> Dear God, I know I'm not right with You. There are sins of many kinds in my life. I now turn away from them and forsake all evil. I ask you, Lord God, ruler of all, to take my life and rule it. Come into my heart, Lord Jesus, and cleanse me and make me right with You. I acknowledge that You are the rightful God and Lord of the universe. Thank You for loving me and caring about me. Thank You for making me Yours and thank You that now I belong to You. In Jesus' name.

If you sincerely made these words your prayer or a prayer like it, you are now a Christian. The Bible is your food, and prayer is your air, as a new creature of God. You need to tell somebody whom you know to be a Christian what you just did. And you need to find a church where you can be a part of the visible Church. I suggest you find a church where the Bible is preached and Christ is the focus.[3]

After we are made right with God by the sacrificial death of Jesus Christ, then we are part of God's kingdom. God's Holy Spirit starts working in us and will continue to do so until we are home in heaven. This process is called sanctification.

All of us who belong to Christ know it to be the greatest joy on earth, when a person becomes a true Christian and starts the journey to heaven (and not via the Celestial Railroad!). We welcome you to the family of God!

---

3.   I recommend that you write to Coral Ridge Ministries and request of them a book by D. James Kennedy entitled *Beginning Again*. This free book will help you understand more about what it means to be a Christian and to live the Christian life. The address is CRM, Box 40, Ft. Lauderdale, FL 33308. The phone number is 954-772-0404. God bless you.

# ACKNOWLEDGMENTS

There are several people I need to thank for this book. Many thanks to Greg Johnson and the whole staff of Alive Communications, who made the book possible in the first place. Secondly, I heartily thank Tracy Webb for his outstanding work in securing permission for many of the stories. I'm also indebted to Dr. Joe Wheeler, editor of the *Christmas In My Heart* series, for direction in permissions-seeking. Special thanks to Ron Kilpatrick and Maureen Breslin for help in finding some of the stories. I am also much appreciative of the helpful staff at Broadman & Holman, in particular, Janis Whipple. I am also thankful to my pastor, Dr. D. James Kennedy for his foreword and the "Merry Tifton" story. Thanks also to the cheerful staff of the Imperial Point Library, Ft. Lauderdale. Finally, I can't thank enough my wife, Kirsti Saebo Newcombe, for her irreplaceable service in finding stories, in translating some, in helping to write some of the introductions, and being my "sounding board." This book reflects a great deal of her toil.

## The Stories

Every attempt has been made to properly credit the sources of any copyrighted material used in this volume. Please inform the editor if any such acknowledgment has been left out by mistake or if any item has been improperly credited. Thank you.

The acknowledgments of the stories are listed in the order in which the stories appear in the book. In the event of multiple stories coming from the same source, the acknowledgments for them all can be found in the first entry from that source.

The Revolt in Heaven, an excerpt from "Declare His Glory in a Suffering World" by Samuel Kamaleson. Included in *Declare His Glory among the Nations,* edited by David M. Howard. Copyright © 1977 by InterVarsity Christian Fellowship of the USA. Used by permission of InterVarsity Press, P. O. Box 1400, Downers Grove, IL 60615.

"Why the Chimes Rang" by Raymond Macdonald Alden. First published, 1909.

"If He Had Not Come" by Nan F. Weeks. Copyright © 1938 (or earlier) from the Keystone Graded Lessons, American Baptist Publication Society. Reprinted with permission of Judson Press, Valley Forge, Pa. 19432-0851. 800-458-3766.

"The Innkeeper of Bethlehem," "The Man Born Blind," and "The Impotent Man at Bethesda" by J. W. G. Ward. Included in *The Glorious Galilean*. First published by Cokesbury Press, Nashville, Tenn., 1936.

"Merry Tifton," by D. James Kennedy. Copyright © 1982. Coral Ridge Ministries, Box 40, Ft. Lauderdale, FL 33308. Reprinted with permission of the author.

"The Creation" and "Go Down Death - A Funeral Sermon," from *God's Trombones* by James Weldon Johnson. Copyright © 1927 by the Viking Press, Inc., renewed © 1955 by Grace Nail Johnson. Used by permission of Viking Penguin, a division of Penguin Books, USA, Inc.

The Startling Painting by Fyodor Dostoevsky, excerpted from *The Idiot,* 1869. Published in the Collected Works, *The Novels of Dostoevsky,* translated by Constance Garnett, 12 vols., 1912–20.

"Alive" by Max Lucado. Excerpted from the book, *No Wonder They Call Him Savior;* Multnomah Books, Questar Publishers; copyright © 1986 by Max Lucado. Reprinted by permission of the publisher.

"The Story of the Faithful Friend and Its Exegesis in a Medieval Sermon." Author unknown. From the appendix of *Three Late Medieval Morality Plays: Mankind, Everyman, Mundus et Infans,* edited by G. A. Lester, W. W. Norton, New York, 1981, 1990. Reprinted by permission. Slightly adapted in modern English by the editor.

The Deaths of the Apostles by John Foxe. Excerpted from *Foxe's Book of Martyrs.* Published in 1563. Slightly adapted in modern English by Jerry and Kirsti Newcombe, 1996.

"In the Arena." Taken from *Loving God* by Charles Colson. Copyright © 1983, 1987 by Charles W. Colson. Used by permission of Zondervan Publishing House.

"The Ministry of Edward Spencer" by Jerry Newcombe. Copyright 1996. Printed by permission of author.

"Father Zossima's Brother" by Fyodor Dostoevsky. Excerpted from *The Brothers Karamazov,* 1881, translated by Constance Garnett. Published in the Collected Works, *The Novels of Dostoevsky,* translated by Constance Garnett, 12 vols., 1912–20.

*In His Steps,* excerpt, by Charles M. Sheldon. First published, 1896. Edited by Jerry Newcombe.

Scripture passages marked (NIV) are taken from the Holy Bible, New International Version. Copyright © 1973, 1978, 1984 by International Bible Society. Used by permission of Zondervan Publishing House. All rights reserved.

The Casket Scenes by William Shakespeare. Summarized by the editor. Excerpted from *The Merchant of Venice.* Circa 1598.

*Paradise Lost* by John Milton. Summarized by the editor and excerpted from *Paradise Lost*, Books 1, 2, and 3. Published, 1674.

*Poor Richard's Almanack* by Benjamin Franklin. Miscellaneous proverbs. Published, 1732.

"Proclamation of a National Fast-Day," March 30, 1863, by Abraham Lincoln. From *Life and Works of Abraham Lincoln, Centenary Edition*, edited by Marion Mills Miller, 9 vols., vol. 9. The Current Literature Publishing Co., New York, 1907.

Our Solid American Citizen by Ralph Linton. Excerpted from *The Study of Man.* Appleton-Century-Crofts, New York. Copyright © 1936.

"The Teapot" and "God Lives" by Hans Christian Andersen (1805–75). Translated by Kirsti Saebo Newcombe. Translation copyright © 1996. Printed by permission of the translator.

"The Good Things of Life," "The First Creche," and "First Hunt" by Arthur Gordon. Included in Gordon's collection, *Through Many Windows.* Copyright © by Fleming H. Revell, a division of Baker Book House Company, Grand Rapids, Mich. Reprinted by permission of the publisher.

"The Healing of Naaman the Leper and the Greed of Gehazi," Saul and David (excerpted from "The Little Boy Looking for Arrows"), David and Bathsheba (excerpted from "The Prophet's Story of the Little Lamb") retold by Jesse Lyman Hurlbut. Published, 1904.

"The Stolen Fruit," Augustine's Struggle with Lust (miscellaneous excerpts), and "Alypius and the Gladiators" are all excerpted from *The Confessions of St. Augustine,* translated by John K. Ryan. Copyright ©

1960 by Doubleday, a division of Bantam Doubleday Dell Publishing Group, Inc. Used by permission of Doubleday.

"The Pardoner's Tale" by Geoffrey Chaucer. Summarized by the editor. Includes a couple of short excerpts from *The Canterbury Tales,* translated into modern English by Nevill Coghill. Copyright © 1951, 1960 by Penguin Books, Baltimore, Md.

"Little Snowdrop" retold by Dinah Maria Mulock Craik (1826–87).

"Iago's Intentions" by William Shakespeare. Excerpted from *Othello.* Summarized by the editor. First published in 1604.

"Headmaster Bard [Baard]" by Bjornstjerne Bjornson (1832-1910). Translated by Kirsti Saebo Newcombe. Translation copyright © 1996. Printed by permission of the translator.

Michael LeFan on Anger and the Diligence of a Polio Victim by Michael LeFan. Excerpted from *Patience, My Foot!* Copyright © 1993 by College Press, Joplin, Mo. Used by permission of the author.

"The Tell-Tale Heart" by Edgar Allan Poe (1809–49).

"The Hammer of God" by G. K. Chesterton. First published in *The Innocence of Father Brown* in 1911.

"Tropical Paradise Lost and Found" retold by Jerry Newcombe. Copyright © 1996. Printed by permission of the author.

The Roman Feast by Henryk Sienkiewicz. Excerpted from *Quo Vadis.* Translated by Jeremiah Curtin. First published 1916 or earlier.

"Freed From Lust" by Steve Gallagher. Excerpted from *Tearing Down the High Places of Sexual Idolatry* (Fair Oaks, Calif.: Pure Life Ministries). Copyright © 1986. Printed by permission of the author.

The Disappearance of Augustus Gloop by Roald Dahl. Excerpted from *Charlie and the Chocolate Factory.* Copyright © 1964 by Alfred A. Knopf, Inc., a division of Random House, Inc., New York. Reprinted with permission from Random House, Inc.

Forty-One Sausages in One Sitting by William Trevor. This is the chapter on Gluttony in *Deadly Sins* by Thomas Pynchon, Mary Gordon, John Updike, William Trevor, Gore Vidal, Richard Howard, A. S. Byatt, and Joyce Carol Oates. Copyright © 1993 by William Morrow and Company, Inc., New York. These essays originally appeared in *The New York Times Book Review.* Copyright © 1993. *The New York Times.* Reprinted with permission from *The New York Times.*

"Lenny's Last Meal" by Robert Newcombe. Copyright © 1996. Printed by permission of the author.

"Betty and the Pigs" by Lily Guzman. Copyright © 1996. Printed by permission of the author.

"The Diary of a Bible" (included in "A Tale of Two Diaries"). Copyright © unknown. Author unknown. This material printed by permission of *The Human Quest* (formerly *The Churchman*). 1074 23 Ave. N. St. Petersburg, FL 33704. 813-894-0097

"How Stonewall Jackson Got His Name: An Account of Dooley Thomas Hudson" by Robert Folsom. Copyright © 1996. Printed by permission of the author.

My Intense Longing to Learn to Read by Booker T. Washington. Excerpted from *Up from Slavery*. Published 1900, 1901.

"The Actor Who Gave His All" by Lee Buck with Dick Schneider. Excerpted from *Tapping Your Secret Source of Power*. Copyright © 1985, Fleming H. Revell, a division of Baker Book House, Grand Rapids, Mich. Reprinted by permission of the author.

Captured by Giant Despair by John Bunyan. Excerpted from *The Pilgrim's Progress,* published in 1678.

"The Celestial Railroad" by Nathaniel Hawthorne. Published in 1843. Slightly edited by Jerry Newcombe.

The Conversion of Adoniram Judson by Eugene Myers Harrison. Excerpted from *GIANTS of the Missionary Trail*. First published in 1945 by Moody Press, Chicago, Ill.

The Healing of the Leper Women by Lew Wallace. Excerpted from *Ben-Hur: A Tale of the Christ*. Published in 1880.

"I Heard the Bells on Christmas Day" by Henry Wadsworth Longfellow. Published in 1862.

The Cave Scene (originally "Sorcery and Sudden Danger") by C. S. Lewis. Excerpted from *Prince Caspian*. Copyright © 1951, 1979 by HarperCollins *Publishers* Limited, London, England. Reprinted with permission from HarperCollins.

Though He Slay Me by B. J. Hoff. Excerpted from *Song of the Silent Harp*. Copyright © 1991 by Bethany House Publishers, Minneapolis, Minn. Reprinted with permission from Bethany House Publishers.

"The Prodigal Son" retold by Charles Dickens (1812–70). Excerpted from *The Life of Our Lord*. Reprinted by Coral Ridge Ministries, Ft. Lauderdale, Fla.

"Terje Vigen" by Henrik Ibsen (1828–1906). Translated by Kirsti Saebo Newcombe. Translation copyright © 1996. Printed by permission of the translator.

"The Mansion" by Henry Van Dyke. Published in 1911.

Alice and the Cheshire-Cat by Lewis Carroll. Excerpted from *Alice in Wonderland*. Published in 1865, 1871.

"Peter Dass Outwits the Devil," traditional Norwegian folktale, translated and retold by Kirsti Saebo Newcombe. Translation copyright © 1996. Printed by permission of the translator.

"Reinert Meets the Cannibals," traditional Norwegian folktale, translated and retold by Kirsti Saebo Newcombe. Translation © copyright 1996. Printed by permission of the translator.

"The Cop and the Anthem" by O. Henry (1862–1910).

"The Innkeeper's Wise Daughter," a folktale from Jewish oral tradition, retold by Peninnah Schram. Included in Schram's *Jewish Stories One Generation Tells Another*. Copyright © 1987, 1993 by Jason Aronson, Inc., Northvale, N.J. Printed by permission of the author.

"The Most Wonderful Story" by Jerry and Kirsti Newcombe. Copyright © 1996. Printed by permission of the author.

All summaries of stories; all introductory and concluding remarks of stories; and all updating of stories by the editor are copyright by the editor, Jerry Newcombe, 1996. Used by permission.